Microsoft Visual C++/CLI
Step by Step

Julian Templeman

ISBN: 978-0-7356-7517-9

Third Printing: July 2014

Printed and bound in the United States of America.

Microsoft Press books are available through booksellers and distributors worldwide. If you need support related to this book, email Microsoft Press Book Support at mspinput@microsoft.com. Please tell us what you think of this book at *http://www.microsoft.com/learning/booksurvey*.

Microsoft and the trademarks listed at *http://www.microsoft.com/about/legal/en/us/IntellectualProperty/ Trademarks/EN-US.aspx* are trademarks of the Microsoft group of companies. All other marks are property of their respective owners.

The example companies, organizations, products, domain names, email addresses, logos, people, places, and events depicted herein are fictitious. No association with any real company, organization, product, domain name, email address, logo, person, place, or event is intended or should be inferred.

Acquisitions and Developmental Editor: Russell Jones

Production Editor: Kara Ebrahim

Technical Reviewer: Luca Regnicoli

Copyeditor: Octal Publishing, Inc.

Indexer: BIM Indexing and Proofreading Services

Cover Design: Twist Creative • Seattle

Cover Composition: Ellie Volckhausen

Illustrator: Rebecca Demarest

[2013-07-26]

I would like to dedicate this book to my wife, Jane, without whose steadfast love and support none of this would be possible.

—Julian Templeman

Contents at a Glance

Introduction   *xxi*

PART I   GETTING STARTED WITH C++ .NET

CHAPTER 1   Hello C++!   3
CHAPTER 2   Introducing object-oriented programming   13
CHAPTER 3   Variables and operators   23
CHAPTER 4   Using functions   37
CHAPTER 5   Decision and loop statements   57
CHAPTER 6   More about classes and objects   77
CHAPTER 7   Controlling object lifetimes   103
CHAPTER 8   Inheritance   121

PART II   MICROSOFT .NET PROGRAMMING BASICS

CHAPTER 9   Value types   143
CHAPTER 10   Operator overloading   159
CHAPTER 11   Exception handling   175
CHAPTER 12   Arrays and collections   197
CHAPTER 13   Properties   229
CHAPTER 14   Delegates and events   245
CHAPTER 15   The .NET Framework class library   263

PART III   USING THE .NET FRAMEWORK

CHAPTER 16   Working with files   281
CHAPTER 17   Reading and writing XML   305
CHAPTER 18   Using ADO.NET   333
CHAPTER 19   Writing a service by using Windows
             Communication Foundation   351
CHAPTER 20   Introducing Windows Store apps   369
CHAPTER 21   More about Windows Store apps   397

PART IV   ADVANCED TOPICS

CHAPTER 22   **Working with unmanaged code**   437

CHAPTER 23   **Attributes and reflection**   453

CHAPTER 24   **Living with COM**   475

Index   *487*

Contents

Introduction . . . . *xxi*

PART I   GETTING STARTED WITH C++ .NET

Chapter 1   Hello C++!   **3**

What is C++/CLI? 3

Your first C++/CLI application 4

The *main* function 4

C++ keywords and identifiers 5

Creating an executable application—theory 6

Editing the application source files 6

Compiling the source files 6

Running and testing the application 7

Creating an executable application—practice 7

Creating a project 8

Editing the C++ source code 9

Building the executable 9

Executing the application 11

Conclusion 11

Quick reference 11

Chapter 2   Introducing object-oriented programming   **13**

What is object-oriented programming? 13

Features of object-oriented programming languages 14

Encapsulation 14

Inheritance 15

Polymorphism 15

Classes and objects 16

Benefits to the development life cycle 16

A simple example 17

Quick reference. 22

Chapter 3   Variables and operators   23

What is a variable? 23

The fundamental data types. 23

Declaring a variable 25

Variable naming 25

Declaring multiple variables 26

Assigning values to variables 26

Handles and pointers. 27

Arrays 28

Constants 28

Typedefs 29

The .NET Framework *String* class 29

Operators and expressions 30

Assignment operators. 30

Arithmetic operators. 30

Relational and logical operators 31

Bitwise operators 32

The ternary operator. 33

Type casting 33

Operator precedence and associativity 34

Quick reference. 35

Chapter 4   Using functions   37

Declaring function prototypes. 38

Declaring a simple function prototype 38

Declaring parameters in a function prototype. 39

Declaring the return type in a function prototype 39

Declaring default values for function parameters 40

Defining function bodies 41

Calling functions. 45

Stepping through the application by using debugger 47

Understanding local and global scope 51

Quick reference. 55

Chapter 5   Decision and loop statements   57

Making decisions by using the *if* statement. 57

Performing one-way tests 57

Performing two-way tests 61

Performing multiway tests 62

Performing nested tests 64

Making decisions by using the *switch* Statement 65

Defining simple *switch* statements 65

Using fall-through in a *switch* statement. .67

Performing loops 68

Using *while* loops. 68

Using *for* loops 70

Using *do-while* loops. 71

Performing unconditional jumps 73

Quick reference. 75

Chapter 6   More about classes and objects   77

Organizing classes into header files and source files 78

Declaring a class in a header file. 79

Implementing a class in a source file 81

Creating objects 83

Initializing objects by using constructors. 84

Defining constructors 84

Member initialization lists. 86

Defining class-wide members. 87

Defining class-wide data members. 88

Defining class-wide member functions 90

Class constructors 92

Using constants in classes 93

    Using class-wide constants. 93

    Using instance constants 94

Defining object relationships 95

    Defining the *LoyaltyScheme* Class. 95

    Implementing the *LoyaltyScheme* class 96

    Creating and using *LoyaltyScheme* objects. 97

    Testing the application 100

Quick reference. 101

Chapter 7   **Controlling object lifetimes**   **103**

The .NET approach to object lifetimes 103

Destruction and finalization 105

    Destructors 105

    Finalizers 106

    Implementing the destructor and finalizer for a class. 107

    Objects and stack semantics 110

    Copy constructors 113

    Relating objects with stack semantics 116

Quick reference. 119

Chapter 8   **Inheritance**   **121**

What is inheritance?. 121

    Inheritance terminology. 122

    Inheritance and code reuse 122

Designing an inheritance hierarchy. 123

    A word on substitutability 123

Defining a base class 124

Defining a derived class. 126

Creating derived class objects 129

Concrete and abstract classes. 130

Overriding member functions 131

Protected access 136

Defining sealed classes. 137

   Abstract and sealed. 137

Defining and using interfaces. 138

Quick reference 139

PART II   MICROSOFT .NET PROGRAMMING BASICS

Chapter 9 **Value types**   **143**

Reference types and value types 143

   The need for value types 144

   Properties of value types 145

Structures 146

   Creating and using a simple struct 146

   Investigating the structure 147

   The differences between structures and classes 149

   Implementing constructors for a structure 149

   Using one structure within another 150

   Copying structures. 152

Enumerations. 153

   Creating and using an enumeration. 153

   Using enumerations in applications 155

   Using memory efficiently 156

Quick reference 156

Chapter 10 **Operator overloading**   **159**

What is operator overloading? 159

   What types need overloaded operators? .160

   What can you overload? 160

   Rules of overloading 161

Overloading operators in managed types 161

   Overloading arithmetic operators. 161

   Using static operator overloads. 163

What functions can you overload?. 166

Implementing logical operators 167

Implementing increment and decrement 171

Operators and reference types 172

Guidelines for providing overloaded operators. 173

Quick reference. 174

Chapter 11 Exception handling 175

What are exceptions?. 175

How do exceptions work?. 177

Exception types 178

Throwing exceptions 178

Handling exceptions. 180

Using the *try* and *catch* construct. 180

Customizing exception handling. 182

Using the exception hierarchy 183

Using exceptions with constructors 184

Nesting and rethrowing exceptions 185

The *finally* block 188

The *catch(...)* block 189

Creating your own exception types. 189

Using *safe_cast* for dynamic casting 191

Using exceptions across languages 192

Quick reference. 195

Chapter 12 Arrays and collections 197

Native C++ arrays 197

Passing arrays to functions. 200

Initializing arrays 202

Multidimensional arrays 202

Dynamic allocation and arrays. 203

Generic types. 205

Managed arrays. 207

The .NET array class 212

    Basic operations on arrays 213

    More advanced array operations 215

    Using enumerators. 218

Other .NET collection classes 219

    The *List<T>* class. 219

    The *SortedList<K,V>* class 222

Generics and templates 224

    The STL/CLR library 224

Quick reference 227

Chapter 13 Properties   **229**

What are properties? 229

    The two kinds of properties. 230

Implementing scalar properties 231

    Errors in properties 232

    Auto-implemented properties. 233

    Read-only and write-only properties. 233

    Properties, inheritance, and interfaces. 235

Implementing indexed properties 236

    The Bank example 236

    Creating *Account* class properties. 239

Adding accounts to the *Bank* class 240

    Implementing the *Add* and *Remove* methods 240

    Implementing an indexed property to retrieve accounts. 241

Quick reference 244

Chapter 14 Delegates and events   **245**

What are delegates? 245

What is the purpose of delegates? 246

    Defining delegates. 247

    Implementing delegates. 247

What are events?. 253

    Implementing an event source class. 254

    Implementing an event receiver 256

    Hooking it all together 258

Quick reference. 262

Chapter 15 The .NET Framework class library   263

What is the .NET Framework?. 263

    The Common Language Runtime. 264

    The Microsoft Intermediate Language. 264

    The Common Type System. 264

    The Common Language Specification 265

    The .NET Framework class library 265

    Assemblies. 266

    Metadata 266

The .NET Framework namespaces 268

    Using namespaces in C++ applications 270

    The *System* namespace. 270

    The *Collections* namespaces. 272

    The *Collections* interfaces 273

    The *Diagnostics* namespace 274

    The *IO* namespace 274

    The *Windows* namespaces 275

    The *Net* namespaces 275

    The *ServiceModel* namespaces 275

    The *Xml* namespaces. 276

    The *Data* namespaces 276

    The *Web* namespaces 277

Quick reference. 278

PART III   USING THE .NET FRAMEWORK

Chapter 16 Working with files   281

The *System::IO* namespace 282

Implementing text I/O by using readers and writers 283

Using *TextWriter* 283

The *FileStream* class 286

Using *TextReader* 287

Working with files and directories 290

Getting information about files and directories 290

Binary I/O 298

The *BinaryWriter* class 298

The *BinaryReader* class 299

Quick reference 303

Chapter 17 Reading and writing XML   305

XML and .NET 305

The .NET XML namespaces. 306

The XML processing classes 306

Parsing XML by using *XmlReader* 307

Parsing XML with validation 315

Writing XML by using *XmlTextWriter* 318

Using *XmlDocument* 322

What is the W3C DOM? 323

The *XmlDocument* class 323

The *XmlNode* class 325

Quick reference 332

Chapter 18 Using ADO.NET   333

What is ADO.NET? 334

ADO.NET data providers 334

ADO.NET namespaces 335

ADO.NET assemblies 336

Creating a connected application 336

    Connecting to a database 337

    Creating and executing a command. 340

    Executing a command that modifies data. 341

    Executing queries and processing the results. 342

Creating a disconnected application. 344

Disconnected operation using a *DataSet*. 345

Quick reference 350

Chapter 19 Writing a service by using Windows Communication
**   Foundation   351**

What is Windows Communication Foundation? .351

    Distributed systems 352

    Services 352

    Connectivity 353

The ABCs of WCF. 353

    Endpoints. 353

    Address 354

    Binding. 355

    Contract. 356

    Message exchange patterns. 357

    Behaviors 358

Creating a service 359

    Writing a service client 361

    Adding metadata to the service 363

    Accessing a service by using a proxy 365

Quick reference. 368

Chapter 20 Introducing Windows Store apps   369

A (brief) history of writing Windows user interface applications. 369

    The Win32 API 369

    Microsoft Foundation Classes 370

    Windows Forms 370

Windows Presentation Foundation. 371

Windows 8 and Windows Store. 371

Which UI library to choose?. 372

Introducing Windows Store apps. 372

Main features of Windows Store apps 373

Writing a Windows Store app. 374

Creating your first Windows Store app 375

Examining the project. 379

Introducing XAML. 380

What is XAML? 380

XAML syntax 381

XAML controls 382

Layout controls. 384

Event handling 389

C++/CX and Windows RT 389

Windows RT. 390

Metadata. 390

C++/CX syntax 391

Common namespaces. 393

Quick reference. 395

Chapter 21 More about Windows Store apps 397

Building the basic calculator. 397

Laying out the number buttons 398

Handling number input 401

Adding arithmetic operations 403

Performing calculations 407

Testing the calculator 410

Improving the graphics. 412

Handling different number bases. 416

Using app bars 425

Adding sharing. 428

Where next? 433

Quick reference. 433

Chapter 22 Working with unmanaged code   437

Managed vs. unmanaged code 437

    Mixed classes 437

    The *GCHandle* type 438

Pinning and boxing. 440

    Interior pointers 441

    Pinning pointers 441

    Boxing and unboxing 442

    Boxing 443

    Unboxing 443

Using P/Invoke to call functions in the Win32 API 444

    The *DllImportAttribute* class. 447

    Passing structures 449

Quick reference. 452

Chapter 23 Attributes and reflection   453

Metadata and attributes 453

    Using ILDASM 454

Using predefined attributes 457

    The AssemblyInfo.cpp file. 457

    Using the predefined attribute classes. 458

Defining your own attributes 461

    Attribute class properties 463

    Design criteria for attribute classes. 463

    Writing a custom attribute 463

Using reflection to obtain attribute data 467

    The *Type* class 467

    Accessing standard attributes 469

    Accessing custom attribute data. 470

Quick reference. 472

Chapter 24 Living with COM 475

COM components and the COM Interop 476

Using COM components from .NET code 476

How do RCWs work? 476

Creating and using RCWs. 477

Handling COM errors 480

Late binding to COM objects. 481

Using .NET components as COM components 483

What must .NET types implement to be used as COM objects? . .483

Quick reference. 485

Index   *487*

Introduction

C++ is a powerful, industrial-strength programming language used in tens of thousands of applications around the world, and this book will show you how to get started using C++ on Windows.

Of all the languages supported by Microsoft, C++ gives you access to the widest range of technologies on the Windows platform, from writing games, through low-level system software, to line-of-business applications. This book is going to introduce you to several of the areas in which C++ is used in Windows development.

For over a decade .NET has become established as the way to write desktop applications for Windows, and it provides a wealth of technologies to support developers. C++/CLI is the variant of C++ that runs in the .NET environment, and you can use it, along with other languages such as C#, to create rich desktop applications.

More recently, Windows 8 has introduced many new features to the Windows operating system, but perhaps the most exciting is the debut of Windows Store applications. These graphical applications are designed to run on touch screen and mobile devices, and provide a completely new way to construct user interfaces on Windows. C++ is one of the main languages supported for Windows Store development, and this book will give you an introduction to these applications and how to develop them in C++/CX, another variant of C++ introduced specifically for this purpose.

Who should read this book

This book exists to help programmers learn how to write applications using C++ on the Windows platform. It will be useful to those who want an introduction to writing .NET applications using C++, as well as to those who want to see how to write Windows Store applications.

If you are specifically interested in Windows Store applications, you may wish to look at *Build Windows 8 Apps with Microsoft Visual C++ Step by Step* by Luca Regnicoli, Paolo Pialorsi, and Roberto Brunetti, published by Microsoft Press.

Assumptions

This book expects that you have some experience of programming in a high-level language, so that you are familiar with concepts such as functions and arrays. It is quite sufficient to have experience in a procedural language such as Visual Basic, and I do not assume that you have any experience of object-oriented programming in general, or of C++ in particular (although any knowledge of a "curly bracket" language will be useful).

Who should not read this book

This book is not suitable for complete beginners to programming. For readers who are completely new to programming and want to learn C++, I recommend starting with a book such as *Programming: Principles and Practice Using C++* by Bjarne Stroustrup, published by Addison-Wesley.

This book is also not suitable for those who want to learn standard C++ or older-style Win32 development, because it concentrates on two Microsoft variants (C++/CLI and C++/CX) and does not cover topics such as the CLR or MFC in any detail.

Organization of this book

This book is divided into four sections.

- Part I, "Getting Started," introduces the main parts of the C++ language, getting you used to coding in C++ and building applications in Visual Studio 2012.

- Part II, "Microsoft .NET Programming Basics," continues by introducing those parts of C++ that are specific to Microsoft's C++/CLI language.

- Part III, "Using the .NET Framework," covers the main features in the .NET Framework libraries used for writing .NET applications. This part includes discussion of working with files, XML and databases, and creating graphical applications.

- Part IV, "Advanced Topics," covers some more advanced material, including details for working with legacy code.

Finding your best starting point in this book

The various sections of this book cover a wide range of technologies associated with C++ on the Windows platform. Depending on your needs and your existing understanding of C++, you may wish to focus on specific areas of the book. Use the following table to determine how best to proceed through the book.

If you are	Follow these steps
New to C++	Read Part I carefully before continuing to the rest of the book.
Familiar with OO programming but not with C++	Read Part I carefully, but you can omit Chapter 2.
Familiar with C++	Review Part I, looking for the differences between standard C++ and C++/CLI.
Familiar with .NET, but not Windows Store applications.	Read Chapters 20 and 21.

Most of the book's chapters include exercises that let you try out the concepts you have just learned. Solutions to these exercises can be downloaded using the companion code link from this book's web page. See the "Code samples" section for details on how to download the companion code.

Conventions and features in this book

This book presents information using conventions designed to make the information readable and easy to follow.

- Each exercise consists of a series of tasks, presented as numbered steps (1, 2, and so on) listing each action you must take to complete the exercise.

- Boxed elements with labels such as "Note" provide additional information or alternative methods for completing a step successfully.

- Text that you type (apart from code blocks) appears in bold.

- A plus sign (+) between two key names means that you must press those keys at the same time. For example, "Press Alt+Tab" means that you hold down the Alt key while you press the Tab key.

- A vertical bar between two or more menu items (e.g., File | Close) means that you should select the first menu or menu item, then the next, and so on.

System requirements

You will need the following hardware and software to complete the practice exercises in this book:

- One of Windows 7, Windows 8, Windows Server 2008 with Service Pack 2, or Windows Server 2008 R2. Note that if you want to build and run the Windows Store applications featured in Chapters 20 and 21, you will need Windows 8.

- Visual Studio 2012, any edition

- A computer that has a 1.6 GHz or faster processor (2 GHz is recommended)

- 1 GB (32 Bit) or 2 GB (64 Bit) RAM

- 3.5 GB of available hard disk space

- 5400 RPM hard disk drive

- DirectX 9 capable video card running at 1024 x 768 or higher-resolution display

- DVD-ROM drive (if installing Visual Studio from DVD)

- Internet connection to download software or chapter examples

Depending on your Windows configuration, you might require Local Administrator rights to install or configure Visual Studio 2012.

Code samples

Most of the chapters in this book include exercises that let you interactively try out new material learned in the main text. All sample projects, in both their pre-exercise and post-exercise formats, can be downloaded from the following page:

http://aka.ms/VCCLISbS/files

Acknowledgments

Producing a book involves a number of people, and I'd like to thank the following in particular.

I'd like to thank all at Microsoft Press and O'Reilly for their help and support, especially Devon Musgrave at Microsoft for inviting me to start this project, and Russell Jones at O'Reilly for providing so much help with writing and editorial matters, and especially his guidance in using the (not always good-tempered) Word templates.

The technical quality of the book has been greatly improved by Luca Regnicoli, who as tech reviewer pointed out numerous errors and omissions. I especially value his input on the Windows Store chapters.

Kara Ebrahim at O'Reilly, along with Dianne Russell and Bob Russell at Octal Publishing, provided excellent editorial support and made sure everything got done on time.

And lastly, I'd like to thank my family, who have put up with all the extra work involved in writing a book, and are probably hoping that this is last one for a while!

Errata and book support

We've made every effort to ensure the accuracy of this book and its companion content. Any errors that have been reported since this book was published are listed on our Microsoft Press site:

> *http://aka.ms/VCCLISbS/errata*

If you find an error that is not already listed, you can report it to us through the same page.

If you need additional support, email Microsoft Press Book Support at *mspinput@microsoft.com*.

Please note that product support for Microsoft software is not offered through the addresses above.

We want to hear from you

At Microsoft Press, your satisfaction is our top priority, and your feedback our most valuable asset. Please tell us what you think of this book at:

http://www.microsoft.com/learning/booksurvey

The survey is short, and we read every one of your comments and ideas. Thanks in advance for your input!

Stay in touch

Let's keep the conversation going! We're on Twitter: *http://twitter.com/MicrosoftPress*

PART I

Getting started with C++ .NET

CHAPTER 1	Hello C++!. 3
CHAPTER 2	Introducing object-oriented programming 13
CHAPTER 3	Variables and operators 23
CHAPTER 4	Using functions. 37
CHAPTER 5	Decision and loop statements. 57
CHAPTER 6	More about classes and objects 77
CHAPTER 7	Controlling object lifetimes 103
CHAPTER 8	Inheritance 121

Hello C++!

After completing this chapter, you will be able to

- Recognize C++ functions.

- Recognize C++ keywords and identifiers.

- Create a C++ application.

Welcome to the exciting world of programming Microsoft .NET with Microsoft Visual C++. This chapter introduces the C++/CLI language and shows you how to perform simple input/output (I/O).

What is C++/CLI?

C++/CLI is a version of the C++ programming language designed to run on the .NET Framework. It has been available since Microsoft Visual Studio 2005 and is the subject of an international standard. You can find details of the ECMA standard at *http://www.ecma-international.org/publications/ standards/Ecma-372.htm*.

To achieve this, some changes had to be made to standard C++. There are some things that you can do in standard C++ that are not permitted in C++/CLI (for example, you cannot inherit from multiple base classes) and there have been some changes to the language geared to support .NET features (such as interfaces and properties) and to work with the .NET Runtime.

Why would you choose to use C++/CLI to write .NET code instead of another .NET language such as C#? Apart from personal preference, there are two very good reasons to choose C++/CLI. The first is for interoperability; C++/CLI makes it simple to incorporate standard C++ code into .NET projects. The second is that we have a .NET version of the C++ Standard Template Library (STL), and so people used to coding against the STL will find it possible to work in the same way in .NET.

Even if neither of these reasons applies to you, C++/CLI is still a perfectly good way to learn about .NET programming because it exposes all of the features that you need to write .NET programs and explore the .NET platform.

Your first C++/CLI application

It's time to get our hands dirty with a simple C++/CLI application. Of course, no programming book would be complete without including the customary "Hello World" application, so let's start with that.

```
using namespace System;

int main()
{
  Console::WriteLine("Hello, World!");
  return 0;
}
```

This short application illustrates some fundamental C++/CLI concepts:

- The first line (which begins with *using*) informs the compiler that you're using the .NET *System* library. Many different libraries could be used in a single project; the *using* statement specifies to the compiler which library you want to use.

- The rest of the application is an example of a C++ *function*. All blocks of code in C++ are called functions—there's no such thing as a procedure or a subroutine. Each C++ function contains the header (the first line of this application) and the function body (all of the text between the braces, { and }). The header shows the return type of the function (in this case *int*, short for *integer*), the name of the function (*main*), and the list of parameters inside round brackets. Note that you still need to include the round brackets even if you don't have anything to pass to the function.

- All statements in C++ are terminated with a semicolon.

Of the six lines of code in the example application, only two contain C++ statements: the *Console* line and the *return* line. The *Console* line outputs characters to the console, and the argument to the function consists of the string that you want to output. The *return* line exits from the function—in this case, the application, because there is only one function—and returns zero, which is the standard value to return when execution is successful.

The *main* function

Why is the only function in the previous example called *main*? The simple answer is that the code won't compile if it isn't! However, it might be more useful to explain how the language works.

A normal C++ application contains many functions (and also many classes, as is discussed in Chapter 2, "Introducing object-oriented programming"). How does the compiler know which function should be called first? Obviously, you can't allow the compiler to just randomly choose a function. The rule is that the compiler always generates code that looks for a function named *main*. If you omit the *main* function, the compiler reports an error and doesn't create a finished executable application.

Free-format languages

C++ falls under the category of a *free-format* language, which means that the compiler ignores all spaces, carriage returns, new-line characters, tabs, form feeds, and so on. Collectively, these characters are referred to as *white space*. The only time the compiler recognizes white space is if it occurs within a string.

Free-format languages give the programmer great scope for using tab or space indenting as a way of organizing application layout. Statements inside a block of code—such as a *for* loop or an *if* statement—are typically indented (often by four space characters). This indentation helps the programmer's eye more easily pick out the contents of the block.

The free-format nature of C++ gives rise to one of the most common (and least useful) arguments in the C++ community: how do you indent the braces? Should they be indented with the code, or should they be left hanging at the beginning of the *if* or *for* statement? There is no right or wrong answer to this question (although some hardened C++ developers might disagree), but a consistent use of either style helps to make your application more readable to humans. As far as the compiler is concerned, your entire application could be written on one line.

So, the compiler will expect a function named *main*. Is that all there is to it? Well, not quite. There are some additional items, such as the return type and parameters being correct, but in the case of *main*, some of the C++ rules are relaxed. In particular, *main* can take parameters that represent the command-line arguments, but you can omit them if you don't want to use the command line.

C++ keywords and identifiers

A C++ *keyword* (also called a *reserved word*) is a word that means something to the compiler. The keywords used in the example application are *using*, *namespace*, and *return*. You're not allowed to use these keywords as variable or function names; the compiler will report an error if you do. You'll find that Visual Studio helps you identify keywords by displaying them in a special color.

An *identifier* is any name that the programmer uses to represent variables and functions. An identifier must start with a letter and must contain only letters, numbers, or underscores. The following are legal C++ identifiers:

- *My_variable*

- *AReallyLongName*

The following are not legal C++ identifiers:

Invalid identifier	Reason for being invalid
0800Number	Must not start with a number
You+Me	Must contain only letters, numbers, and underscores (the plus sign is the culprit here)
return	Must not be a reserved word

Outside of these restrictions, any identifier will work. However, some choices are not recommended, such as the following:

Identifier	Reason it's not recommended
main	Could be confused with the function main.
INT	Too close to the reserved word int.
B4ugotxtme	Just too cryptic!
_identifier1	Underscores at the beginning of names are allowed, but they are not recommended because compilers often use leading underscores when creating internal variable names, and they are also used for variables in system code. To avoid potential naming conflicts, you should not use leading underscores.

Creating an executable application—theory

Several stages are required to build an executable application; Microsoft Visual Studio 2012 helps you accomplish this by automating them. To examine and understand these stages, however, let's look at them briefly. You'll see these stages again later in the chapter when we build our first application.

Editing the application source files

Before you can create an application, you must write something. Visual Studio 2012 provides an integrated C++ editor, complete with color syntax highlighting and Microsoft IntelliSense to show function parameter information and provide word completion.

Compiling the source files

The C++/CLI compiler is the tool for converting text source files into something that can be executed by a computer processor. The compiler takes your source files (which usually have a *.cpp* extension) and builds them into either a stand-alone executable file (with a *.exe* extension) or a library file to be used in other projects (with a *.dll* extension).

Standard C++ and C

If you have ever worked with standard C++ or C, you might be familiar with the idea of compiling to object files and then linking with libraries to build the final executable file—which is commonly referred to simply as an executable. Although you can compile to the equivalent of an object file (called a *module* in the .NET world) and then link those together by using a tool called the *assembly linker*, Visual Studio takes you straight from source to executable without you seeing the intermediate step.

Running and testing the application

After you have successfully built the application, you need to run it and test it.

For many development environments, running and testing is often the most difficult part of the application development cycle. However, Visual Studio 2012 has yet another ace up its sleeve: the integrated debugger. The debugger has a rich set of features with which you can easily perform run-time debugging, such as setting *breakpoints* and *variable watches*.

Creating an executable application—practice

Go ahead and start Visual Studio 2012. An invitingly blank window appears on your screen.

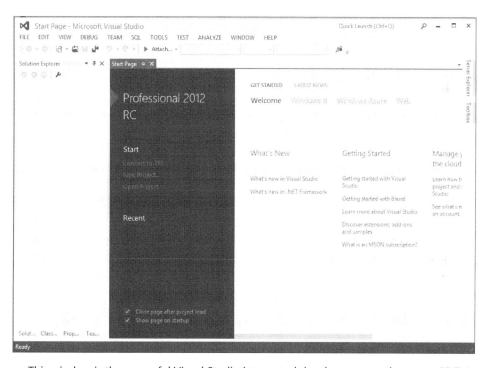

This window is the powerful Visual Studio integrated development environment (IDE). It contains all the tools you'll need to create full-featured, easy-to-use applications.

 Note This book was written by using the Release Candidate (RC) version of Visual Studio 2012. As a result, screen shots and other details might differ from the version you're using when you read this.

Creating a project

The first task is to create a new project for the "Hello, World" program.

1. In Visual Studio, on the File menu, point to New, and then click Project. (Alternatively, you can press Ctrl+Shift+N.)

 Note I am using the Professional version of Visual Studio 2012. If you are using other versions, the way in which you create a project might be different. For example, in the Express version, you will find New Project on the File menu.

The New Project dialog box opens.

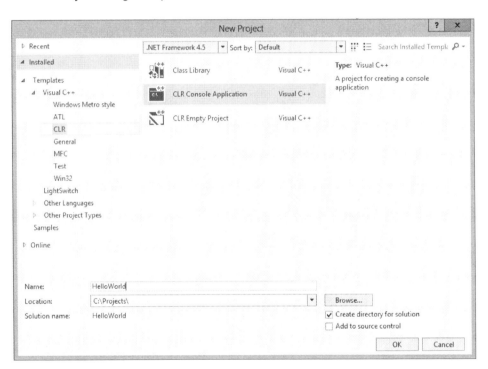

2. In the navigation pane on the left, under Templates, click Visual C++, and then click CLR. In the center pane, click CLR Console Application and then, toward the bottom of the dialog box, in the Name box, type **HelloWorld**.

 Note Depending on how Visual Studio has been set up, you might find Visual C++ under the Other Languages node.

3. Click the Location list and select a location for your new project or click Browse and navigate to an appropriate directory.

4. Click OK to create the project.

The wizard correctly initializes all the compiler settings for a console project.

Editing the C++ source code

The wizard creates a project for you with all the files needed for a simple console application. It also opens the main source file in the editor that contains just the code we want.

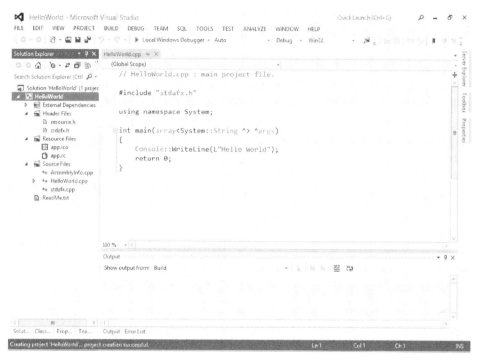

Notice that the keywords automatically appear in blue (provided that you spell them correctly).

There are a few things in the automatically generated source code that we don't need, so let's remove them. This will give you some practice in using the editor as well as making the code easier to understand. The application is not going to receive any command-line arguments when you run it, so remove everything between the opening and closing parentheses following *main*—in this example, *array<System::String ^> ^args*. In addition, the "L" before the *"Hello World"* string isn't necessary either (for reasons that I'll explain later), so you can remove that, as well.

Building the executable

The next step is to build the executable. The term *build* in Visual Studio 2012 refers to compiling and linking the application. Visual Studio compiles any source files that have changed since the last build and—if no compile errors were generated—performs a link.

To build the executable, on the Build menu, click Build Solution or press F7.

Note The shortcut keys might differ depending on the version of Visual Studio you are using. For example, in the Ultimate edition, the shortcut is F6.

An Output window opens near the bottom of the Visual Studio window, showing the build progress. If no errors are encountered, the message *Build: 1 succeeded, 0 failed, 0 up-to-date, 0 skipped* will appear in the Output window. If this window is closed, you can open it by selecting Output from the View menu.

If any problems occur, the Error List window will contain a list of errors and warnings.

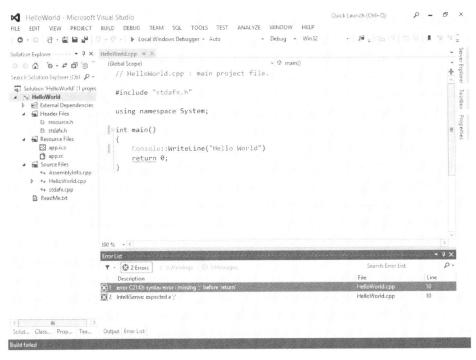

You can double-click the error line in the Error List window to place the cursor at the line in the source file where the compiler encountered the error. Fix the error (you might have misspelled a keyword or forgotten a semicolon) and rebuild the project. If the Error List pane is closed, you can open it by selecting Error List from the View menu.

How should you treat warnings?

Always treat warnings as errors—in other words, get rid of them. Warnings are there for a reason; they're telling you that your code is not correct.

Executing the application

After you've eliminated all errors and you've successfully built the project, you can finally execute the application. On the Debug menu, click Start Without Debugging to run the application. You can also press Ctrl+F5 to execute the application.

You'll see the output of your application, with the message "Press any key to continue" at the bottom of the output. This line is added by the IDE so that the console window doesn't simply disappear when the application has finished running.

Conclusion

Although the example in this chapter isn't the most exciting application ever written, it demonstrates some key C++ development points. It introduces the Visual Studio 2012 IDE and the ability to compile and link a application, and it serves as an introduction to the C++/CLI language.

Now, there's no turning back. Every new C++/CLI and Visual Studio 2012 feature that you learn about will fire your imagination to learn more and be increasingly productive. Software development is an exciting world.

Finally, don't forget to have some fun. Go back and try a few variations on the example application, click a few menus, and take some time to become familiar with the environment.

Quick reference

To	Do this
Create a new project in Visual Studio 2012.	Click File | New | Project, or press Ctrl+Shift+N. In the Express version, on the File menu, click New Project.
Add a file to a project.	Click File | New | File, or press Ctrl+N.
Build a Visual Studio 2012 project.	Click Build | Build Solution, or press Ctrl+Shift+B.
Execute a program from within Visual Studio 2012.	Click Debug | Start Without Debugging, or press Ctrl+F5.

CHAPTER 2

Introducing object-oriented programming

After completing this chapter, you will be able to

- Describe the key concepts of object-oriented programming.

- Understand how these concepts are supported by C++ language constructs.

- Understand the major development benefits of object-oriented programming.

- Create and use simple classes.

What is object-oriented programming?

Object-oriented programming is a paradigm that provides a natural way to develop many kinds of systems. We perceive the world as consisting of objects: tables, chairs, computers, cars, bank accounts, football games, and so on. It is a natural human trait to try to organize these objects, arranging them into some form of classification and choosing to highlight certain features of objects in preference to others. So, dogs and cats are mammals, toasters and refrigerators are appliances, swimming and tennis are sports, Toyotas and Fords are cars, trucks and cars are vehicles, and so on.

There can be many levels to these categories and many ways to classify the objects in the world. How people classify things depends to a large extent on what they want to do with them as well as the relevant features of the objects themselves. For example, a retailer of household appliances is likely to use different categories—possibly deeper and richer—for its products than a typical homeowner. When grouping objects into classification schemes, we also tend to highlight certain attributes of objects in preference to others. For instance, to an engineer, a car's color might not matter, but it might figure heavily in the mental model of car classifications used by a Ferrari salesperson.

Object-oriented programming lets us build hierarchies of objects, creating them and defining how they are related. As long ago as the 1960s, researchers realized that many computer programs modeled entities that can be named, and that their properties and behavior can be described. Examples of such objects might be bank accounts, arrays, files, and users, all of which are analogous to objects in the real world.

Object-oriented programming can crudely be characterized as identifying the objects relevant to the problem, organizing them into hierarchies, adding attributes to the objects to describe the features relevant to the problem context, and adding functions (methods) to the objects such that they can perform their required tasks. The details are a little more complicated, but essentially, it is a simple process.

Yet, simple doesn't necessarily mean easy. A collection of objects could potentially be classified in many ways. The ability to identify the important attributes of objects and to form good abstractions and appropriate hierarchies is crucial. Even within the context of a problem domain, it's sometimes hard to determine the correct levels of abstraction and suitable classification hierarchies. Just deciding which class or grouping an object belongs to can be very difficult. As philosopher Ludwig Wittgenstein pointed out in his 1953 book *Philosophical Investigations*, some objects will bear more of a family resemblance to a concept than others; for example, hockey and tennis are more obviously sports than are chess and synchronized swimming.

Features of object-oriented programming languages

I've already pointed out that object-oriented programming means defining and building hierarchies of objects and defining their properties and behavior. You can do this to a certain extent in any programming language, just the same as you could, theoretically, take a trip over the Rockies in a golf cart, but it is much easier to do object-oriented programming if you use a language that is designed to support object-oriented programming methods.

Object-oriented programming languages such as C++ and C# are characterized by three key features: *encapsulation*, *inheritance*, and *polymorphism*. These features support this natural process of identifying and classifying objects. Let's take a closer look at each one.

Encapsulation

One of the problems faced by software developers is that the systems we are developing are becoming increasingly larger and more complex. Encapsulation helps to keep things manageable by breaking an application down into small, self-contained entities. For example, if you're building an accounting system, you'll probably need objects to represent accounts and invoices. After you've developed the *Account* class, you no longer need to worry about the details of the implementation of the class. You can use the class anywhere in your application in much the same way you would use a built-in type, such as an integer. The class exposes the essential features of the *Account* object while hiding the implementation details.

The account's name and the state of its balance are some of the attributes of the object in which the client is interested and needs to know. Details of how the account name is stored—whether it's an array of 50 characters or a string object, or the fact that the account's balance is maintained as a currency variable—are irrelevant to the client. The process of hiding the data structures and implementation details of an object from other objects in the system is called *encapsulation* (sometimes also known as *data hiding*), and it prevents the other objects from accessing details about which they don't need to know. Encapsulation makes large programs easier to comprehend; data hiding makes them more robust.

Objects can interact with other objects through only their publicly exposed attributes and methods. The more attributes and methods that are publicly exposed, the more difficult it will be to modify the class without affecting the code that uses the class. When done properly, the inner workings of a class can be changed without affecting the code that uses objects created, or *instantiated*, from that class. The programmer would have to worry only about the methods in the class that accessed that variable rather than worry about all the places in the application that an object instantiated from that class might be called.

Inheritance

The natural tendency for humans to classify objects into hierarchies is useful from a programmer's perspective and is supported in object-oriented languages, including C++, by inheritance. Inheritance provides two benefits to the C++ programmer. First, and most important, it lets you build hierarchies that express the *"is a"* relationships between types. Suppose that you have two classes, *SavingsAccount* and *CheckingAccount*, both of which are derived from the parent *Account* class. If you have a function that requires an *Account* as an argument, you can pass it a *SavingsAccount* or a *CheckingAccount* because both classes are types of *Account*. *Account* is a general classification, and *CheckingAccount* and *SavingsAccount* are more specific types. The second benefit of object-oriented programming is that classes can inherit features from classes higher in the hierarchy. Instead of developing new classes from scratch, new classes can inherit the functionality of existing classes and then modify or extend this functionality. The parent class from which the new class inherits is known as the *base class*, and the new class is known as the *derived class*.

One of the major tasks facing developers is finding appropriate classifications for the objects and classes in their programs. For example, if you need to develop classes for a driving game, it makes more sense for you to develop a general car class and then use this class as a base class for specific car types such as sportscar or truck. These derived classes would then extend or modify the general car class by adding new attributes and methods or by overriding existing methods. Composing objects from subobjects—for example, a car consisting of an engine and a chassis—can also simplify the development effort. Doing it this way, each of the objects is simpler and therefore easier to design and implement than the collective whole.

Polymorphism

The third feature of object-oriented programming languages is *polymorphism*, which is Greek for "many forms." It is quite a hard concept to define, so I'll use some examples to show you what polymorphism is and leave the precise definitions to more academic writers.

Polymorphism essentially means that classes can have the same behavior but implement it in different ways. Consider several different types of vehicle: they all need to be started, so in programming terms, we could say that all vehicles have "start" functionality. Exactly *how* starting is implemented depends on the vehicle. If it is a Ford Model T, starting will mean manually cranking the starting handle at the front of the vehicle, but if it is a modern car, starting will mean turning the key in the ignition. If the vehicle is a steam locomotive, starting will be a very different and more complex process, indeed.

As another example, consider the aforementioned *SavingsAccount* and *CheckingAccount* types. All types derived from *Account* share certain functionality, such as the ability to deposit, withdraw, and query the balance. They might implement them in different ways because *CheckingAccount* might permit an overdraft, whereas *SavingsAccount* might accrue interest, but they all work the same way. This means that if I'm passed an *Account*, it doesn't matter exactly what type of account it is; I can still deposit funds, withdraw funds, and query the balance. This functionality is useful in programming terms because it gives you the ability to work with generic object types—accounts and vehicles— when you're not concerned with the way in which each class implements functionality.

Classes and objects

Up to this point in the chapter, the terms "class" and "object" have been used fairly interchangeably. However, classes and objects aren't the same thing, and we need to clarify the differences between these terms. As the name implies, object-oriented programming is about objects. An *object* is composed of data that describes the object and the operations that can be performed on the object. However, when you create an application in C++, you define classes, not objects.

A *class* is a user-defined type; it encapsulates both the data and the methods that work on that data. With the exception of static functions, you cannot use classes directly. A class is like a template, which is used to create (instantiate) objects. Just as you have to declare an *int* variable before you can use it, you also have to instantiate an object of the class before you can use it.

For example, you would not define an *Animal* object. Instead, you would define an *Animal* class along with its attributes and methods. The class represents the concept, so the *Animal* class does not represent a specific animal but the class of all animals. When you want to use an *Animal* object, you have to instantiate an *Animal* object from the class. The class can be considered as the abstract representation of an entity, whereas the instantiation of the class—the object—is the concrete representation.

Benefits to the development life cycle

There are three key benefits to object-oriented programming: *comprehensibility*, *reusability*, and *extensibility*. Breaking code down into classes makes it more comprehensible by imposing a structure as programs grow larger and larger. The ideal is to assemble object-oriented systems from prewritten classes and to make the required modifications to support the new requirements by using inheritance and composition to derive new classes from the existing classes. The existing classes are reused as building blocks and not altered in any way. Creating systems from reusable components naturally leads to higher productivity, which is probably the most frequently cited benefit of object-oriented approaches. Object-oriented programming should also result in higher-quality systems. When you reuse classes, it means that you are using code that has already been tested and proven in earlier projects; thus, it is likely to contain fewer bugs than classes developed from scratch. Over time, any bugs that might have existed have been found and fixed in these classes, whereas code that is written from scratch has yet to pass through the same bug detection and fixing process.

The features (encapsulation, inheritance, and polymorphism) of object-oriented programming also provide benefits. Encapsulation makes it easier to scale up from small systems to large systems. For the most part, regardless of the size of the system, the developer is simply creating objects. Large systems might require more objects than small systems, but the level of complexity facing the developer is not significantly increased. Inheritance helps to improve the flexibility and extensibility of systems, hence reducing their costs to maintain. Deriving new classes from existing classes provides additional functionality and makes it possible to extend the software without altering the existing classes.

Finally, data hiding also leads to more secure systems. The state of an object can be modified only by its publicly exposed methods, which increases the predictability of object behavior.

A simple example

The following simple example should serve to show you how to create a class, instantiate objects, and access member functions and attributes.

1. Start Microsoft Visual Studio 2012.

2. On the File menu, point to New, and then click Project.

   The New Project dialog box opens.

3. In the navigation pane on the left, under Templates, click Visual C++, and then click CLR.

4. In the center pane choose CLR Console Application.

5. Toward the bottom of the dialog box, in the Name box, type **Animals**.

6. Click the Location box and select a location for the new project (or click Browse to find it), and then click OK.

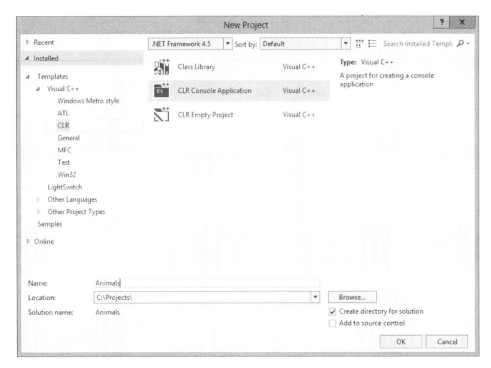

7. The file Animals.cpp should already be open in the editor. If it is not, in Solution Explorer, in the Source Files folder, double-click the Animals.cpp file.

8. Immediately under the *using namespace System;* line, add the following class definition:

```
ref class Animal
{
    int legs;
    String ^name;
};
```

To declare a class in C++, you use the keywords *ref class* followed by a name for the class—*Animal* in this example—and then you list all the member variables and functions for the class between opening and closing braces ({ and }).

So far, you have created an *Animal* class with an *int* variable for the number of its legs and a *String* variable for its name. As it stands, no other application or class will be able to access these variables. The members of a class—data and methods—are private by default and can only be accessed by methods of the class itself. C++ provides three access modifiers, *public*, *private*, and *protected*, which you use to specify the visibility of the various members of the class.

9. Add the keyword *public* followed by a colon (:) on a new line between the opening brace and the first variable declaration.

```
ref class Animal
{
public:
    int legs:
    String ^name;
};
```

By declaring the variables after the keyword *public*, you make both of them accessible. However, it is not usually a good idea to allow other classes and parts of your application access to the variables of a class.

As discussed earlier in the section on encapsulation, it's better to keep the implementation details of a class hidden from users of that class and to control the access to the class's data through functions. In the next step, we use the keyword *private* to prevent direct access to the *String* variable of the class. We'll leave the *int* variable *legs* with public access, simply to show how it can then be directly accessed by the main application.

10. Add the keyword *private* followed by a colon (:) between the first *int* variable and the second *String* variable.

```
ref class Animal
{
public:
    int legs;
private:
    String ^name;
};
```

To provide access to the private *String* variable, public accessor functions and methods need to be added to the class to allow other functions to manipulate its value.

11. After the declaration of the *int* variable and before the *private* access modifier, add the following method declarations or implementation lines:

```
void SetName(String ^nm)
{
   name = nm;
}

String^ GetName()
{
   return name;
}
```

Because these methods are small functions, it's easiest to declare and implement them as *inline functions*. Inline functions are explained further in Chapter 6, "More about classes and objects," when we go into classes in greater detail.

You have probably noticed the *ref* keyword. This C++/CLI keyword simplifies the interaction with .NET Framework components. By placing *ref* in front of the *class* keyword, the class becomes a managed class. When the object is instantiated, it is created on the Common Language Runtime (CLR) heap. The lifetime of an object instantiated from the class is managed by the .NET Framework's garbage collector. When the object goes out of scope, the memory used by the object is garbage-collected automatically. *ref* classes are known as *reference types* because the variable does not actually contain the object; rather it is a pointer to the memory location of the object, known as a *handle*.

However, there are performance issues to consider when using reference types. The memory has to be allocated from the managed heap, which could force a garbage collection to occur. In addition, reference types must be accessed via their handles, affecting both the size and speed of the compiled application.

Because of these performance issues, the .NET Framework also supports *value* types. Value types are objects created on the stack. The variable contains the object itself rather than a handle to the object. Hence, the variable doesn't have to be dereferenced to manipulate the object, which of course improves performance. To declare a value type class, the *value* keyword should be used instead of the *ref* keyword. In this case, the variables would have been created on the stack. Instead of declaring handles for this class and then creating the objects on the CLR heap, the objects are declared in the same way as the built-in C++ types, and the member variables are accessed by the dot operator.

Now that you have written the *Animal* class, your application can use it just as the application would use a built-in type.

1. In the *main* function, delete the following line:

   ```
   Console::WriteLine(L"Hello World");
   ```

2. Declare and create two *Animal* objects in your *main* function.

   ```
   Animal cat, dog;
   ```

3. Use the member function *SetName* to assign the names Cat and Dog to the respective *cat* and *dog* objects, and set the *legs* variable for both objects to 4.

   ```
   cat.SetName("Cat");
   cat.legs = 4;
   dog.SetName("Dog");
   dog.legs = 4;
   ```

   To access the member variables and functions of an object, you use the dot operator (.). You can read this as "set the name of the cat to 'Cat'," with the dot operator relating the function to the object on which it is operating.

   Having created a couple of *Animal* objects and assigned data to them, you are now going to display that data on the screen.

4. Add the following lines:

```
Console::WriteLine("Animal 1");
Console::Write("Name:    ");
Console::WriteLine(cat.GetName());
Console::Write("Legs:    ");
Console::WriteLine(cat.legs);
Console::WriteLine();
Console::WriteLine("Animal 2");
Console::Write("Name:    ");
Console::WriteLine(dog.GetName());
Console::Write("Legs:   ");
Console::WriteLine(dog.legs);
Console::WriteLine();
```

Now, it's time to build the application.

5. On the Build menu, click Build Solution or use the keyboard shortcut F6.

In case you've had any problems putting the application together from the fragments in the preceding steps, the entire application is listed here:

```
#include "stdafx.h"

using namespace System;

ref class Animal
{
public:
    int legs;

    void SetName(String ^nm)
    { name = nm; }

    String^ GetName() { return name; }
private:
    String ^name;
};

int main(array<System::String ^> ^args)
{
    Animal cat, dog;

    cat.SetName("Cat");
    cat.legs = 4;
    dog.SetName("Dog");
    dog.legs = 4;
    Console::WriteLine("Animal 1");
    Console::Write("Name:    ");
    Console::WriteLine(cat.GetName());
    Console::Write("Legs:    ");
    Console::WriteLine(cat.legs);
    Console::WriteLine();
    Console::WriteLine("Animal 2");
    Console::Write("Name:    ");
    Console::WriteLine(dog.GetName());
```

```
        Console::Write("Legs:    ");
        Console::WriteLine(dog.legs);
        Console::WriteLine();
        return 0;
    }
```

6. If the build was successful, run the application by clicking Start Without Debugging on the Debug menu, or use the keyboard shortcut Ctrl+F5.

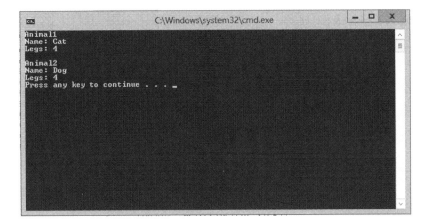

Quick reference

To	Do this
Create a class.	Use the keyword *class*.
Control the visibility of variables and methods.	Use the access control keywords *public*, *private*, or *protected*, followed by a colon (:).
Declare a reference type class.	Place the *ref* keyword before the *class* specifier.
Declare a value type class.	Place the *value* keyword before the *class* specifier.
Instantiate a reference type class object.	Use the name of the class when declaring an object; for example: `Animal cat;`

CHAPTER 3

Variables and operators

After completing this chapter, you will be able to:

- Declare (create) variables.

- Use the built-in C++ data types.

- Use the Microsoft .NET Framework String class.

- Assign values to a variable.

- Create expressions by using the C++ operators.

- Cast (change) the type of a variable.

In Chapter 2 "Introducing object-oriented programming," you looked at the advantages of object-oriented programming and developed a simple application to illustrate the creation and use of classes.

In this chapter, you'll take a closer look at how to create and use variables, the fundamental data types of C++, how to access and use classes from the .NET Framework, and how to create expressions by using C++ operators.

What is a variable?

Variables are locations in memory where data can be temporarily stored for use by the application. They have a name, a type, and a value. The value of the variable can be changed during the execution of the application; hence, the name variable. Before you can use a variable, you must declare it: you must specify its type, and you must give it a name. The type of a variable defines the allowable range of values that the variable can hold and the operations that you can perform on it.

The fundamental data types

C++ has a built-in set of data types, as outlined in the following table.

Type	Description	Comments
bool	A Boolean type that can contain the values true or false	
char, __int8	A single-byte integral type, often used to hold ASCII values	Values can range from –128 to +127.
short, __int16	An integral type; stores whole numbers	Values can range from –32,768 to +32,767. An unsigned short can range from 0 to 65,535.
int, __int32	An integral type; stores whole numbers	Values can range from –2,147,483,648 to 2,147,483,647. An unsigned int can range from 0 to 4,294,967,295.
long	An integral type like *int*, except on many compilers, it's twice the size	In Microsoft Visual C++, the *long* is the same size as the *int*. Therefore, it can only store the same range of values.
long long, __int64	An integral type	Values can range from –9,223,372,036,854,775,808 to 9,223,372,036,854,775,807.
float	Stores floating-point numbers; for example, 3.7	In Visual C++, the *float* stores up to seven decimal places. The range of values is 3.4E+/-38.
double	Stores floating-point numbers like the *float* but with greater precision and more accuracy	The *double* can store up to 15 decimal places. The range of values is 1.7E+/-308
wchar_t	A wide character or multibyte character type	

In some cases you'll see that there is a C++ name (for example, *int*) and a Microsoft-specific equivalent (*__int32*). The two names are equivalent, and it is most common to use the C++ name.

From these built-in types, you can construct other types, as you'll see in this chapter:

- Handle types; for example, *int^*

- Array types; for example, *int[]*

- Reference types; for example, *double%*

Or, you can construct user-defined types by creating data structures and classes. Classes were introduced in Chapter 2 and are elaborated upon in Chapter 6, "More about classes and objects." Data structures (structs) are covered in Chapter 9, "Value types."

C++/CLI data types

If you have ever looked at C++ outside the Microsoft .NET environment, there is one big difference of which you need to be aware. In "classic" C++, the sizes of the basic data types are not fixed: an *int* can be 4 bytes, 8 bytes, or indeed any size that makes sense for the platform on which it is running. In the .NET version, the sizes of the basic types are fixed so that (for example) *int*s are always 32 bits.

Declaring a variable

As I mentioned earlier, you must declare variables before you can use them. A simple declaration consists of a type, followed by one or more variable names separated by commas and terminated by a semicolon, as shown in the following example:

```
int primeNumber;
double x, y, z;
```

You can give each variable a qualifier before the type (for example, *unsigned*). You can also place an initializer after the variable name to give it an initial value (for example, *int i = 0*). The qualifier and the initializer are optional and are not required to appear in the declaration, but the base type and variable name must be present. The declaration is terminated by a semicolon.

```
[qualifier] type name [initializer];
unsigned int i;        // An unsigned integer variable i, note the
                       // qualifier limiting the variable to
                       // positive numbers.
long salary = 0;       // A long variable initialized to zero.
double y;              // A double variable without qualifier or
                       // initializer.
```

When you declare a variable, the compiler does the following

- Allocates enough memory to store the variable of that type and to associate the name of the variable with that memory location.

- Reserves the name of the variable to prevent it from being used by other variables within the same *scope*.

 Note Scope refers to that part of the code for which a variable is visible—in other words, where it can be used. The concept of scope is explained more in Chapter 4, "Using functions."

- Ensures that the variable is used in a way consistent with its type. For example, if you have declared a variable as a *char*, you can't store the value 3.7 in it.

Variable naming

A C++ variable name can be any combination of letters, numbers, and underscores, as long as the first character of the variable name is a letter or an underscore. Although C++ does not place any restrictions on your choice of variable names, they should be meaningful, and you should be consistent in your naming conventions to increase the readability of your code. C++ is case-sensitive. This means that *myvariable* and *myVariable* are two separate variables. However, it's not a good idea to differentiate variables solely on the basis of case; doing so could lead to confusion. It would be easy to type a letter in the wrong case and end up using a completely wrong variable!

> **Note** As is mentioned in Chapter 1, "Hello C++!," it's not a good idea to create identifiers that begin with two underscores or an underscore followed by a capital letter (for example, _A). Microsoft uses this naming convention to specify macros and Microsoft-specific keywords, so starting your variables with these combinations could lead to name conflicts.

Declaring multiple variables

You can declare several variables of the same type in the same statement simply by separating them with commas, as demonstrated in the following:

```
int x = 10, y, z = 11;
```

This statement creates three integers called *x*, *y*, and *z*. The first integer is initialized to 10 and the third to 11, whereas the second is not initialized.

Assigning values to variables

You assign a value to a variable by using the assignment operator = (the equal sign). The value on the right side of the operator is stored in the variable, which is on the left side. When assigning a value to a variable, the value must belong to the same type as the variable, it must be a type for which C++ will perform an assignment conversion (such as between float and integral types), or it must be explicitly converted (cast) to the correct type.

Assignment conversions

Assignment conversions occur when variables on opposite sides of an equal sign are of different types and the compiler can convert between the two types without any possible loss of data. For instance, assigning an *int* to a *double* results in an assignment conversion because conceptually all the compiler has to do is to add .0 to the integer to make the conversion.

You might occasionally need to force the compiler to perform a conversion that it otherwise wouldn't do. For example, dividing two integers results in an integer result: if you want a floating-point result, you can instruct the compiler to convert one of the values to a double, as illustrated here:

```
double result = double(640) / 480;
```

You give the name of the type to which to convert, followed by the value in parentheses. This process is called *casting*, and it can be rather dangerous because you're directing the compiler to apply a conversion that it otherwise would not do, and you'd better be sure you're correct.

```
int x;
float y;
double z;
x = 1;
z = x;
y = 3.56;
x = y;     // Assignment conversion from float to int
           // results in loss of data.
           // The integer 3 is stored in the variable x.
```

In this final case the compiler will generate the warning "C4244: '=' conversion from 'float' to 'int' possible loss of data." The reason for this is because the assignment to an integer will lose the fractional part, so 3.56 will be truncated to 3.

Handles and pointers

In standard C++, a pointer is a variable that holds the memory address of another variable or function, which means that you can use a pointer to refer indirectly to a variable.

In C++/CLI, however, the runtime is managing memory on your behalf, and it reserves the right to move things around to maximize the available free memory. This means that an object might not stay at the same address throughout its lifetime; thus, the address stored in your pointer might become out of date, leading to problems if you try to use it.

For this reason pointers, in the traditional C++ sense, are not used in C++/CLI. Instead, you use *handles* (also known as *tracking handles*), which also contain the address of a variable but which will be updated by the runtime if it has to move the variable around.

Although a handle contains an address and therefore can store a memory address of any data type, handle variables are declared to be data-type specific. A handle to a *Person* object can't store the address of an *Account*. A handle variable is declared in the same way as the data-type variable, but the handle operator ^ (caret character) is prepended to the variable name:

```
Person ^pp;          // handle to a Person
Account ^ac;         // handle to an Account
```

 Note It is in fact possible to use pointers in some circumstances in C++/CLI, but that is beyond the scope for this introductory discussion.

You typically create an object dynamically and obtain a handle to it by using the *gcnew* operator, as illustrated here:

```
Person ^pp = gcnew Person("Fred");
```

This code instructs the runtime to create a new *Person* object, passing in the string "Fred" as initialization data, and return a handle to the object it has created.

When you access a member of an object through a handle, you use the pointer operator (->), which is discussed in more detail in the following chapters.

Arrays

An array is a collection of data-storage locations, each of which holds the same type of data, such as all integers or all doubles. Arrays are very useful when you want to represent a collection of values (such as the number of days in each month or the names of company employees) and you know how many you need to store.

Unlike classic C++, arrays in C++/CLI are objects that know how much data they are managing. This makes them safer than traditional C++ arrays because any attempt to read or write past the end of the array results in a run-time error, but does not corrupt memory.

Each storage location is called an *element* of the array. Elements of the array are accessed by an index, which starts at zero and continues up to one less than the array bound. Why not start the index from one? This is to preserve compatibility with other C-type languages, which all start array indexing from zero.

To declare an array, you need to specify the type of item that you are going to store. You create array objects dynamically by using the *gcnew* operator.

```
array<int> ^arr = gcnew array<int>(10);    // Declare an array of ten integers.
int x;
arr[0] = 23;       // The first element in the array starts at offset 0
arr[9] = 21;       // The last element in the array starts at offset 9
x = arr[0];        // Use an element from the array
```

Constants

Like variables, constants are named data-storage locations. However, unlike a variable, the value of a constant can't be changed after it has been declared. It has to be initialized when it's created and can't be assigned a new value later. C++ has two types of constants: *literal* and *symbolic*.

A literal constant is simply a value typed into the application. The statements in the following code assign the literals 40 and Dog to the respective variables *noOfEmployees* and *name*:

```
noOfEmployees = 40;
name = "Dog";
```

A symbolic constant is a constant that is represented by a name. You define it in exactly the same way as a variable, but the qualifier must start with the keyword *const* and the variable must be initialized. After declaration, you can use the constant name anywhere that you can use a variable of that type, as shown in the following:

```
const unsigned long noOfFullTimeEmployees = 49;
const unsigned long noOfPartTimeEmployees = 234;
unsigned long noOfEmployees;
noOfEmployees = noOfFullTimeEmployees + noOfPartTimeEmployees;
```

There are a couple of advantages to using symbolic constants rather than literal constants:

- The symbolic names make the application more readable. The symbolic constant *noOfFull TimeEmployees* is more meaningful than the literal constant *49*.

- It's easier to change a single symbolic constant declaration than to find and replace all occurrences of a literal in a application.

However, using symbolic constants instead of literals can be taken too far. It is not necessary to replace all literals with constants. There are some constants that are intuitively obvious to everyone and that are not going to change; for example, the number of days in a week or months in a year. These values can be left as literals without reducing the readability or maintainability of the code.

Typedefs

A *typedef* is a user-defined synonym for an existing type. To create a synonym for a type, you use the keyword *typedef* followed by the name of the type and the new name you are defining. Because *typedef* is a C++ statement, you also need a closing semicolon:

```
typedef unsigned int positiveNumber;
```

This *typedef* declares *positiveNumber* to be a synonym of *unsigned int* and can be used in a declaration instead of the actual type name:

```
positiveNumber one, two;
```

The .NET Framework *String* class

The *String* class is not a built-in data type like *int* or *long*; it is a part of the .NET Framework. Because *String* isn't a built-in type, you must include some files in your project before the compiler will let you use it. Code that wants to use the *String* class needs to include the following line at the top of its source code file:

```
using namespace System;
```

This line makes it easier to use certain .NET classes. Because *String* is in the *System* namespace, its full name is *System::String*, but a *using namespace* statement such as this makes it possible for you to use the name without qualification. This will be explained in more detail later on.

The *String* class contains a large number of methods to simplify manipulating strings, such as *Insert* and *Replace*.

> **Note** After you initialize a *String* object, it is immutable: It can't be changed after it is created. The member functions of the *String* class that appear to alter strings, such as *Insert* and *Replace*, actually return a new *String* object, which contains the modified string. If you need to make repeated changes to a string, you should use the *StringBuilder* class, adding a *using namespace* statement for the *System::Text* namespace to simplify access.

Operators and expressions

Expressions are built by using operators that work with data—the *operands*—to give a result. Look at this example:

```
remuneration = salary + bonus;
```

Here the addition operator + (plus sign) is used to add the operands *salary* and *bonus*, and the assignment operator = (equal sign) is used to store the total in the *remuneration* variable.

Assignment operators

You use an assignment expression to assign a value to a variable. All expressions return a value when evaluated, and the value of the assignment expression becomes the new value of the object on the left side. This functionality makes it possible to assign the same value to a group of variables.

```
noOfMammals = noOfDogs = noOfCats = 0;
```

In this example, all three variables—*noOfMammals*, *noOfDogs*, and *noOfCats*—are set to 0.

Arithmetic operators

C++ has 12 arithmetic operators, 5 of which operate like the standard mathematical operators: the addition operator + (the plus sign), the subtraction operator − (the minus sign), the multiplication operator * (the asterisk), the division operator / (the slash), and the modulus operator % (the percent sign), which returns the remainder after division.

```
result = 4 + 2 - 3;   // result = 3
result = 4 * 5;       // result = 20
remainder = 7 % 3;    // remainder = 1
```

In addition, there are a number of arithmetic assignment operators, each of which consists of the operator and the = (equal sign): so the addition assignment operator += is a plus sign with an equal sign, and we also have −=, *=, /=, %=. These operators are shorthand forms that combine the corresponding mathematical operation with the assignment operation. So, the following two statements are identical:

```
a = a + 5;
a += 5;
```

The addition assignment operator is a shortcut operators; thus, there is no difference between the two statements. In both statements, an addition is performed, followed by an assignment. The second form is just a shorter way of expressing a frequently used operation.

The increment and decrement operators are similar shorthand operators, but these operators only add or subtract 1 from the value of the variable.

```
a++; // Adds 1 to the value of the variable a
a--; // Subtracts 1 from the value of the variable a
```

There are two forms of the increment and decrement operators: the prefix form $++a$ or $--a$, and the postfix forms $a++$ or $a--$. Although both forms add or subtract 1, in the prefix form, the mathematical operation is performed before the variable is used in the expression; in the postfix form, the variable is incremented or decremented after the variable has been used in the expression.

```
int a, b, c;
a = b = c = 0;
b = ++a;   // a = 1, b = 1
c = a++;   // c = 1, a = 2
```

In this code fragment, the final values of the variables are $a = 2$, $b = 1$, and $c = 1$. The prefix increment operator expression added 1 to the value of a before assigning the value of the variable a to the variable b. The postfix increment operator expression assigned the value of the variable a to the variable c and then incremented the value of the variable a by 1.

Relational and logical operators

Relational operators are used to compare two values or expressions, returning a value of true or false. C++ has six relational operators, as shown in the following code:

```
a > b    // returns true if a is greater than b.
a >= b   // returns true if a is greater than or equal to b.
a < b    // returns true if a is less than b.
a <= b   // returns true if a is less than or equal to b.
a == b   // returns true if a is equal to b.
a != b   // returns true if a is not equal to b.
```

A logical operator is used to relate two relational expressions. C++ has three logical operators: the AND operator && (two ampersands), the OR operator || (two pipes), and the NOT operator ! (an exclamation point). The AND operator relates two expressions, both of which must be true for the operator to return a true value. The OR operator returns true if either of the two expressions evaluates to true.

```
a && b                 // returns true if both a and b are true
(a > b) && (a < c)     // returns true if a is greater than b and a
                       // is less than c
a || b                 // returns true if either a or b are true
(a > b) || (a < c)     // returns true if either a is greater than b
                       // or a is less than c
```

The evaluation of a relational expression stops as soon as the logical value of the whole expression is determined, a feature known as *short-circuit evaluation*. For example, the expression *expr1 && expr2* is true only if both *expr1* and *expr2* are true. If *expr1* is false, the final value of the expression must be false, and therefore, *expr2* is not evaluated.

The NOT operator returns the negation of the Boolean value of its operand:

```
!a     // returns false if a is true
       // returns true if a is false
```

These operators are most often used in decision or loop structures, which are discussed in Chapter 5, "Decision and loop statements."

Bitwise operators

C++/CLI has six bitwise operators: the AND operator & (an ampersand), the OR operator | (a vertical bar), the exclusive OR operator ^ (a caret), the complement operator ~ (a tilde), the right-shift operator >> (two right angle brackets), and the left-shift operator << (two left angle brackets). These operators work on the individual bits of the byte and can only be applied to integral operands—the types *char*, *short*, *int*, and *long*. The bitwise AND operator compares the bits of two operands; if the bit in the same position for each operand is 1, the resulting bit is 1; if, however, either bit is 0 the resulting bit is set to 0. This operator is often used to mask off bits.

The bitwise OR operator compares the bits of two operands. If either bit is 1, the corresponding bit of the result is 1, and if both bits are 0, the corresponding bit of the result is set to 0. The bitwise OR operator is often used to turn on bits, flags, or options.

The exclusive OR operator sets the result bit to 1 only if one of the operands has the corresponding bit set to 1. If the corresponding bit of both operands is 1 or 0, the bit is set to 0.

The complement operator reverses the bit setting of the operand. If the bit is 1, it is set to 0; if the bit is 0, it is set to 1.

The left-shift operator moves the bit pattern of its left operand to the left by the number of bits specified by its right operand. The bits vacated by the left shift are filled with zeros. The right-shift operator moves the bit pattern of its right operand to the right by the number of bits specified by its right operand. If the variable is an unsigned data type, the vacated bits will be filled with zeros; if the variable is signed, the vacated bits will be filled with the sign bit.

```
int a;
a = 5;
a = a << 2;     // The bits of a will be shifted two bits to the left
                // and the value of 20 assigned to a.
```

```
a = 5;
a = a >> 2;     // The bits of a will be shifted two bits to the
                // right and the value of 1 assigned to a.
```

The ternary operator

The ternary operator *?:* (a question mark and a colon) acts like an inline *if* statement. (See Chapter 5 for more information on *if* statements.) The expression to the left of the question mark is evaluated; if it is true, the value or expression between the question mark and the colon will be returned. If it is false, the value or expression after the colon will be returned.

```
int a;
bool b;
b = true;
a = b ? 1 : 2;   // b is true, so a is assigned 1.
b = false;
a = b ? 1 : 2;   // b is false, so a is assigned 2.
```

Type casting

C++/CLI supports the C-style cast operator, whereby the type to which you want to convert the expression is placed in parentheses in front of the expression; for example, (float) 7. It also supports five C++ cast operators:

- *static_cast<>*

- *const_cast<>*

- *dynamic_cast<>*

- *safe_cast<>*

- *reinterpret_cast<>*

The *static_cast<>* operator changes the data type of the variable, with the type to which you want to cast being placed in the angle brackets. For example, if an expression needs to convert an *int* to a *double*, the number should be cast by using the *static_cast<double>* operator. Here's an example:

```
int a = 10;

double b;

b = (int) a;                // old C-style cast

b = static_cast<double>(a); // C++ static cast
```

You use the *dynamic_cast<>* operator to cast objects down or across the inheritance hierarchy. The *const_cast<>* operator works with pointers, and references can be used to add or remove the *const* qualification of the variable. The *safe_cast<>* operator is an extension added to C++/CLI; it performs the same function as *dynamic_cast<>* but throws an exception if the cast fails. Using the *reinterpret_cast<>* operator, you can convert any pointer to a pointer of another type. This particular operator is not used that often in application code.

Operator precedence and associativity

There are two ways by which the expression *2 + 3 * 4* could be evaluated: It could be evaluated as (2 + 3) * 4, yielding a value of 20, or it could be evaluated as 2 + (3 * 4), yielding a value of 14.

The rules of operator precedence specify an unambiguous evaluation of expressions. Operators higher in the hierarchy are given precedence over operators lower in the hierarchy. Because the * operator is higher than the + operator, the second interpretation of the above expression, 2 + (3 * 4), would be evaluated. For situations in which two operators are at the same level in the hierarchy, the order of evaluation proceeds from left to right. Hence, *2 * 3 / 2 * 3* would be evaluated as ((2 * 3) / 2) * 3, giving a value of 9. Parentheses can be used to group operators and override the precedence hierarchy. For example, *(2 * 3) / (2 * 3)* results in a value of 1. Many people use parentheses even when they are not strictly required, simply to clarify their intentions. The following table shows the hierarchy of precedence from highest to lowest. Operators in the same row of the table share the same level of precedence.

Operator	Name
:: [] ()	Scope resolution, subscripting, function calls
static_cast<> const_cast<> dynamic_cast<> reinterpret_cast<> safe_cast<>	Casting operators
sizeof ++ — ^ ! – + & *	sizeof(), increment, decrement, complement, not, unary minus, unary plus, address of, dereference
* / %	Arithmetic operators
+ -	
<< >>	Bit-shifting operators
< <= => >	Logical inequality operators
== !=	
&	Bitwise AND
^	Exclusive OR
|	Bitwise OR
&&	Logical AND
||	Logical OR
?:	Ternary operator
= += -+ *= /= %= <<= >>= &= != ^=	
,	Comma

Quick reference

To	Do this

Declare a variable.	Specify the type, followed by spaces and then the variable name, followed by a semicolon. For example:
	
	`int number1;`
	`long longNumber1;`

Assign values to a variable.	Use the assignment operator =.
Group homogenous data together.	Use an array.
Prevent data from being changed.	Make the variable a constant. For example: `const int x = 10;`
Restrict the values a variable can accept to a small set.	Declare an enumerated constant, and declare the variable to be of that type.
Access a *String* class.	Use the .NET *String* class.
Convert one data type to another.	Use the *static_cast<>* operator.
Override default operator precedence, or make the code more readable.	Use parentheses to group operators.

CHAPTER 4

Using functions

After completing this chapter, you will be able to:

- Declare function prototypes.

- Define function bodies.

- Call functions.

- Deal with local and global variable scope.

- Define and use overloaded functions.

B y now, you should be fairly comfortable with basic C++/CLI syntax. You've seen how to declare variables, write statements, use operators, and perform simple console output. However, as your programs begin to grow larger, you need to organize your code to cope with the growing complexity.

In this chapter, you'll learn how to divide a C++/CLI application into functions. First, you'll see how to declare function prototypes to introduce the functions to the compiler. Next, you'll see how to define function bodies to carry out the required processing. For example, you might write a function to calculate the expected growth on an investment or to extract the user's password from a logon screen. Finally, you'll see how to call a function from elsewhere in your application.

Why use functions?

There are many good reasons for dividing an application into functions. Here are three of them:

- Each function is usually quite short and discrete. It's easier to write an application as a series of functions than as a single, long script because you can concentrate on one function at a time.

- It's also easier to read and debug an application that contains lots of small functions than one that contains a single, long function because you don't have to remember what the entire application is doing.

- Functions are reusable. After you've written a function, you can call it whenever you need it in your application, which reduces coding effort and therefore improves developer productivity.

Declaring function prototypes

A function prototype is a single-line statement that introduces the name of a function to the compiler. The prototype also indicates what types of parameters can be passed into the function and what type of value the function returns. The combination of information about a function's name and parameters is called the *function signature*.

Declaring a simple function prototype

The following example shows a simple function prototype:

```
void DisplayWelcome();
```

In this example, the name of the function is *DisplayWelcome*. The parentheses are required to indicate that this is a function. The parentheses are empty in this example, which means that the function doesn't take any parameters. The *void* keyword at the beginning of the function prototype indicates that the function doesn't return a value; presumably, the function just displays a welcome message on the screen.

> **Note** Some programming languages differentiate between functions (which return a value) and subroutines (which do not return a value). For example, Microsoft Visual Basic .NET uses the *Function* keyword for functions and the *Sub* keyword for subroutines. C++ only has functions; use the *void* return type if the function doesn't return a value. Also, notice the semicolon at the end of the function prototype. The semicolon is a statement terminator, and it marks the end of the function prototype. A function prototype doesn't give you any indication as to what the function does; it just provides the function signature.

A note on function naming

Some languages have very strong naming conventions that guide how you should construct function and variable names. C++ has never had such a universal convention, but if you're writing C++/CLI code, you would be wise to adopt the convention used in the Microsoft .NET libraries. Function names should start with a capital letter, and individual words within the name should also be capitalized, as in *DisplayWelcome* or *CreateNewCustomerOrder*. The exception to this convention is the entry point *main*, which is traditionally typed in lowercase letters.

In this exercise, you will declare a simple function prototype in a C++/CLI application. The function does not take any parameters, and it does not return a value, either.

1. Start Visual Studio 2012 and create a new CLR Console Application project named **InvestmentPlanner**.

   After the project is created, the source file appears in the editor window.

2. At the top of the file, immediately below the *using namespace System;* line, add the following function prototype:

```
void DisplayWelcome();
```

This line is the function prototype you saw earlier. You place function prototypes near the top of the source file so that they are visible to the rest of the code in the file.

3. On the Build menu, click Build Solution to build your application and check that there are no syntax errors.

There's no point in running the application yet because you haven't implemented or called the *DisplayWelcome* function. You'll do that later in this chapter.

Declaring parameters in a function prototype

Functions can take parameters to make them more generic. You must declare the data types for these parameters in the function prototype.

In this exercise, you will declare a function prototype that uses parameters.

1. Continue working with the project you created in the previous exercise.

2. Add the following function prototype immediately below the *void DisplayWelcome()* line:

```
void DisplayProjectedValue(double amount, int years, double rate);
```

This function prototype declares a function named *DisplayProjectedValue*. The function takes three parameters: a *double*, an *int*, and another *double*. The compiler uses this information to ensure that the function is always called with the correct number and types of parameters.

 Tip Parameter names are optional in the function prototype. Strictly speaking, you could omit the parameter names and just specify the parameter types. However, parameter names help to convey the meaning of the parameters, so it's good practice to use them.

3. Build your application to check the syntax.

Declaring the return type in a function prototype

As well as specifying input parameters for a function, you must also specify a return type for the function. As you saw earlier, the *void* return type indicates that the function does not return a value.

In this exercise, you will see how to specify a non-*void* return type for a function.

1. Continue working with the project from the previous exercise.

2. Add the following function prototype immediately below the *void DisplayProjectedValue()* line:

```
double GetInvestmentAmount();
```

This function prototype declares a function named *GetInvestmentAmount*. The function doesn't take any parameters, but it returns a double.

3. Add another function prototype as follows, immediately below the *double GetInvestment Amount()* line:

```
int GetInvestmentPeriod(int min, int max);
```

This example shows how to declare a function that takes parameters and returns a value. The *GetInvestmentPeriod* function takes two *int* parameters and returns an *int*.

> **Note** The parameter types and return type are independent of one another. The fact that the *GetInvestmentPeriod* parameters and return type are all *int*s is entirely coincidental. It's quite easy to imagine a function whose parameter types and return type are different, as shown in this example:
>
> ```
> double CalculateAverageValue(int number1, int number2);
> ```

4. Build your application.

Declaring default values for function parameters

When you declare a function prototype, you can specify default values for some or all of its parameters. Default values are useful for parameters that usually have the same value each time the function is called. Specifying a default value for a function parameter means that you can omit the parameter value when you call the function; the compiler will substitute the default value on your behalf.

In this exercise, you will define default parameters in one of the function prototypes you declared earlier.

1. Continue working with the project from the previous exercise.

2. Find the following function prototype:

```
int GetInvestmentPeriod(int min, int max);
```

3. Modify the function prototype as follows to define default parameter values:

```
int GetInvestmentPeriod(int min=10, int max=25);
```

This function prototype has two parameters named *min* and *max*. The parameters are followed by = (the equal sign) and then a default value. We have defined a default value of 10 for the *min* parameter and a default value of 25 for the *max* parameter. You'll see how to call this function in the section "Calling functions" later in this chapter.

4. Build your application.

Defining function bodies

In the previous section, you learned how to declare function prototypes. Recall that a function prototype specifies the name of a function, its parameter list, and its return type. However, function prototypes do not contain any executable statements; they do not inform you as to what the function will do when it is called.

To provide the behavior for a function, you must define a function body. The function body contains executable statements to perform the desired operations in the function. In this section, you will define function bodies for all the function prototypes introduced earlier.

Defining a simple function body

The following example shows a simple function body, corresponding to the *DisplayWelcome* function prototype from earlier in chapter:

```
void DisplayWelcome()
{
    Console::WriteLine("-------------------------------------");
    Console::WriteLine(
        "Welcome to your friendly Investment Planner");
    Console::WriteLine("-------------------------------------");
    return;
}
```

Notice that the first line of the function body is identical to the function prototype, except that there is no semicolon. This first line is known as the *function header*.

After the function header, a pair of braces ({}) encloses the executable statements for the function body. In this example, the *DisplayWelcome* function displays a simple welcome message on the screen. In the next two sections you'll see more complex functions that perform console input and mathematical calculations.

The *return* keyword at the end of the function causes flow of control to return to the calling function. In this example, the *return* keyword is superfluous because the closing brace of the function acts as an implicit return. However, you can use *return* in other locations in a function, such as within an *if* statement, to return prematurely from a function. You'll see more about the *if* statement in Chapter 5, "Decision and loop statements."

In this exercise, you will add the *DisplayWelcome* function body to your C++/CLI application.

1. Continue working with the project you created earlier in this chapter.

2. Locate the end of the *main* function. On the next line, define the *DisplayWelcome* function body as follows:

```
void DisplayWelcome()
{
    Console::WriteLine("------------------------------");
    Console::WriteLine(
        "Welcome to your friendly Investment Planner");
```

```
    Console::WriteLine("--------------------------------");
    return;
}
```

3. Build your application. You shouldn't get any compiler errors.

> **Note** You can define function bodies in any order in C++/CLI. For example, you can place the *DisplayWelcome* function body before or after the *main* function body. However, functions cannot be nested. You can't define one function body inside the braces (({})) of another function.

Defining a function body that uses parameters

When you define a function body that uses parameters, you must define exactly the same number and types of parameters as in the function prototype. This is quite reasonable: The whole point of the function prototype is to introduce the exact signature of the function.

> **Tip** The function body can use different parameter names than the prototype because the parameter names in the prototype are there just for documentation. However, for consistency, you should use the same parameter names in the prototype and the function body.

In this exercise, you will define a function body for the *DisplayProjectedValue* function. You saw the prototype for this function earlier.

```
void DisplayProjectedValue(double amount, int years, double rate);
```

The function body will have the same signature as the prototype and will calculate the projected value of an investment after a specified number of years at a particular growth rate.

1. Continue working with the project from the previous exercise.

2. Scroll to the end of the source code and add the following lines—this is the start of the *DisplayProjectedValue* function body:

```
void DisplayProjectedValue(double amount, int years, double rate)
{
```

3. Define some local variables within the function:

```
double rateFraction = 1 + (rate/100);
double finalAmount = amount * Math::Pow(rateFraction, years);
finalAmount = Math::Round(finalAmount, 2);
```

Here, the *rateFraction* variable holds the growth rate as a fractional value. For example, if the rate is 6 percent, *rateFraction* will be 1.06.

The expression *Math::Pow(rateFraction, years)* shows how to raise a number to a power in C++/CLI. For example, *Math::Pow(1.06, 3)* is equivalent to 1.06 * 1.06 * 1.06.

The expression *Math::Round(finalAmount, 2)* rounds *finalAmount* to two decimal places. For example, if *finalAmount* is 1000.775, the rounded value will be 1000.78.

4. Add the following statements to the function to display the result of the calculations:

```
Console::Write("Investment amount: ");
Console::WriteLine(amount);
Console::Write("Growth rate [%]: ");
Console::WriteLine(rate);
Console::Write("Period [years]: ");
Console::WriteLine(years);
Console::Write("Projected final value of investment: ");
Console::WriteLine(finalAmount);
return;
}
```

5. Build your application.

Defining a function body that returns a value

When you define a function with a non-*void* return type, you must return an appropriate value from the function. To return a value, use the *return* keyword followed by the value that you want to return.

> **Note** If you forget to return a value, you'll get an error when the compiler reaches the closing brace of the function. This point is where the compiler realizes you haven't returned a value from the function.

In this exercise, you will define a function body for the *GetInvestmentAmount* function. Here is the prototype for the function, as you saw earlier:

```
double GetInvestmentAmount();
```

The function asks the user how much money she wants to invest. It returns this value as a *double* data type.

You will also define a function body for the *GetInvestmentPeriod* function. The prototype for this function is as follows:

```
int GetInvestmentPeriod(int min=10, int max=25);
```

The function asks the user how long she wants to invest the money. It returns this value as an *int* value.

1. Continue working with the project from the previous exercise.

2. Scroll to the end of the source code and define the *GetInvestmentAmount* function body as follows:

```
double GetInvestmentAmount()
{
    Console::Write("How much money do you want to invest? ");

    String ^input = Console::ReadLine();
    double amount = Convert::ToDouble(input);
    return amount;
}
```

The first statement displays a prompt message on the console, asking the user how much money she wants to invest. The *Console::ReadLine* function call reads a line of text from the keyboard, and the result is assigned to a *String* variable.

The *Convert::ToDouble* function call parses the *String* and converts it to a *double* value. The *return* statement returns this value back to the calling function.

> **Tip** You can declare local variables anywhere in a function. For example, here the *input* and *amount* variables are declared halfway down the *GetInvestmentAmount* function. Typically, you should declare variables at the point where they are first needed in the function, which is different from the C programming language, for which you have to declare local variables at the start of a block.

3. Add the following function body:

```
int GetInvestmentPeriod(int min, int max)
{
    Console::Write("Over how many years [");
    Console::Write("min=");
    Console::Write(min);
    Console::Write(", max=");
    Console::Write(max);
    Console::Write("] ? ");

    String ^input = Console::ReadLine();
    int years = Convert::ToInt32(input);
    return years;
}
```

The *Console::Write* function calls ask the user to enter a value between *min* and *max*. These values are supplied as parameters into the *GetInvestmentPeriod* function.

The *Console::ReadLine* function call reads the user's input as a *String*, and the *Convert::ToInt32* function call converts this value into a 32-bit integer. The *return* statement returns this value to the calling function.

Note The function prototype for *GetInvestmentPeriod* declared default values for the *min* and *max* parameters. The default value for *min* is 10, and the default value for *max* is 25. Default values are specified only in the function prototype—you don't mention these default values in the function body. If you accidentally define the default values in the function body as well as in the function prototype, you'll get a compiler error at the function body.

4. Build your application.

Calling functions

Now that you have defined all the function bodies in the sample application, the last step is to call the functions at the appropriate place in the application.

To call a function, specify its name followed by a pair of parentheses. For example, you can call the *DisplayWelcome* function as follows:

```
DisplayWelcome();
```

This is a simple example because the function doesn't take any parameters or return a value.

If you want to call a function that returns a value, you can assign the return value to a variable. The following example calls the *GetInvestmentAmount* function and assigns the return value (a *double*) to a local variable named *sum*:

```
double sum = GetInvestmentAmount();
```

Note You can ignore the return value from a function if you want. When you call the function, leave out the assignment operator on the left side of the function name. The function still returns the value, but the value is discarded.

If you want to call a function that takes parameters, pass the parameter values between the parentheses in the function call. The following example calls the *DisplayProjectedValue* function, passing in three literal values as parameters:

```
DisplayProjectedValue(10000, 25, 6.0);
```

Note You don't specify the parameter data types when you call a function. Just provide the parameter values.

The following example shows how to call a function that takes parameters and returns a value. In this example, you call the *GetInvestmentPeriod* function to get a value between 5 and 25. You assign the return value to a local *int* variable named *period*:

```
int period = GetInvestmentPeriod(5, 25);
```

Calling functions in the sample application

In this exercise, you will extend your sample application to include the function calls you've just seen.

1. Continue working with the project from the previous exercise.

2. Locate the *main* function and then replace the line that prints "Hello, world" with the following statement, which calls the *DisplayWelcome* function:

    ```
    DisplayWelcome();
    ```

3. Add the following statements to display an illustration of investment growth.

    ```
    Console::WriteLine("\nIllustration...");
    DisplayProjectedValue(10000, 25, 6.0);
    ```

    The *DisplayProjectedValue* function call displays the value of 10,000 after 25 years at a growth rate of 6 percent.

4. Next add the following statements to ask the user how much he wants to invest and for how long.

    ```
    Console::WriteLine("\nEnter details for your investment:");
    double sum = GetInvestmentAmount();
    int period = GetInvestmentPeriod(5, 25);
    ```

    The *GetInvestmentAmount* and *GetInvestmentPeriod* function calls return these values.

> **Note** The *GetInvestmentPeriod* function has default values for each of its parameters. (The first parameter has a default value of 10, and the second parameter has a default value of 25.) You can use these default values when you call the function. For example, the following function call uses the default value for the second parameter:
>
> ```
> int period = GetInvestmentPeriod(5);   // First parameter is 5;
>                                        // second parameter
>                                        // defaults to 25.
> ```
>
> If you use a default value for a parameter, you must use the default values for each subsequent parameter in the parameter list. For example, the following function call is invalid:
>
> ```
> int period = GetInvestmentPeriod(, 20);   // Try to use default value
>                                           // for just the first
>                                           // parameter - illegal.
> ```

5. Add the following statements to calculate and display the projected final value of this investment, assuming a growth rate of 6 percent:

```
Console::WriteLine("\nYour plan...");
DisplayProjectedValue(sum, period, 6.0);
```

6. Build your application and fix any compiler errors. On the Debug menu, click Start Without Debugging to run the application. You should see output similar to the following:

```
Welcome to your Friendly Investment Planner

Illustration:
Amount: 10000
Rate (%): 6
Period (years): 25
Projected final amount: 42918.71
Enter details for your investment:
How much money do you want to invest?
```

Stepping through the application by using debugger

In this exercise, you will step through the application by using the debugger. Doing so will help you understand how the flow of control passes from one function to another in your application. This exercise also illustrates the concept of variable scope. You will see how local variables in a function come into scope during the function's execution and disappear from scope at the end of the function.

1. Open the project from the previous exercise.

2. Locate the *main* function.

3. In the gray border to the left of the code, click next to the *DisplayWelcome* function call to insert a debug breakpoint. A red dot appears in the border, as shown in the graphic that follows.

 Tip If you add a breakpoint in the wrong place, simply click again on the red dot to remove it.

```
InvestmentPlanner.cpp + ×
(Global Scope)                                           ▼  ⊙  main(array<System::String^>^ args)                    ▼

   ⊟int main(array<System::String ^> ^args)
    {
●       DisplayWelcome();

        Console::WriteLine("\nIllustration: ");
        DisplayProjectedValue(10000, 25, 6.0);

        Console::WriteLine("Enter details for your investment:");
        double sum = GetInvestmentAmount();
        int period = GetInvestmentPeriod(5, 25);

        Console::WriteLine("\nYour plan:");
        DisplayProjectedValue(sum, period, 6.0);

        return 0;
    }

   ⊟void DisplayWelcome()
    {
        Console::WriteLine("------------------------------------------------");
        Console::WriteLine("Welcome to your friendly Investment Planner");
100 %   ▼  <                                      ▓                                          >
```

4. Start the debugging session by pressing F5.

   After the application loads, it executes and stops at the breakpoint in the *main* function.

```
InvestmentPlanner.cpp + ×
(Global Scope)                                           ▼  ⊙  main(array<System::String^>^ args)                    ▼

   ⊟int main(array<System::String ^> ^args)
    {
⇨       DisplayWelcome();

        Console::WriteLine("\nIllustration: ");
        DisplayProjectedValue(10000, 25, 6.0);

        Console::WriteLine("Enter details for your investment:");
        double sum = GetInvestmentAmount();
        int period = GetInvestmentPeriod(5, 25);

        Console::WriteLine("\nYour plan:");
        DisplayProjectedValue(sum, period, 6.0);

        return 0;
    }

   ⊟void DisplayWelcome()
    {
100 %   ▼  <                                      ▓                                          >
```

A yellow arrow appears in the margin next to the *DisplayWelcome* function call. The yellow arrow indicates that this is the next statement to be executed.

5. Press F11 to step into the *DisplayWelcome* function.

   The debugger calls the *DisplayWelcome* function and displays a yellow arrow at the start of that function.

```
InvestmentPlanner.cpp + X
(Global Scope)                          ▼ ☺ DisplayWelcome()
        DisplayProjectedValue(sum, period, 6.0);

            return 0;
        }

    ⊟void DisplayWelcome()
        {
⇨           Console::WriteLine("-------------------------------------------------");
            Console::WriteLine("Welcome to your Friendly Investment Planner");
            Console::WriteLine("-------------------------------------------------");
        }

    ⊟void DisplayProjectedValue(double amount, int years, double rate)
        {
            double rateFraction = 1 + (rate/100);
            double finalAmount = amount * Math::Pow(rateFraction, years);
            finalAmount = Math::Round(finalAmount, 2);

            Console::Write("Amount: ");
            Console::WriteLine(amount);
            Console::Write("Rate (%): ");
100 %    ▼ ◄
```

Note You can also use the Debug toolbar to control the debugger. To display the Debug toolbar, on the View menu, point to Toolbars and then click Debug from the list of toolbars that appears. Each of the debug function keys mentioned in the remainder of this exercise has an equivalent Debug toolbar button.

6. Press F10 several times to step over each statement one at a time in the *DisplayWelcome* function.

This causes a welcome message to be displayed in the console window. At the end of the function, the debugger returns you to the *main* function. The yellow arrow indicates the next statement to execute in *main*.

```
InvestmentPlanner.cpp + X
(Global Scope)                          ▼ ☺ main(array<System::String^>^ args)
        void DisplayWelcome();
        void DisplayProjectedValue(double amount, int years, double rate);
        double GetInvestmentAmount();
        int GetInvestmentPeriod(int min=10, int max=25);

    ⊟int main(array<System::String ^> ^args)
        {
●           DisplayWelcome();

⇨           Console::WriteLine("\nIllustration: ");
            DisplayProjectedValue(10000, 25, 6.0);

            Console::WriteLine("Enter details for your investment:");
            double sum = GetInvestmentAmount();
            int period = GetInvestmentPeriod(5, 25);

            Console::WriteLine("\nYour plan:");
            DisplayProjectedValue(sum, period, 6.0);

            return 0;
100 %    ▼ ◄
```

7. Press F10 to step over the *Console::WriteLine* function.

   The debugger executes the *Console::WriteLine* function but doesn't take you through it step by step. The yellow arrow moves on to the *DisplayProjectedValue* function call in *main*.

8. Press F11 to step into the *DisplayProjectedValue* function. On the Debug menu, point to Windows, and then click Locals.

   The local variables in this function appear.

```
InvestmentPlanner.cpp    + ×
(Global Scope)                                    ⚙ DisplayProjectedValue(double amount, int years, double
    {
        Console::WriteLine("---------------------------------------'
        Console::WriteLine("Welcome to your Friendly Investment Planner'
        Console::WriteLine("---------------------------------------'
    }

    void DisplayProjectedValue(double amount, int years, double rate)
    {
        double rateFraction = 1 + (rate/100);
        double finalAmount = amount * Math::Pow(rateFraction, years);
        finalAmount = Math::Round(finalAmount, 2);

        Console::Write("Amount: ");
        Console::WriteLine(amount);
        Console::Write("Rate (%): ");
        Console::WriteLine(rate);
```

Name	Value	Type
amount	10000.000000000000	double
years	25	int
rate	6.0000000000000000	double
finalAmount	0.00000000000000000	double
rateFraction	0.00000000000000000	double

   The Locals window displays five local variables. The first three variables—*amount*, *years*, and *rate*—are the function parameters. These variables are already initialized with the values you passed into the function.

   The last two variables—*finalAmount* and *rateFraction*—do not have meaningful values because the variables haven't been assigned a value yet. In fact, the debugger is a little misleading here because the *finalAmount* and *rateFraction* variables haven't even been declared yet. These variables don't really exist until the variable declaration statements further on in the function.

9. Press F10 several times to step over the statements in the *DisplayProjectedValue* function. Observe how the *finalAmount* and *rateFraction* variables change during the function. (The debugger displays values that were changed during the execution of the previous statement in red for prominence.) Take a look at the console window to see what is displayed.

10. Keep pressing F10 until you reach the end of the *DisplayProjectedValue* function and return to *main*.

11. In *main*, press F10 to step over the *Console::WriteLine* statement.

12. Press F11 to step into the *GetInvestmentAmount* function. Step through the statements in this function. When the debugger executes the *ReadLine* statement, the console window appears and you are asked to enter a number. Type a number such as **20** and then press Enter.

13. Keep stepping through the *GetInvestmentAmount* function until you return to main.

14. Press F10 one more time and then examine the local variables in *main*. Notice that the return value from *GetInvestmentAmount* has been assigned to the *sum* local variable in *main*.

```
InvestmentPlanner.cpp ⊕ X
(Global Scope)                              ▾  Ⓘ main(array<System::String^>^ args)    ▾
    double GetInvestmentAmount();
    int GetInvestmentPeriod(int min=10, int max=25);

⊟int main(array<System::String ^> ^args)
    {
●        DisplayWelcome();

         Console::WriteLine("\nIllustration: ");
         DisplayProjectedValue(10000, 25, 6.0);

         Console::WriteLine("Enter details for your investment:");
         double sum = GetInvestmentAmount();
⇨        int period = GetInvestmentPeriod(5, 25);

         Console::WriteLine("\nYour plan:");
         DisplayProjectedValue(sum, period, 6.0);

         return 0;
    }

⊟void DisplayWelcome()
100 %  ▾  <                              ▦                              >
Locals                                                                ▾ ⌐ ×
  Name                  Value                             Type
   ⬥ args               {Length=0}                        array<Sy
   ⬥ sum                12000.000000000000                double
   ⬥ period             0                                 int
```

15. Continue stepping through the application in this manner until the application terminates.

Tip If the debugger takes you into a function that you're not interested in stepping through, press Shift+F11 to step out of the function. If you just want to run the application without stopping at all, press F5.

Understanding local and global scope

The previous exercise demonstrated how each function defines its own scope for local variables. The local variables are created during function execution and are automatically destroyed at the end of the function, which means you can quite happily have variables with the same name in different functions without interference.

It's also possible to declare variables globally, outside of any function. Global variables are visible in all function bodies that come after the global variable definition in your source file. You can use global variables as a rudimentary way of sharing information between multiple functions.

> **Important** Global variables are generally considered bad programming practice, especially in object-oriented languages such as C++. Global variables have too much visibility. Because global variables can often be used in several functions, if one becomes corrupt, it can be difficult to pinpoint where the problem occurred. Global variables also introduce too much dependency between functions.
>
> For these reasons, you should use global variables sparingly. A better way of sharing information between functions is to pass parameters and return values, as you saw earlier in this chapter.

In this exercise, you will define a global variable in your application. You will use this global variable in several functions to illustrate its global scope.

1. Continue working with the project from the previous exercise.

2. Before the start of the *main* function, define a global integer variable named *numberOf YourFunctionsCalled*, as follows:

```
int numberOfYourFunctionsCalled = 0;
```

3. Find the *DisplayWelcome* function in your code. At the start of this function, increment the *numberOfYourFunctionsCalled* variable, as shown in the following.

```
InvestmentPlanner.cpp  X
(Global Scope)                                    DisplayProjectedValue(double amount, int years, double rate)
    using namespace System;

    void DisplayWelcome();
    void DisplayProjectedValue(double amount, int years, double rate);
    double GetInvestmentAmount();
    int GetInvestmentPeriod(int min=10, int max=25);
    void DisplayProjectedValue(double amount, int years);

    int numberOfYourFunctionsCalled = 0;

    int main(array<System::String ^> ^args) { ... }

    void DisplayWelcome()
    {
        numberOfYourFunctionsCalled++;

        Console::WriteLine("---------------------------------------------");
        Console::WriteLine("Welcome to your Friendly Investment Planner");
        Console::WriteLine("---------------------------------------------");
    }

    void DisplayProjectedValue(double amount, int years, double rate)
```

Note You can click the minus sign (–) symbol to the left of the code to collapse a block of code. To view a collapsed block, click the plus sign (+) to expand it again. This can make it easier to work with code by hiding functions that are not of interest at the moment. In the preceding screen shot, the *main* function has been collapsed.

4. Add a similar statement to the start of every function in your application.

5. Modify the *main* function. At the end of this function, just before the *return* statement, display the value of the *numberOfYourFunctionsCalled* variable.

```
InvestmentPlanner.cpp  ⊞ X
(Global Scope)                                    ▼ ☺ main(array<System::String^>^ args)
    int numberOfYourFunctionsCalled = 0;

⊟int main(array<System::String ^> ^args)
    {
        DisplayWelcome();

        Console::WriteLine("\nIllustration: ");
        DisplayProjectedValue(10000, 25, 6.0);

        Console::WriteLine("Enter details for your investment:");
        double sum = GetInvestmentAmount();
        int period = GetInvestmentPeriod(5, 25);

        Console::WriteLine("\nYour plan:");
        DisplayProjectedValue(sum, period, 6.0);

        Console::Write("Number of your functions called: ");
        Console::WriteLine(numberOfYourFunctionsCalled);

        return 0;
    }
```

6. Build and run your application. How many of your functions are called during the application?

Overloading functions

With C++/CLI, you can provide many functions with the same name, as long as each function has a different parameter list. This process is known as *function overloading*. Function overloading is useful if you have several different ways of performing a particular operation based on different input parameters.

For example, you might want to provide an *Average* function to find the average value of two *double* values, and you might have another *Average* function to find the average value of an array of integers. You can define two functions to support these requirements. Give each function the same name, *Average*, to emphasize the common purpose of these functions. Define different parameter lists for the functions to differentiate one from another.

```
double Average(double number1, double number2);
double Average(int array[], int arraySize);
```

You must still implement both of these functions—there is no magic here! When you call the *Average* function, the compiler deduces which version of the function to call based on the parameter values you supply.

> **Note** If you define overloaded functions, the functions must have different parameter lists. If you define overloaded functions that differ only in their return type, you'll get a compiler error.

In this exercise, you will define an overloaded version of the *DisplayProjectedValue* function. The new version calculates a random growth rate between 0 and 20 percent rather than use a specific growth rate.

1. Continue working with the project from the previous exercise.

2. Add the following function prototype at the start of your code, below the existing prototype for *DisplayProjectedValue*:

```
void DisplayProjectedValue(double amount, int years);
```

3. In the *main* function, locate the second call to the *DisplayProjectedValue* function. Modify the function call so that you pass only two parameters into the function.

```
DisplayProjectedValue(sum, period);
```

4. Define the new *DisplayProjectedValue* function body as follows, placing it after the existing *DisplayProjectedValue* function:

```
void DisplayProjectedValue(double amount, int years)
{
    numberOfYourFunctionsCalled++;

    Random r;
    int randomRate = r.Next(0, 20);
    DisplayProjectedValue(amount, years, randomRate);
}
```

> **Tip** You now have two overloaded *DisplayProjectedValue* functions. It is good practice to keep overloaded functions together in the source code.

This function uses the *Random* class to calculate a random number between 0 and 20. The function passes the random number into the original version of the *DisplayProjectedValue* function to calculate the value of the investment using this random rate.

5. Define breakpoints at the start of both of the *DisplayProjectedValue* functions.

6. Build the application and start it in the debugger.

7. Observe which versions of *DisplayProjectedValue* are called as your application executes. See what random number the application uses for your growth rate.

8. Run the application several times to verify that the growth rate really is random.

Quick reference

To	Do this
Declare a function prototype.	Specify the return type of the function, followed by the function name, followed by the parameter list enclosed in parentheses. Remember to include the semicolon at the end of the function prototype. For example: `double MyFunction(int p1, short p2);`
Define default parameters.	Define default parameters in the function prototype, if required. Use an = operator, followed by the default value. For example: `double MyFunction(int p1, short p2=100);`

Define a function body.	Specify the return type of the function, followed by the function name, followed by the parameter list enclosed in parentheses. Do not specify default parameters here. Define the function body within braces. For example:
	
	`double MyFunction(int p1, short p2)`
	`{`
	`   int n = p1 + p2;`
	`   ...`
	`}`

Return a value from a function.	Use the *return* keyword, followed by the value that you want to return. For example: `return (p1 + p2) / 2.00;`
Call a function.	Specify the function name and pass parameter values within parentheses. If the function returns a value, you can assign it to a variable. For example: `double result = MyFunction(100, 175);`

Define and use global variables.	Define the global variable outside of any function. Use the variable in any subsequent function in the source file. For example:
	
	`int myGlobal = 0;`
	
	`void MyFunction()`
	`{`
	`   myGlobal++;`
	`   ...`
	`}`

To	Do this
Define and use overloaded functions.	Define several functions with the same name but different parameter lists. Implement each function. Call the version you want, using appropriate parameter values. For example:

```
// Prototypes
void MyFunction(int p1);
void MyFunction(double p1, double p2);
...
// Function calls
MyFunction(100);
MyFunction(2.5, 7.5);
...
// Function bodies
void MyFunction(int p1)
{
  ...
}
void MyFunction(double p1, double p2)
{
  ...
}
```

CHAPTER 5

Decision and loop statements

After completing this chapter, you will be able to:

- Make decisions by using the *if* statement.

- Make multiway decisions by using the *switch* statement.

- Perform loops by using the *while*, *for*, and *do-while* statements.

- Perform unconditional jumps in a loop by using the *break* and *continue* statements.

All high-level languages provide keywords with which you can make decisions and perform loops. C++ is no exception. C++ provides the *if* statement and the *switch* statement for making decisions, and it provides the *while*, *for*, and *do-while* statements for performing loops. In addition, C++ provides the *break* statement to exit a loop immediately and the *continue* statement to return to the start of the loop for the next iteration.

In this chapter, you will see how to use these statements to control the flow of execution through a C++/CLI application.

Making decisions by using the *if* statement

The most common way to make a decision in C++/CLI is to use the *if* statement. You can use the *if* statement to perform a one-way test, a two-way test, a multiway test, or a nested test. Let's consider a simple one-way test first.

Performing one-way tests

The following example shows how to define a one-way test in C++/CLI:

```
if (number < 0)
    Console::WriteLine("The number is negative");
Console::WriteLine("The end");
```

The *if* keyword is followed by a conditional expression, which must be enclosed in parentheses. If the conditional expression evaluates to true, the next statement is executed, which in this example will display the message "The number is negative". Notice that the message "The end" will always be displayed, regardless of the outcome of the test, because it is outside the body of the *if* statement.

Note There is no semicolon after the closing parenthesis in the *if* test. It is a common C++ programming error to put one in by mistake, as shown here:

```
if (number < 0);    // Note the spurious semicolon
```

This statement is equivalent to the following statement, which is probably not what you intended:

```
if (number < 0)
    ;    // Null if-body - do nothing if number < 0
```

If you want to include more than one statement in the *if* body, enclose the if body in braces (({})), as follows:

```
if (number < 0)
{
    Console::Write("The number ");
    Console::Write(number);
    Console::WriteLine(" is negative");
}
Console::WriteLine("The end");
```

Many developers reckon that it is good practice to enclose the *if* body in braces, even if it only consists of a single statement. This means that the code will still be correct if you (or another developer) add more statements to the *if* body in the future.

In this exercise, you will create a new application to perform one-way tests. As this chapter progresses, you will extend the application to use more complex decision-making constructs and to perform loops. For now, the application asks the user to enter a date and then it performs simple validation and displays the date in a user-friendly format on the console.

1. Start Visual Studio 2012 and create a new CLR Console Application project. Name the application **CalendarAssistant**.

2. At the top of the source code file, immediately below the *using namespace System;* line, add the following function prototypes (you will implement all these functions during this chapter):

```
int GetYear();
int GetMonth();
int GetDay(int year, int month);
void DisplayDate(int year, int month, int day);
```

3. At the end of the file, after the end of the *main* function, implement the *GetYear* function as follows:

```
int GetYear()
{
    Console::Write("Year? ");
    String ^input = Console::ReadLine();
    int year = Convert::ToInt32(input);
    return year;
}
```

4. Implement the *GetMonth* function as follows:

```
int GetMonth()
{
    Console::Write("Month? ");
    String ^input = Console::ReadLine();
    int month = Convert::ToInt32(input);
    return month;
}
```

This is a simplified implementation; later in this chapter, you will enhance the function to en-sure that the user enters a valid month.

5. Implement the *GetDay* function as follows:

```
int GetDay(int year, int month)
{
    Console::Write("Day? ");
    String ^input = Console::ReadLine();
    int day = Convert::ToInt32(input);
    return day;
}
```

Later, you will enhance this function to ensure that the user enters a valid day for the given year and month.

6. Implement the *DisplayDate* function as shown in the following code to display the date as three numbers:

```
void DisplayDate(int year, int month, int day)
{
    Console::WriteLine("\nThis is the date you entered:");
    Console::Write(year);
    Console::Write("-");
    Console::Write(month);
    Console::Write("-");
    Console::Write(day);
    Console::WriteLine();
}
```

Later in this chapter you will enhance this function to display the date in a more user-friendly format.

7. Add the following code inside the *main* method, immediately before the *return 0;* Line:

```
Console::WriteLine("Welcome to your calendar assistant");
Console::WriteLine("\nPlease enter a date");
int year = GetYear();
int month = GetMonth();
int day = GetDay(year, month);
```

```
// Simplified test for now – assume there are 31 days in
// every month :-)
if (month >= 1 && month <= 12 && day >= 1 && day <= 31)
{
    DisplayDate(year, month, day);
}
Console::WriteLine("\nThe end\n");
```

This code asks the user to enter a year, month, and day. If the date passes a simplified validation test, the date is displayed on the console. If the date is invalid, it is not displayed at all.

> **Note** This *if* statement combines several tests by using the logical AND operator *&&*.
> As you learned in Chapter 3, "Variables and operators," logical tests are performed
> from left to right. Testing stops as soon as the final outcome has been established.
> For example, if the month is 0, there is no point performing the other tests—the
> date is definitely invalid. This is known as *short-circuit evaluation*.

8. Build the application and fix any compiler errors that you might have.

9. Run the application. Type in valid numbers for the year, month, and day (for example, **2012**, **7**, and **22**).

    The application displays the messages shown in the following screen shot:

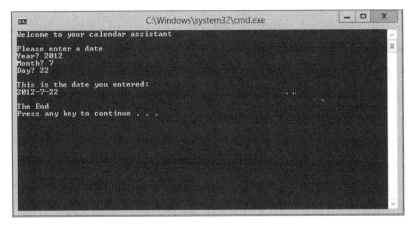

    Observe that the application displays the date because it is valid. The message "The End" also
    appears at the end of the program.

10. Run the application again, but this time, type an invalid date (for example, **2012**, **2**, and **33**).
    The application displays the messages shown in the following screen shot:

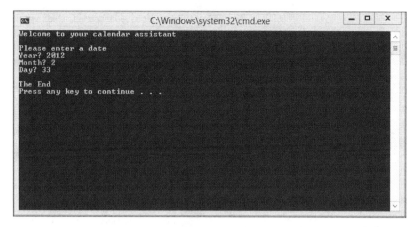

Notice that because the date you typed was invalid, the application doesn't display it. Instead, it just displays "The End." You can make the application more user-friendly by displaying an error message if the date is invalid. To do so, you need to use a two-way test.

Performing two-way tests

The following code shows how to define a two-way test for the Calendar Assistant application:

```
if (month >= 1 && month <= 12 && day >= 1 && day <= 31)
{
    DisplayDate(year, month, day);
}
else
{
    Console::WriteLine("Invalid date");
}
Console::WriteLine("\nThe end\n");
```

The *else* body defines what action to perform if the test condition fails.

In this exercise, you will enhance your Calendar Assistant application to display an error message if an invalid date is entered.

1. Continue working with the project from the previous exercise.

2. Modify the *main* function, replacing the simple *if* with an *if-else* statement to test for valid or invalid dates.

```
if (month >= 1 && month <= 12 && day >= 1 && day <= 31)
{
    DisplayDate(year, month, day);
}
else
{
    Console::WriteLine("Invalid date");
}
Console::WriteLine("\nThe end\n");
```

3. Build and run the application. Type an invalid date such as **2001**, **0**, and **31**.

   The application now displays an error message, as demonstrated in the following screen shot:

```
C:\Windows\system32\cmd.exe                        _  □  X

Welcome to your calendar assistant

Please enter a date
Year? 2012
Month? 2
Day? 33
Invalid date

The End
Press any key to continue . . .
```

Performing multiway tests

You can arrange *if-else* statements in a cascading fashion to perform multiway decision making.

The following code shows how to use a multiway test to determine the maximum number of days (*maxDay*) in a month:

```
int maxDay;
if (month == 4 || month == 6 || month == 9 || month == 11)
{
    maxDay = 30;
}
else if (month == 2)
{
    maxDay = 28;
}
else
{
    maxDay = 31;
}
```

This code specifies that if the month is April, June, September, or November, set *maxDay* to 30. If the month is February, *maxDay* is set to 28. (We'll ignore leap years for now!) If the month is anything else, set *maxDay* to 31.

> **Note** There is a space between the keywords *else* and *if* because they are distinct keywords. This is unlike Microsoft Visual Basic .NET, which uses the single keyword *ElseIf*.

In this exercise, you will enhance your Calendar Assistant application to display the maximum number of days in the user's chosen month.

1. Continue working with the project from the previous exercise.

2. Replace the *GetDay* function with the following code so that it uses an *if-else-if* statement to determine the maximum allowable number of days.

```
int GetDay(int year, int month)
{
    int maxDay;
    if (month == 4 || month == 6 || month == 9 || month == 11)
    {
        maxDay = 30;
    }
    else if (month == 2)
    {
        maxDay = 28;
    }
    else
    {
        maxDay = 31;
    }
    Console::Write("Day [1 to ");
    Console::Write(maxDay);
    Console::Write("]? ");

    String ^input = Console::ReadLine();
    int day = Convert::ToInt32(input);
    return day;
}
```

3. Build and run the application. Type the year **2012** and the month **1**.

   The application prompts you to enter a day between 1 and 31, as illustrated in the following screen shot:

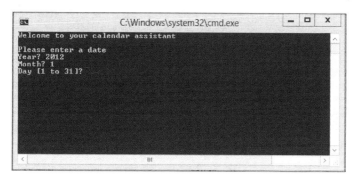

4. Type a valid day and close the console window when the date is displayed.

5. Run the application again. Type the year **2012** and the month **2**.

   The application prompts you to enter a day between 1 and 28, as shown here:

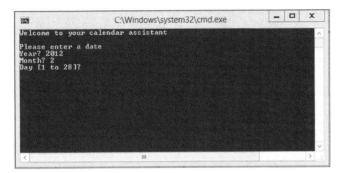

6. Type a valid day and close the console window when the date is displayed. (Don't worry about the date validation in *main:* You will remove it later and replace it with more comprehensive validation in the *GetMonth* and *GetDay* functions.)

Performing nested tests

It is possible to nest tests within one another. This makes it possible for you to perform more complex logical operations. The following code shows how to use nested tests to accommodate leap years correctly in the Calendar Assistant application:

```
int maxDay;
if (month == 4 || month == 6 || month == 9 || month == 11)
{
    maxDay = 30;
}
else if (month == 2)
{
    bool isLeapYear = (year % 4 == 0 && year % 100 != 0) || (year % 400 == 0);
    if (isLeapYear)
    {
        maxDay = 29;
    }
    else
    {
        maxDay = 28;
    }
}
else
{
    maxDay = 31;
}
```

If the month is February, you define a *bool* variable to determine if the year is a leap year. A year is a leap year if it is evenly divisible by 4 but not evenly divisible by 100 (except years that are evenly divisible by 400, which are leap years). The following table shows some examples of leap years and non–leap years.

Year	Leap year?
1996	Yes
1997	No
1900	No
2000	Yes

You then use a nested *if* statement to test the *bool* variable *isLeapYear* so that you can assign an appropriate value to *maxDay*.

> **Note** There is no explicit test in the nested *if* statement. The condition *if (isLeapYear)* is equivalent to *if (isLeapYear != false)*.

In this exercise, you will enhance your Calendar Assistant application to deal correctly with leap years.

1. Continue working with the project from the previous exercise.

2. Modify the *GetDay* function, replacing the *if…else if…else* statements to match the block of code just described to test for leap years.

3. Build and run the application. Type the year **1996** and the month **2**. The application prompts you to enter a day between 1 and 29. Type a valid day and then when the date is displayed, close the console window.

4. Run the application again. Type the year **1997** and the month **2**. Verify that the application prompts you to enter a day between 1 and 28.

5. Run the application several more times using the test data from the previous table.

Making decisions by using the *switch* Statement

Now that you have seen how the *if* statement works, let's take a look at the *switch* statement. Using the *switch* statement, you can test a single variable and execute one of several branches depending on the variable's value.

Defining simple *switch* statements

The example that follows shows the syntax for the *switch* statement. The *switch* statement tests the *numberOfSides* in a shape and displays a message to describe that shape.

```
int numberOfSides;    // Number of sides in a shape
...
switch (numberOfSides)
{
    case 3:  Console::Write("Triangle");      break;
    case 4:  Console::Write("Quadrilateral"); break;
    case 5:  Console::Write("Pentagon");      break;
    case 6:  Console::Write("Hexagon");       break;
    case 7:  Console::Write("Septagon");      break;
    case 8:  Console::Write("Octagon");       break;
    case 9:  Console::Write("Nonagon");       break;
    case 10: Console::Write("Decagon");       break;
    default: Console::Write("Polygon");       break;
}
```

The *switch* keyword is followed by an expression in parentheses. This expression must evaluate to an integer, a character, or an enumeration value. The body of the switch consists of a series of case branches, each of which comprises the keyword *case*, a value, and a colon.

The value identifying a case branch must be a constant of integer type. This means that integer numbers, enumeration values, and characters are allowed. For example, *5* and *a* are valid, but *abc* is not because it is a string literal.

Note Each case label specifies a single literal value. You can't specify multiple values, you can't define a range of values, and the values must be known at compile time. This means that you can't, for instance, say *case foo*, where *foo* is a variable whose value will only be known when the application executes.

Each case branch can contain any number of statements. At the end of each branch, use a *break* statement to exit the *switch* statement.

Note There is normally no need to use braces around the code in a case branch. The break statement marks the end of each case branch. However, you do need to use braces if you need to declare a variable within the branch code.

You can define an optional *default* branch in the *switch* statement. The *default* branch will be executed if the expression doesn't match any of the case labels.

Tip It's good practice to define a *default* branch even if you don't have any specific processing to perform. Including the *default* branch shows that you haven't just forgotten it. Also, the *default* branch can help you trap unexpected values and display a suitable warning to the user.

In this exercise, you will enhance your Calendar Assistant application to display the month as a string such as January or February.

1. Continue working with the project from the previous exercise.

2. Modify the *DisplayDate* function. Rather than display the month as an integer, replace the *Console::Write(month)* statement with a *switch* statement that displays the month as a string.

```
switch (month)
{
    case 1:  Console::Write("January");   break;
    case 2:  Console::Write("February");  break;
    case 3:  Console::Write("March");     break;
    case 4:  Console::Write("April");     break;
    case 5:  Console::Write("May");       break;
    case 6:  Console::Write("June");      break;
    case 7:  Console::Write("July");      break;
    case 8:  Console::Write("August");    break;
    case 9:  Console::Write("September"); break;
    case 10: Console::Write("October");   break;
    case 11: Console::Write("November");  break;
    case 12: Console::Write("December");  break;
    default: Console::Write("Unknown");   break;
}
```

3. Build the application.

4. Run the application several times, typing a different month each time. Verify that the application displays the correct month name each time.

Using fall-through in a *switch* statement

If you omit the *break* statement at the end of a case branch, flow of control continues on to the next statement. This process is called *fall-through*. This can be useful to avoid duplication of code, but be careful not to do it accidentally.

The following example illustrates why fall-through might be useful. This example tests a lowercase letter to see if it is a vowel or a consonant:

```
char lowercaseLetter;   // Single lowercase letter, for example 'a'
...
switch (lowercaseLetter)
{
    case 'a':
    case 'e':
    case 'i':
    case 'o':
    case 'u':  Console::Write("Vowel"); break;

    default:   Console::Write("Consonant"); break;
}
```

There is no *break* statement in the first four case labels. As a result, the flow of control passes on to the next executable statement to display the message *Vowel*. The *default* branch deals with all the other letters and displays the message *Consonant*.

In this exercise, you will enhance your Calendar Assistant application to display the season for the user's date.

1. Continue working with the project from the previous exercise.

2. Modify the *DisplayDate* function. After displaying the year, month, and day, add the following code after the line *Console::Write(day)* to display the season:

```
switch (month)
{
    case 12:
    case 1:
    case 2:  Console::WriteLine(" [Winter]"); break;

    case 3:
    case 4:
    case 5:  Console::WriteLine(" [Spring]"); break;

    case 6:
    case 7:
    case 8:  Console::WriteLine(" [Summer]"); break;

    case 9:
    case 10:
    case 11: Console::WriteLine(" [Fall]"); break;
}
```

3. Build the application.

4. Run the application several times, typing a different month each time. Verify that the application displays the correct season name each time.

Performing loops

For the rest of this chapter, you'll see how to perform loops in C++/CLI. You'll also see how to perform unconditional jumps in a loop by using the *break* and *continue* statements.

C++ has three main loop constructs: the *while* loop, the *for* loop, and the *do-while* loop.

 Note There is actually a fourth loop type, the *for-each* loop, but I'll leave discussing that until we get to arrays.

Let's look at the *while* loop first.

Using *while* loops

A *while* loop continues executing its body for as long as the condition in parentheses evaluates to true. The following example shows how to write a simple *while* loop in C++/CLI:

```
int count = 1;
while (count <= 5)
{
    Console::WriteLine(count * count);
    count++;
}
Console::WriteLine("The end");
```

You must follow the *while* keyword with a conditional expression enclosed in parentheses. As long as the conditional expression evaluates to true, the *while* body executes. After the loop body has been executed, control returns to the *while* statement and the conditional expression is tested again. This sequence continues until the test evaluates to false.

You must, of course, remember to include some kind of update statement in the loop so that it will terminate eventually. In this example *count++* is incrementing the loop counter. If you don't provide an update statement, the loop will iterate forever, which probably isn't what you want.

The preceding example displays the following output:

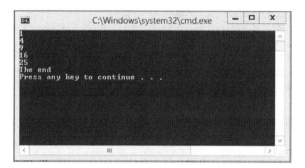

In this exercise, you will enhance your Calendar Assistant application so that the user can type five dates.

1. Continue working with the project from the previous exercise.

2. Modify the code in the *main* function by replacing the entire body of the function with the following code:

```
Console::WriteLine("Welcome to your calendar assistant");

int count = 1;     // Declare and initialize the loop counter
while (count <= 5)    // Test the loop counter
{
    Console::Write("\nPlease enter a date ");
    Console::WriteLine(count);

    int year = GetYear();
    int month = GetMonth();
    int day = GetDay(year, month);
    DisplayDate(year, month, day);

    count++;    // Increment the loop counter
}
```

3. Build and run the application. The application prompts you to enter the first date. After you have typed this date, the application prompts you to enter the second date. This process continues until you have typed five dates, at which point the application closes, as depicted in the following screen shot:

```
C:\Windows\system32\cmd.exe                    _ □ X

This is the date you entered:
2012-April-2
[Spring]

Please enter a date
Year? 2012
Month? 5
Day [1 to 31]? 12

This is the date you entered:
2012-May-12
[Spring]

Please enter a date
Year? 2012
Month? 8
Day [1 to 31]? 21

This is the date you entered:
2012-August-21
[Summer]

The End
Press any key to continue . . .
```

Using *for* loops

The *for* loop is an alternative to the *while* loop. It provides more control over the way in which the loop executes.

The following example shows how to write a simple *for* loop in C++/CLI. This example has exactly the same effect as the *while* loop.

```
for (int count = 1; count <= 5; count++)
{
    Console::WriteLine(count * count);
}

Console::WriteLine("The end");
```

The parentheses after the *for* keyword contain three expressions separated by semicolons. The first expression performs loop initialization, such as initializing the loop counter. This initialization expression is executed once only, at the start of the loop.

 Note You can declare loop variables in the first expression of the *for* statement. The preceding example illustrates this technique. The count variable is local to the *for* statement and goes out of scope when the loop terminates.

The second expression statement defines a test. If the test evaluates to *true*, the loop body is executed, but if it is *false*, the loop finishes and control passes to the statement that follows the closing parenthesis. After the loop body has been executed, the final expression in the *for* statement is executed; this expression performs loop update operations, such as incrementing the loop counter.

Note The *for* statement is very flexible. You can omit any of the three expressions in the *for* construct as long as you retain the semicolon separators. You can even omit all three expressions, as in *for(; ;)*, which represents an infinite loop

The preceding example displays the output shown in the following screen shot.

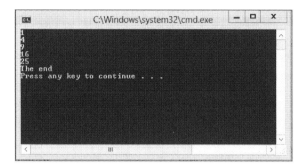

In this exercise, you will modify your Calendar Assistant application so that it uses a *for* loop rather than a *while* loop to obtain five dates from the user.

1. Continue working with the project from the previous exercise.

2. Modify the code in the *main* function to use a *for* loop rather than a *while* loop, as shown here:

```
Console::WriteLine("Welcome to your calendar assistant");

for (int count = 1; count <= 5; count++)
{
    Console::Write("\nPlease enter date ");
    Console::WriteLine(count);

    int year = GetYear();
    int month = GetMonth();
    int day = GetDay(year, month);
    DisplayDate(year, month, day);
}
```

Notice that there is no *count++* statement after displaying the date. This is because the *for* statement takes care of incrementing the loop counter.

3. Build and run the application. The application asks you to enter five dates, as before.

Using *do-while* loops

The third loop construct you'll look at here is the *do-while* loop (remember, there's still the *for-each* loop, which you will meet later). The *do-while* loop is fundamentally different from the *while* and *for* loops because the test comes at the end of the loop body, which means that the loop body is always executed at least once.

The following example shows how to write a simple *do-while* loop in C++/CLI. This example generates random numbers between 1 and 6, inclusive, to simulate a die. It then counts how many throws are needed to get a 6.

```
Random ^r = gcnew Random();
int randomNumber;
int throws = 0;
do
{
    randomNumber = r->Next(1, 7);
    Console::WriteLine(randomNumber);
    throws++;
}
while (randomNumber != 6);

Console::Write("You took ");
Console::Write(throws);
Console::WriteLine(" tries to get a 6");
```

The loop starts with the *do* keyword, followed by the loop body, followed by the *while* keyword and the test condition. A semicolon is required after the closing parenthesis of the test condition.

The preceding example displays the output shown in the following screen shot:

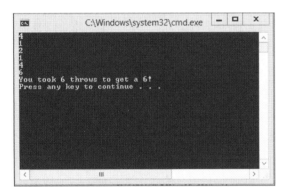

In this exercise, you will modify your Calendar Assistant application so that it performs input validation, which is a typical use of the *do-while* loop.

1. Continue working with the project from the previous exercise.

2. Modify the *GetMonth* function as follows, which forces the user to type a valid month:

```
int GetMonth()
{
    int month = 0;
    do
    {
        Console::Write("Month [1 to 12]? ");
        String ^input = Console::ReadLine();
        month = Convert::ToInt32(input);
    }
```

```
        while (month < 1 || month > 12);
        return month;
    }
```

3. Modify the *GetDay* function as follows, which forces the user to type a valid day:

```
int GetDay(int year, int month)
{
    int day = 0;
    int maxDay;

    // Calculate maxDay, as before (code not shown here) … … …

    do
    {
        Console::Write("Day [1 to ");
        Console::Write(maxDay);
        Console::Write("]? ");
        String ^input = Console::ReadLine();
        day = Convert::ToInt32(input);
    }
    while (day < 1 || day > maxDay);
    return day;
}
```

4. Build and run the application.

5. Try to type an invalid month. The application keeps asking you to enter another month until you type a value between 1 and 12, inclusive.

6. Try to type an invalid day. The application keeps asking you to enter another day until you type a valid number (which depends on your chosen year and month).

Performing unconditional jumps

C++/CLI provides two keywords—*break* and *continue*—with which you can jump unconditionally within a loop. The *break* statement causes you to exit the loop immediately. The *continue* statement abandons the current iteration and goes back to the top of the loop ready for the next iteration.

> **Note** The *break* and *continue* statements can make it difficult to understand the logical flow through a loop. Use *break* and *continue* sparingly to avoid complicating your code unnecessarily.

In this exercise, you will modify the main loop in your Calendar Assistant application. You will give the user the chance to break from the loop prematurely, skip the current date and continue on to the next one, or display the current date as normal.

1. Continue working with the project from the previous exercise.

2. Modify the *main* function as follows, which gives the user the option to *break* or *continue* if desired:

```
Console::WriteLine("Welcome to your calendar assistant");
for (int count = 1; count <= 5; count++)
{
    Console::Write("\nPlease enter date ");
    Console::WriteLine(count);
    int year = GetYear();
    int month = GetMonth();
    int day = GetDay(year, month);

    Console::Write("Press B (break), C (continue), or ");
    Console::Write("anything else to display date ");
    String ^input = Console::ReadLine();
    if (input->Equals("B"))
    {
        break;
    }
    else if (input->Equals("C"))
    {
        continue;
    }
    DisplayDate(year, month, day);
}
```

> **Note** The *Equals* method is used here to check that two strings contain the same content. You will see another (and more idiomatic) way to do this using the == operator when we discuss operator overloading.

3. Build and run the application.

4. After you type the first date, you are asked whether you want to break or continue. Press X (or any other key except B or C) and then press Enter to display the date as normal.

5. Type the second date, and then press C followed by Enter, which causes the *continue* statement to be executed.

The *continue* statement abandons the current iteration without displaying your date. Instead, you are asked to type the third date.

6. Type the third date and then press B, which causes the *break* statement to be executed. The break statement terminates the entire loop.

Quick reference

To	Do this
Perform a one-way test.	Use the *if* keyword followed by a test enclosed in parentheses. You must enclose the *if* body in braces if it contains more than one statement. For example: ```\nif (n < 0)\n{\n Console::Write("The number ");\n Console::Write(n);\n Console::WriteLine(" is negative");\n}\n```
Perform a two-way test.	Use an *if-else* construct. For example: ```\nif (n < 0)\n{\n Console::Write("Negative");\n}\nelse\n{\n Console::Write("Not negative");\n}\n```
Perform a multiway test.	Use an *if-else-if* construct. For example: ```\nif (n < 0)\n{\n Console::Write("Negative");\n}\nelse if (n == 0)\n{\n Console::Write("Zero");\n}\nelse\n{\n Console::Write("Positive");\n}\n```
Test a single expression against a finite set of constant values.	Use the *switch* keyword followed by an integral expression enclosed in parentheses. Define case branches for each value you want to test against, and define a default branch for all other values. Use the *break* statement to close a branch. For example: ```\nint dayNumber; // 0=Sun, 1=Mon, etc.\n...\nswitch (dayNumber)\n{\ncase 0:\ncase 6:\n Console::Write("Weekend");\n break;\ndefault:\n Console::Write("Weekday");\n break;\n}\n```
Perform iteration by using the *while* loop.	Use the *while* keyword followed by a test enclosed in parentheses. For example: ```\nint n = 10;\nwhile (n >= 0)\n{\n Console::WriteLine(n);\n n--;\n}\n```

To	Do this
Perform iteration by using the *for* loop.	Use the *for* keyword followed by a pair of parentheses. Within the parentheses, define an initialization expression, followed by a test expression, followed by an update expression. Use semicolons to separate these expressions. For example: ```\nfor (int n = 10; n >= 0; n--)\n{\n Console::WriteLine(n);\n}\n```
Perform iteration by using the *do-while* loop.	Use the *do* keyword, followed by the loop body, followed by the *while* keyword and the test condition. Terminate the loop with a semicolon. For example: ```\nint n;\ndo\n{\n String^ input = Console::ReadLine();\n n = Convert::ToInt32(input);\n} while (n > 100);\n```
Terminate a loop prematurely.	Use the *break* statement inside any loop. For example: ```\nfor (int n = 0; n < 1000; n++)\n{\n int square = n * n;\n if (square > 3500)\n {\n break;\n }\n Console::WriteLine(square);\n}\n```
Abandon a loop iteration and continue with the next iteration.	Use the *continue* statement inside any loop. For example: ```\nfor (int n = 0; n < 1000; n++)\n{\n int square = n * n;\n if (square % 2 == 0)\n {\n continue;\n }\n Console::WriteLine(square);\n}\n```

CHAPTER 6

More about classes and objects

After completing this chapter, you will be able to:

- Organize classes into header files and source files.

- Create objects.

- Define constructors to initialize an object.

- Define class-wide members by using the *static* keyword.

- Define relationships between objects in an application.

Chapter 2, "Introducing object-oriented programming," discusses how C++ is an object-oriented programming language. Recall from that chapter that you define classes to represent the important types of entities in your application, and you create objects as instances of these classes. For example, a Human Resources application might define classes such as *Employee* and *Contract*. When the application is running, it might create a new *Employee* object every time a new employee joins the company and a new *Contract* object to describe the employee's terms of employment.

This chapter builds on the introduction to classes and objects in Chapter 2. In this chapter, you'll see how to organize classes into header files and source files, which makes it possible for you to keep a clean separation between a class definition and its implementation. You'll also learn how to provide constructors to initialize new objects when they're created.

Most of the data members and member functions in a class are *instance members* because they belong to specific instances of the class. It's also possible to define *class members*, which belong to the class as a whole. You'll see how to define class members in this chapter by using the *static* keyword.

Finally, you'll see how to create object relationships in C++. This concept is important in object-oriented programming because it facilitates objects communicating with one another in a running application.

Organizing classes into header files and source files

Chapter 2 shows you how to define a simple class and implement all its member functions inline. Let's refresh your memory by considering the following class, which represents a credit card account:

```
ref class CreditCardAccount
{
public:
    void PrintStatement()
    {
        Console::Write("Credit card balance: ");
        Console::WriteLine(currentBalance);
    }
private:
    double currentBalance;
};
```

The *CreditCardAccount* class contains a single member function named *PrintStatement*. This function has been declared public, so it can be accessed by other parts of the application. The class also contains a single data member named *currentBalance*, which has been declared private to preserve encapsulation.

Notice that the class definition contains the full body of the *PrintStatement* function not just its prototype. This is known as an *inline function*. Inline functions are fine for small functions but can carry an overhead if used too much, and they can also make the class definition hard to understand. Imagine a class containing 100 functions, all of which are declared inline. The class definition would be very long, and it might be difficult to understand the structure of the code. A common solution in C++ is to divide the class definition into two parts: a header file and a source file, as shown in the following figure.

```
class CreditCardAccount
{
public:
    void PrintStatement();
private:
    double currentBalance;
};
```

CreditCardAccount.h

```
#include "CreditCardAccount.h"

void CreditCardAccount::PrintStatement()
{
    Console::Write("Credit card balance: ");
    Console::WriteLine(currentBalance);
}
```

CreditCardAccount.cpp

Note You can use any file names you like for the header file and source file. Most developers use the same name as the class, with the standard file extensions .h (for the header file) and .cpp (for the source file.)

The header file, CreditCardAccount.h, contains the *class declaration*. Notice that the class declaration now contains *function prototypes* rather than function bodies. These prototypes make the header file easier to read because the function signatures are more prominent.

The source file, CreditCardAccount.cpp, contains the *class definition*, which consists of all the function bodies for the class. Each function must be prefixed by the name of the class to which it belongs, followed by two colons, as follows:

```
void CreditCardAccount::PrintStatement()
{
    ... function body ...
}
```

The double-colon syntax (::) is the C++ *scope resolution operator.* In this example, the scope resolution operator tells us that the *PrintStatement* function belongs to the *CreditCardAccount* class.

The reason for this should be clear: How is the compiler to know that this is the *PrintStatement* function that is part of *CreditCardAccount* as opposed to some other *PrintStatement* function?

Note You must provide an *#include* statement at the start of the source file to include the header file for the class. For example, CreditCardAccount.cpp has an *#include* statement to include CreditCardAccount.h. The compiler needs the information in this header file to compile the function bodies in the source file, for example, to check that the spelling and number of arguments in *PrintStatement* matches the declaration.

Declaring a class in a header file

In this exercise, you will create a new application and define a *CreditCardAccount* class in a header file. (You will implement the class in the exercise that follows.)

1. Start Visual Studio 2012 and create a new CLR Console Application project named **CreditOrganizer**.

2. On the Project menu, click Add New Item.

3. In the Add New Item dialog box, in the pane on the left, select Visual C++ and then, in the center pane, click Header File (.h).

4. Toward the bottom of the dialog box, in the Name box, type **CreditCardAccount.h**, and then click Add.

   Visual Studio creates an empty header file.

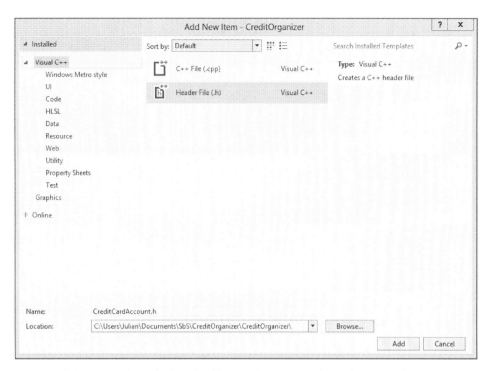

5. Type the following code in the header file to define the *CreditCardAccount* class:

```
ref class CreditCardAccount
{
public:
    void SetCreditLimit(double amount);
    bool MakePurchase(double amount);
    void MakeRepayment(double amount);
    void PrintStatement();
    long GetAccountNumber();

private:
    long accountNumber;
    double currentBalance;
    double creditLimit;
};
```

Every credit card account has a unique account number, a current balance, and a credit limit. The *SetCreditLimit* member function will be used to initialize the credit limit for the account. You can use the *MakePurchase* member function to make a purchase on the credit card. This function returns true if the purchase is allowed, or false if the purchase would cause the credit limit to be exceeded. The *MakeRepayment* member function repays some or all of the outstanding balance. The *PrintStatement* member function displays a statement for the account. And finally, the *GetAccountNumber* member function returns the number for the account.

6. Build the application and fix any compiler errors.

Implementing a class in a source file

In this exercise, you will implement the *CreditCardAccount* class in a source file.

1. Continue using the project from the previous exercise.

2. On the Project menu, click Add New Item.

3. In the Add New Item dialog box, in the pane on the left, select Visual C++ and then, in the center pane, click C++ File (.cpp).

4. Toward the bottom of the dialog box, in the Name box, type **CreditCardAccount.cpp**, and then click Add.

    Visual Studio creates an empty source file.

5. Add two *#include* statements at the beginning of the file, as follows:

    ```
    #include "stdafx.h"
    #include "CreditCardAccount.h"
    ```

    The file stdafx.h is a header file that can include other standard header files; you include stdafx.h at the start of every source file in your project.

    CreditCardAccount.h contains the class definition for *CreditCardAccount*. You include this header file here so that the compiler can check your implementation of the *CreditCardAccount* class.

6. Add the following code so that you can use classes and data types defined in the *System* namespace:

    ```
    #using <mscorlib.dll>
    using namespace System;
    ```

    The *#using <mscorlib.dll>* preprocessor directive imports the Microsoft Intermediate Language (MSIL) file mscorlib.dll so that you can use managed data and managed constructs defined in this library file.

    The *using namespace System* statement helps you to use classes and data types defined in the *System* namespace. Specifically, you will use the *Console* class to display messages on the console.

7. Implement the *CreditCardAccount::SetCreditLimit* member function, as shown here:

    ```
    void CreditCardAccount::SetCreditLimit(double amount)
    {
      creditLimit = amount;
    }
    ```

8. Implement the *CreditCardAccount::MakePurchase* member function as follows:

```
bool CreditCardAccount::MakePurchase(double amount)
{
    if (currentBalance + amount > creditLimit)
    {
        return false;
    }
    else
    {
        currentBalance += amount;
        return true;
    }
}
```

This function is called when the card owner attempts to make a purchase by using the credit card. The *amount* parameter indicates the amount of the purchase. The function tests whether the purchase would exceed the *creditLimit* data member, returning *false* if it would. Otherwise, the function adds the amount to the *currentBalance* data member and returns *true*.

 Note Member functions have unrestricted access to all the members in the class, including private members.

9. Implement the *CreditCardAccount::MakeRepayment* member function as follows:

```
void CreditCardAccount::MakeRepayment(double amount)
{
    currentBalance -= amount;
}
```

This function gives the user the opportunity to pay off some or all of the outstanding balance.

10. Implement the *CreditCardAccount::PrintStatement* member function as follows:

```
void CreditCardAccount::PrintStatement()
{
    Console::Write("Current balance: ");
    Console::WriteLine(currentBalance);
}
```

This function displays information about the current state of the account.

11. Implement the *GetAccountNumber* member function as follows:

```
long CreditCardAccount::GetAccountNumber()
{
    return accountNumber;
}
```

12. Build the application and fix any compiler errors.

Creating objects

After you have defined and implemented a class, you are ready to begin creating objects.

The following code shows how to create an object and call its public member functions:

```
CreditCardAccount ^myAccount;          // Declare a handle
myAccount = gcnew CreditCardAccount;   // Create a new
                                       // CreditCardAccount object
myAccount->MakePurchase(100);          // Use the -> operator to invoke
                                       // member functions
myAccount->MakeRepayment(70);
myAccount->PrintStatement();
...
```

The *gcnew* operator creates a new object of the *CreditCardAccount* class and returns a handle to this new object. The handle is used with the -> operator to invoke member functions on the new object.

> **Note** If you forget to delete an object of a managed class, the garbage collector is responsible for disposing of it. In Chapter 7, "Controlling object lifetimes," you can see how this works as well as how you can work with the garbage collector to ensure that your objects are tidied up correctly at the end of their lives.

In this exercise, you will create a new *CreditCardAccount* object, invoke its member functions, and delete the object when it is no longer required.

1. Continue using the project from the previous exercise.

2. If the file CreditOrganizer.cpp is not visible in the editor window, find the file in the Solution Explorer, and then double-click the name to display it in the editor.

3. Just after the *#include "stdafx.h"* line, add another *#include* directive as follows:

```
#include "CreditCardAccount.h"
```

This line makes it possible for you to create and use *CreditCardAccount* objects in this source file.

Replace the body of the *main* function with the following code:

```
CreditCardAccount ^myAccount;          // Declare a handle
myAccount = gcnew CreditCardAccount;   // Create a new CreditCardAccount object
myAccount->SetCreditLimit(1000);
myAccount->MakePurchase(1000);         // Use the -> operator to invoke member functions
myAccount->MakeRepayment(700);
myAccount->PrintStatement();
long num = myAccount->GetAccountNumber();
Console::Write("Account number: ");
Console::WriteLine(num);
```

4. Build the application and fix any compiler errors.

5. Run the application by pressing Ctrl+F5.

The application creates a *CreditCardAccount* object, makes a purchase and a repayment, and prints a statement. However, the account number displays as zero, as illustrated in the following screen shot:

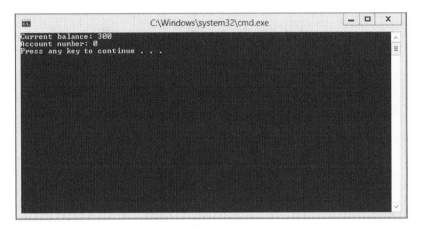

The reason for this is because the members of the *CreditCardAccount* object are initialized to zero when it's created. However, it doesn't really make sense to have an account without a number, so we'd like to ensure that every account is created with an account number.

You do this by defining a *constructor* in the *CreditCardAccount* class. The constructor is a member function that initializes new objects when they're created. Chapter 7 shows you how to tidy up objects just before they are destroyed.

Initializing objects by using constructors

In this section, you will see how to define constructor functions for a class.

Defining constructors

A constructor is a special member function that is called automatically when an object is created. The purpose of the constructor is to initialize the object to bring it into an operational state. You declare the prototype for the constructor in the class definition. The following example declares a simple constructor for the *CreditCardAccount* class:

```
ref class CreditCardAccount
{
public:
    CreditCardAccount();
    // ... Other members, as before
};
```

There are several important points to notice here. First, a constructor must have the same name as the class; this is how the compiler recognizes it as a constructor. Also, a constructor cannot specify a return type—not even *void*. If you do specify a return type for a constructor, you will get a compiler error.

You can implement the constructor in the source file as follows:

```
CreditCardAccount::CreditCardAccount()
{
    accountNumber = 1234;
    currentBalance = 0;
    creditLimit = 3000;
}
```

Note Although this example has set all three fields, the compiler will arrange for fields to be set to a default value. This is zero for numeric types, false for Booleans, and a "null" value for handles.

This simple constructor initializes every new *CreditCardAccount* object with the same values. A more realistic approach is to define a constructor that takes parameters so that each object can be initialized with different values.

Note You can provide any number of constructors in a class, as long as each constructor has a distinct parameter list. This is an example of *function overloading*.

In this exercise, you will add a constructor to the *CreditCardAccount* class. The constructor takes two parameters specifying the account number and credit limit for the new account. The current balance is always initialized to 0 for each new account, so there is no need to supply a parameter for this data member.

1. Continue using the project from the previous exercise.

2. Open CreditCardAccount.h and declare a public constructor as follows:

```
ref class CreditCardAccount
{
public:
    CreditCardAccount(long number, double limit);
    // ... Other members, as before
};
```

Tip Ensure that the constructor is public. If you make it private by mistake, you won't be able to create *CreditCardAccount* objects in your application.

3. Open CreditCardAccount.cpp and implement the constructor as follows:

```
CreditCardAccount::CreditCardAccount(long number, double limit)
{
    accountNumber = number;
    creditLimit = limit;
    currentBalance = 0.0;
}
```

4. Open CreditOrganizer.cpp and modify the statement that creates the *CreditCardAccount* object as follows:

```
myAccount = gcnew CreditCardAccount(12345, 2500);
```

This statement creates a new *CreditCardAccount* object and passes the values 12345 and 2500 into the *CreditCardAccount* constructor. The constructor uses these parameter values to initialize the *accountNumber* and *creditLimit* data members, respectively.

5. Build the application, fix any compiler errors, and then run the application.

The application now displays meaningful information for the account number, as demonstrated in the following screen shot:

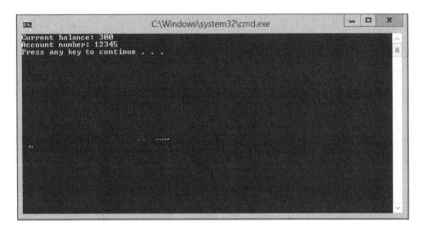

Member initialization lists

There's an alternative syntax for initializing data members in a constructor using a member initialization list, as follows:

```
CreditCardAccount::CreditCardAccount(long number, double limit)
     : accountNumber(number), creditLimit (limit), currentBalance(0.0)
{
}
```

The colon on the second line is followed by a comma-separated list of data members. For each data member, an initial value is provided in parentheses. Observe that the body of the constructor is now empty because we have nothing else to do—this is quite normal.

It is considered better practice to use a member initialization list rather than initializing members in the constructor body. There are also some situations in which you must use a member initialization list. You'll see such an example in Chapter 8, "Inheritance," when you delve into that subject.

Defining class-wide members

The data members and member functions currently defined in the *CreditCardAccount* class are instance members. Each *CreditCardAccount* instance has its own *accountNumber*, *currentBalance*, and *creditLimit*. Likewise, when you invoke member functions such as *MakePurchase*, *MakeRepayment*, and *PrintStatement*, you must specify which *CreditCardAccount* instance you're using, as shown in the following figure.

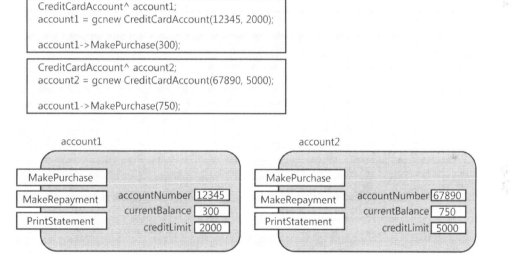

With C++, you can also define class-wide members that logically belong to the entire class rather than to a specific instance. For example, you can define a class-wide data member named *interestRate* that holds the interest rate for all accounts. Similarly, you can provide class-wide member functions called *SetInterestRate* and *GetInterestRate* to work with the interest rate, as shown in the following figure.

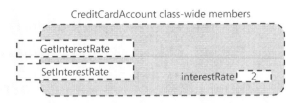

CreditCardAccount class-wide members

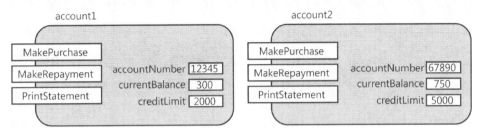

Let's see how to define class-wide data members and member functions.

Defining class-wide data members

To define a class-wide data member, use the *static* keyword, as demonstrated in the following code:

```
ref class CreditCardAccount
{
private:
    static int numberOfAccounts = 0;          // Declare class-wide data member
    // ... Other members, as before
};
```

This declaration informs the compiler that there is a class-wide data member named *numberOf Accounts* and initializes it to zero.

Note Like any other member of a class, if you do not initialize *numberOfAccounts* explicitly, the default initial value will be 0.

In this exercise, you will add a static *numberOfAccounts* data member to the *CreditCardAccount* class. You will increment this data member every time a new *CreditCardAccount* object is created.

1. Continue using the project from the previous exercise.

2. Open CreditCardAccount.h and declare the static *numberOfAccounts* data member as follows:

```
class CreditCardAccount
{
private:
```

```
        static int numberOfAccounts = 0;
        // ... Other members, as before
};
```

3. Open CreditCardAccount.cpp and modify the *CreditCardAccount* constructor so that it increments *numberOfAccounts* every time a new *CreditCardAccount* object is created.

```
CreditCardAccount::CreditCardAccount(long number, double limit)
{
    accountNumber = number;
    creditLimit = limit;
    currentBalance = 0.0;
    numberOfAccounts++;
    Console::Write("This is account number ");
    Console::WriteLine(numberOfAccounts);
}
```

4. Open CreditOrganizer.cpp and modify the main function so that it creates and uses several
   CreditCardAccount objects.

```
Console::WriteLine("Creating first object");
CreditCardAccount ^account1;
account1 = gcnew CreditCardAccount(12345, 2000);
account1->MakePurchase(300);
account1->PrintStatement();
Console::WriteLine("\nCreating second object");
CreditCardAccount ^account2;
account2 = gcnew CreditCardAccount(67890, 5000);
account2->MakePurchase(750);
account2->PrintStatement();
```

5. Build the application, fix any compiler errors, and then run the application.

   Every time a new *CreditCardAccount* object is created, the application increments *numberOf
   Accounts* and displays its latest value.

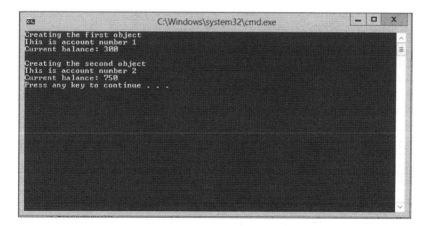

Defining class-wide member functions

It can be dangerous to make data members public; preferably, you want to give users access through member functions. To give access to a static data member, you can define a static member function. To define a class-wide member function, use the *static* keyword in the function declaration like this:

```
ref class CreditCardAccount
{
public:
    static int GetNumberOfAccounts();
    // ... Other members, as before
};
```

Implement the function in the source file to match the code snippet that follows. Keep in mind that you don't use the *static* keyword on the implementation, but only on the declaration inside the class definition.

```
int CreditCardAccount::GetNumberOfAccounts()
{
    return numberOfAccounts;
}
```

 Note Because it is not associated with an instance but with the class as a whole, a static member function can only access static class members. For example, *GetNumberOfAccounts* can access *numberOfAccounts*, but it cannot access *accountNumber*, *currentBalance*, or *creditLimit*, because they are part of an instance.

To call a static member function, use the class name rather than a particular instance, as shown in this example:

```
int n = CreditCardAccount::GetNumberOfAccounts();
```

The use of the class name emphasizes the fact that *GetNumberOfAccounts* is a class-wide member function rather than an instance member function.

 Note You have seen the syntax *ClassName::FunctionName* before. Every time you display a message on the console, you use a statement such as *Console::WriteLine("Hello world")*. This statement calls the static member function *WriteLine* on the *Console* class.

In this exercise, you will define a static *GetNumberOfAccounts* member function in the *Credit CardAccount* class. You will then call this function several times in *main*.

1. Continue using the project from the previous exercise.

2. Open CreditCardAccount.h and declare the *GetNumberOfAccounts* function as follows:

```
ref class CreditCardAccount
{
public:
    static int GetNumberOfAccounts();
    // ... Other members, as before
};
```

3. Open CreditCardAccount.cpp and implement the *GetNumberOfAccounts* function as follows:

```
int CreditCardAccount::GetNumberOfAccounts()
{
    return numberOfAccounts;
}
```

4. Open CreditOrganizer.cpp and modify the main function so that it calls *GetNumberOf Accounts* at various stages during execution.

```
int n = CreditCardAccount::GetNumberOfAccounts();
Console::Write("Number of accounts initially: ");
Console::WriteLine(n);
Console::WriteLine("\nCreating first object");
CreditCardAccount ^account1;
account1 = gcnew CreditCardAccount(12345, 2000);
account1->MakePurchase(300);
account1->PrintStatement();
Console::WriteLine("\nCreating second object");
CreditCardAccount ^account2;
account2 = gcnew CreditCardAccount(67890, 5000);
account2->MakePurchase(750);
account2->PrintStatement();
n = CreditCardAccount::GetNumberOfAccounts();
Console::Write("\nNumber of accounts now: ");
Console::WriteLine(n);
```

5. Build the application, fix any compiler errors, and then run the application.

   The application displays the messages depicted in the following screen shot:

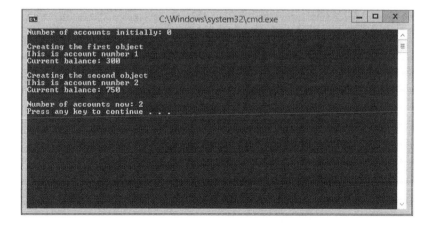

Class constructors

Suppose that you have a class-wide member but you cannot give it a value until run time. For example, you want to set the interest rate for the *CreditCardAccount* class to the current rate at the time the application starts.

Unlike standard C++, C++/CLI embodies the concept of a *static constructor*. An ordinary constructor is used to initialize instance members when an object is created; a static constructor is used to do *once-only initialization* for a class. You use them to do any setup that is needed before your class is used, and it is guaranteed to run before the class is used. This means that it is called before any objects of that type are created or before any static members of the class are used. It is as if the compiler makes sure that the static constructor is called the first time it meets a mention of the name *CreditCardAccount*.

A static constructor is like a normal constructor: it has the same name as the class, and no return type. In addition, static constructors have the *static* modifier and do not take any arguments:

```
ref class MyClass
{
public:
    static MyClass() { ... }
    ...
};
```

You can easily rewrite the *CreditCardAccount* class so that is uses a static constructor to initialize an *interestRate* member.

1. Continue using the project from the previous exercise.

2. Open CreditCardAccount.h and add a declaration for a private member called *interestRate*.

   ```
   static double interestRate;
   ```

3. Add the declaration for a static constructor in the public section of the class declaration.

   ```
   static CreditCardAccount();
   ```

4. Open CreditCardAccount.cpp and add the implementation of the static constructor. The call to *WriteLine* will help you see when the constructor is called.

   ```
   static CreditCardAccount::CreditCardAccount()
   {
       interestRate = 4.5;
       Console::WriteLine("Static constructor called");
   }
   ```

   Be aware that you need the *static* keyword here. You don't normally use *static* outside the class declaration, but in this case it is needed so that the compiler can determine that this is the static constructor.

5. Build and run the application. Here is the code that you should have at the top of *main*:

```
int n = CreditCardAccount::GetNumberOfAccounts();
Console::Write("Number of account initially:");
Console::WriteLine(n);
Console::WriteLine("\nCreating first object");
CreditCardAccount ^account1;
account1 = gcnew CreditCardAccount(12345, 2000);
```

The output from running the application appears as follows:

```
Static constructor called
Number of accounts initially: 0
```

You can see from this that the static constructor is called immediately before the first object is created.

Using constants in classes

You will often find that you need to represent constant values in your classes, members whose value cannot change as execution proceeds. These constants might be of two types:

■ Those which are constant and common to every object in the class. For example, a *Car* class might have a *numberOfWheels* member that is common to every *Car* instance and which has a fixed value of 4.

■ Those that are constant, but might be different for each object. For example, a *BankAccount* object has an account number; this is individual to each instance but cannot be changed after it has been set.

Using class-wide constants

A class-wide constant represents a value that is common to all instances of a class. For our *Credit Account* example, suppose that this kind of credit card account has a name, such as "Super Platinum Card." This name will apply to all cards of the same type, so it logically belongs to the class rather than each instance. Let us further suppose that the name associated with the card class isn't going to change. This makes it a candidate for a class-wide constant.

You can create a class-wide constant by using the *literal* keyword, as shown here:

```
literal String ^name = "Super Platinum Card";
```

A *literal* can have an initial value placed in the class definition. If you do this, it must be a value that the compiler can calculate. In other words, it can't depend on something that will only be known at run time.

Let's see how to add the *name* to the *CreditAccount* class.

1. Continue using the project from the previous exercise.

2. Open CreditAccount.h and add the declaration of a *literal* to the public section of the class declaration.

    ```
    literal String ^name = "Super Platinum Card";
    ```

    Because *name* is a constant, we can make it *public* because there is no danger that anyone can modify it. You can declare literals of built-in types, ref types, and value types.

3. You can access the literal through the class name. Add the following code to display the *name* to the start of *main*, before you create any *CreditCardAccount* objects:

    ```
    Console::Write("Card name is ");
    Console::WriteLine(CreditCardAccount::name);
    ```

    Because the *name* belongs to the class, you do not have to have any instances in existence in order to use it.

4. Build and run the application to see the value of the name printed out.

Literals and *const*

In standard C++, you would use a *static const* member to represent a class-wide constant. Although C++/CLI supports this, constants declared in this way are not recognized as compile-time constants if the class is accessed via a *#using* statement. Therefore, you are recommended to use *literal*, because members declared in this way behave as expected.

Using instance constants

You can use the *initonly* keyword to mark a data member as per-instance constant. A data member marked as *initonly* can have its value set in the constructor for the class but cannot be modified after that. The following short exercise shows you how to use *initonly* in the *CreditCardAccount* class.

1. Open CreditAccount.h and add *initonly* to the declaration of *accountNumber*.

    ```
    initonly long accountNumber;
    ```

2. Build the application.

    It should run exactly the same as before because you are setting the value for *accountNumber* in the constructor, as required by *initonly*.

3. Open CreditAccount.cpp and try to assign a new value to *accountNumber* in one of the other member functions, such as *SetCreditLimit*.

4. Notice that *accountNumber* is underlined in red, and if you hover over the variable name, a ToolTip appears, informing you that the variable cannot be modified here.

5. Remove this line of code before continuing!

Defining object relationships

For the remainder of this chapter, you will see how to define relationships between objects in a C++/CLI application. Applications typically contain many objects, and these objects communicate with one another to achieve the overall functionality needed in the application.

To illustrate object relationships, you will add a new class named *LoyaltyScheme* to your credit card application. With the *LoyaltyScheme* class, credit card owners can collect bonus points when they use their credit card. These points act as a reward for the customer's loyal use of the credit card.

When a *CreditCardAccount* object is first created, it doesn't have a *LoyaltyScheme* object. The *LoyaltyScheme* object is created when *CreditCardAccount* reaches 50 percent of its credit limit. Subsequently, every $10 spent using the credit card will add one bonus point to the *LoyaltyScheme* object, as long as the account stays above the 50 percent mark.

To achieve this functionality, you will complete the following exercises:

- Define the *LoyaltyScheme* class
- Implement the *LoyaltyScheme* class
- Create and use *LoyaltyScheme* objects
- Test the application

Defining the *LoyaltyScheme* Class

In this exercise, you will define the *LoyaltyScheme* class in a new header file named LoyaltyScheme.h.

1. Continue using the project from the previous exercise.

2. On the Project menu, click Add New Item.

3. In the Add New Item dialog box, select the template Header File (.h). In the Name box, type **LoyaltyScheme.h**, and then click Add.

4. Type the following code in the header file to define the *LoyaltyScheme* class:

```
ref class LoyaltyScheme
{
public:
    LoyaltyScheme();                // Constructor
    void EarnPointsOnAmount(double amountSpent);    // Earn one point per $10 spent
    void RedeemPoints(int points); // Redeem points
    int GetPoints();                // Return the value of totalPoints
private:
    int totalPoints;                // Total points earned so far
};
```

5. Build the application and fix any compiler errors.

Implementing the *LoyaltyScheme* class

In this exercise, you will implement the *LoyaltyScheme* class in a new source file named LoyaltyScheme.cpp.

1. Continue using the project from the previous exercise.

2. On the Project menu, click Add New Item.

3. In the Add New Item dialog box, select the template C++ File (.cpp). In the Name box, type **LoyaltyScheme.cpp**, and then click Add.

   Visual Studio creates an empty source file.

4. Add two *#include* statements at the beginning of the file, as shown here:

```
#include "stdafx.h"
#include "LoyaltyScheme.h"
```

5. Add the following code to expose the *System* namespace:

```
#using <mscorlib.dll>
using namespace System;
```

6. Implement the *LoyaltyScheme* constructor as follows:

```
LoyaltyScheme::LoyaltyScheme()
{
    Console::WriteLine("Congratulations, you now qualify for"
                        " bonus points");
    totalPoints = 0;
}
```

7. Implement the *EarnPointsOnAmount* member function as follows:

```
void LoyaltyScheme::EarnPointsOnAmount(double amountSpent)
{
    int points = (int)(amountSpent/10);
    totalPoints += points;
    Console::Write("New bonus points earned: ");
    Console::WriteLine(points);
}
```

The syntax *(int)(amountSpent/10)* divides the amount spent by 10 and converts the value to an *int*.

8. Implement the *RedeemPoints* member function as follows:

```
void LoyaltyScheme::RedeemPoints(int points)
{
    if (points <= totalPoints)
    {
        totalPoints -= points;
    }
    else
    {
        totalPoints = 0;
    }
}
```

This function makes it possible for the user to redeem some or all of the accrued bonus points.

9. Implement the *GetPoints* member function as follows:

```
int LoyaltyScheme::GetPoints()
{
    return totalPoints;
}
```

10. Build the application and fix any compiler errors.

Creating and using *LoyaltyScheme* objects

In this exercise, you will extend the *CreditCardAccount* class to support the loyalty scheme functionality.

1. Continue using the project from the previous exercise.

2. Open CreditCardAccount.h. At the beginning of the file, add an *#include* directive as follows:

```
#include "LoyaltyScheme.h"
```

This makes it possible for you to use the *LoyaltyScheme* class in this header file.

3. Add a private data member to the *CreditCardAccount* class as follows:

```
LoyaltyScheme ^scheme;     // Handle to a LoyaltyScheme object
```

This handle represents an association between a *CreditCardAccount* object and a *LoyaltyScheme* object.

4. Add a public member function to the *CreditCardAccount* class as follows:

```
void RedeemLoyaltyPoints();
```

This function acts as a wrapper to the *RedeemPoints* function in the *LoyaltyScheme* class. When you want to redeem loyalty points, you call *RedeemLoyaltyPoints* on your *CreditCard Account* object. This function calls *RedeemPoints* on the underlying *LoyaltyScheme* object to do the work.

> **Note** Relying on another object to do some work for you is an example of *delegation*. The *CreditCardAccount* object delegates the management of loyalty points to the *LoyaltyScheme* object.

5. Open CreditCardAccount.cpp and find the *CreditCardAccount* constructor. Add the following statement in the constructor body:

```
scheme = nullptr;
```

This statement sets the initial value of the *scheme* handle to *nullptr*. This is a special value for a handle, indicating that the handle doesn't yet point to an object. In our application, the *scheme* object won't be created until the credit card balance reaches 50 percent of the credit limit.

> **Note** There is a big difference between not initializing the *scheme* handle at all and initializing it to *nullptr*. Although the compiler is good at detecting attempts to use uninitialized variables, it is good practice to explicitly initialize handles to null.

6. Modify the *MakePurchase* function to match the code that follows to collect bonus points when the credit card balance reaches 50 percent of the credit limit:

```
bool CreditCardAccount::MakePurchase(double amount)
{
    if (currentBalance + amount > creditLimit)
    {
        return false;
    }
    else
    {
        currentBalance += amount;

        // If current balance is 50% (or more) of credit limit...
        if (currentBalance >= creditLimit / 2)
```

```
        {
            // If LoyaltyScheme object doesn't exist yet...
            if (scheme == nullptr)
            {
                // Create it
                scheme = gcnew LoyaltyScheme();
            }
            else
            {
                // LoyaltyScheme already exists,
                // so accrue bonus points
                scheme->EarnPointsOnAmount(amount);
            }
        }
        return true;
    }
}
```

7. Implement the *RedeemLoyaltyPoints* function as shown in the code that follows. *Redeem LoyaltyPoints* is a new member function by which the user can redeem some or all of the loyalty points in the associated *LoyaltyScheme* object.

```
void CreditCardAccount::RedeemLoyaltyPoints()
{
    // If the LoyaltyScheme object doesn't exist yet...
    if (scheme == nullptr)
    {
        // Display an error message
        Console::WriteLine("Sorry, you do not have a "
                            "loyalty scheme yet");
    }
    else
    {
        // Tell the user how many points are currently available
        Console::Write("Points available: ");
        Console::Write( scheme->GetPoints() );
        Console::Write(". How many points do you want "
                        " to redeem? ");
        // Ask the user how many points they want to redeem
        String ^input = Console::ReadLine();
        int points = Convert::ToInt32(input);
        // Redeem the points
        scheme->RedeemPoints(points);
        // Tell the user how many points are left
        Console::Write("Points remaining: ");
        Console::WriteLine( scheme->GetPoints() );
    }
}
```

Note It's important to check the value of the *scheme* handle before you use it. If you forget to check the value and the handle is still null, your application will crash at run time. This is a very common error in C++ applications.

8. Build the application and fix any compiler errors.

Testing the application

In this exercise, you will modify the code in CreditOrganizer.cpp to test the loyalty scheme functionality.

1. Continue using the project from the previous exercise.

2. Open CreditOrganizer.cpp and modify the *main* function as follows:

```
Console::WriteLine("Creating account object");
CreditCardAccount ^account1;
account1 = gcnew CreditCardAccount(12345, 2000);
Console::WriteLine("\nMaking a purchase (300)");
account1->MakePurchase(300);
Console::WriteLine("\nMaking a purchase (700)");
account1->MakePurchase(700);
Console::WriteLine("\nMaking a purchase (500)");
account1->MakePurchase(500);
Console::WriteLine("\nRedeeming points");
account1->RedeemLoyaltyPoints();
```

3. Build the application and fix any compiler errors.

4. Run the application.

The application creates a *CreditCardAccount* object and makes various purchases. When the credit card balance reaches $1,000, a *LoyaltyScheme* object is created. Subsequent purchases collect a loyalty point for every $10 spent.

When you try to redeem loyalty points, the application informs you of how many points are available and asks how many you want to redeem. Type a value such as **36** and press Enter. The application displays how many points are left.

The following screen shot shows the messages displayed on the console during the application.

```
Creating account object
This is account number 1

Making a purchase (300)

Making a purchase (700)
Congratulations! You now qualify for bonus points

Making a purchase (500)
New bonus points earned: 50

Redeeming loyalty points
Points available: 50
How many points do you want to redeem? 30
Points remaining: 20
Press any key to continue . . .
```

Quick reference

To	Do this

Define a class.	Add a header file to your project. Define the class in the header file. For example:
	
	`ref class MyClass`
	`{`
	`public:`
	`    void MyFunction();`
	`private:`
	`    int myData;`
	`};`

Implement a class.	Add a source file to your project. In the source file, use a *#include* statement to include the header file that contains the class definition. Then implement the member functions in the source file. For example:
	
	`#include "MyHeader.h"`
	`void MyClass::MyFunction()`
	`{`
	`    myData = myData * 2;`
	`}`

Provide a constructor for a class.	Declare the constructor in the header file, and implement it in the source file. The constructor must have the same name as the class and cannot return a value. However, a constructor can take parameters. For example:
	
	`// Header file`
	`ref class MyClass`
	`{`
	`public:`
	`    MyClass(int n);`
	`    ...`
	`};`
	`// Source file`
	`MyClass::MyClass(int n)`
	`{`
	`    myData = n;`
	`}`

To	Do this
| Create instances of a class. | Create an object by using the *gcnew* keyword, passing parameters into the constructor, if necessary. Assign the resulting handle to a variable of the appropriate type. For example:<br><br>```
MyClass^ myObject;
myObject = gcnew myClass(100);
myObject->MyFunction();
``` |
| Define class-wide (static) data members. | Declare the data member by using the *static* keyword, initializing it, if appropriate. For example:<br><br>```
ref class MyClass {
private:
    static int myClassData = 0;
    ...
};
``` |
| Define and use class-wide (static) member functions. | Declare the member function by using the *static* keyword. Implement the member function in the source file. Call the function by using the syntax *ClassName::FunctionName*. For example:<br><br>```
// Header file
ref class MyClass
{
public:
    static void MyClassFunction();
    ...
};
// Source file
void MyClass::MyClassFunction()
{
    myClassData++;
}
// Client code
MyClass::MyClassFunction();
``` |
| Define relationships between classes. | Define all the required classes and use handles to denote relationships between objects. For example, if an instance of class A needs to point to an instance of class B, use the following:<br><br>```
ref class B
{
    ...
};

ref class A
{
    ...
private:
    B^ handleToB;
};
``` |

CHAPTER 7

Controlling object lifetimes

After completing this chapter, you will be able to:

- Describe how Microsoft .NET memory management differs from traditional C++ memory management.

- Provide finalizers and destructors for your classes.

- Create objects by using stack semantics.

Now that you know how to create objects in C++/CLI by using the *gcnew* operator, it's time to learn how to control object lifetimes as well as another way to create and use objects.

The .NET approach to object lifetimes

We've seen what happens at the start of an object's life, but what happens when an object is no longer required?

There are two things that need to happen when an object comes to the end of its life:

- You might want to do some clean-up before the object is destroyed, such as writing data back to a database

- The object's memory needs to be reclaimed by the runtime

Let's see how this is done in C++/CLI. In .NET, like Java and many other modern languages, the runtime is responsible for ensuring that memory from dead objects is reclaimed. The component that does this is called the *garbage collector*. The runtime keeps track of handles to objects, and when an object can no longer be referenced through any handle, it is unreachable and is a candidate for garbage collection.

This means that programmers need to keep several things in mind:

- Objects are always used through handles, because that's the way that the system keeps track of them.

- An object will always be available as long as there is at least one handle to it.

- You cannot tell when an object's memory will be reclaimed; this is up to the garbage collector.

.NET garbage collection

The garbage collection mechanism in the .NET Framework is very sophisticated, but you don't need to know much about the details to use C++/CLI. In fact, it's designed to work fine without any intervention from you at all. However, if you're interested to know a little more about what's happening, read on.

Memory for objects is allocated from the *managed heap*, an area of memory that the .NET runtime uses to store dynamically allocated objects. Every allocation takes some space from the heap, and it's possible that at some point heap memory will be exhausted, or (more likely) there won't be a piece large enough for the new allocation. If a request for memory fails, the garbage collector will be invoked to see if there are any unreferenced objects whose memory can be reclaimed to free up some heap memory.

The basic process is as follows:

- Find all the objects that are still alive. This means starting with handles to objects in the code. Then, follow any handles to other objects that they might have. This repeats to the end of each chain of objects.

- When all the live objects have been marked, assume that all the rest of memory is garbage.

- Move the live objects, compacting them to create the maximum amount of free space.

- Fix up the handles to the live objects so that they point to new locations.

This should explain why you refer to objects by using handles: not only does it let the runtime track what is using an object, it also isolates the user from where exactly in memory the object is right at the moment.

In reality, it's not quite that simple. Garbage collection is expensive and affects the operation of your applications, so it's best to not run a collection on the whole of memory if you don't have to. When designing .NET, Microsoft discovered an interesting fact: the longer an object lives, the longer it is likely to live. In other words, applications tend to have a lot of objects that come and go rapidly, and others that live for a long time.

This led them to the idea of *generations*. Every dynamically created .NET object belongs to a generation, and each generation has its own area of the managed heap. Objects belong to generation 0 when they are created; if generation 0 fills up, no more new objects can be created. At this point, the garbage collector runs on the generation 0 objects only. Any objects that survive this collection are promoted to generation 1, and generation 0 is cleared ready for more new objects. Microsoft's observation was that many objects live and die in generation 0, so longer-lived objects can be left alone.

At present, the .NET garbage collector has three generations (0, 1, and 2). You usually let the garbage collector decide when to perform a collection and which generation to collect, but you can use the *System::GC::Collect* static method to force a collection if you know you'll have a lot of reclaimable objects in your code. With *Collect*, you can run a default collection or specify a particular generation. If you're interested in finding out to which generation a particular object belongs to, you can use the *System::GC::GetGeneration* method, passing in an object reference.

Destruction and finalization

Before we can start looking at code, let's introduce two new terms. *Finalization* is what happens when an object's memory is about to be reclaimed and is under the control of the garbage collector. You can provide code to be executed at this point, in the form of a *finalizer* method on your class.

But it might be that you know definitely at some point in the code that you no longer need the object, and you would like it to tidy itself up there and then. For example, if you are working with a *Customer* object, you might want the object to save its data back to the database when you've finished with it. This is called *destruction*, and you can provide a *destructor* method in your class.

With C++/CLI, you can provide code to be executed at both these points in an object's lifecycle, as you will see in the following sections.

Destructors

A destructor is executed when you no longer need an object. To provide a destructor for a class, add a member function that has the same name as the class but is preceded by a tilde character (~).

```
ref class MyClass
{
public:
    MyClass();        // constructor
    ~MyClass();       // destructor
};
```

You can signal that you no longer need an object by calling *delete* on a handle to the object.

```
// Create an Account
Account ^acc = gcnew Account();

// Use the Account

// We no longer need the Account
delete acc;
```

At this point in the code the destructor is called; thus, you know exactly where and when the object has ceased to operate.

Here are three points you should note about destructors:

- Like the constructor, they have no return type, and it is an error to give them one.

- They do not take any arguments, which means they cannot be overloaded.

- Destructors are usually public members of a class. If you make them private, you might not be able to destroy objects of that type.

Finalizers

Finalizers are called when the garbage collector finally reclaims the object's memory. You will need a finalizer if you have unmanaged resources, such as pointers to unmanaged classes, file handles, window handles, graphic device contexts, and so on. If you don't have any of those—and you'll only tend to do that when you are working with unmanaged code—you probably don't need a finalizer.

A finalizer is a member function that has the same name as the class but is preceded by an exclamation mark (!).

```
ref class MyClass
{
public:
    MyClass();      // constructor
    !MyClass();     // finalizer
};
```

You can see that finalizers obey the same rules as destructors; they have the same name as the class and don't have a return type or take arguments.

A few points about finalizers

There are three things that you should be aware of when using finalizers.

First, don't define a finalizer for your class if you don't have anything for it to do. In most cases, adding an empty function to a class will have little effect, but that isn't the case for finalizers. If the garbage collector sees that your class implements a finalizer, it knows that it has to run this before reclaiming objects of that type, and this slows down the collection process.

Second, no guarantee is made as to the order in which finalizers will run, which can be problematic if objects have dependencies on one another. Suppose that two objects, *A* and *B*, both have a finalizer, and that both of them update a data resource. Both finalizers will be called when the objects are destroyed, but you can't know which one will be called first. This means that you can't determine in what order data will be written to the data resource, which could cause a problem.

And third, finalizers aren't called during application termination for objects that are still live, such as those being used by background threads or those created during the execution of a finalizer. Although all system resources will be freed up when the application exits, objects that don't have their finalizers called might not get a chance to clean up properly.

This might give you the impression that finalizers should be avoided. Although they are useful in some situations, you will find that you can normally do whatever cleanup you require in the destructor.

Implementing the destructor and finalizer for a class

In this exercise, you will see how to create and use the finalizer and destructor for a class.

1. Start Visual Studio 2012 and create a new CLR Console Application called **Lifetimes**.

2. On the Project menu, click Add New Item.

3. In the Add New Item dialog box, in the pane on the left, select Visual C++, and then, in the center pane, click Header File (.h).

4. Toward the bottom of the dialog box, in the Name field, type **MyClass.h**, and then click Add.

> **Note** Another way that you can open the Add New Item dialog box is to right-click the project name in Solution Explorer and then, in the shortcut menu that appears, point to Add, and then click New Item.

5. Open the header file and add the declaration for a class that has a constructor, a destructor, a finalizer, and a single work method, which you will call to show that the object can be used.

    ```
    using namespace System;

    ref class MyClass
    {
        String ^name;
    public:
        MyClass(String ^objectName);    // constructor
        ~MyClass();                     // destructor
        !MyClass();                     // finalizer
        void DoSomething();             // 'work' method
    };
    ```

6. Repeat steps 2 through 4, but this time add a source file called **MyClass.cpp** to the project. Open the file and add #include statements for stdafx.h and MyClass.h.

    ```
    #include "stdafx.h"
    using namespace std;

    #include "MyClass.h"
    ```

7. Implement the constructor so that it stores the name in the data member and prints a message to show that has been called.

    ```
    MyClass::MyClass(String ^objectName)
    {
        name = objectName;
        Console::WriteLine("Constructor called for {0}", name);
    }
    ```

Note Up to this point, you have used multiple *Write* and *WriteLine* statements to build up a line of output. This exercise introduces a more efficient way: call *WriteLine* or *Write* with a string that contains text and markers that consist of a number in braces, such as *{0}* and *{1}*. The string should be followed by a list of items that you want to print out. The first item will be output in place of *{0}*, the second in place of *{1}*, and so on. We will use this from now on to save typing (and paper!).

8. Implement the destructor to print a message to show that has been called.

```
MyClass::~MyClass()
{
    Console::WriteLine("Destructor called for {0}", name);
}
```

9. Implement the finalizer to print a message to show that it has been called.

```
MyClass::!MyClass()
{
    Console::WriteLine("Finalizer called for {0}", name);
}
```

10. Implement the *DoSomething* method to print out a message. This is to show that the object has been used between creation and destruction.

```
void MyClass::DoSomething()
{
    Console::WriteLine("DoSomething called for {0}", name);
}
```

11. Build the project and fix any compiler errors.

Using the finalizer

In this exercise you will see how the finalizer for a class is called.

1. Continue using the project from the previous exercise.

2. Open Lifetimes.cpp and in the *main* method of the application, create an object by using *gcnew*, and then call *DoSomething*. Remember to add a *#include* for *MyClass.h, as shown here*:

```
#include "MyClass.h"

int main(array<System::String^>^ args)
{
    MyClass ^m1 = gcnew MyClass("m1");
    m1->DoSomething();

    Console::WriteLine();
    Console::WriteLine("End of program");
    Console::WriteLine();
    return 0;
}
```

3. Build and run the application.

Output similar to the following appears:

```
Constructor for m1
DoSomething called

End of Program

Finalizer called for m1
```

When you create an object, its constructor is called. If the application finishes and the object hasn't been destroyed, the garbage collector will call the finalizer to clear up any unmanaged resources associated with the object.

Using the destructor

In this exercise you will see how the destructor for a class is called.

1. Continue using the project from the previous exercise.

2. Edit the code so that you explicitly delete the object after using it. Do this by inserting a call to *delete* after the call to *DoSomething*.

```
MyClass ^m1 = gcnew MyClass("m1");
m1->DoSomething();
delete m1;
```

3. Build and run the application.

Output similar to the following appears:

```
Constructor called for m1
DoSomething called for m1
Destructor called for m1

End of Program
```

Notice that two things have happened: first, the destructor has been called at the point where you called delete; second, the finalizer was not called at the end of the application.

The destructor being called when you call *delete* means that you have complete control over when objects tidy themselves up. This *deterministic destruction* is a hallmark of traditional C++, and it is the basis of many common C++ coding idioms. You should make a habit of calling *delete* on your object handles when you no longer need them.

We also saw that as a result of calling *delete*, the finalizer wasn't executed. The garbage collector decides that you have dealt with the disposal of an object if its destructor has been executed, and so it doesn't need to execute its finalizer. This means that if you do have a finalizer, you should call it from the destructor to ensure that all unmanaged resources are freed up no matter how your objects exit.

```
MyClass::~MyClass()
{
    // Free up managed resources: this will be done anyway by the runtime
    // Now call the finalizer to free unmanaged resources
    this->!MyClass()
}
```

Objects and stack semantics

It might seem rather tedious to have to create objects by using *gcnew* and then call *delete* on the handles when you have finished using them. After all, wasn't the idea of garbage collection supposed to be that you didn't have to keep track of your objects when you finished with them?

It is important not to confuse the concept of an object tidying up after itself with the runtime reclaiming the object's memory; the two are independent of one another. You might want to say what an object does to tidy up when you have finished with it but not really care when the garbage collector decides to reclaim its memory. In this case, you would implement a destructor, which you can then call by using *delete*.

Traditional C++ object creation and destruction

Traditional C++ objects can also have destructors and be dynamically created and destroyed in a manner very similar to the one to which you have become accustomed. They use *new* instead of *gcnew*, but the mechanism is very similar.

There is, however, another way by which objects can be created in standard C++, and that is to create them on the stack as local objects, such as illustrated in the following:

```
MyClass m("m3");
m.DoSomething();
```

You can see two differences from C++/CLI code here. The more obvious of them is that you don't use *gcnew* and you don't create a handle. This syntax creates an object called *m*, and the constructor parameters are passed after the object name in the same way as they were passed to *gcnew* when creating an object dynamically. The second obvious difference is that members of the object are accessed by using the dot operator (.) rather than ->.

There is one important consequence to creating objects in this way, apart from it taking slightly less typing. When you create an object in this manner, its destructor is called automatically at the end of the block of code. This is shown in the following code sample:

```
{
    MyClass m("m3");
    m.DoSomething();
}  // Destructor for m is called here
```

Such objects are sometimes called *automatic objects* because they are automatically destroyed when they go out of scope.

> **Note** In C++, *scope* refers to where in the code an object is visible. It is often related to an object's lifetime. In this case, *m* cannot be seen outside the block, so it goes *out of scope* at the final brace.

This is a huge benefit to programmers: you can create an object and then know exactly where and when it will be destroyed and tidy itself up without the need for you to call *delete*. In standard C++ these objects are created in an area of memory called the *stack*, and so we say that these objects exhibit *stack semantics*.

Creating objects with stack semantics

In C++/CLI, you can create your objects in the same way, as you will see in the next exercise.

> **Note** In C++/CLI, these objects are not actually declared on the stack. This notation is a convenience that makes it possible for you to work with objects in the traditional C++ way, but under the hood, our objects are still created and managed by using handles.

1. Continue using the project from the previous exercise.

2. Edit the *main* function by adding code to create and use another object, placing it before the "end of program" *WriteLine* calls. Ensure that you create this object by using stack semantics.

   ```
   MyClass m2("m2");
   m2.DoSomething();
   ```

3. Build and run the application.

   After the output for *m1*, you should see output similar to the following:

   ```
   Constructor called for m2
   DoSomething called for m2

   End of Program
   Destructor called for m2
   ```

You create and use the object, but do not manually delete it. The destructor is called automatically when execution passes the end curly bracket in the function.

> **Note** You can create most types of objects by using stack semantics, but you cannot do this for *String*s or *array*s. For those types you must use *gcnew* to get a handle, and you access the objects by using the -> operator.

The Resource Acquisition Is Initialization idiom

Resource Acquisition Is Initialization (RAII) is an awkward phrase that is used to describe a very common programming style in C++, one that is useful in many circumstances. You will find that you often want an object to do something when you create it and then do a matching action when the object dies. For example, open a file and then ensure that it is closed, or read data from a database and then ensure that it is updated.

In C++, you can pair up these actions by performing the action in a constructor and then performing the matching action in the destructor. In this way, you can be certain that the matching action will be performed without you having to remember to do it.

Here's an example: suppose that you want to change the cursor to an hourglass before starting a long-running operation and then revert to the arrow cursor upon completion. You could code it up like this:

```
void DoLongOperation()
{
    SetCursorToHourglass();

    // Lots of complex code...

    SetCursorToArrow();
}
```

That is fine, but what if you forget to switch the cursor back? Or more likely, what happens if an error occurs and the *SetCursorToArrow* line is never executed? You are left with the cursor stuck as an hourglass, and the user becomes annoyed.

One solution is to create a small helper class. This carries out one task: it sets the cursor to an hourglass in its constructor and then sets it back to the arrow in its destructor.

```
ref class BusyCursorHelper
{
public:
    BusyCursorHelper { SetCursorToHourglass(); }
    ~BusyCursorHelper { SetCursorToArrow(); }
};
```

You can now recode *DoLongOperation* to match the following:

```
void DoLongOperation()
{
    BusyCursorHelper bch();

    // Lots of complex code...
}
```

The object is created and sets the cursor. At the final brace, it is destroyed, and that sets the cursor back to an arrow. Importantly (and as is demonstrated in Chapter 11, "Exception handling") this even happens if there is an error.

This example of the RIAA idiom—doing something in the constructor and undoing it in the destructor—shows how sometimes you might create a class simply for the side-effects you get when using it.

Copy constructors

A copy constructor is a special kind of constructor function that takes an object of the same type as its argument. In other words, you can create an object as a copy of another one. In this section you'll see how to write and use a copy constructor, but you'll also learn about two other important concepts: dereferencing and tracking references.

Do I need a copy constructor?

Standard C++ makes heavy use of copy constructors because they are needed to support proper memory management. Referring to *ref* objects through handles, coupled with garbage collection, means that you don't need copy constructors nearly as often in C++/CLI

In standard C++ the compiler will give you a default copy constructor if you do not provide one. This is not the case in C++/CLI, so if you want to provide copy construction for your classes, you will need to write a copy constructor.

Let's start by analyzing what happens in the following piece of code:

```
ref class MyClass
{
    int value;
    String ^str;
public:
    MyClass(int v, String ^s) : value(v), str(s) {}
    int getValue() { return value; }
    String ^getString() { return str; }
};

int main(array<System::String ^> ^args)
{
    Console::WriteLine("Copy Construction");
```

```
MyClass ^one = gcnew MyClass(3, "abc");
MyClass ^two = one;

Console::WriteLine("Value: {0}, str: {1}", two->getValue(), two->getString());

    return 0;
}
```

If you run this code, it prints out Value: 3, str: abc. The handle *one* points to a new *MyClass* object created through *gcnew*. The handle *two* is simply a copy of *one*; in other words, it points to the same object as *one*. Copying a handle doesn't copy the object to which it points. And, if you modify the value member of *two*, the value for *one* will be changed, as well, because they are referring to the same object.

Suppose, though, that we did want to make *two* a copy of *one*. In that case, we would provide a copy constructor for the class, which would look like this:

```
MyClass(const MyClass %other)
{
    value = other.value;
    str = other.str;
}
```

The constructor takes another *MyClass* object and copies its members. The *value* is an *int*, so a copy of the value is made. The *str* member is a handle to a string, but because strings are immutable, it doesn't matter that we're pointing to the same one.

But, look more closely at the declaration of the argument: What is a *const MyClass%*? The percent (%) symbol introduces what is called a *tracking reference*. A handle lets you refer to an object indirectly, and you use the -> operator to access members. A tracking reference is really an alias, another name for a variable. Consider this code fragment:

```
int i = 5;
int %ri = i;    // ri is a tracking reference
```

Printing out *ri* prints "5", because *ri* and *i* refer to the same variable. In many ways references are safer than handles because it is possible to have a handle that hasn't been assigned, but it is difficult to create an uninitialized reference.

You can have references to built-in types, to managed objects, and to handles. When you have a tracking reference to a managed object, the runtime ensures that it always refers to the right location in memory, even if the garbage collector moves things around.

> **Note** In the same way that a handle is the C++/CLI version of a standard C++ pointer, a tracking reference is the C++/CLI version of a standard C++ reference. It differs from a standard reference because the garbage collector can relocate the object being referred to during memory compaction.

So, we now know that the copy constructor takes a tracking reference to an object rather than a handle. The reference is marked as *const* because it lets us make copies of constant *MyClass* objects, which the compiler otherwise would not allow.

The other construct that we need to cover is *dereferencing*. Here's another code fragment:

```
MyClass ^m = gcnew MyClass();
MyClass %rm = *m;
```

The first line creates a *MyClass* object by using *gcnew* and returns a handle to it. The second line returns a reference to *m* by using the dereference operator, "*" (the asterisk character). You can read *m as "what m points to."

However, this still hasn't created a copy: *m* and *rm* are still referring to the same object in memory. But, what about this code?

```
MyClass mm = *m;
```

Here, *mm* is a *MyClass* with stack semantics, and the code is saying "create me a new object, *mm*, as a copy of the one to which *m* is pointing." It is at this point that the copy constructor is invoked.

This exercise shows you how to implement a copy constructor for a class.

1. Create a new CLR Console Application named **CopyCon**.

2. Add the following class definition before the *main* function:

```
ref class MyClass
{
    int value;
    String ^str;
public:
    MyClass(int v, String ^s) : value(v), str(s) {}

    MyClass(const MyClass %other)
    {
        Console::WriteLine("copy con called");
        value = other.value;
        str = other.str;
    }

    int getValue() { return value; }
    void setValue(int v) { value = v; }
    String ^getString() { return str; }
};
```

MyClass has two data members: an *int* and a *String* handle. The normal constructor initializes these two from the values passed in, and you can use the simple getter functions to retrieve the values later on.

3. Implement the main function to create and use *MyClass* objects:

```
int main(array<System::String ^> ^args)
{
    Console::WriteLine("Copy Construction");

    MyClass ^one = gcnew MyClass(3, "abc");
    MyClass ^two = one;

    Console::WriteLine("Value: {0}, str: {1}", two->getValue(), two->getString());

    MyClass three = *one;
    three.setValue(4);
    Console::WriteLine("Value of one: {0}", one->getValue());
    Console::WriteLine("Value of three: {0}", three.getValue());

    return 0;
}
```

The handle *one* is created to point to a *MyClass* object, and the handle *two* is a copy of *one*. You can verify this by printing out the data by using the *two* handle. The object *three* is created by dereferencing *one*, which creates a copy. You can verify that this is the case by changing the data in *three* and showing that it hasn't changed the data in *one*.

4. Build and run the application. Check that you understand the output.

Relating objects with stack semantics

It is common for objects to be composed of other objects. For example, a *Person* might have an *Address*, or a *Rectangle* might be composed of two *Points*. Consider the *Rectangle* as an example. Because the *Points* are part of the *Rectangle*, it is reasonable to expect that when a *Rectangle* object is destroyed, its *Points* are destroyed, as well. If you declare the objects by using stack semantics, you can easily ensure that this happens.

In this exercise, you will see how to compose objects so that they are destroyed correctly.

1. Create a new CLR Console Application project with a suitable name.

2. Add a header file called Geometry.h to the project.

3. Edit the header file to define two classes: *Rectangle* and *Point*. Note that a *Rectangle* is composed of two *Points*.

```
using namespace System;

ref class Point
{
public:
    Point();
    ~Point();
};
```

```
ref class Rectangle
{
    Point p1, p2;
public:
    Rectangle();
    ~Rectangle();
};
```

4. Add a source file called Geometry.cpp to the project and implement the *Point* and *Rectangle* class members.

```
#include "stdafx.h"
using namespace System;

#include "Geometry.h"

Point::Point()
{
    Console::WriteLine("Point constructor called");
}

Point::~Point()
{
    Console::WriteLine("Point destructor called");
}

Rectangle::Rectangle()
{
    Console::WriteLine("Rectangle constructor called");
}

Rectangle::~Rectangle()
{
    Console::WriteLine("Rectangle destructor called");
}
```

5. Edit *main* to create a *Rectangle* object by using stack semantics. Remember to add a *#include* for *Geometry.h*, as shown in the following:

```
#include "Geometry.h"

int main(array<System::String^>^ args)
{
    Rectangle r;

    Console::WriteLine();
    Console::WriteLine("End of program");
    Console::WriteLine();
    return 0;
}
```

6. Build and run the application.

You should see output similar to the following:

```
Point constructor called
Point constructor called
Rectangle constructor called

End of program

Rectangle destructor called
Point destructor called
Point destructor called
```

You can see from this output that the *Point* members of the *Rectangle* are constructed before the *Rectangle*'s constructor is called. If you think about it, this is quite logical: when initializing itself, the *Rectangle* might want to use the *Point*s to set some other properties, such as its area or diagonal length. So, it makes sense for the composed objects to be constructed before the constructor for the outer object is executed.

The destructors are called in reverse order, with the *Rectangle* destructor being called before the destructors for the *Point*s. The *Point* objects are not destroyed until you can be sure that the *Rectangle* no longer needs them.

> **Note** If you want to create an object that takes no arguments in the constructor, do not put empty parentheses after the variable name.
>
> ```
> Rectangle r();  // This won't work
> ```
>
> If you do this, you will get a warning (C4930) and the application will not give the correct output when you run it. The reason is that the compiler takes this as a function prototype declaration rather than a variable declaration. It is not helpful behavior, but has been a part of traditional C++ since the earliest implementations.

When to use handles?

If you want a class to contain another object—as in the preceding *Rectangle/Point* exercise—you have a choice of how to represent the composed object. You could use an object, as you did in the exercise, or you could use a handle to an object, as in the following code.

```
ref class Rectangle
{
    Point ^p1;
    Point ^p2;
    ...
};
```

What is the difference between these two, and why might you choose one over the other?

The one you choose depends on the nature of the relationship between the two objects. It is beyond the scope of this book to give a full explanation of object-oriented design, but here are a couple of examples to introduce you to the ideas.

The questions you need to ask are the following:

- Is the contained object a part of its container, such that it has no independent existence?

- Is the contained object shared with anyone else?

- Could you swap the contained object for another one?

- Can the contained object live on after its container?

Consider the case of an object that represents a business meeting. This has properties such as description, date and time, but it also has a location, which is represented by a *Location* object. The *Location* object holds all the details about a meeting room: where it is, the phone number, how many people it can hold, whether it has conference facilities, and so on.

Obviously many meetings can use the same *Location* at different times, so they will have a reference to the same *Location* object. It is also possible that the meeting can be moved, so you need to be able to change the *Location*. And obviously, the *Location* doesn't cease to exist when a meeting is over. This makes it a sensible idea to use a handle to a *Location* object in the *Meeting* class.

As a second example, consider the *Rectangle/Point* exercise again. The *Points* are parts of the *Rectangle*; they will disappear when the *Rectangle* object reaches the end of its life. There is no way that we are going to share a *Point* with anyone else, and so it makes sense that *Points* are contained within the *Rectangle*.

Quick reference

To	Do this

Define a destructor for a class.	Add a member function that has the same name as the class but prefixed with a tilde (~). For example:
	
	``MyClass::~MyClass()
	{
	    . . .
	}```

Define a finalizer for a class.	Add a member function that has the same name as the class but prefixed with an exclamation mark (!). For example:
	
	``MyClass::!MyClass()
	{
	    . . .
	}```

Destroy a dynamically created object.	Call *delete* on the handle to the object. For example: ```MyClass ^m = gcnew MyClass(); . . . delete m;```

To	Do this

Create an object with stack semantics.	Declare it as you would a built-in type, passing any constructor arguments in parentheses. For example:
	
	``cpp
	MyClass m1("argument1");
	``

Create an object with stack semantics that has no arguments.	Declare it as you would a built-in type, but do not use empty parentheses. For example:
	
	``cpp
	MyClass m3; // correct
	MyClass m4(); // wrong
	``

Call methods on objects with stack semantics.	Use the dot operator. For example:
	
	``cpp
	MyClass m5;
	m5.DoSomething();
	``

Compose an object that might be shared or changed.	Include them by using handles. For example:
	
	``cpp
	ref class Meeting
	{
	    Location ^location;
	    ...
	};
	``

Compose an object whose lifetime is bound to its container.	Include them by using stack semantics. For example:
	
	``cpp
	ref class Rectangle
	{
	    Point p1;
	    Point p2;
	    ...
	};
	``

CHAPTER 8

Inheritance

After completing this chapter, you will be able to:

- Describe the importance of inheritance in object-oriented programming.

- Define a base class.

- Define a derived class.

- Access base-class members from the derived class.

- Use the *virtual* keyword to achieve polymorphism.

- Define abstract classes and abstract methods.

- Define sealed classes.

- Use interfaces.

In this chapter, you will learn how to use all aspects of inheritance in C++/CLI. You will see how to define base classes and derived classes, and you will find out how to use these classes effectively in your application.

What is inheritance?

Inheritance is an important concept in object-oriented programming, helping us relate and classify types in a way that makes our applications more type-safe, flexible, and extensible.

> **Note** *Type-safe* means that the type system makes it easy to use the correct type in the correct place, and it's easy for the compiler to spot any mistakes that you make.

As an example, consider cars, trucks, and buses. All of these are types of vehicles: we can say that a car "is a" vehicle and that a sports car "is a" car. We tend to classify the world in terms of more general and more specific types all the time: A manager is also an employee; a savings account is an account; and so on.

How we view things depends on the job we need to do. If I just need to drive down the block, I could use any kind of car; for example, a sports car would do, as would an SUV—as long as it is a car. But, if I need to take my family to the airport, a sports car won't do: I need to be more specific.

Inheritance lets you use this classification mechanism in your code. If I am writing an application to monitor traffic flow, I might have a function to count the number of vehicles passing a given point. Using inheritance, the compiler knows that cars, trucks, and buses are all vehicles, so I can pass all of those to the function.

The advantages of inheritance are well documented, resulting in better-structured code that is easier to work with and maintain.

Inheritance terminology

When you use inheritance you are dealing with an "is a" relationship between a parent class and one or more child classes. You will find that there are several terms used to describe this relationship, including the following:

- C++ tends to use the term *base* and *derived* classes.

- Java uses *superclass* and *subclass*.

- Other languages might use *parent* and *child*.

Using the correct terms for your language is, of course, not as important as getting the relationships correct.

Inheritance and code reuse

Suppose that you are designing a *Vehicle* class and some classes that derive from it. You will put the things that are common to all vehicles in the *Vehicle* class, using the derived classes to implement those features that make them unique.

The derived classes inherit the functionality of the *Vehicle* class. They have to; otherwise, they would not be *Vehicles*. This means that after you have implemented functionality in the *Vehicle* class, you don't have to duplicate it in the derived classes.

It is very important to understand that code reuse is not the main reason for inheritance. Although it is useful, the main reason why you want to use inheritance is to define relationships between types. If you happen to also gain the benefit of code reuse, this is a bonus. If you use inheritance solely for code reuse, you risk building incorrect inheritance models.

Designing an inheritance hierarchy

Before you start writing any code to use inheritance in C++, you should spend some time designing the inheritance hierarchy. Identify classes that have common behavior, and consider whether these classes would benefit from using inheritance.

In this chapter, you will define and implement an inheritance hierarchy representing different types of bank accounts. The following illustration shows how the classes will be arranged in the inheritance hierarchy:

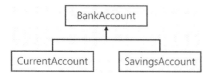

Note This illustration uses Unified Modeling Language (UML) notation to represent inheritance. Each box in this diagram is a class. The arrow pointing to *BankAccount* denotes inheritance in UML.

BankAccount is the base class. It defines common data members and member functions that are common to all kinds of bank accounts.

CurrentAccount and *SavingsAccount* are derived classes, representing specific types of bank account. These derived classes inherit all the data members and member functions from *BankAccount*, and they can add extra data members and member functions, as required.

CurrentAccount and *SavingsAccount* can also override member functions defined in *BankAccount*. For example, the *BankAccount* class might have a method named *CanDebit* to indicate whether a certain amount of money can be debited from the account. The policy rules for allowing debits are different for each type of account; therefore, *CurrentAccount* and *SavingsAccount* can override the *CanDebit* method to perform the required processing for each type of account.

You will define and implement all three of these classes during this chapter. Let's begin with the base class, *BankAccount*.

A word on substitutability

Substitutability means that everywhere you want a base class object, you can use a derived class object. For example, if I ask you to bring me a vehicle (base class), a car or a truck (derived class) will suffice because I wasn't specific. I expect, however, that anything you bring me is a vehicle, and as a minimum does everything that a vehicle can do.

For this reason, derived classes can add functionality over and above their base class, and can redefine operations that they inherit, but they are not allowed to remove functionality.

You can regard the functionality provided by the base class as a contract that the derived class must honor. If it doesn't, it is not substitutable for the base class, and the inheritance relationship is not proper.

Defining a base class

When you define a base class, you can start it by defining the common member functions that will be required by all the derived classes. After you have defined these member functions, add data members to support their implementation. Then, provide one or more constructors to initialize these data members.

 Tip Always start by deciding what it is that a class must do, and then think about what data members are needed to support these operations.

In this exercise, you will create a new application and define the *BankAccount* class. The *BankAccount* class will be the base class for all types of bank accounts in the application.

In *BankAccount*, you will define the common member functions and data members that apply for all types of bank accounts. You will also define a constructor and destructor for this class.

1. Start Visual Studio 2012 and create a new CLR Console Application project named **BigBank**.

2. On the Project menu, click Add New Item.

3. In the Add New Item dialog box, in the pane on the left, select Visual C++, and then, in the center pane, click Header File (.h).

4. Toward the bottom of the dialog box, in the Name box, type **BankAccount.h**, and then click Add.

 Note Another way that you can open the Add New Item dialog box is to right-click the project name in Solution Explorer and then, in the shortcut menu that appears, point to Add, and then click New Item.

5. Define the *BankAccount* class as follows:

```
#pragma once

using namespace System;
```

```
ref class BankAccount
{
public:
    BankAccount(String ^holder);
    void Credit(double amount);
    void Debit(double amount);
    double GetBalance();
private:
    String ^accountHolder;
    double balance;
};
```

Tip The *#pragma once* compiler directive specifies that this header file will be processed only once by the compiler during a build. This directive is particularly useful for frequently included header files, such as those containing base-class definitions.

If you omit the *#pragma once* directive, you will almost certainly get a compiler error when you try to build the application later on because BankAccount.h will be included in several different places in the application, and the compiler will generate an error if it sees the *BankAccount* class declaration more than once.

Working with floating-point values

In this simple example, the code uses a *double* to hold the balance. Although this is fine in this case because we're not actually concerned that the balance is accurate, you would never use a *double* in any place where a floating-point value needs to be exact, such as in banking calculations.

The reason for this is that arithmetic on *float* and *double* values is subject to rounding errors. Because of the way in which these types are implemented, some values cannot be represented exactly. It is similar to the way in which 1/3 cannot be exactly represented as a decimal (it is a repeating value, 0.33333..., which never terminates). This means that arithmetic on such values ends up accumulating errors due to the approximations involved. These can be very small, but in some applications they are significant.

Not only might values be inexact, but because of this, it might not be possible to compare values exactly. Two variables that ought to have the same value might be slightly different because of accumulated errors during their calculation.

In more serious code, you should use the *System::Decimal* type, which provides an exact representation of floating-point values and is not subject to rounding errors. The downside is that operations are less efficient than those using *float* or *double*.

6. Repeat steps 2 through 4, but this time add a new C++ source file named **BankAccount.cpp** to the project.

7. Type the following code in the source file to implement the *BankAccount* class:

```
#include "stdafx.h"
#include "BankAccount.h"

BankAccount::BankAccount(String ^holder)
: accountHolder(holder), balance(0.0)
{
}

void BankAccount::Credit(double amount)
{
    balance += amount;
}

void BankAccount::Debit(double amount)
{
    balance -= amount;
}

double BankAccount::GetBalance()
{
    return balance;
}
```

 Note The constructor uses a member initialization list to initialize the *BankAccount* data members, which is the preferred syntax for initializing data members in a constructor. Furthermore, it's the only way to invoke base-class constructors, which will become apparent when you define the *CurrentAccount* and *SavingsAccount* classes shortly.

8. Build the application and fix any compiler errors.

Defining a derived class

To define a derived class in C++/CLI, use the following syntax:

```
ref class MyDerivedClass : MyBaseClass
{
    ...
};
```

The colon in the class definition indicates inheritance. Following the colon, you specify the name of the base class.

Note In standard C++ you would put one of the keywords *public*, *protected*, or *private* after the colon and before the base class name. C++/CLI (and all other Microsoft .NET languages) only support public inheritance, so you do not need to use the *public* keyword. It is not an error if you use it, but be aware that it is not required.

Inheritance and *System::Object*

In .NET, every class derives ultimately from the *System::Object* class. If you don't specify a base class, the class you create will implicitly have "*: System::Object*" added to its declaration. This means that every object you create "is a" *System::Object*, and also that all classes inherit the common functionality that *Object* provides, such as the *ToString* function.

In this exercise, you will define and implement the *CurrentAccount* and *SavingsAccount* classes. *CurrentAccount* will inherit from *BankAccount*, which means that there is no need to reimplement inherited member functions such as *Credit* and *Debit*. Likewise, there is no need to redefine inherited data members such as *accountHolder* and *balance*. All you need to define in *CurrentAccount* are additional member functions and data members, which apply specifically to current accounts.

SavingsAccount will have an interest rate associated with it. Because the interest rate is common to all *SavingsAccount* objects, it makes sense to make it a static member of the class.

1.   Continue using the project from the previous exercise.

2.   Add a new header file to the project named **CurrentAccount.h**.

3.   Type the following code in the header file to define the *CurrentAccount* class:

```
#pragma once

#include "BankAccount.h"

ref class CurrentAccount : BankAccount
{
public:
    CurrentAccount(String ^holder, double limit);
    void ChangeOverdraftLimit(double newLimit);
    double GetOverdraftLimit();
private:
    double overdraftLimit;
};
```

Notice the *#include "BankAccount.h"* directive. This directive is required because *BankAccount* is the base class of *CurrentAccount*. The compiler needs to know how *BankAccount* is defined to compile the *CurrentAccount* class.

Also notice that the *CurrentAccount* constructor takes two parameters; the first parameter initializes the account holder's name (defined in *BankAccount*), and the second initializes the *overdraftLimit* (defined in *CurrentAccount*).

4. Add a new C++ source file to the project named **CurrentAccount.cpp**.

5. Type the following code in the source file to implement the *CurrentAccount* class:

```
#include "stdafx.h"
#include "CurrentAccount.h"

CurrentAccount::CurrentAccount(String ^holder, double limit)
    : BankAccount(holder), overdraftLimit(limit)
{
}

void CurrentAccount::ChangeOverdraftLimit(double newLimit)
{
    overdraftLimit = newLimit;
}

double CurrentAccount::GetOverdraftLimit()
{
    return overdraftLimit;
}
```

The most important thing to note about this code is the *CurrentAccount* constructor. The member initialization list includes the syntax *BankAccount(holder)*. This calls the constructor in the base class, *BankAccount*, to initialize inherited data members. If you take a look in BankAccount.cpp, you'll see that the *BankAccount* constructor requires a *String^* parameter to set the account holder's name. The balance is always set to 0 initially.

 Note The derived-class constructor must call the base-class constructor by using the member initialization list syntax. If you forget to call the base-class constructor, the compiler will attempt to call a no-argument constructor in the base class on your behalf; if there isn't a no-argument constructor in the base class, you'll get a compiler error.

6. Add a header file to the project named **SavingsAccount.h**.

7. Add the following declaration for the *SavingsAccount* class to the file:

```
#pragma once

#include "BankAccount.h"

ref class SavingsAccount : BankAccount
{
public:
    SavingsAccount(String ^holder);
    static void SetInterestRate(double rate);
    static double GetInterestRate();
```

```
private:
    static double interestRate;
};
```

8. Add a source file to the project named **SavingsAccount.cpp**.

9. Add the following code to the file to implement the *SavingsAccount* class:

```
#include "stdafx.h"

#include "SavingsAccount.h"

SavingsAccount::SavingsAccount(String ^holder) : BankAccount(holder) { }

void SavingsAccount::SetInterestRate(double rate)
{
    interestRate = rate;
}

double SavingsAccount::GetInterestRate()
{
    return interestRate;
}
```

10. Build the application and fix any compiler errors.

Creating derived class objects

In this exercise, you will see how to create and use objects of a derived class.

1. Continue using the project from the previous exercise.

2. Open BigBank.cpp and add *#includes* for the *CurrentAccount* and *SavingsAccount* header files.

```
#include "CurrentAccount.h"
#include "SavingsAccount.h"
```

> **Note** There is no need to explicitly write *#include "BankAccount.h"* because this header file is already included in CurrentAccount.h and SavingsAccount.h.

3. Delete the "Hello World" line from *main*. Add code to create a *CurrentAccount* object and exercise it.

```
CurrentAccount acc("Me", 2000.0);
acc.Credit(100.0);

double balance = acc.GetBalance();
double overdraft = acc.GetOverdraftLimit();

Console::WriteLine("Balance: {0}", balance);
Console::WriteLine("Overdraft: {0}", overdraft);
```

You can see that the *CurrentAccount* object gives you access to the *Credit* and *GetBalance* member functions from *Account*. It also gives you access to its own *GetOverdraftLimit* function.

4. Add code to *main* to create a *SavingsAccount*.

```
SavingsAccount::SetInterestRate(2.5);
SavingsAccount sacc("You");
double rate = sacc.GetInterestRate();

Console::WriteLine("Interest rate: {0}", rate);
```

5. Build and run the application.

   You should see the interest rate printed, showing that you can access a static member through either the class name or through an object.

6. Build and run the application.

   You should see output similar to this:

```
Balance: 100
Overdraft: 2000
Interest Rate: 2.5
```

Concrete and abstract classes

When you define an inheritance hierarchy, the base class acts as a repository for the common member functions and data members required by derived classes. However, the base class often doesn't represent a real object.

Consider the bank account example we've been developing in this chapter. When you walk into a bank to open an account, you have to specify what type of account you want (checking account or savings account). You can't just open a "bank account."

In similar fashion, when programming, you should prevent generic *BankAccount* objects from being created. You should allow only derived classes such as *CurrentAccount* and *SavingsAccount* to be instantiated. To accomplish this in C++/CLI, declare the *BankAccount* class as an *abstract* class, as demonstrated in the following:

```
ref class BankAccount abstract
{
    // ... Class body, as before
};
```

Observe how the *abstract* modifier appears after the class name.

In this exercise, you will modify the *BankAccount* class as just described to make it an abstract class. You will then write some code in the *main* function in the application to create and use *CurrentAccount* and *SavingsAccount* objects.

1. Continue using the project from the previous exercise.

2. Open BankAccount.h and change the *BankAccount* class definition by adding the *abstract* keyword.

```
ref class BankAccount abstract
{
   ...
};
```

3. Open BigBank.cpp to edit the *main* function for the application.

4. Inside the *main* function, try to create a *BankAccount* object as follows:

```
BankAccount genericAccount("Fred");
```

IntelliSense flags an error, which confirms the fact that you cannot create instances of an abstract class.

5. Delete the statement you created in Step 4.

Overriding member functions

When you define a base class, you must consider whether derived classes will need to override any of your base-class member functions. For each member function in the base class, there are three possibilities:

- The base-class function is suitable for all derived classes. Derived classes will never need to override the member function with customized behavior. The *Credit* and *GetBalance* member functions in *BankAccount* fit this scenario. These functions will work the same way for all derived classes. Here's an example:

```
ref class BankAccount abstract
{
public:
    void Credit(double amount);   // This function cannot be overridden
    double GetBalance();          // Neither can this one
    ...
};
```

- The base-class function performs some task, but derived classes might need to override the function to provide customized behavior. To make it possible to override a base-class function, you must declare the function by using the *virtual* keyword in the base-class definition, as shown in this example:

```
ref class BankAccount abstract
{
public:
    virtual String ^ToString() override;  // This function can be overridden
    ...
};
```

This function declaration uses both the *virtual* and *override* keywords. We have seen how *virtual* indicates that a derived class can override this function. The *override* keyword must be used when you are overriding a function from a base class; in this case, *ToString* is defined in the ultimate base class, *System::Object*, and so we use *override* to show that we are intending to override this function and haven't just added a function that looks exactly the same.

If by some chance you want to add a function that looks like a base class function but does not override it, you would use the *new* modifier:

```
// This function does not override ToString
virtual String ^ToString() new;
```

- The base-class function specifies some operation that is required by all derived classes, but each derived class needs to perform the operation in a significantly different way. There is no sensible common behavior you can define in the base class. To do this, you declare the base-class member function as abstract. C++ calls these *pure virtual functions*.

  There are two ways to denote a pure virtual function. The first comes from standard C++ and involves putting "= 0" at the end of the function declaration. The second way, introduced by C++/CLI, is to add the *abstract* keyword. Here's an example:

```
ref class BankAccount abstract
{
public:
    // Declare a pure virtual function using standard C++ syntax
    virtual void Debit(double amount) = 0;

    // Declare a pure virtual function using C++/CLI syntax
    virtual void Debit(double amount) abstract;
    ...
};
```

 Note Including a pure virtual function in a class means that it must be abstract, although the opposite is not necessarily true: a class can be abstract without having any pure virtual functions. If a derived class does not implement the function, it too must be abstract.

In this exercise, you will define a *ToString* member function in the *BankAccount* class. You will declare this function as virtual to give derived classes the opportunity to override the function if they want to. You will also modify the way in which debits are handled so that derived classes decide whether a withdrawal can be made.

1. Continue using the project from the previous exercise.

2. Open BankAccount.h and add the following public function declarations to the *BankAccount* class:

```
// Derived classes can override this function
virtual String ^ToString() override;
// Derived classes must override this function
// You can use '=0' instead of 'abstract'
virtual bool CanDebit(double amount) abstract;
```

3. Open BankAccount.cpp and implement the *ToString* function as follows:

```
String ^BankAccount::ToString()
{
    String ^result = gcnew String("Account holder: ");
    result = String::Concat(result, accountHolder);
    result = String::Concat(result, ", Balance: ");
    result = String::Concat(result, balance.ToString());
    return result;
}
```

Observe the use of the *String::Concat* function, which is used for joining strings together.

4. Modify the *Debit* member function as follows:

```
bool BankAccount::Debit(double amount)
{
    if (CanDebit(amount))
    {
        balance -= amount;
        return true;
    }
    else
    {
        return false;
    }
}
```

Notice that *Debit* now calls *CanDebit* to verify that the debit is allowed. *CanDebit* isn't implemented in *BankAccount*, but all derived classes are obliged to provide this function. At run time, the correct version of *CanDebit* is called depending on the type of bank account being used for the debit operation—polymorphism in action! We have also changed the return type of *Debit* so that calling code can determine whether the debit worked.

5. Change the prototype for *Debit* in BankAccount.h so that it returns a *bool*.

6. Open CurrentAccount.h and add the following public function declarations to the *Current Account* class:

```
// Choose to override ToString
virtual String ^ToString() override;
// Have to override CanDebit
virtual bool CanDebit(double amount) override;
```

Notice the use of the *override* keyword. This instructs the compiler that you are intending to override a function from the base class and haven't just added a function that happens to look exactly the same.

7. Open CurrentAccount.cpp and implement the *ToString* function as follows:

```
String ^CurrentAccount::ToString()
{
    String ^result = BankAccount::ToString();
    result = String::Concat(result, ", Overdraft Limit: ");
    result = String::Concat(result, overdraftLimit.ToString());
    return result;
}
```

The *BankAccount::ToString()* syntax calls the *ToString* function in the base class (*BankAccount*). This call returns a string containing the account holder's name and balance. We concatenate the *overdraftLimit* value to this string and return it.

8. Still in CurrentAccount.cpp, implement the *CanDebit* function as follows:

```
bool CurrentAccount::CanDebit(double amount)
{
    return (amount <= GetBalance() + overdraftLimit);
}
```

There are two things to note about this code. First, we need to call the *GetBalance* function to get the current balance. Just because we inherit from *BankAccount* doesn't mean that we can access its private *balance* member.

Second, notice the way in which the *return* statement is written, returning the result of the expression directly. We could have used an *if* statement to check the condition and return true or false, but this code is shorter while being no less readable, and that is something that C++ coders like.

9. Open SavingsAccount.h and add the following public function declaration to the *Savings Account* class:

```
virtual bool CanDebit(double amount) override;
```

You are obliged to override *CanDebit* because it's a pure virtual function. However, you do not have to override *ToString*, because the base class (*BankAccount*) provides a default implementation of this function. The *SavingsAccount* class chooses not to override *ToString*.

10. Open SavingsAccount.cpp and implement the *CanDebit* function as follows:

```
bool SavingsAccount::CanDebit(double amount)
{
    return (amount <= GetBalance() / 10);
}
```

This function makes it possible for the user to withdraw one-tenth of the current balance.

11. Open BigBank.cpp and replace the existing code in the *main* function with the following:

```
Console::WriteLine("Testing the CurrentAccount");
CurrentAccount current("Jane", 100);
current.Credit(500);

// Should be accepted
if (current.Debit(550) == true)
{
    Console::WriteLine("Debit(550) OK");
}
else
{
    Console::WriteLine("Debit(550) failed");
}

// Should be declined
if (current.Debit(100) == true)
{
    Console::WriteLine("Debit(100) OK");
}
else
{
    Console::WriteLine("Debit(100) failed");
}

Console::WriteLine(current.ToString());

Console::WriteLine("\nTesting the SavingsAccount");
SavingsAccount savings("Fred");
savings.Credit(500);

// Should be accepted
if (savings.Debit(50) == true)
{
    Console::WriteLine("Debit(50) OK");
}
else
{
    Console::WriteLine("Debit(50) failed");
}

// Should be declined
if (savings.Debit(46) == true)
{
    Console::WriteLine("Debit(46) OK");
}
else
{
    Console::WriteLine("Debit(46) failed");
}

Console::WriteLine(savings.ToString());

return 0;
```

12. Build and run the application. Check that the output is what you expect.

13. Create a breakpoint on the first statement in the *main* function and then start the application in the debugger. Step through the application one statement at a time, stepping into each function to see which version is called during execution.

Protected access

You have used two access levels for class members so far: *private* and *public*. You know that *private* members cannot be used outside the defining class, whereas *public* members can be used by anyone. Inheritance, however, introduces a relationship between two classes, and there is a need for an access level that grants access to derived classes. The *protected* access level is less restrictive than *private* but more restrictive than *public*.

Any members that are defined as *protected* can be used in the base class, and in any class that derives from it.

 Tip You should only make member functions protected, not data members. The data belonging to a class is the responsibility of that class, and it should not allow direct modification by derived classes.

In this example, you will add a protected member function to the *BankAccount* class. Suppose that *BankAccount* has a *RoutingInstructions* function that details how a given size of debit or credit should be handled for a particular account. This function is not to be accessed by users of the class but might be of use to derived classes.

1. Continue using the project from the previous exercise.

2. Open BankAccount.h and add the following *protected* function declaration to the *BankAccount* class:

```
protected:
    String ^RoutingInstructions(double amount);
```

 Note The order in which you specify the *public*, *private*, and *protected* sections of a class declaration does not matter, although many people will put the *public* section first because that is the most important section from the point of view of users of the class.

3. Open BankAccount.cpp and add the definition of *RoutingInstructions*.

```
String ^BankAccount::RoutingInstructions(double amount)
{
    return "Some string…";
}
```

4. Open CurrentAccount.cpp and modify the *CanDebit* function so that it calls *RoutingInstructions*. You should not see any warnings from the compiler, because *CurrentAccount* is allowed to call this function.

```
bool CurrentAccount::CanDebit(double amount)
{
    String ^details = RoutingInstructions(amount);
    return (amount <= GetBalance() + overdraftLimit);
}
```

5. Open BigBank.cpp and try adding a call to *RoutingInstructions* on either the *SavingsAccount* or *CurrentAccount* objects.

   IntelliSense flags an error because you are not allowed to call this function from an unrelated class. If you build the project, you will get error C3767 ('BankAccount::RoutingInstructions': candidate function(s) not accessible)

Defining sealed classes

In C++/CLI, you can define a class as *sealed*, which means that the class cannot be used as a base class. Defining a class as sealed is useful if it performs operations that you don't want customized in derived classes, but it is also useful in another, less obvious way. If a class is sealed, the compiler knows that it will not have any derived classes. Because this means that there will be no calls to virtual functions, the compiler might be able to generate more efficient code.

To mark a class as sealed, use the *sealed* keyword in the class definition as follows:

```
ref class MyClass sealed
{
    // ... Class body, as before
};
```

Abstract and sealed

It might appear at first sight that *abstract* and *sealed* are opposites: one means that a class has to have derived classes to be useful, whereas the other means that you can't derive classes. It is, however, possible to use *abstract* and *sealed* together on a class.

Suppose that you have a class that only contains static (class-level) members. It would make sense to say that you do not want objects of this type, because there are no object-level functions. Making the class *abstract* prevents instantiation. In addition, you might want to prevent anyone from adding extra functions to your class, which *sealed* does.

 Note You can specify the *sealed* and *abstract* modifiers in any order.

Defining and using interfaces

Interfaces are an important programming construct in .NET; therefore, you need to be able to use them in C++/CLI. You have already learned about pure virtual functions, which are specified in a base class but implemented by a derived class. Imagine that you have a class that only contains pure virtual functions, such as the following:

```
ref class XmlWriter
{
public:
    virtual void ReadFromXmlFile(String ^filename) = 0;
    virtual void WriteToXmlFile(String ^filename) = 0;
};
```

This class specifies how to convert data to and from XML, and it is implemented by derived classes to suit their particular data. You could use the following:

```
ref class MyData : XmlWriter
{
public:
    void ReadFromXmlFile(String ^filename) override
    {
        // Read my data
    }

    void WriteToXmlFile(String ^filename) override
    {
        // Write my data
    }
};
```

An interface is similar, and you could rewrite the *XmlWriter* class as follows:

```
interface class IXmlWriter
{
    void ReadFromXmlFile(String ^filename);
    void WriteToXmlFile(String ^filename);
};
```

The definition of the derived class also needs to be changed. You need to specify the interface name, and declare the functions as *virtual*.

```
ref class MyData : IXmlWriter
{
public:
    virtual void ReadFromXmlFile(String ^filename)
    {
        // Read my data
    }

    virtual void WriteToXmlFile(String ^filename)
    {
        // Write my data
    }
};
```

You can see that you inherit from an interface in the same way that you inherit from a class. However, there are a number of differences between a class and an interface:

- A class can contain implementation and data members; an interface cannot.

- All members of an interface are *public* and *abstract* by definition.

- Interface names should start with an "I" (capital i) by convention.

- A class can only inherit from one base class, but it can implement as many interfaces as it wants.

If you have used standard C++, you might know that a class can inherit from many base classes. This feature is called *multiple inheritance*. .NET only allows you to inherit from one base class, but because you can implement as many interfaces as necessary, you can get the benefits of multiple inheritance.

Interfaces are very important in .NET, not least of which because they are cross-language. You can define an interface in C++ and implement it in C#. More important than that, they provide a way to specify a contract, which one class implements, and another uses. Neither class might have knowledge of the other, but they can communicate because they both know about and use the interface contract. You will see many examples of interfaces as you progress through the rest of the book.

Quick reference

To	Do this

Define an abstract base class.	Use the *abstract* keyword in the class definition. For example:
	
	``ref class MyBase abstract
	{
	...
	};```

Define a derived class.	In the derived-class definition, use a colon followed by the name of the base class. For example:
	
	``ref class MyDerived : MyBase
	{
	...
	};```

Construct derived objects.	In the derived-class constructor, use a member initialization list to call the base-class constructor. For example:
	
	``MyDerived::MyDerived(int bdata, int ddata)
	    : MyBase(bdata), derivedData(ddata)
	{
	...
	}```

To	Do this

Enable derived classes to access members in the base class while denying access to unrelated classes.	Declare the members as protected in the base class. For example:
	<pre>ref class MyBase abstract
	{
	protected:
	    void functionVisibleToDerivedClass;
	    ...
	};</pre>

Define overridable member functions in the base class.	Declare the member functions as virtual in the base class. For example:
	<pre>ref class MyBase abstract
	{
	protected:
	    virtual void myOverridableFunction();
	    ...
	};</pre>

Specify base-class member functions that must be over-ridden by derived classes.	Declare the member functions as virtual in the base class. After the closing parenthesis, append = 0 or *abstract*. For example:
	<pre>ref class MyBase abstract
	{
	protected:
	    virtual void myMustBeOverridden() = 0;
	    ...
	};</pre>

To prevent a class being used as a base class.	Use the *sealed* keyword in the class definition. For example:
	<pre>ref class MySealedClass sealed
	{
	    ...
	};</pre>

Define an interface.	Use the *interface class* keyword, and start the interface name with "I". Do not provide any bodies for the functions you define. For example:
	<pre>interface class IMyInterface {
	    void function1(int n);
	    int function2(double d);
	};</pre>

Implement an interface.	Use the same syntax as for inheritance. Implement all the required functions in your class. For example:
	<pre>ref class MyImplementingClass
	        : IMyInterface
	{ public:
	    void function1(int n);
	    int function2(double d);
	
	    // Other members, as needed
	    ...
	};</pre>

Microsoft .NET programming basics

CHAPTER 9   Value types 143

CHAPTER 10   Operator overloading 159

CHAPTER 11   Exception handling 175

CHAPTER 12   Arrays and collections. 197

CHAPTER 13   Properties 229

CHAPTER 14   Delegates and events 245

CHAPTER 15   The .NET Framework class library 263

Value types

After completing this chapter, you will be able to:

- Distinguish between reference and value types.

- Work with structures.

- Work with enumerations.

In preceding chapters, you learned about object-oriented programming and how to apply it within the Microsoft .NET Framework. You've seen how many data types within .NET are represented by classes, and you've learned how to create and use your own classes. However, not every data type in .NET is a class, and now you're going to meet the other fundamental building block of .NET types—the value type.

In this chapter, you'll discover what value types are and how they differ from the reference types you've already met. You will also learn about two important value types, structures and enumerations, which will be useful in your own code.

Reference types and value types

Let's summarize what you've learned about classes so far. Classes are known as *reference types* because you always access objects by using reference variables, known as *handles*. Consider the following line of code:

```
MyClass ^pc = gcnew MyClass();
```

In this example, *pc* is a reference variable by which we can refer to the *MyClass* object created by the *gcnew* operator. Accessing objects by using references in this way makes it possible for the .NET garbage-collection mechanism to reclaim the resources used by an object when there are no longer any references to it. This feature of .NET makes for efficient memory usage and means that you won't suffer from one of the traditional problems of C++ applications: memory leaks.

The second thing you've learned about classes is that they consist of data members and member functions. Data members represent the state of the object, and it's good practice to make them private to the class. Member functions provide the behavior of the object, and they use the data members to determine how to respond. All operations on objects are done by calling member functions, using the -> operator, as in the following line of code:

```
result = pc->DoOperation();
```

You also saw how with C++/CLI, you can use *stack semantics* to create objects, making it look as if they are traditional C++ local variables, and how you can use the dot operator (.) to access members, as demonstrated here:

```
MyClass m;
result = m.DoOperation();
```

In fact, they work in exactly the same way as objects you create by using *gcnew*.

The need for value types

So, how are value types different from reference types, and why do we need them? As the name "value type" implies, they have been designed to hold values, such as integers, floating-point numbers, Booleans, and characters. Anything that is basically a wrapper around a simple value—and is less than about 16 bytes in size—is a good candidate for a value type.

We need value types because we want simple values to be used as efficiently as possible, but we also want them to be usable as objects. Using values as objects is a problem with object-oriented languages because if basic types are represented as objects, all operations (such as addition and multiplication of integers) must be done by calling functions, which isn't efficient at all. On the other hand, if basic types are not represented as objects, operations on them can be very efficient, but we can't use them where objects are needed.

.NET gets around this problem with value types, which are represented and used as efficiently as built-in types, but which can also be used as objects when necessary. You don't need to know this is happening most of the time. This process is called *boxing*, and it is discussed in Chapter 22, "Working with unmanaged code."

The following table summarizes the most common value types provided by the .NET Framework.

Value type	Description	C++/CLI equivalent
Byte	An 8-bit unsigned integer	*unsigned char*
SByte	An 8-bit signed integer	*char*
Int16	A 16-bit signed integer	*short*
Int32	A 32-bit signed integer	*int* or *long*
Int64	A 64-bit signed integer	*__int64* or *long long*
UInt16	A 16-bit unsigned integer	*unsigned short*
UInt32	A 32-bit unsigned integer	*unsigned int* or *unsigned long*

Value type	Description	C++/CLI equivalent
UInt64	A 64-bit unsigned integer	unsigned __int64 or unsigned long long
Single	A single-precision, 32-bit floating-point number	float
Double	A double-precision, 64-bit floating-point number	double
Boolean	A Boolean value	bool
Char	A 16-bit Unicode character	wchar_t
IntPtr	A signed integer used to represent pointers	No built-in type
UIntPtr	An unsigned integer used to represent pointers	No built-in type

Note that the C++ equivalents are simply names for the types—aliases, if you like— that fit better with C++ syntax. Although it's more natural to use the native language equivalents, you could use the underlying .NET types, instead, which means that the following two lines of code mean exactly the same thing:

```
int n = 0;      // use managed C++ type
Int32 n = 0;    // use .NET native type
```

Properties of value types

A value type is a type that inherits from the *System::ValueType* class. Value types have several special properties:

- Value types are stored on the stack (unlike references, which are stored on the run-time heap).

- Value types are not garbage collected.

- Instances of value types are always accessed directly (unlike reference types, which are accessed through references). Direct access means that you don't use the *gcnew* operator when creating instances.

- Copying value types copies the value, rather than the reference.

- Value types can't be used as base classes for inheritance.

As you can see, value types behave just like the standard built-in types such as *int* and *char*, and they are just as efficient to use. As mentioned in the previous section, the main difference between value types and built-in types is that value types can also be treated as objects when necessary.

Although you can't add new basic types to the language, you can create your own value types in the form of structures and enumerations. We'll explore these in the rest of this chapter.

Structures

Structures (commonly referred to as structs) provide a way to create the compound data or record types that you might have come across in other programming languages. Similar to classes, structures can contain member functions, data members, and other .NET features that you'll learn about in later chapters, but there's one important difference: structures are value types, not reference types. Therefore, if you have a value type that needs to have some internal structure, such as a point with X and Y coordinates, you can implement it by using a *struct*.

Creating and using a simple struct

The following exercise shows how to create a structure representing a point with X and Y coordinates, how to create instances of the structure, and how to use the instances in code.

> **Note** Both standard C++ and C++/CLI use the *struct* keyword to define structures. This chapter discusses the use of .NET (managed) structs rather than the traditional *struct*. Declaring .NET structures has the advantage of working within the .NET world and also makes it possible for you to exchange structures with other .NET languages.

1. Start Microsoft Visual Studio 2012 and create a new CLR Console Application project named **Structs**.

2. At the top of the Structs.cpp file, immediately below the *using namespace System;* line, add the following structure definition:

```
// The Point structure definition
value struct Point
{
    int x, y;
};
```

The *value* and *struct* keywords start a structure definition, and you'll notice that structures look very similar to classes in the way that they are defined. The body of the structure is enclosed in braces and finishes with a semicolon, and the *public* and *private* keywords can be used to set the access level for structure members.

Notice the use of the *value* keyword here. This keyword instructs the compiler that this is a .NET value type and not a traditional C++ structure. It's important that you remember to use *value* when defining your structures.

This simple structure represents a point on a graph, so it has two integer data members representing the X and Y coordinates.

Note In standard C++ the only difference between a *struct* and a *class* is in the default access level. Members of a class are *private* by default, whereas members of a struct are *public*, unless marked otherwise. This has been carried over into C++/CLI, so there is no need to make structure members public.

3. To create and initialize a *Point* object, add the following lines to the *main* function of your application:

```
// Create a Point
Point p1;

// Initialize its members
p1.x = 10;
p1.y = 20;
```

Notice that the code doesn't use the *gcnew* operator. The *gcnew* operator is used to create references to objects, and value types aren't accessed by reference. Instead, a *Point* has been created on the program stack, and you access it directly as *p1*. Because the data members are public at this point, you can access them by using the familiar dot notation.

4. Add two lines to print out the value of one of the structure members, like this:

```
Console::WriteLine("p1.x is {0}", p1.x);
```

5. Compile and run the application.

At this point, you should see the output "p1.x is 10".

Investigating the structure

In this exercise, you will run the application under control of the debugger so that you can look at the structure of the value type you have created.

1. If you closed the Structs project, open it again and open the source file Structs.cpp.

2. Insert a debug breakpoint by clicking in the gray border to the left of the code. Click next to the declaration of *p1*.

A red dot appears in the border, as illustrated in the screen shot that follows.

```
Structs.cpp + X
(Global Scope)                                           ▼  ⊙ main(array<System::String^>^ args)                ▼
                                                                                                                ✛
    using namespace System;                                                                                     ⌃

  ⊟value struct Point
   {
       int x, y;
   };

  ⊟int main(array<System::String ^> ^args)
   {
  ●     Point p1;
        p1.x = 10;
        p1.y = 20;

        Console::WriteLine("p1.x is {0}", p1.x);

        return 0;
   }                                                                                                            ⌄
100 %  ▼ <                                                                                                    >
```

3. Press F5 to start the debugging session.

   After the application loads, it executes and stops at the breakpoint. You can now use the Locals pane at the bottom of the window to look at the structure of the *Point* type.

   You should see an entry for the variable *p1*. Any type that has internal structure—such as *Point*—is indicated by a plus sign (+) to the left of the variable name.

4. Click the plus sign to expand the structure.

   The Locals pane opens, appearing similar to the one shown in the following screen shot:

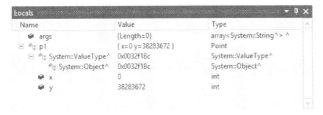

   You can see that *p1* has three entries below it. The first shows that it's derived from *System::ValueType*, which is in turn derived from *System::Object*. The other two are the *x* and *y* members, which are both 32-bit integers. At this point in in the code, the structure hasn't been fully initialized, so they don't contain sensible values.

5. Press F10 three times to initialize *p1* and execute the next two assignment statements.

   This action results in *p1* being initialized, and you will see the values of *x* and *y* change to reflect the values you set. The values also change from black to red in the Locals pane, showing that they were changed in the previous execution step.

6. Continue pressing F10 to single-step through the code, examining the changes that occur to *p1* as you execute each line. When you're done, discontinue debugging by clicking the Stop Debugging button on the toolbar (the dark-red square), clicking the Stop Debugging command on the Debug menu, or pressing Shift+F5.

The differences between structures and classes

Structures and classes have several fundamental differences:

- You can't initialize members in a structure definition. If you need to provide initialization for a structure type, you must provide a constructor.

- You can't override the default no-argument constructor for a structure. This is because the runtime automatically sets all members of a structure to their default values: 0 for numeric types, and false for Booleans.

- Structures can't have destructors or finalizers, because they aren't garbage collected.

- Inheritance isn't applicable to structures, so they can't inherit from anything else and you can't use them as a base class.

- Structures can implement interfaces.

Implementing constructors for a structure

In this next exercise, you will add a constructor to the *Point* structure so that instances can be initialized on creation.

1. Continue using the project from the previous exercise.

2. Add a constructor to your *Point* structure so that the code looks like this:

```
value struct Point
{
    int x, y;
    Point(int xVal, int yVal) { x = xVal; y = yVal; }
}
```

The constructor takes two *int* values and uses them to initialize the *x* and *y* data members. In this case, the arguments are simply being copied into the data members, but it would be simple to add some checking to ensure that the data passed in is correct.

 Note Anyone who has used C++ before will be familiar with the use of default arguments on constructors. You can't use default arguments on managed types in C++/CLI, so you need to provide an explicit default constructor.

3. You can now add extra code to your *main* function to create initialized *Point*s.

```
Point p2(10,20);    // use the second constructor to set x
                    // to 10 and y to 20
Console::WriteLine("p2.x is {0}", p2.x);
```

4. Build and run the application. Check that the result is what you expect.

Using one structure within another

It's possible—and often useful—to use one structure within another. Imagine that you have a structure named *Person* for describing a person. The structure contains the name and date of birth, among other data. You could use separate fields for each item, but you could also make the date entries into another structure and refer to it inside *Person*. Here's an example:

```
// A Date structure containing day, month and year
value struct Date
{
    int dd, mm, yyyy;
};

// A Person structure containing a Date member
value struct Person
{
    String ^name;
    Date DOB;
};
```

You can see how the *Date* structure contains three members representing the day, month, and year. This structure is quite general, so you could use it in other applications. The *Person* structure contains a *String* reference to hold the name, and a *Date* object to hold the date of birth.

In this exercise, you'll use these two classes to investigate how structure data members work.

1. Create a new CLR Console Application project named **Person**.

2. At the top of the file, immediately below the *using namespace System;* line, add the structure definitions for *Date* and *Person*.

3. In the *main* function, create a *Person* object. Remember that you don't use *gcnew*, because structures are value types.

```
// Create a Person
Person p1;
```

4. Fill in the values for the fields.

```
// Fill in the name
p1.name = "Fred";
p1.DOB.dd = 10;
p1.DOB.mm = 3;
p1.DOB.yyyy = 1960;
```

Notice how structure data members are accessed. Because the *DOB* member has members of its own, you simply extend the dot notation to another level to access its members. You can continue this nesting to as many levels as you like, although it is unusual to go much deeper than you've done here.

5. You can also initialize all the members of *Person* in one line. Remove the four initialization lines you entered in step 4 and then change the line where you create the *Person*.

```
Person p1 = {"Fred", {10, 3, 1960}};
```

Can you see what is going on here? The data in the braces—called an *aggregate initializer*—provides data for the initialization of the structure. The *Person* structure contains two items: a *String* and a *Date*. Therefore, there are two items in the list. Because *Date* has members of its own, its entries are also enclosed in braces.

> **Note** Use of an aggregate initializer is an alternative to using a constructor and can be handy where there's no checking to be done on the data.

6. If you decide that the date of birth is wrong, you can simply create a new *Date* and copy it into the *Person* object, such as in the following:

```
// Create a new Date
Date newDOB = {1, 4, 1955};
p1.DOB = newDOB;
```

The new *Date* takes the values specified in the initializer and then copies it into the *Person* object, overwriting the values in the *Date* that's already there.

7. You can see the configuration of the *Person* structure by running the application under control of the debugger. Place a breakpoint in the application at the line where *p1* is created by clicking in the gray margin to the left of the code.

8. Press F5 to start the debugging session.

After the application loads, it executes and stops at the breakpoint. You can now use the Locals pane at the bottom of the window to look at the structure of the *Person* type.

9. Click the plus sign to the left of *p1* in the Locals pane to expand the structure of Person.

Observe that it has Name and DOB members, and if you click the plus sign to the left of DOB, you can expand its structure, as well.

10. Press F10 to step through the code until all the members are initialized.

The members of *p1* display in red as each value changes.

11. When you've finished, press Shift+F5 to stop debugging or, on the toolbar, click the Stop Debugging button.

Finally, let's consider nested structure definitions. If you don't want to use the *Date* structure anywhere except inside your *Person* structure, you can define *Date* inside *Person*, as shown here:

```
// A Person structure containing a Date structure
value struct Person
{
    String ^name;
    value struct Date
    {
        int dd, mm, yyyy;
    };
    Date DOB;
};
```

You create *Person* variables and access their members exactly the same as before. The big difference is that the *Date* structure is now a part of *Person*, so you can't create *Date* variables on their own.

Copying structures

Because structures are value types, copying them makes a copy of the values they contain. Contrast this behavior with classes, for which copying objects results in references being copied.

```
Person p1;
Person p2;
...
p2 = p1;    // p1's data is copied into p2
MyClass m1;
MyClass m2;
...
m2 = m1;    // m2 and m1 now refer to the same object.
            // No data is copied.
```

Note You can't use a reference type as a member of a structure, because structures aren't garbage-collected; a reference member would have to take part in garbage collection.

Enumerations

An enumeration (commonly referred to as enum) is a set of named integer constants. Enumerations are especially suitable for representing types that can take one of a set of fixed values such as the days of the week or the months of the year. Enumerations are value types, and they derive from the abstract *System::Enum* class, which in turn derives from *System::ValueType*.

Creating and using an enumeration

In the following exercise, you will create an enumeration to hold values representing the days of the week and then use it in an application.

1. Create a new CLR Console Application project named **Enums**.

2. At the top of the Enums.cpp file, immediately below the *using namespace System;* line, add the following structure definition:

```
// The Weekday enum definition
public enum class WeekDay
{
    Monday, Tuesday, Wednesday, Thursday, Friday,
    Saturday, Sunday
};
```

The *enum class* keywords start an enumeration definition, and you'll notice that, once again, enums are defined similarly to classes. The body of the enumeration is enclosed in braces and finishes with a semicolon. The use of the *enum* and *class* keywords indicates to the compiler that this is a value type and not a traditional C++ enumeration.

The enumeration itself consists of a comma-separated set of names, each of which represents an integer constant.

3. You create enumeration variables the same as you create any other type. To create and initialize a *WeekDay* object, add the following lines to the *main* function of your application:

```
// Create a WeekDay
WeekDay w = WeekDay::Monday;
```

As with structures, the code doesn't use the *gcnew* operator. An enumeration variable of type *WeekDay* has been created on the program stack, and you access it directly as *w*. Notice how the enumeration variable is initialized with one of the members of the enumeration. This syntax is how you initialize enumeration variables and how you can change their values later on.

> **Note** In C++/CLI, unlike in standard C++, enumeration members must be qualified with the name of their type. It is an error to just say *Monday* rather than *WeekDay::Monday*.

4. Try printing out the value of the *WeekDay* object like this:

```
Console::WriteLine("Value of w is {0}", (int)w);
```

The value 0 should be printed. Each of the named constants making up the enumeration represents an integer value. By default, these values start from 0 and increase by one for each subsequent member of the enumeration. You can test this output by changing the value that you initially assigned to *w*, for example, *WeekDay::Saturday*. When you run the code again, the value 5 should print.

You must cast the enumeration to an *int* in order to be able to print it; you will get an error if you try to print the enumeration without casting it.

5. It would be good to be able to print out the symbol associated with the enumeration as well as its numeric value. You can do this using the *Format* member of the *Enum* base class, as in the following example:

```
String ^s = Enum::Format(WeekDay::typeid, w, "G");
Console::WriteLine("The day is {0}", s);
```

Format needs to be informed as to the type of the enumeration, which you do it by using *Enum::typeid* and the value itself. The "G" indicates the format for the conversion: this is general format, which means a string.

Note Ensure that you qualify your enumeration with either *public* or *private*. If you don't, you will get an error (C2664) when you try to use *Enum::Format*. This is because the new C++ standard (C++11, which this version of Microsoft C++ supports) has a new enumeration type; if the compiler does not see *public* or *private* on an enumeration declaration, it assumes that you have declared a C++11 enumeration.

More about enumerations

Even though the value given to an enumeration is an integer, there's no implicit conversion between enumerations and integers. If you consider the following lines of code, you'll understand why:

```
//** This code won't compile! **//
// '1' would mean Tuesday
w = 1;
// What would '8' mean?
w = 8;
```

If converting between integers and enumerations were allowed, it would be possible to put invalid values into the enumeration. If you do want to convert between integers and enumeration values, you need to use an explicit cast to inform the compiler as to what you want to do, such as in the following example:

```
int day = static_cast<int>(w);
```

You can also use a cast to go the other way, from integer to enumeration, but that isn't good practice.

You don't have to rely on the default numeric values that are assigned to the enumeration members. Suppose that you want the integer equivalents of the weekdays to range from 1 through 7 instead of 0 through 6; simply assign 1 to the *Monday* member, as shown here:

```
public enum class WeekDay
{
    Monday = 1, Tuesday, Wednesday, Thursday, Friday,
    Saturday, Sunday
};
```

The enumeration now starts with 1, and because you haven't given any other values for the remaining members, they are numbered 2 through 7.

If you want, you can give a completely discontinuous series of values for the enumeration members, as in this example:

```
public enum class StatusCodes
{
    OK=0, FileNotFound=2, AccessDenied=5, InvalidHandle=6,
    OutOfMemory=8
};
```

Using enumerations in applications

In this exercise, you'll see how to use an enumeration to control application execution by using it in a switch statement.

1. Continue using the project from the previous exercise. If you've closed it, on the File menu, click Open Solution to open the project again.

2. After the *WriteLine* statements, add the following *switch* statement code:

```
// Switch on the weekday
switch(w)
{
case WeekDay::Monday:
    Console::WriteLine("It's a Monday!");
    break;
case WeekDay::Tuesday:
    Console::WriteLine("It's a Tuesday!");
    break;
case WeekDay::Wednesday:
    Console::WriteLine("It's a Wednesday!");
    break;
default:
    Console::WriteLine("It's some other day...");
}
```

You are allowed to use an enumeration variable as a switch control variable because it's basically an integer. Likewise, you can use the names of enumeration members as switch case labels because they're also integers. The example code has cases for *Monday* through *Wednesday*; everything else is handled by the default case. Remember to put the *break* statements in after the code for each case, or the application won't behave as you expect.

Using memory efficiently

By default, an *enum* is an *int*, and therefore, enumerations are 32 bits in size, which gives you a range of values of –2,147,483,648 through 2,147,483,647. If you're going to use only small values for enumeration members, memory will be wasted if each variable takes up 32 bits. For this reason, it's possible to base an enumeration on any integer type. In the case of our *WeekDay* example, all our values can quite happily fit into 1 byte. Thus, you could base the *enum* on a *char*, as shown here:

```
// WeekDay variables are one byte in size
public enum class WeekDay : char
{
    Monday = 1, Tuesday, Wednesday, Thursday, Friday,
    Saturday, Sunday
};
```

Quick reference

To	Do this

Create a structure.	Use *value struct*, followed by the name of the structure and the body in braces, followed by a semicolon. For example:
	
	`value struct Point3D`
	`{`
	`    int x, y, z;`
	`};`

Initialize structure members.	Create a constructor, which is a function that has the same name as the structure. For example:
	
	`value struct Point3D`
	`{`
	`    int x, y, z;`
	`    Point3D(int xVal, int yVal, int zVal)`
	`    {`
	`        x=xVal;`
	`        y=yVal;`
	`        z=zVal;`
	`    }`
	`};`
	
	You can also use an aggregate initializer:
	
	`Point3D p1 = { 10, 20, 30 };`

Access structure members.	Use the dot notation. For example:
	
	`p1.x = 10;`
	`myPerson.DOB.dd = 20;`

To	Do this

Create an enumeration.	Use *enum class*, followed by the name of the enumeration and the body in braces, followed by a semicolon. For example:
	
	``
	enum class Seasons
	{
	    Spring, Summer, Autumn, Winter
	};
	``

Control the values used for enumeration members.	Assign values to the members in the enumeration definition. For example:
	
	``
	enum class Seasons
	{
	    Spring=1, Summer, Autumn, Winter
	};
	``

Base enumerations on other integer types.	Put a colon and the type name after the enumeration name. For example:
	
	``
	enum class Seasons : char
	{
	    Spring, Summer, Autumn, Winter
	};
	``

Operator overloading

After completing this chapter, you will be able to:

- Describe what operator overloading is.

- Decide which classes should support operator overloading.

- Recognize what you can and can't overload.

- Describe guidelines for providing overloaded operators.

- Explain how to implement operator overloads.

You've already seen how to construct classes and structures, provide member functions in your types, and use these functions in applications. In this chapter, you're going to find out about a special category of member functions called overloaded operator functions, with which you can add extra functionality so that your types can be used more naturally and intuitively.

Note If you've encountered operator overloading in C++ before, you will find that there are many similarities when using C++/CLI. There are also a number of differences, so read carefully!

What is operator overloading?

Chapter 3, "Variables and operators," introduces the operators provided by the C++ language. The problem is that those operators work only with the built-in types, and now, you're starting to use classes and structures to define your own data types. This means that if you want to add or compare objects of types that you've created, you can't use the + and == operators because the compiler doesn't know how to apply them to your objects.

Operator overloading is a C++ feature by which you can define operators to work with your types, which can often lead to a more natural style of programming, so instead of writing

```
object3 = object1.Add(object2);
```

you can write this:

```
object3 = object1 + object2;
```

What types need overloaded operators?

In general, overloaded operators are needed by classes that wrap simple values. Types can be split into three broad classifications, as shown in the following table.

Classification	Defining characteristics	Examples
Values	Values wrap data; if two objects contain the same data, those objects are identical.	*String*, *Matrix*, *Date*, and *Time*
Services	Services can have little or no state data. They provide services through their member functions.	*CreditCardCheck* and *AddressLookup*
Entities	Entities have an identity that is unique for each object.	*BankAccount* (identified by account number) and *Person* (identified by Social Security number)

Values are the classes for which you'll most often find yourself implementing overloaded operators. You can imagine wanting to implement +, >, ==, and other operators for types such as *Date* and *String*, but it's harder to see when you might want them for the other classifications. Service types, which have little or no state, don't tend to need operators: What would comparing two *AddressLookup* objects mean? Entity types might have some operators, but their meaning might not be intuitive. You could use == to check two *BankAccounts* for equality, but what would that mean? There's more on equality later on in this chapter; first, let's move on to see how operator overloading works.

What can you overload?

You learned about the rich set of operators that C++ supports in Chapter 3. You can overload many of these, but there are some restrictions. Traditional C++ won't let you overload several of the more esoteric operators, such as *sizeof* and the member-of dot operator. C++/CLI extends the list and adds a number of other C++ operators that can't be overloaded, including ->, (), and [].

The main reason for this restriction is that the Common Language Specification (CLS) is designed for use across languages, and as such, it will support a set of operators that are useful to all Microsoft .NET languages rather than support operators that are specific to C++. You'll see later exactly which operators .NET lets you overload.

Rules of overloading

Several rules apply when overloading operators. The problem is that you can implement operators to mean whatever you like, so some rules are needed to impose a few limits and to prevent creating an impossible job for the compiler.

- You cannot define any new operators. Even if you think that %% would make a neat new operator, you can't add it.

- You can't change the *arity*, the number of operands taken by an operator. You might think it would be really useful to create a unary / operator, but the division operator always has to have two operands.

- You can't change the precedence or associativity of operators. So, * (multiplication) always takes precedence over + (addition), regardless of what they are actually implemented to mean for a type.

Overloading operators in managed types

Let's start by adding operator overloading to value types and then move on to reference types. You already know that value types are the types most likely to need operator overloading.

Overloading arithmetic operators

In this exercise, you'll see how to implement operators in a value type. The exercise also introduces many of the techniques you'll need to use when adding operator overloading to your own types.

1. Start Microsoft Visual Studio 2012 and create a new CLR Console Application project named **Overload**.

2. At the top of the Overload.cpp file, immediately below the *using namespace System;* line, add the following *struct* definition:

```
// The IntVal struct definition
value struct IntVal
{
private:
    int value;
public:
    IntVal(int v) : value(v) { }
    int getVal() { return value; }
};
```

This simple *struct* is the one you'll use throughout these exercises. It simply wraps an *int* and then provides a constructor for creating and initializing *IntVal* objects and a *get* function for accessing the data member. Chapter 9, "Value types," explains that the keyword *value* makes *IntVal* a .NET value type rather than a traditional C++ structure.

3. Create three *IntVal* objects, replacing the body of the *main* function with the following code:

```
IntVal one(1);
IntVal two(2);
IntVal three;    // will get zero value
```

Because value types always have a default constructor, *three* will be initialized to zero.

4. Try adding *one* and *two* and assigning the result to *three*, followed by a *WriteLine* statement to print the value of *three*.

```
three = one + two;
Console::WriteLine(three.getVal());
```

When you build the application, you get an error (C2676), informing you that the compiler can't find a "+" operator that works with your objects.

5. Implement the "+" operator for *IntVal* by adding the following function to the *struct* definition, placing it after the *getVal* function:

```
IntVal operator+(IntVal rhs)
{
    IntVal result(value + rhs.value);
    return result;
}
```

Let's analyze this function. An overloaded operator is represented by a function whose name starts with *operator*, which also has the operator symbol appended to it. So, the == operator would be represented by a function called *operator==*, the > operator by *operator>*, and so on.

When the compiler sees the code

```
one + two
```

it is actually calling the function you define, like this:

```
one.operator+(two)
```

Thus, a binary operator (one that takes two operands) is represented by a member function that takes one argument, the right-hand side of the + operation. A unary operator (one that takes a single operand, such as the "−" in −1) is represented by a function that takes no arguments.

Now, let's look at how the operator is implemented. The result of *one* + *two* is not *one* or *two*, but a new value that represents their sum. In the code, therefore, we create a new object that is initialized with the sum of the two values and return it.

6. Build the application again.

You should find that the compilation is successful because the compiler can find a "+" that works with *IntVal* objects. If you run the application, you should see the value "3" printed out.

Now that you've seen how to implement addition, it should be easy for you to implement the other arithmetic operators. Indeed, because this class represents a simple integer value, you probably should implement them so that they are consistent with the behavior of integers.

> **Tip** The last sentence in the previous paragraph introduces a very important point: It is up to you to define all the operators that make your type work properly. See the section "Guidelines for providing overloaded operators" at the end of the chapter for more details.

Using static operator overloads

Becasue *IntVal* is basically just an *int* wrapped up in a *struct*, it would seem reasonable to want to do this:

```
three = one + 2;
```

You can easily add an overload of *operator+* that takes an *int*, such as in the following:

```
IntVal operator+(int rhs)
{
    IntVal result(value + rhs);
    return result;
}
```

How about this next example? The rules of basic addition dictate that this should be equivalent:

```
three = 2 + one;
```

If you try this, however, it will not work, because the compiler cannot find a function that takes an *int* as its left operand. But you cannot add such a function to *IntVal*, because such functions always have to have an object as their left operand.

The solution is to create a static operator overload in the *IntVal* class, and you would do this for any binary operator that is symmetrical (for example, you would expect a == 3 to be the same as 3 == a)

This exercise shows you how to add a static addition operator to the *IntVal* class.

1. Continue using the project from the previous exercise.

2. Add a line to the *main* function that tries to use an *int* as the left operand. Verify that it doesn't compile:

```
three = 2 + one;
```

3. Add a static version of *operator+* to *IntVal*:

```
static IntVal operator+(int lhs, IntVal rhs) {
    IntVal result(lhs + rhs.value);
    return result;
}
```

Remember that static members belong to a class (or structure) as a whole rather than to any one object. This means that they aren't associated with an object, and so they need to be passed to both operands.

If you want, you can implement three overloads of the static operator, one for *(IntVal, IntVal)*, one for *(IntVal, int)*, and one for *(int, IntVal)*, and not have the non-static version at all. But, it turns out that there is a much neater solution, which you will see in the exercise that follows this one.

4. Add the following function to the *struct*, placing it after the *getVal* function:

```
static operator IntVal(int v)
{
    return IntVal(v);
}
```

This is an example of a *conversion operator*, a function that directs the compiler how to convert to and from a type. This function instructs the compiler how to get from an *int* to an *IntVal* by creating an *IntVal* and initializing it with the *int*. In effect, you are saying to the compiler, "If you see an *int* but you want an *IntVal*, here's what to do." If you don't have such a conversion operator, the compiler won't be able to perform the conversion.

Conversions and C++/CLI

Standard C++ embodies the concept of *converting constructors*. If you defined *IntVal* as a standard C++ structure, the constructor that takes an *int* would allow the compiler to implicitly convert *int*s to *IntVal*s wherever it is needed. Microsoft decided to disallow this implicit conversion in C++/CLI, so even if you have a suitable constructor, you have to provide a conversion operator to signal the compiler that it can perform the conversion.

This next exercise shows you how the conversion operator makes it possible to use a single *operator+* function that works with all combinations of *IntVal* and *int*.

1. Delete any existing *operator+* functions and replace them with this single one:

```
static IntVal operator+(IntVal lhs, IntVal rhs) {
    IntVal result(lhs.value + rhs.value);
    return result;
}
```

This function adds two *IntVal*s, but it also copes with an *int* as either the right or left operand because we've now instructed the compiler that it can convert between *int* and *IntVal*.

2. Edit the code in *main* to test all the possible options:

```
three = one + two;
Console::WriteLine("three is {0}", three.value);

three = one + 2;
Console::WriteLine("three is {0}", three.value);

three = 2 + one;
Console::WriteLine("three is {0}", three.value);
```

You can verify that the conversion is occurring by using the debugger.

3. Place a breakpoint in the code by clicking in the gray margin to the left of the three = 2 + one line.

4. Press F5 to start the debugging session.

After the application loads, it executes and stops at the breakpoint. At this point, scroll up and place another breakpoint at the first line of the *operator+* function.

5. Press F11.

This brings you to the *operator+* function at the breakpoint. At the bottom of the window, in the Locals pane, look at the values. Observe that both *lhs* and *rhs* are *IntVals*, showing that the *int* has been converted for you.

You can see that—provided that your types implement the correct constructors and conversion operators—you can sometimes use one operator overload to perform a family of operations.

6. When you are done, discontinue the debugging session either by pressing the dark-red square on the Debug toolbar, by clicking Stop Debugging on the Debug menu, or by pressing Shift+F5.

Overloading compound assignment operators

C++ has a number of compound assignment operators, such as "+=" and "−=", with which you can use x += 2 as shorthand for x = x + 2. In standard C++, they are considered completely separate operators; you don't get "+=" just because you have overloaded the "+" and "=" operators.

In C++/CLI, the compound assignment operators are synthesized for you. This means that x += 2 is rewritten as x = x + 2 so that your overloaded "+" operator can be used.

What functions can you overload?

You can overload most operators in C++, including all the common ones such as the arithmetic and logical operators. However, .NET places a premium on interoperability between languages: whenever you use classes from the .NET Framework, such as *String*, you are using code written in C#, and it is quite possible that someone using C# or Visual Basic .NET might want to use your C++/CLI types in their code. If you know that your code is never going to be used by any other language, you can skip the rest of this section.

The CLS defines those features that a language is required to support. A lot of this is only of interest to language implementers, but one thing that interests us here is the list of operators that CLS-compliant languages are required to support.

If your intent is that your overloaded operators should be able to be used in other .NET languages, you need to follow several rules:

- Operator functions must be static members of the class or structure.

- Value types must be passed or returned by value.

- Ref types must be passed or returned by reference.

If your operators don't follow these rules, they are too closely affiliated with C++ and will not work in the wider .NET world.

Following is the list of CLS-compliant operators. If you implement any of these, you can expect them to be usable from other .NET languages. Because some languages don't have a concept of operator overloading, each operator has a .NET function name, in the same way that *Int32* is the .NET type that underlies *int*.

CLS name	C++ operator function
op_AddressOf	*operator&*
op_LogicalNot	*operator!*
op_OnesComplement	*operator~*
op_PointerDereference	*operator**
op_UnaryNegation	*operator-*
op_UnaryPlus	*operator+*
op_Addition	*operator+*
op_BitwiseAnd	*operator&*
op_BitwiseOr	*operator|*
op_Comma	*operator,*
op_Decrement	*operator--*
op_Division	*operator/*
op_Equality	*operator==*
op_ExclusiveOr	*operator^*

CLS name	C++ operator function
op_GreaterThan	operator>
op_GreaterThanOrEqual	operator>=
op_Increment	operator++
op_Inequality	operator!=
op_LeftShift	operator<<
op_LessThan	operator<
op_LessThanOrEqual	operator<=
op_LogicalAnd	operator&&
op_LogicalOr	operator||
op_Modulus	operator%
op_Multiply	operator*
op_RightShift	operator>>
op_Subtraction	operator-

Note You cannot overload the *gcnew* and *delete* operators as you can in standard C++. This is because memory allocation is the job of the .NET runtime, and you are not allowed to take this task over yourself.

Implementing logical operators

We've dealt with the arithmetic operators, so let's continue by considering the logical and comparison operators. C++ offers a set of comparison operators, which are summarized in the following table:

Operator	Description
==	Equality
!=	Inequality
>	Greater than
>=	Greater than or equal to
<	Less than
<=	Less than or equal to

Implementing these operators is simple and follows the model of the addition operator in the previous examples. Here's how to implement the equality operator (==):

1. Using the same project as in the previous exercises, find the *operator+* function in your code and add the following function after it:

```
static bool operator==(IntVal lhs, IntVal rhs) {
    return lhs.value == rhs.value;
}
```

The function follows the same pattern as the *operator+*. It is a static member of the *IntVal* structure, but this time it returns a *Boolean*, just as you'd expect a logical operator to do, and it makes its decision based on the internal structure of its two operands.

2. Add some test code to *main* to test the new operation:

```
if (three == 3)
    Console::WriteLine("All is OK");
else
    Console::WriteLine("Something is very wrong!");
```

3. Build and run the application to verify that the operator is working as you expect.

4. If you implement equality you need to implement inequality, as well, so add a definition for *operator!=* to *IntVal*:

```
static bool operator!=(IntVal lhs, IntVal rhs) {
    return !(lhs == rhs);
}
```

Notice how this is implemented: it uses *operator==* to compare the two objects and then uses the logical NOT operator to negate the result. Delegating the comparison to *operator==* rather than comparing the internals of the objects themselves is not only slightly less typing, but if the internal structure of *IntVal* were to change, you only have to change the *operator==* function and you have automatically updated *operator!=*, as well.

5. Add some test code for this new operator.

```
if (three != 3)
    Console::WriteLine("Something is wrong!");
else
    Console::WriteLine("Inequality working OK");
```

6. Build and run the application to ensure that all is working correctly.

The other logical operators (<, <=, >, and >=) can be overloaded in a similar way, and you can make use of the same shortcut when implementing them.

What is equality?

Deciding whether to implement == and != depends on the type you're writing, and it might not be a simple decision. For some types the choice is obvious: consider a *Point* type that has *x* and *y* coordinates. In this case, two *Point*s are equal if their *x* and *y* members have the same value.

What about a *Currency* class that has a value and a currency type? You might say that two *Currency* objects are the same if both the value and the currency are identical. Likewise, you might decide that two objects are the same if their values are the same when converted to a common base currency such as dollars or Euros. Both approaches are equally valid; it's up to you to choose one and document it.

There might also be classes for which any notion of equality is artificial. Consider a *Bank Account* class: what would equality mean? Two accounts can't be completely identical because they have different, unique account numbers. You might choose something that counts as equality (such as having the same balance) but there is no obvious meaning. You might well decide that equality is not meaningful for such types.

As a final point, remember that testing for equality can pose problems for floating-point values. It is well known that computations on these types can introduce rounding errors in the final decimal places; thus, two values which should be identical might not test as equal.

One way around this is to define such values as being equal if they are within a tolerance; for example:

```
if (Math::Abs(value1 - value2) < 0.00001)
    // they are equal
else
    // they are not
```

The *Math::Abs* function is a static member of the *Math* class that returns the absolute value of its operand.

Implementing *Equals*

All types in .NET ultimately inherit from the *System::Object* class. This class provides several functions that all .NET types inherit, and the one that is particularly relevant to our discussion of equality is the *Equals* function.

With *Object::Equals*, types can provide a way to compare content, as opposed to comparing references. This is the same job that you've been doing by implementing the == operator, but it works for languages that don't support operator overloading. This means that if your types are going to be used from other .NET languages, you need to implement the *Equals* function.

In this exercise, you will implement *Equals* for the *IntVal* structure:

1. Continue using the same project. Add the following function to the end of the *IntVal* structure definition:

```
virtual bool Equals(Object ^other) override
{
    IntVal ^obj = dynamic_cast<IntVal^>(other);
    if (obj == nullptr)
        return false;

    return value == obj->value;
}
```

This function is more complex than the others you've looked at, so you might want to compile the code to ensure that you haven't made any coding errors. Let's examine the code line by line. The function is inherited from *System::Object*, so you need to use both the *virtual* and *override* modifiers to show that you are overriding a base class virtual function. *Equals* takes a handle to an *Object* as its argument because it is inherited by all classes and so can be used to compare any type at all.

The first thing you need to do is to use *dynamic_cast* to convert the *Object* handle into an *IntVal* handle.

 Note *dynamic_cast* is a C++ casting mechanism that performs a cast at run time, returning a *nullptr* if the types don't match.

If the handle passed in wasn't an *IntVal*, the cast will return null. You know that two objects of different types can't be equal, so you can return *false* immediately. If the result is not null, we have an *IntVal*. Comparison is then simply a case of comparing the fields of the two objects to see if they are the same.

2. Test the *Equals* function by creating some *IntVal* objects and checking if they are equal:

```
IntVal four(4), anotherFour(4), five(5);

if (four.Equals(anotherFour))
    Console::WriteLine("All is OK");
else
    Console::WriteLine("Something is wrong...");

if (four.Equals(five))
    Console::WriteLine("Something is very wrong!");
else
    Console::WriteLine("All is OK");
```

You might wonder how an *IntVal* object is turned into an *Object* handle in the call to *Equals*. If the compiler sees a value type being used where a reference type is wanted, it automatically wraps it in an object wrapper, a process called *boxing*, which is discussed in more detail in Chapter 22 "Working with unmanaged code."

3. Build and run the application to ensure the results are what you expect.

Points about *Equals*

System::ValueType, the base type for all structures, implements a version of *Equals*. This means that you don't actually need to provide your own, but you might want to because the inherited version can be very slow. It uses a feature called *reflection* to examine objects at run time, find their data members, and compare them. If you find that the performance of *Equals* is a concern, you now know how to provide your own version.

If you do override *Equals*, you should also consider overriding the *GetHashCode* function, as well. A *hashcode* is an integer value that represents an object. It is used when storing data in dictionaries. If two objects are "equal," they should have the same hashcode. Calculating hashcodes is beyond the scope of this book.

Implementing increment and decrement

As a final example, this section shows you how to overload the increment and decrement operators (++ and −−). As is discussed in Chapter 3, the built-in ++ and −− operators are used to increment and decrement the value of integer variables. You can overload them for your own types, and it makes sense to use them wherever you have the idea of incrementing or decrementing. For example, if you had a *Date* type, you could overload ++ and −− to add or subtract a day from the current date, adjusting the month and year as appropriate.

You also saw how these operators can be placed before or after the variable. If placed before (called *pre-increment* and *pre-decrement*), the value will be adjusted before the variable is used in the expression. If placed after (*post-increment* and *post-decrement*), the original value is used in the expression, and the value adjusted after it has been used.

In standard C++, you would provide two operator overloads each for ++ and −−, one each for the pre-increment and post-increment cases. In C++/CLI, you implement the overload of each operator as a single static member, and this does for both cases.

1. Continue with the same project. Add the following method to the *IntVal* structure:

```
static IntVal operator++(IntVal i)
{
    i.value++;
    return i;
}
```

The static function takes a single *IntVal* as its argument, increments its value, and then returns it.

2. Test out the operator in code, such as the following:

```
IntVal first(3);

IntVal next = ++first;    // pre-increment
Console::WriteLine("pre-inc, next = {0}, first = {1}",
    next.value, first.value);

next = first++;    // post-increment
Console::WriteLine("post-inc, next = {0}, first = {1}",
    next.value, first.value);
```

3. Build and run the application.

The following output displays, showing that your operator is working in both pre and post-increment situations:

```
pre-inc, next = 4, first = 4;
post-inc, next = 4, first = 5;
```

The variable first started with the value 3. The pre-increment changed it to 4 and then used it in the assignment. The post-increment did the assignment and then increased the value.

After you have implemented the increment operator, it will be simple to employ decrement in the same way.

Operators and reference types

Implementing operators for reference types is very similar to implementing them for value types, the main difference being that you need to deal with handles to objects. As an example, here is part of the *IntVal* structure, re-implemented as a *ref* type rather than a *value* type:

```
ref struct IntVal
{
    int value;

    IntVal(int v) : value(v) { }

    static operator IntVal^(int v)
    {
        return gcnew IntVal(v);
    }

    static IntVal^ operator+(IntVal ^lhs, IntVal ^rhs) {
        IntVal^ result = gcnew IntVal(lhs->value + rhs->value);
        return result;
    }
};
```

```
int main(array<System::String ^> ^args)
{
    IntVal ^one = gcnew IntVal(1);
    IntVal ^two = gcnew IntVal(2);

    IntVal ^three = one + two;
    Console::WriteLine("Three is {0}", three->value);

    IntVal ^anotherThree = 1 + two;
    Console::WriteLine("anotherThree is {0}", anotherThree->value);

    return 0;
}
```

You can see how objects and the dot operator have been replaced by handles and ->, and objects are created by using *gcnew*. Apart from that, the code is substantially the same.

Guidelines for providing overloaded operators

The most important guideline to keep in mind is that *overloaded operators must make intuitive sense for a class*. For instance, if you have a *String* class, using + to concatenate the *String*s is pretty intuitive. You might get some agreement that –, as in s2 – s1, would mean "look for s1 within s2, and if you find it, remove it." However, what could the * operator mean when applied to two *Strings*? There's no obvious meaning, and you're only going to confuse people if you provide it. So, ensure that the operators you provide for your types are the ones that people expect to find.

The second guideline is *operator usage must be consistent*. In other words, if you overload ==, ensure that you overload !=, as well. The same goes for < and >, ++ and —, and so on.

The third guideline is *don't overload obscure operators or ones that change the semantics of the language*. Operators such as the comma are obscure, and few people know how they work, so it isn't a good idea to overload them. Other operators, such as the logical AND and OR operators (&& and ||), can cause problems. In earlier chapters, you learned about the *if* statement and how expressions joined by && and || are only evaluated if necessary. As a result, some expressions in an *if* statement might never be evaluated. If you overload the AND and OR operators, the whole of the expression will have to be evaluated, which changes the way the *if* works.

Quick reference

To	Do this
Overload operators.	Implement a function having the name operator with the operator symbol appended. For example: ```\nIntVal operator+(IntVal other)\n{\n . . .\n}\n```
Overload operators for value types.	Pass arguments and return values as value objects.
Overload operators for reference types.	Pass arguments and return values as handles.
Implement equality tests.	Overload == and != and provide an overload of Equals for the benefit of other .NET languages.

Exception handling

After completing this chapter, you will be able to:

- Explain what exceptions are.

- Recognize the different types of exceptions that can be used in C++/CLI.

- Describe how to generate exceptions.

- Explain how to handle exceptions.

- Create your own exception classes.

N ow that you know how to construct classes and value types and use them in programming, this chapter introduces you to exception handling, a powerful way of managing errors within C++ applications.

What are exceptions?

Exceptions are an error-handling mechanism employed extensively in C++ and several other modern programming languages. Traditionally, error and status information is passed around by using function return values and parameters, as demonstrated in the following:

```
// Pass status back as return value
bool bOK = doSomething();

// Pass status back in a parameter
int status;
doSomething(arg1, arg2, &status);
```

Note The "&" (ampersand character) denotes a reference in standard C++, in the same way that "%" denotes a tracking reference in C++/CLI.

Although this is a tried-and-tested way of passing status information around, it suffers from several drawbacks:

- You can't force the programmer to do anything about the error.

- The programmer doesn't even have to check the error code.

- If you're deep within in a series of nested calls, you must set each status flag and back out manually.

- It's very difficult to pass back status information from something that doesn't take arguments or return a value.

Exceptions provide an alternative error-handling mechanism, which gives you three main advantages over traditional return-value error handling:

- **Exceptions can't be ignored**   If an exception isn't handled at some point, the application will terminate, which makes exceptions suitable for handling critical errors.

- **Exceptions don't have to be handled at the point where the exception occurs**   An error can occur many levels of function call deep within an application, and there might not be a way to fix the problem at the point at which the error occurs. Exceptions make it possible for you to handle the error anywhere up the call stack. (See the upcoming sidebar "The call stack and exceptions.")

- **Exceptions provide a useful way to signal errors when a return value can't be used**   There are two particular places in C++ where return values can't be used: constructors don't use them, and overloaded operators can't have their return value overloaded to use for error and status information. Exceptions are particularly useful in these situations because they give you a means to sidestep the normal return-value mechanism.

The call stack and exceptions

At any point in an application, the call stack holds information about which functions have been called to get to the current point. The call stack is used in three main ways by applications: during execution to control calling and returning from functions, by the debugger, and during exception handling.

The handler for an exception can occur in the routine in which the exception was thrown. It can also occur in any routine above it in the call stack, and, at run time, each routine in the call stack is checked to see if it implements a suitable handler. If nothing suitable has been found by the time the top of the stack has been reached, the application terminates.

In .NET, exceptions have one other significant advantage: They can be used across languages. Because exceptions are part of the underlying Microsoft .NET Framework, it's possible to throw an exception in C++/CLI code and catch it in Microsoft Visual Basic .NET, something that isn't possible outside the .NET environment.

As is the case with any other error mechanism, you'll tend to trigger exceptions by making errors in your code. However, you can also generate exceptions yourself if necessary, as you'll see shortly.

How do exceptions work?

When an error condition occurs, the programmer can generate an exception by using the *throw* keyword, and the exception is tagged with a piece of data that identifies exactly what has happened. At this point, normal execution stops and the exception-handling code built in to the application begins looking for a handler. It looks in the currently executing routine, and if it finds a suitable handler, the handler is executed and the application continues. If it doesn't find a handler in the current routine, the exception-handling code moves one level up the call stack and checks for a suitable handler there. This process carries on until either the application finds a handler or it reaches the top level in the call stack—the *main* function. If nothing has been found by this time, the application terminates with an "unhandled exception" message.

Here's an example of how an unhandled exception appears to you. You've probably seen a lot of these already! Look at the following simple code fragment:

```
Console::WriteLine("Exception Test");
int top = 3;
int bottom = 0;

int result = top / bottom;
Console::WriteLine("Result is {0}", result);
```

It's easy to see that this code is going to cause a divide-by-zero error, and when it is executed, you see the result shown in the following screen shot:

You can see that the divide-by-zero has resulted in an exception being generated. Because I didn't handle it in the code, the application has been terminated, and the final output never makes it to the screen. Notice the form of the standard message: it informs you as to what happened (a *System::DivideByZeroException* error), presents an error message, and then gives you a stack trace that directs you to where the error occurred (in this case, in the *main* function at line 13 in the Exception-Test.cpp file).

System::DivideByZeroException denotes the kind of object that was passed in the exception. A lot of exception classes are provided in the *System* namespace, and it's also likely that you'll make up your own based on the *System::Exception* base class, as you'll see later in the chapter.

Exception types

Exception handling is slightly complicated in that you might encounter three different types of exception handling when using C++/CLI: traditional C++ exceptions, C++/CLI exceptions, and Microsoft Windows Structured Exception Handling (SEH). Traditional C++ exceptions form the basis of all exception handling in C++. C++/CLI adds the ability to use managed types (for example, *ref* classes and *value* types) in exceptions, and you can mix them with traditional exceptions. C++/CLI also extends exception handling by adding the concept of a *finally* block, which I discuss in the section "The *finally* block" later in the chapter. The third sort of exception handling, SEH, is a form of exception handling built in to Windows operating systems that is independent from C++. I won't talk any more about SEH here, except to note that you can interact with it from C++.

Throwing exceptions

Let's start our exploration of exceptions by discussing how to generate, or *throw*, them. You'll end up generating far more exceptions by accident than by design, but you need to know how to generate your own when errors occur in your application.

What can you throw?

In traditional C++, you can attach any type of object to an exception, so you can use built-in types (such as *int* and *double*) as well as structures and objects. If you throw objects in C++, you usually throw and catch them by reference.

.NET languages throw and catch objects that are of types inheriting from the *System::Exception* base class, so although you can throw built-in types, you should use *Exception*-derived objects when you're writing .NET code.

When should you throw?

You should use exceptions to signal conditions that are in some way exceptional; in other words, situations that are unusual, and which definitely need attention by the caller. Don't use exceptions for normal flow of control in your application. For example, throwing an exception because your code can't find a file that ought to be present is fine; using an exception to signal that you've read to the end of a file isn't, because that is a normal and expected occurrence, not an exceptional one.

How do you know what to throw? There are a large number of exception classes in the *System* namespace, all of which derive from *Exception*. A number of those you'll commonly encounter are listed in the following table. You should be able to find the exception class to suit your purposes, and if you can't, it's always possible to derive your own exception classes from *System::Exception*.

Exception class	Description
System::ApplicationException	Thrown when a non-fatal application error occurs.
System::ArgumentException	Thrown when one of the arguments to a function is invalid. Subclasses include *System::ArgumentNullException* and *System::ArgumentOutOfRangeException.*
System::ArithmeticException	Thrown to indicate an error in an arithmetic, casting, or conversion operation. Subclasses include *Sytem::DivideByZeroException* and *System::OverflowException.*
System::Exception	The base class of all exception types.
System::IndexOutOfRangeException	Thrown when an array index is out of range.
System::InvalidCastException	Thrown when an invalid cast or conversion is attempted.
System::MemberAccessException	Thrown when an attempt is made to dynamically access a member that doesn't exist. Subclasses include *Sytem::MissingFieldException* and *Sytem::Missing MethodException.*
System::NotSupportedException	Thrown when a method is invoked that isn't supported.
System::NullReferenceException	Thrown when an attempt is made to dereference a null reference.
System::OutOfMemoryException	Thrown when memory cannot be allocated.
System::SystemException	The base class for exceptions that the user can be expected to handle. Subclasses include *ArgumentException* and *ArithmeticException.*
System::TypeLoadException	Thrown when the Common Language Runtime (CLR) cannot find an assembly or a type within an assembly, or cannot load the type. Subclasses include *System::DllNotFoundException.*

The following exercise shows you how to generate an exception. In the section that follows, you'll go on to see how to catch and process the exception.

1. Start Microsoft Visual Studio 2012 and create a new CLR Console Application project named **Throwing**.

2. Immediately after the using *namespace System;* line and immediately before *main*, add the following function definition:

```
void func(int a)
{
    if (a <= 0)
        throw gcnew ArgumentException("Aaargh!");
}
```

This simple function takes an integer argument, and if its value is less than 0, it throws an exception. In this case, I'm creating a new *System::ArgumentException* object, initializing it with a string, and then throwing it.

3. Insert code to test the behavior by adding the following code to the *main* function:

```
Console::WriteLine("Throw Test");
Console::WriteLine("Calling with a=3");
func(3);
Console::WriteLine("Calling with a=0");
func(0);
Console::WriteLine("All done");
```

The code calls the function twice, once with a valid value and once with 0, which should trigger the exception.

4. Compile and run the application, and you should see something similar to the following screen shot:

```
Throw Test
Calling with a=3
Calling with a=0

Unhandled Exception: System.ArgumentException: Aaaargh!
   at func(Int32 a) in c:\users\julian\documents\sbs\throwing\throwing\throwing.
cpp:line 10
   at main(String[] args) in c:\users\julian\documents\sbs\throwing\throwing\thr
owing.cpp:line 20
   at mainCRTStartupStrArray(String[] arguments) in f:\dd\vctools\crt_bld\self_x
86\crt\src\mcrtexe.cpp:line 301
Press any key to continue . . .
```

The application has called the function once without incident, but the second call has triggered an exception. As before, you get a message and a stack trace. This time the message is the string used to initialize the exception object and the stack trace has two levels, showing that the exception was triggered at line 10 in the *func* function, which was called from the *main* function at line 20.

 Note The precise line number you see reported in the exception stack trace depends on exactly how you typed in and formatted your code.

Handling exceptions

Now that you've seen how to generate exceptions, let's move on to handling them.

Using the *try* and *catch* construct

You catch exceptions and process them by using the *try/catch* construct, which has the following form:

```
try
{
    // code that may fail
}
catch(TypeOne ^one)
{
    // handle this exception
}
```

```
catch(TypeTwo ^two)
{
    // handle this exception
}
```

Code that you suspect might fail is enclosed in a *try* block that is followed by one or more handlers in the form of *catch* blocks. Each *catch* block looks a little like a function definition, with *catch* followed by a type in parentheses, which represents the type that will be caught and processed by the *catch* block. In the preceding code, the first *catch* block handles exceptions tagged with a *TypeOne*^ object, whereas the second block handles those tagged with a *TypeTwo*^ object.

> **Note** *try* and *catch* blocks form a single construct. You can't have a *try* block without at least one *catch* block, you can't have a *catch* block without a *try* block, and you can't put anything in between them.

You can chain as many *catch* blocks together as there are exception types to catch, as long as you have at least one.

The following exercise shows you the basics of handling exceptions, using the example from the previous exercise as a basis.

1. Continue using the project from the previous exercise

2. Modify the *main* function to look like the following:

```
Console::WriteLine("Throw Test");

try
{
    int a = 3;
    Console::WriteLine("Calling with a=3");
    func(a);
    Console::WriteLine("Calling with a=0");
    a = 0;
    func(a);
}
catch(System::ArgumentException ^ex)
{
    Console::WriteLine("Exception was {0}", ex);
}
Console::WriteLine("All done");
```

The calls to the function are enclosed in a *try* block, which is followed by a single *catch* block. When the second call to the function fails, the exception-handling mechanism takes over. It can't find a handler in the function where the error originated, so it walks one level up the call stack and comes out in the *try* block.

At this point, the runtime wants to go off looking for a handler. As part of this process, it puts the program stack back to where it was at the start of the *try* block. In other words, it unwinds the stack, which means that it destroys any variables that have been created on the stack within the *try* block, so you can't use them in the *catch* block. You need to keep this in mind when writing exception handlers and declare any variables you need to use in the *catch* block outside the corresponding *try*.

When the stack has been unwound, the code looks at the *catch* blocks associated with this *try* block to see whether there is one that has an argument type that matches what was thrown. In this case, you have a match, so the contents of the *catch* block are executed. If there wasn't a suitable *catch* block, the runtime would try to move up another level of the call stack and then would fail and terminate the application.

3. Execute this code.

    You should see something very similar to the following screen shot:

```
Throw Test
Calling with a=3
Calling with a=0
Exception was System.ArgumentException: Aaaargh!
   at func(Int32 a) in c:\users\julian\documents\sbs\throwing\throwing\throwing.
cpp:line 10
   at main(String[] args) in c:\users\julian\documents\sbs\throwing\throwing\thr
owing.cpp:line 23
All done
Press any key to continue . . .
```

The second function call has generated an exception that has been caught by the *catch* block, which has printed out "Exception was:" plus the exception details. In contrast to what happened in the previous exercise, the final "All done" message is now printed. This illustrates an important point about exception handling: After a *catch* block has been executed, application execution continues after the *catch* block as if nothing had happened. If there are any other *catch* blocks chained to the one that is executed, they're ignored.

4. Try changing the second call so that it passes in a positive value. You'll find that the *catch* block isn't executed at all. If a *try* block finishes without any exception occurring, execution skips all the *catch* blocks associated with the *try* block.

Customizing exception handling

Just printing out the exception object results in the type-plus-message-plus-stack trace that you saw when the exception was unhandled. You can use properties of the *Exception* class to control what is printed, as shown in the following table:

System::Exception property	Description
Message	Returns a string containing the message associated with this exception.
StackTrace	Returns a string containing the stack trace details.
Source	Returns a string containing the name of the object or application that caused the error. By default, this is the name of the assembly.

Here's a brief exercise that demonstrates the use of *Exception* class properties:

1. Continue using the project from the previous exercise. Edit the *main* function to set *a* back to zero before the second call to *func*.

2. Edit the *catch* statement in the *main* function to read as follows:

```
catch(System::ArgumentException ^ex)
{
    Console::WriteLine("Exception was {0}", ex->Message);
}
```

3. Build and run the application.

   You should see a result like this:

   ```
   Exception was Aaargh!
   ```

In a similar way, you could use *StackTrace* to retrieve and print the stack trace information.

Using the exception hierarchy

The exception classes form a hierarchy based on *System::Exception*, and you can use this hierarchy to simplify your exception handling. As an example, consider *System::ArithmeticException*, which inherits from *System::Exception* and has subclasses that include *System::DivideByZeroException* and *System::OverflowException*. Now, look at the following code:

```
try
{
    // do some arithmetic operation
}
catch(System::ArithmeticException ^aex)
{
    // handle this exception
}
catch(System::DivideByZeroException ^dex)
{
    // handle this exception
}
```

Suppose that a *DivideByZeroException* is thrown. You might expect it to be caught by the second catch block, but it will, in fact, be caught by the first one. This is because according to the inheritance hierarchy, a *DivideByZeroException* is an *ArithmeticException*, so the type of the first catch block matches. To get the behavior you expect when using more than one catch block, you need to rank the catch blocks from most specific to most general.

Tip The compiler will give you warning C4286 if you have the catch blocks in the wrong order. This works for both managed and unmanaged code.

So, if you just want to catch all arithmetic exceptions, you can simply put in a handler for *ArithmeticException*, and all exceptions from derived classes will be caught. In the most general case, you can simply add a handler for *Exception*, and all managed exceptions will be caught.

Using exceptions with constructors

In the section "What are exceptions?" earlier in this chapter, I mentioned one of the advantages of exceptions is that they make it possible for you to signal an error where there's no way to return a value. They're very useful for reporting errors in constructors, which, as you now know, don't have a return value.

In the following exercise, you'll see how to define a simple class that uses an exception to report errors from its constructor, and you'll also see how to check for exceptions when creating objects of this type.

1. Create a new CLR Console Application project named **CtorTest**.

2. Immediately after the *using namespace System;* line and immediately before *main*, add the following class definition:

```
ref class Test
{
    String ^str;
public:
    Test(String ^s)
    {
        if (s == nullptr || s == "")
            throw gcnew System::ArgumentException("Argument null or blank");
        else
            str = s;
    }
};
```

The *ref* keyword makes this class managed, and this managed class has one simple data member, a handle to a managed *String*. At construction time, this handle must not be null or point to a blank string, so the constructor checks the handle and throws an exception if the test fails. If the handle passes the test, construction continues.

> **Note** The *nullptr* keyword represents a null value for a handle; it must be used where a null value is required. This is in contrast to standard C++, in which you can use a numeric "0" to represent a null pointer.

3. Try creating an object in the *main* function, as shown in the following:

```
int main()
{
    Console::WriteLine("Exceptions in Constructors");
    // Create a null handle to test the exception handling
    String ^s = nullptr;

    Test ^t = nullptr;

    // Try creating an object
    try
    {
        t = gcnew Test(s);
    }
    catch(System::ArgumentException ^ex)
    {
        Console::WriteLine("Exception: {0}",
                            ex->Message);
    }

    Console::WriteLine("Object construction finished");
    return 0;
}
```

Notice that the call to *gcnew* is enclosed in a *try* block. If something is wrong with the *String* handle (as it is here), the *Test* constructor will throw an exception that will be caught by the *catch* block.

4. Build and run the application, and you will see the output from the *catch* block. Try modifying the declaration of the string so that it points to a blank string (initialize it with ""), and then try a nonblank string (for example, "hello") to check that the exception is thrown correctly.

Nesting and rethrowing exceptions

Now that you've seen how to use the *try/catch* construct, let's move on to cover some more advanced uses. The first of these are nesting and rethrowing exceptions.

As the name implies, nesting exceptions means including one *try/catch* construct within another, which can provide a useful way to handle error conditions. It works as you might expect:

```
try        // outer try block
{
    try        // inner try block
    {
        // Do something
    }
    catch(SomeException ^ex1)
    {
        Console::WriteLine("Exception: {0}", ex1->Message);
    }
}
```

```
catch(OtherException ^ex2)
{
    Console::WriteLine("Exception: {0}", ex2->Message);
}
```

If an exception occurs within the inner *try* block that is of type *SomeException^*, it will be handled by the inner *catch* block and execution will continue after the end of the inner *catch* block, as usual. The outer *catch* block will not be executed in this case because the error has already been adequately handled.

If an exception occurs within the inner *try* block that is of type *OtherException^*, it won't be handled by the inner *catch* block, so it will be passed to the outer *try* and *catch* construct, where it is processed by the outer *catch* block.

 Note You can nest *try* and *catch* constructs to several levels, but it's unusual to go more than two levels deep because it can overcomplicate the structure of the code.

Rethrowing an exception means just that—handling an exception in a *catch* block and then throwing it again so that it can be handled somewhere else. The following exercise shows how to catch an exception and rethrow it.

1. Create a new CLR Console Application project named **Rethrow**.

2. Immediately after the *using namespace System;* line and immediately before *main*, add the following function definition:

```
void func(int a)
{
    try
    {
        if (a <= 0)
            throw gcnew ArgumentException("Aaargh!");
    }
    catch(ArgumentException ^ex)
    {
        Console::WriteLine("Exception caught in func()");
    }
}
```

This function is basically the same simple function to which you were introduced at the start of the chapter. It throws a *System::ArgumentException* when it has passed a negative argument. The difference here is that the exception is being caught within the function.

3. Modify the *main* function so that it looks like this:

```
Console::WriteLine("Throw Test");

try
{
    int n = 0;
    Console::WriteLine("Calling with n=0");
    func(n);
}
catch(ArgumentException ^ex)
{
    Console::WriteLine("Exception caught in main()");
}
Console::WriteLine("All done");
```

If you run this code, you'll find that the exception is caught locally in *func* and the *catch* block in *main* doesn't execute.

4. Modify the definition of *func* so that it rethrows the exception after handling it.

```
void func(int a)
{
    try
    {
      if (a <= 0)
          throw gcnew ArgumentException("Aargh!");
    }
    catch(ArgumentException ^ex)
    {
        Console::WriteLine("Exception caught in func()");
        throw;    // rethrow the exception
    }
}
```

Using *throw* without an argument rethrows the current exception, and it can be used in this way only within a *catch* block. At this point, the runtime goes off looking for another handler, which means moving up the call stack to the *main* function, where the exception is caught a second time.

5. Build and run this application.

The "Exception caught in func()" and "Exception caught in main()" messages print, demonstrating that the exception has been handled twice.

Note that you don't have to rethrow the same exception; it's quite usual to catch one type of exception, handle it, and then rethrow an exception of another type. You'll see an example of this in the section "Creating your own exception types" later in this chapter.

The *finally* block

C++/CLI adds a new construct to traditional C++ exception handling: the *finally* block. The purpose of this block is to let you clean up after an exception has occurred, and the following short exercise shows how it works.

1. Continue using the project from the previous exercise.

2. Modify the main function so that it looks like the following, adding a *finally* block after the *catch* block:

```
Console::WriteLine("Throw Test");

try
{
    int n = 3;
    Console::WriteLine("Calling with n=3");
    func(n);
    Console::WriteLine("Calling with n=0");
    n = 0;
    func(n);
}
catch(System::ArgumentException ^ex)
{
    Console::WriteLine("Exception was {0}", ex);
}
finally
{
    Console::WriteLine("This is the finally block");
}

Console::WriteLine("All done");
```

   If you try executing the code, you'll find that the *finally* block is executed after the *catch* block.

3. Modify the *main* function so that the second call doesn't cause an exception, either by changing the value or by commenting it out. When you run the application again, you'll see that the *finally* block is still executed, even though there was no error.

The purpose of this block is to ensure that if you do something in the *try* block—such as opening a file or allocating some memory—you'll be able to tidy up whether an exception occurs or not because the *finally* block is always executed when execution leaves a *try* block. This construct gives you a way to clean up what might otherwise require duplicate code.

The *catch(...)* block

Standard C++ has a construct that can be used to catch any exception that goes past. Here's how it works:

```
try
{
    // do some arithmetic operation
}
catch(System::ArithmeticException ^pex)
{
    // handle this exception
}
catch(...)
{
    // handle any exception
}
```

If an exception doesn't match the first *catch* block, it will be caught by the second one, no matter what type it is. The problem is that you lose any information about the exception, because the *catch(...)* block doesn't have an argument.

 Note Even though you can't tell what kind of exception you are handling inside a *catch(...)* block, if you rethrow from within the block, a properly typed object will be thrown to handlers higher in the call stack.

If you want this functionality when using C++/CLI, use a *catch* block that has an *Exception^* as its argument, which will catch any managed exception object.

Creating your own exception types

You've already seen how all the exception types are derived from the *System::Exception* class. If you can't find one that suits your needs in the standard exception hierarchy, you can easily derive your own class from *Exception* and use it in your code. The following exercise shows you how to derive a new exception class and how to use it in code.

1. Create a new CLR Console Application project named **OwnException**.

2. Add the following class definition immediately after the *using namespace System;* line:

```
// User-defined exception class
ref class MyException : System::Exception
{
public:
    int errNo;
    MyException(String ^msg, int num) : Exception(msg), errNo(num) {}
};
```

This custom exception class is a managed class that inherits from *System::Exception*, and it extends *Exception* by adding a single field to hold an error number. The class constructor takes a message and a number, and passes the message string back to the base class.

> **Note** I've made the *errNo* field public. Although you're normally advised to make all data members of classes private, you can make a case for having public data members in certain circumstances. After you've created an *Exception* object and passed it back to the client, do you care what the client does with it? Exceptions are "fire and forget" objects, and you're normally not concerned with the integrity of their state after they leave your code in a throw statement.

3. Add the following function definition immediately after the class definition:

```
void func(int a)
{
    try
    {
        if (a <= 0)
            throw gcnew ArgumentException("Argument <= 0");
    }
    catch(System::ArgumentException ^ex)
    {
        Console::WriteLine("Caught ArgumentException in func()");
        throw gcnew MyException(ex->Message, 1000);
    }
}
```

The function checks its argument and throws a *System::ArgumentException* if it finds a negative value. This exception is caught locally, and a message is printed. Now, I decide that I really want to handle the exception elsewhere, so I create a new *MyException* object and throw it, initializing it with the message from the original *ArgumentException*.

4. Test the exception handling by calling the function in the application's *main* routine.

```
int main()
{
    Console::WriteLine("Custom Exceptions");
    try
    {
        func(0);
    }
    catch(MyException ^ex)
    {
        Console::WriteLine("Caught MyException in main()");
        Console::WriteLine("Message is '{0}'", ex->Message);
        Console::WriteLine("ErrNo is {0}", ex->errNo);
    }

    return 0;
}
```

Calling the function with a 0 value triggers the exception, which is handled in the function itself, and the exception is then rethrown to be handled in the *main* function. You can see in the following screen shot how the exception has been caught in both places.

```
Custom Exceptions
Caught ArgumentException in func()
Caught MyException in main()
Message is 'Argument <= 0'
ErrNo is 1000
Press any key to continue . . .
```

Using *safe_cast* for dynamic casting

C++ supports casting, which is when you instruct the compiler to convert one type to another for use in an expression. Although casting can be useful, it can also be dangerous because you're overriding what the code would naturally direct the compiler to do. The *safe_cast* keyword was introduced in C++/CLI to help make the operation safer. The following code fragment shows how some conversion operations can be unsafe:

```
// Define the Vehicle and Car classes
ref class Vehicle {};
ref class Car : Vehicle {};
ref class Truck : Vehicle {};
ref class Bus : Vehicle {};
...
Car ^pc = gcnew Car();   // Create a Car
Vehicle ^pv = pc;        // Point to it using a Vehicle handle - OK
...
Car ^pc2 = pv;           // Copy pv into another Car^ handle - not OK!
```

The compiler raises an error on the last line, complaining that it can't convert a *Vehicle^* to a *Car^*. The problem is that a *Vehicle* handle could point to any object derived from *Vehicle* such as a *Truck* or a *Bus*. Implicitly casting from a *Car* to a *Vehicle* is fine because a *Car* is a *Vehicle*; going the other way doesn't work because not every *Vehicle* is a *Car*. One way around this issue is to use the *safe_cast* construct, such as in the following:

```
try
{
    Car ^pc2 = safe_cast<Car^>(pv);
}
catch(System::InvalidCastException ^pce)
{
    Console::WriteLine("Cast failed");
}
```

At run time, *safe_cast* checks the object on the other end of the handle to see if it has the same type as the object to which you're trying to cast. If it does, the cast works; if it doesn't, an *Invalid CastException* is thrown.

Note Experienced C++ programmers will realize that *safe_cast* is very similar to the *dynamic_cast* construct supported by standard C++. The difference is that *safe_cast* throws an exception if the cast fails, whereas *dynamic_cast* returns a null value.

Using exceptions across languages

One of the great things about managed exceptions in C++/CLI is that they work across languages, so now you can, for example, throw an exception in C++/CLI and catch it in a Visual Basic application. No longer are exceptions simply a C++ feature, and this ability to harmonize error handling across code written in different languages makes mixed-language programming much easier than it has been in the past.

 Note In .NET you should throw exception objects that derive from *System::Exception*. Standard C++ allows you to throw and catch any kind of value, such as *ints* and *doubles*. If you do this and the exception is thrown to non-C++ code, your value will be wrapped in a *RuntimeWrappedException* object.

In the final example in this chapter, you will create a C++ class in a dynamic-link library (DLL) and then use the class in a Visual Basic.NET application.

 Note You will need to have Visual Basic.NET installed to complete the second part of this example.

1. Start Visual Studio 2012 and open a new Visual C++ project. This time, choose a Class Library project from the CLR section: this is used when you want to create a DLL rather than an EXE. I called the project MyClass; you can name it what you like, but make a note of the name.

   You'll find that you've created a project that defines a namespace called *MyClass*, containing a single class called *Class1*. It's this class that you'll edit, adding a method that can be called from a Visual Basic client.

2. The project will contain a number of files, among them MyClass.h and MyClass.cpp, which are used to hold the definition and implementation of the *Class1* class. Open MyClass.h and add the *Test* function so that it looks like the following code:

```
// MyClass.h

#pragma once

using namespace System;
```

```
namespace MyClass
{
    public ref class Class1
    {
    public:
        void Test(int n)
        {
            if (n < 0)
                throw gcnew ArgumentException(
                    "Argument must be positive");
        }
    };
}
```

The *Test* method should look familiar by now: it simply checks its argument and throws an exception if it's less than 0.

3. Build the project.

   You end up with a DLL called MyClass.dll being created in the project's Debug directory.

4. Close the project (by clicking Close Solution on the File menu) and create a new Visual Basic Console Application project named **Tester**. Before you can use the DLL you just created, you have to add a reference to it to the project. To do so, open Solution Explorer (using the Solution Explorer item on the View menu if it isn't visible) and right-click the project name.

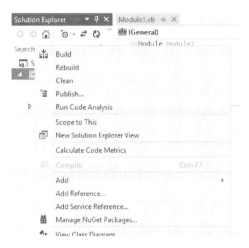

5. On the shortcut menu that appears, click Add Reference. In the Reference Manager dialog box that opens, click Browse and search for the DLL you built in step 3. Ensure that it's added to the Selected Components pane and then click OK.

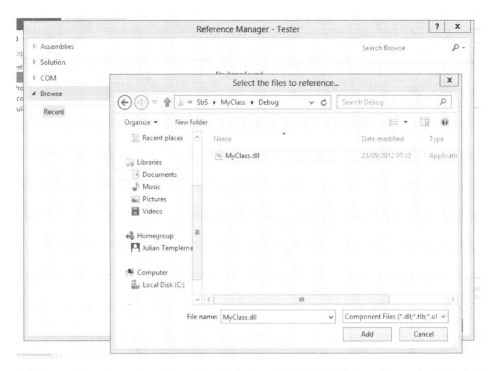

6. Add the code to the project. Open Module1.vb and edit the *Main* function so that it looks like the following code:

```
' Application to demonstrate cross-language exception handling
Imports [MyClass]

Module Module1
  Sub Main()
    Dim obj As New Class1()

    Try
      obj.Test(-1)
    Catch ex As ArgumentException
      Console.WriteLine("Exception: " & ex.Message)
    End Try

    Console.WriteLine("All done")
  End Sub
End Module
```

The first line imports the *MyClass* namespace into the application. This line does the same job as *using namespace* does in C++, so you don't have to fully qualify the name *Class1* when it appears. The first line in the *Main* function creates a new *Class1* object; this is equivalent to creating an object in C++ by using *gcnew*. The call to the *Test* function is enclosed in a *Try* and *Catch* construct, and you can see the similarity between the way exceptions are handled in Visual Basic and C++. The main difference is that in Visual Basic, the *Catch* blocks are inside the *Try* block.

Note Even if you don't know Visual Basic, it should be obvious that the structure of the code is quite similar to C++/CLI, and you are using exactly the same .NET Framework types.

7. Build the application and execute it.

   Passing –1 through as the argument triggers the exception, and you should see the message printed out in the *Catch* block.

Quick reference

To	Do this
Generate an exception.	Use the *throw* keyword, using a handle to a managed type as the argument. For example: ```throw gcnew SomeException();```

Catch an exception.	Use the *try/catch* construct, surrounding the code that might fail with a *try* block, followed by one or more *catch* blocks. Remember that you catch exceptions by reference, so you must use a handle. For example:
	
	```try {```
	``` // code that might fail```
	```}```
	```catch(SomeException ^se)```
	```{```
	``` // handle the exception```
	```}```

Catch more than one exception.	Chain *catch* blocks together. For example:
	
	```catch(SomeException ^ex)```
	```{```
	``` // handle the exception```
	```}```
	```catch(SomeOtherException ^ex2)```
	```{```
	``` // handle the exception```
	```}```

Catch a family of exceptions.	Use the base class of the exceptions that you want to catch in the catch block; for example, *ArithmeticException* will catch *DivideByZeroException* and several others.
Catch every exception.	Use a *catch* block that takes *Exception^* as a parameter, which will catch every type that is derived from *Exception*.
Handle exceptions at more than one point in a program.	Use *throw* to rethrow exceptions from one catch block to another.
Create your own exceptions.	Derive from the *Exception* class, adding your own members.

Arrays and collections

After completing this chapter, you will be able to:

■ Implement arrays in C++.

■ Create single-dimensional and multidimensional arrays.

■ Create and use managed arrays.

■ Understand what generic types are.

■ Use the features of the *System::Array* class.

■ Use the collection classes provided by the .NET Framework.

■ Describe what the STL/CLR library is.

This chapter concerns itself with data structures. You'll learn about arrays and other collection classes, and you'll learn how to use them in your applications. In the first part of the chapter, you're going to learn about two sorts of arrays: the native arrays provided by the C++ language, and the Microsoft .NET managed arrays, which use functionality inherited from the .NET Framework.

The second part of the chapter looks more widely at the range of collection classes provided by the .NET Framework, discussing their characteristics and showing you how and when to use them. The chapter concludes with a brief introduction to the STL/CLR library.

Native C++ arrays

Native arrays are those provided as part of the C++ language, and they are based on the arrays that C++ inherited from C. Although native arrays are designed to be fast and efficient, there are draw-backs associated with using them, as you'll see shortly.

This first exercise introduces you to C++ native arrays by showing you how to create an array of value types and how to use the array.

1. Start Microsoft Visual Studio 2012 and create a new CLR Console Application project named **TradArray**.

2. Open the source file Trad.cpp and edit the *main* function to match the following:

```
const size_t SIZE = 10;

int main(array<System::String ^> ^args)
{
    Console::WriteLine("Traditional Arrays");

    // Create an array
    int arr[SIZE];
    Console::WriteLine("Size in main: {0}", sizeof(arr));

    // Fill the array
    for(size_t i=0; i<SIZE; i++)
        arr[i] = i*2;

    return 0;
}
```

The first line declares a constant that represents the size of the array. Using symbolic constants in this fashion is preferable to using the integer literal "10" in the code. Not only does it make explicit just what the 10 represents, but should you want to change the size of the array, you only have to change the value in one place.

The type *size_t* is a *typedef* for *unsigned int*. This is used where you want to denote sizes, dimensions, or quantities. It is good practice to use *size_t* rather than *int*. Also note the wide-spread convention of using capitalized names for constants.

The array is created by specifying a type, a name, and a size enclosed in square brackets ([]). Here, the array is named *arr*, and it holds ten *int* values. All arrays are created by using the same syntax, as shown here:

```
// Create an array of six doubles
double arr[6];
// Create an array of two char*'s
char* arr[2];
```

Here's the first important point about native arrays: after you've created an array, you can't resize it, so you need to know how many elements you require before you start. If you don't know how many elements you're going to need, you might be better off using a .NET collection, which is discussed later in this chapter.

> **Note** The array size has to be known at compile time, so, for example, you can't ask the user for a value and then use that value to specify an array dimension at run time. However, it's common to create constants, either by using preprocessor *#define* declarations or by declaring *const* variables, and using them to specify array dimensions.

As you can see from the loop in the preceding code, array elements are accessed by using square brackets that contain the index. Here's the second important point about native arrays: indexing starts at zero rather than one, so the valid range of indices for an array is from zero to one less than the size of the array. In other words, for a 10-element array, valid indices are [0] to [9].

3. Add a second loop to print out the array's contents after filling it.

```
// Print its contents
for(size_t j=0; j<10; j++)
    Console::WriteLine(arr[j]);
```

4. Build and run the application.

The values print, one to a line, as shown in the following screen shot, and you also see that the size of the array is 40, representing 10 *int*s of 4 bytes each:

What happens if you change the range of the second loop so that it tries to print the element at [10]?

5. Alter the code in the second loop to look like the following:

```
// Print its contents
for(size_t j=0; j<=10; j++)
    Console::WriteLine(arr[j]);
```

Notice the less-than-or-equal-to (<=) condition. The effect of this condition is to try to print 11 elements rather than 10. Compile and run the program, and you should see output similar to the following:

Notice the random value that's been printed at the end of the list. Here's the third important point about native arrays: bounds aren't checked. Native arrays in C++ aren't objects, and therefore they have no knowledge of how many elements they contain. It's up to you to keep within the bounds of the array; if you don't, you risk corrupting data or crashing your application.

Passing arrays to functions

Passing arrays to functions introduces a complication because the function has no knowledge about the size of the array it has been passed. As you'll see shortly, when you pass an array to a function, you pass only the starting address, which means that you have to figure out some way of passing the size information along with the array when you call the function. Normally this is accomplished in one of two ways:

- Pass the size as an explicit parameter to the function call.

- Ensure that the array is always terminated by a unique marker value so that the function can determine when the end of the data has been reached.

How do native arrays work?

A native array in C++ isn't an object; it's simply a collection of values strung together in memory. So, a 10-element array of integers consists of 10 integers, one after the other, in memory. The name of the array represents the address of the first element, so when you declare an array like this:

```
int foo[10];
```

you're instructing the compiler to reserve memory large enough to hold 10 integers and return you the address as *foo*. When you access an array element, you're actually specifying the offset from this address; thus, *foo[1]* means "offset one *int* from the address foo, and use what is stored there." This explains why array indexing starts from 0: an index of 0 denotes an offset of zero from the start address, so it means the first element.

As soon as the compiler has allocated the space, it works from that point forward relative to this starting address. When you provide an offset in terms of an array index, the compiler generates code to access that piece of memory. And, if you have it wrong and stepped outside the bounds of the allocated memory, you can end up reading or writing somewhere inappropriate.

Although this might seem dangerous—and indeed, it is—in fact, it is sometimes both desirable and necessary behavior, for reasons that unfortunately I have neither the time nor space to explain in proper detail here. Trying to read or write off the end of an array is called a *buffer overrun*. This has been the cause of many serious bugs in C and C++ applications. Some malicious individuals have used these bugs to create attacks against applications, and there are many well-documented exploits that use buffer overruns. Tools do exist to check that applications aren't misbehaving, but they can't catch everything, and so you have to be very careful to check your use of array indices.

Let's investigate passing an array to a function.

1. Continue with the project from the previous exercise.

2. Add the following function definition immediately after the *using namespace System;* line:

```
void func(int arr[], size_t size)
{
    Console::WriteLine("Size in func: {0}", sizeof(arr));
    for(size_t i=0; i<size; i++)
        Console::WriteLine(arr[i]);
}
```

The first argument to the function alerts the compiler that the address of an array is going to be passed, which is equivalent to passing a pointer. It's very common to see *int** used, instead. The second argument passes the size of the array—in effect, the amount of memory pointed to by the first argument. The function prints out the array by using the size, just as before.

3. Call the function from the *main* routine, as shown here:

```
func(arr, 10);
```

What if the array size needs to be changed at some point? You can make your code more robust by calculating the number of elements in the array automatically by using the *sizeof* operator, like this:

```
func(arr, sizeof(arr)/sizeof(arr[0]));
```

The *sizeof* operator returns the size of its argument in bytes, where the argument can be a variable name or a type name. Using *sizeof* on an array returns the total size of the array in bytes, in this case, 40 bytes. When divided by the size of one element—4 bytes—you're left with the number of elements in the array.

4. Build and run the application.

The right values print out as well as the fact that the array is of size 4 bytes. This reflects the fact that it is passed to the function as a pointer.

Initializing arrays

It's possible to initialize arrays at the point of declaration, as shown in the following syntax fragment:

```
int arr[4] = { 1, 2, 3, 4 };
```

The values to be used for initialization are provided as a comma-separated list in braces ({}) on the right side of an assignment; these values are known as an aggregate initializer. The compiler is clever enough to figure out how many values are in the list, and it will dimension the array to fit if you don't provide a value.

```
// Dimension the array automatically
int arr[] = { 1, 2, 3, 4 };
```

If you give a dimension and then provide too many values, you'll get a compiler error. If you don't provide enough values, the initial values you give will be used to initialize the array starting from element zero, and the remaining elements will be set to zero.

Multidimensional arrays

Multidimensional arrays in C++ are an extension of the single-dimensional variety. The following short exercise shows how to create and use a two-dimensional array.

1. Create a new CLR Console Application project named **MultiD**.

2. Open the source file MultiD.cpp and add the following code to the *main* function:

```
int main(array<System::String ^> ^args)
{
    Console::WriteLine("Multidimensional Arrays");

    // Create a 2D array
    int arr[2][3];

    // Fill the array
    for(int i=0; i<2; i++)
        for(int j=0; j<3; j++)
            arr[i][j] = (i+1)*(j+1);

    return 0;
}
```

Observe that a two-dimensional array is declared by using two sets of square brackets. You don't put the two values inside one set of brackets, as you do in many other languages, and for higher-order arrays, you simply add more sets of square brackets. As with single-dimensional arrays, you have to provide the size at compile time, and the indices of each dimension vary from zero to one less than the declared size. Array elements are also accessed by using two sets of square brackets.

3. Print out the array by using an extension of the method for printing out the elements of the single-dimensional array, as follows:

```
// Print the array content
for(int i=0; i<2; i++)
{
    for(int j=0; j<3; j++)
        Console::Write("{0} ", arr[i][j]);

    Console::WriteLine();
}
```

Notice that one row of the array is printed on one line. The inner loop prints a single row by using repeated calls to *Console::Write*. After each row has been output, a call to *Console::WriteLine* outputs a new line.

To pass a multidimensional array to a function, use two empty sets of square brackets (for example, *int arr[][]*) and specify the dimension information, as before.

Dynamic allocation and arrays

So far, all arrays in this chapter have had a fixed size allocated at compile time. It is possible—and very common—to create arrays dynamically at run time by using the *new* operator. The array you create still has a fixed size, but this size can be specified at run time when you know how many elements you need. The following exercise shows how to create an array dynamically and then use it.

1. Create a new CLR Console Application project named **Dynamic**.

2. Open the source file Dynamic.cpp and edit the *main* function as shown:

```
const size_t SIZE = 10;

int main(array<System::String ^> ^args)
{
    Console::WriteLine("Dynamic Arrays");

    // Create an array dynamically
    int *pa = new int[SIZE];

    // Fill the array
    for(size_t i=0; i<SIZE; i++)
        pa[i] = i*2;

    // Print the array content
    for(size_t j=0; j<SIZE; j++)
        Console::WriteLine(pa[j]);

    // Get rid of the array once we're finished with it
    delete [] pa;

    return 0;
}
```

You've previously used the *gcnew* operator to create .NET reference types; the *new* operator is used in traditional C++ code in a similar way to allocate memory dynamically at run time. The syntax is *new*, followed by the type of the array and then the dimension enclosed in square brackets. After the array has been created, you're returned a pointer to the start of the array. Pointers work in a similar way to handles, but they use an asterisk (*) instead of a caret.

You can see that dynamic arrays are accessed in exactly the same way as statically allocated arrays, using the square-bracket notation. This use of a pointer with array notation underlines the relationship between pointers and arrays, as explained in the sidebar "How do native arrays work?" earlier in this chapter.

Notice the call to *delete* just before the program exits. Allocating an array dynamically in traditional C++ doesn't create a managed object, so there is no garbage collection associated with this array. Therefore, to use memory efficiently, you must remember to deallocate memory as soon as you've finished with the array. There are two versions of *delete*: one to delete single objects (*delete*), and one for arrays (*delete []*).

When deleting an array, you need to use the *delete []* version. If you forget the square brackets, your application might well still run, but according to the standard, the result of calling single-element *delete* on an array is undefined.

Strictly speaking, the call is unnecessary here because all allocated memory is freed up when the application exits. However, in any real-world application, you need to manage your memory carefully to ensure that all memory is freed up at an appropriate point.

 Note After you've called *delete* on a pointer, you must not use the pointer again, because the memory it points to is no longer allocated to you. If you try to use a pointer after freeing up the memory it points to, you can expect to get a run-time error.

Problems with manual memory management

Manual memory management is widely considered to be the single biggest cause of bugs in C and C++ programs, and it's the driving force behind the development of the garbage-collection mechanisms in languages such as C# and Java. If it's up to the programmers to call *delete* on every piece of memory they allocate, mistakes are going to be made.

There are two main problems associated with manual memory management:

- **Not freeing up memory**   If you don't free up memory when you have finished with it, you create a *memory leak*. Although this problem is normally the less serious of the two, it results in an application taking up more memory than it needs. In extreme cases, the amount of extra memory consumed by an application can reach the point where it begins to interfere with other applications or even the operating system.

- **Freeing up memory inappropriately**   In a complex application, it might not be obvious where a particular piece of memory should be freed up or whose responsibility it is to free it. If *delete* is called too soon and another piece of code tries to use the dynamically allocated array, you can expect a run-time error. The same is true if anyone attempts to call *delete* on the same pointer more than once.

Although manual memory allocation using *new* and *delete* makes it possible for you to manage memory very precisely, these two problems were the impetus behind the development of garbage collectors, which make the system track the use of dynamically allocated memory and free it up when no one else is using it.

Generic types

Before we talk about the .NET array and collection classes, we need to introduce the concept of *generic types*. This is a complex topic, and we cannot cover it in great depth, but this section provides enough detail for you to understand why generic types are useful and how they work. You will also find that you use generic types far more often than you create them, so I will focus on how to use the generic types you will encounter in .NET.

Perhaps the easiest way to introduce generic types is through an example. Suppose that you want to create a class that will hold a list of object handles. When you begin designing the class, you will soon realize that it doesn't matter what type the objects in the list are, as long as they are *ref* types and you can get a handle to them. A list of *String^* will work in exactly the same way as a list of *Person^* or a list of *Vehicle^*. In fact, you can say that your list class will work with *T^*, where *T* is any reference type.

This is what generic types give you the flexibility to do. You can write a class in terms of *T^*, and only decide what *T* is going to be when you use it. Here is what a (very) partial definition of such a generic list class might look like:

```
generic <typename T>
ref class MyList
{
public:
    void Add(T obj);
    T GetAtIndex(int idx);
    ...
};
```

The class definition begins with the *generic* keyword, which alerts the compiler that you're starting a generic type. The *<typename T>* then informs the compiler that *T* is a type parameter, a placeholder that will be filled in later and which must be the name of a type. You can then implement the class in terms of *T*, using it in member declarations, and for function parameter and return types.

Note It is possible (and quite common) for a generic type to have more than one type parameter. For example, a dictionary of key/value pairs will have one parameter for the key type and a second for the value type, which would be denoted by *<typename K, typename V>*.

To use this type in code, you need to specify to the compiler what *T* will be by providing as a type name in angle brackets:

```
MyList<String^> ^listOfString = gcnew MyList<String^>();
```

This line informs the compiler that we want a list of *String^*, and the compiler will ensure that the object will only work with *String^*. Any attempt to add another type results in a compile-time error. The types created from a generic type by specifying a type parameter are called *constructed types*.

Note When this code is compiled, a generic version of the class is added to the assembly, and constructed types are created at run time, as needed. This is important because it means that it is not necessary to know when compiling the original *MyList<T>* code what types it will be used with at run time.

Managed arrays

The .NET Framework library contains an array class that provides a managed equivalent of a standard C++ array but without the disadvantages. A managed array is an object that is allocated on the managed heap and subject to the normal garbage-collection rules.

> **Note** Unlike standard C++ arrays, indexing is not just a way of specifying an offset from an address.

Creating a managed array is quite different from creating a standard C++ array. You declare a managed array by using the *array* keyword, as in the following examples:

```
array<int> ^arr1;
array<double, 2> ^arr2;
array<Person^> ^arr3;
```

Observe that all of these are declared as handles. This is because an array is a managed object, and you always interact with arrays through handles. So, *arr1* is a handle to a 1D array of integers; *arr2* is a handle to a 2D array of doubles; and *arr3* is a handle to an array of *Person* handles.

> **Note** The <> syntax indicates that the array is a generic type. The array class is written so that it can represent an array of any type of object, and you specify the type it is to contain in angle brackets at the time of declaration.

The general syntax for declaration is

```
array<type, rank> handle_name;
```

where rank is the number of dimensions (although for a 1D array, you can omit the rank). So, we could declare some arrays as follows:

```
array<int> ^intArray = gcnew array<int>(5);
array<String^> ^stringArray = gcnew array<String^>(10);
```

The first line declares an array of 5 *int*s, whereas the second declares an array of 10 *String* handles. You might recognize this second type from the *main* function that you've seen in all the examples.

This exercise shows you how to create and iterate over an array of *int*s.

1. Create a new CLR Console Application project named **IntArray**.

2. Add the following code to *main* to create an array of *int*s and then fill it with some squares:

```
array<int> ^intArray = gcnew array<int>(5);
for (int i=0; i<intArray->Length; i++)
    intArray[i] = i*i;
```

Notice how you access the array elements by using the square-bracket notation, with the index starting at zero, just as in traditional arrays. There is no reason why indexing must start from zero, but it is traditional for languages in the C family.

3. Add another loop to print out the values.

```
for (int i=0; i<intArray->Length; i++)
    Console::WriteLine("Element {0} is {1}", i, intArray[i]);
```

4. Build and run the application, and verify that the values are printed.

5. Modify the loop so that it tries to read off the end of the array.

```
for (int i=0; i<intArray->Length+1; i++)
```

6. Build and run the application again.

This time you should get an exception because the array object knows how many elements it has, and it won't let you try to access an element that doesn't exist.

This is an important difference between traditional and managed arrays. The managed array is holding a set of values for you, knows exactly how many it has, and isn't going to let you access an element that doesn't exist.

Initialization

You saw earlier how a traditional C++ array can be initialized by using an aggregate initializer. You can do the same with managed arrays, so we can write the following:

```
array<int> ^intArray = gcnew array<int>(3) { 1, 2, 3 };
```

As you might expect, the compiler is clever enough to work out the size of the array from the initializer, so you can omit the dimension, as demonstrated in the following:

```
array<int> ^intArray = gcnew array<int>() { 1, 2, 3 };
```

And, just like traditional arrays, you can omit the entire *gcnew* expression because the compiler knows from the left side of the statement that you want an *array<int>*, as illustrated here:

```
array<int> ^intArray = { 1, 2, 3 };
```

Arrays and reference types

Arrays of reference types are slightly different to arrays of value types. Remember that reference types are always accessed through a handle. This means that an array of reference types is actually going to be an array of handles.

You can see this by examining the main function of any application you've written so far. If you look at the definition of *main*, the first line should look like this:

```
int main(array<System::String ^> ^args)
```

The *args* argument is a handle to an array of *String* handles, and you will become very accustomed to seeing this "double caret" pattern as you work with managed arrays.

The following exercise shows you how to create and use an array of reference types. In this example, you will use the *System::String* class, but you can easily substitute a reference type of your own.

1. Create a new CLR Console Application named **RefArray**.

2. Edit the *main* function to match the following:

```
const size_t SIZE = 5;

int main(array<System::String ^> ^args)
{
    Console::WriteLine("Arrays of Reference Types");

    // Create an array of String references
    array<String ^> ^arr = gcnew array<String ^>(SIZE);

    // Explicitly assign a string to element zero
    arr[0] = gcnew String("abc");

    // Implicitly assign a string to element one
    arr[1] = "def";

    // Print the content
    for (size_t i=0; i<SIZE; i++)
        if (arr[i] == nullptr)
            Console::WriteLine("null");
        else
            Console::WriteLine(arr[i]);
}
```

3. Compile and run the application, ensuring that the values are printed as you expected.

    You should see two strings printed first, followed by three nulls. This is because the array object sets the *String* handles to *null* when it is created, and you have only assigned to two of them.

You can also use an aggregate initializer with reference types, so you could have initialized the array like this:

```
array<String ^> ^arr = gcnew array<String^>(SIZE) {
        gcnew String("abc"),
        gcnew String("def") };
```

Using the *for each* loop with arrays

In .NET code, there is a better way to iterate over arrays than using a counted *for* loop: the *for each* loop. With *for each*, you can iterate over a collection without having to maintain a counter. Here's what a *for each* loop looks like:

```
for each (String ^s in arr)
{
    // use s
}
```

Each time around the loop, an element from the array is assigned to the *String s*, so that you can use it within the body of the loop. You do not have to know how big the array is, and don't have to initialize and maintain a counter. Not having to do this means that there is less chance to get an off-by-one error in your code.

There is another advantage to using the *for each* loop that might not be immediately apparent. This loop doesn't only work with arrays; it works with any collection that implements the *IEnumerator* interface. This means that you can use the same programming construct to iterate over very different kinds of collection.

Enumerators

Enumerators are the .NET implementation of the Iterator design pattern, which provides an abstract way to iterate over any collection. In .NET, arrays and other collection types do this by implementing the *IEnumerator* interface, which has the following three members:

- The *MoveNext* method, which moves to the next element in the collection, returning *false* when there are no more

- The *Current* property, which returns the item currently being pointed to by the enumerator

- The *Reset* method, which resets the pointer to just before the start

When you create an enumerator, it is positioned just before the first element. Calling *MoveNext* until it returns *false* is guaranteed to visit each element in the collection once, although with some collections, the order of traversal is not guaranteed.

Using an enumerator means that you do not have to be concerned with the underlying collection type, meaning (for instance) that the implementation could be changed to use a linked list rather than an array, and the calling code would not have to change.

Note, however, that you can only read collections through an enumerator. If you want to modify elements while you traverse the collection, you will have to use a counted *for* loop.

This short exercise shows you how to use a *for each* loop:

1. Continue with the project from the previous exercise.

2. Modify the code that prints out the contents of the array to use a *for each* loop:

```
for each (String ^s in arr) {
    if (s == nullptr)
        Console::WriteLine("null");
    else
        Console::WriteLine(s);
}
```

3. Build and run the application to ensure that you see the same output.

Multidimensional arrays

Just as in standard C++, you can create multidimensional arrays in C++/CLI. Unlike standard C++, however, you don't provide extra pairs of square brackets, but instead specify the dimension inside the angle brackets. For example, here is how you would declare a two-dimensional array of *int*s:

```
array<int,2> ^array2D = gcnew array<int,2>(3, 3);
```

Because you have two dimensions, you need to specify two values in the constructor to set the values for each dimension.

You also obviously need to give two values when specifying an element in a 2D array, but in C++/CLI, you place both inside a single pair of square brackets:

```
array2d[1,1] = 7;
```

As you would expect, indexes start from zero in all dimensions, and you can generalize the creation and use of these arrays to any number of dimensions you like.

You can use aggregate initializers with multidimensional arrays, and you use nested curly brackets to show which values belong to which row of the array:

```
array<int, 2> ^array3d = {
    { 1, 2, 3 },
    { 4, 5, 6 },
    { 7, 8, 9 }
};
```

The .NET array class

Managed arrays in the .NET Framework all inherit from *System::Array*, which means that every managed array has a number of useful properties and methods. These properties and methods are summarized in the following two tables.

Property	Description
IsFixedSize	Returns true if the array has a fixed size. Always returns true, unless overridden by a derived class.
IsReadOnly	Returns true if the array is read-only. Always returns false, unless overridden by a derived class.
IsSynchronized	Returns true if the array is thread-safe (synchronized). Always returns false, unless overridden by a derived class.
Length	Returns the total number of elements in all dimensions of the array as a 32-bit integer.
LongLength	Returns the total number of elements in all dimensions of the array as a 64 bit integer.
Rank	Returns the number of dimensions in the array.
SyncRoot	Returns a pointer to an object that can be used to synchronize access to the array.

Method	Description
AsReadOnly	Returns a read-only wrapper for an array.
BinarySearch	Static method that searches a single-dimensional array for a value by using a binary search algorithm.
Clear	Static method that sets all or part of an array to zero or a null reference.
Clone	Creates a shallow copy of the array.
Copy	Static method that copies all or part of one array to another array, performing type downcasting as required.
CopyTo	Method that copies all or part of one single-dimensional array to another.
Exists	Determines whether the array contains elements that match a condition.
Find	Return the first element of the array that matches a condition.
FindAll	Return all the elements of the array that match a condition.
FindLast	Return the last element of the array that matches a condition.
ForEach	Performs an action on each element of the array.
GetEnumerator	Returns an enumerator for the array. See the section "Using enumerators" later in this chapter for details.
GetLength	Returns the number of elements in a specified dimension as an integer.
GetLowerBound	Returns the lower bound of a specified dimension as an integer.

Method	Description
GetUpperBound	Returns the upper bound of a specified dimension as an integer.
GetValue	Returns the value at a specified position in a single-dimensional or multidimensional array.
IndexOf	Static method that returns the index of the first occurrence of an element in an array or a part of an array.
Initialize	Initializes an array of value types by calling the default constructor of the value type. This method must not be used on arrays of reference types.
LastIndexOf	Static method that returns the index of the last occurrence of an element in an array or a part of an array.
Resize	Resize the array to the specified number of elements.
Reverse	Static method that reverses the order of the elements in all or part of a single-dimensional array.
SetValue	Sets an array element to a specified value.
Sort	Static method that sorts the elements in a single-dimensional array.
TrueForAll	Determines whether every element of the array matches a condition.

Basic operations on arrays

Unlike traditional C++ arrays, managed arrays are objects, and they "know" how many dimensions they have and how many elements they contain. The following exercise introduces you to some of the basic functionality in the *System::Array* class.

1. Create a new CLR Console Application project named **SysArray**.

2. At the top of the *main* function, add declarations for some loop counters and a two-dimensional array of 32-bit integers, as demonstrated in the following:

```
// Declare loop counters
int i,j,k;

// Create a multidimensional array of ints
array<int, 2> ^arr = gcnew array<int, 2>(3,2);
```

This is the array that you'll use for exploring the features of the *System::Array* class in the rest of this section.

3. Because this is a managed array, it inherits directly from *System::Array*, so you can use the *Rank* and *Length* properties of the *Array* class to find out the rank (number of dimensions) and total length of the array. Add the following code to the *main* function:

```
Console::WriteLine("Rank is {0}", arr->Rank);
Console::WriteLine("Length is {0}", arr->Length);
```

When you run this code, you should find that the rank is two and the total length is six, which matches the declaration.

4. The *GetLength* method—not to be confused with the *Length* property—returns the size of any one dimension of the array, so you can print out the sizes of each dimension, as presented here:

```
// Print out the array dimension information
for (i=0; i<arr->Rank; i++)
    Console::WriteLine("Dimension {0} is of size {1}", i, arr->GetLength(i));
```

Now that you have an array and can find out how large each dimension is, you need to know how to get and set elements in the array.

5. Add the following nested loops to the end of your code:

```
// Fill the array with values
for (j=0; j<arr->GetLength(0); j++)
    for (k=0; k<arr->GetLength(1); k++)
        arr[j,k] = (j+1)*(k+1);
```

The outer loop iterates over the rows, whereas the inner loop iterates over the columns, and the [x,y] notation is used to reference the array elements. The *Array* class also has the *SetValue* method, which provides an alternative way of setting values for those languages that don't support the array notation style of C++.

```
// Put '10' in array element [1,1]
arr->SetValue(10, 1, 1);
```

6. Print out the values in the array by using a similar pair of nested loops.

```
// Print out the array data
for (j=arr->GetLowerBound(0); j<=arr->GetUpperBound(0); j++)
    for (k=arr->GetLowerBound(1); k<=arr->GetUpperBound(1); k++)
        Console::WriteLine("pn[{0},{1}] = {2}", j, k, arr[j,k]);
```

Again, the outer loop iterates over the rows, and the inner loop iterates over the columns. In this case, the *GetLowerBound* and *GetUpperBound* methods return the indices of the lower and upper bounds. The argument to *GetUpperBound* and *GetLowerBound* is the dimension of the array whose bound you want to find. In C++, the lower bound is invariably 0 and the upper bound can be obtained by using the *GetLength* method, so these are mainly useful in other languages for which it might be common to have arrays with arbitrary lower and upper bounds.

7. Build and run the application. Check that the results are what you expect.

More advanced array operations

You can now create arrays, find out how many dimensions they have and how large they are, and get and set values. This section introduces some of the more advanced operations supported by the *Array* class, such as copying, searching, and sorting.

Copying array elements

The following exercise shows you how to use the *Copy* method to copy part of one array to another.

1. Continue with the project from the previous exercise.

2. At the end of the *main* function, create a second two-dimensional array the same size and type as the original.

   ```
   // Create another multidimensional array of ints
   array<int, 2> ^arr2 = gcnew array<int, 2>(3,2);
   ```

3. Add some code to fill the new array with a constant value.

   ```
   // Fill the array with a constant value
   for (j=0; j<arr2->GetLength(0); j++)
       for (k=0; k<arr2->GetLength(1); k++)
           arr2[j,k] = 47;
   ```

4. To copy some values over from the first array to the second, use the static *Copy* method.

   ```
   // Copy two values from arr to arr2
   System::Array::Copy(arr,0, arr2,2, 2);
   ```

   Using this method, you can copy all or part of one array into another. The first two arguments are the source array and the index from which to start copying. The second two are the destination array and the starting index at which elements are to be replaced. The final argument is the number of elements to be copied. In this case, you've copied two elements from *arr* into the middle of *arr2*, which you'll be able to see if you add code to print the contents of *arr2*, such as in the following example:

   ```
   for(j=arr2->GetLowerbound(0); j<=arr2->GetUpperBound(0); j++)
       for(k=arr2->GetLowerbound(1); k<=arr2->GetUpperBound(1); k++)
           Console::WriteLine("pn[{0},{1}] = {2}", j, k, arr2[j,k]);
   ```

5. Build and run the application.

Searching

It's common to want to search an array to see whether it contains a specific entry, and you can do so by using the *IndexOf* and *LastIndexOf* methods.

1. Create a new CLR Console Application project named **Strings**.

2. Open the Strings.cpp source file and add the following code to the top of the *main* function to create an array of strings:

```
// Create an array of strings
array<String ^> ^sa = { "Dog", "Cat", "Elephant", "Gerbil", "Dog",
    "Horse", "Pig", "Cat" };

// Check the length
Console::WriteLine("sa has length {0}", sa->Length);
```

3. The *IndexOf* and *LastIndexOf* functions both let you search to determine whether a particular object occurs in the array. Add the following code to the *main* function:

```
// Search for a value
String ^s = "Dog";

int pos = Array::IndexOf(sa, s);
Console::WriteLine("Index of s in sa is {0}", pos);

// Search for the next occurrence
pos = Array::IndexOf(sa, s, pos+1);
Console::WriteLine("Next index of s in sa is {0}", pos);
```

The call to *IndexOf* finds the first occurrence of the string "Dog" in the array and returns its index, which in this case is 0. The second call, to an overload of *IndexOf*, searches for an occurrence beginning at a given offset. Because the search is starting just past the first occurrence, the index returned is that of the second occurrence, which is 4. A third overload lets you search within a portion of the array.

> **Note** If the value isn't found, the index returned will be one less than the lower bound of the array, which in C++ will usually mean a value of –1.

LastIndexOf works in the same way as *IndexOf*, but it starts searching from the other end of the array.

4. Build and run the application.

Sorting

The static *Array::Sort* method and its overloads give you a way to sort an array or a part of an array, whereas *Array::Reverse* lets you reverse the order of elements. Try adding the following code to the *main* routine:

```
Array::Sort(sa);
Array::Reverse(sa);
for each (String ^s in sa)
    Console::WriteLine(s);
```

When you run the application, you should see the elements of the array printed in reverse order, from *Pig* back to *Cat*.

One valuable overload to *Sort* makes it possible for you to provide two arrays, one of which contains keys used to define the sort order. Here's an exercise to show you how this works.

1. Continue with the project from the previous exercise.

   The *sa* array currently contains the following entries:

   ```
   Pig
   Horse
   Gerbil
   Elephant
   Dog
   Dog
   Cat
   Cat
   ```

2. After the calls to *Sort* and *Reverse*, add a new array.

   ```
   array<int> ^keys = { 6, 4, 3, 5, 2, 2, 1, 1 };
   ```

   This array contains the keys that you're going to use to sort the array of animal names. They reflect my preferences—cats are number one, while pigs come in at number six—so feel free to change them as you like.

3. Add another call to *Sort*, specifying both arrays.

   ```
   Array::Sort(keys, sa);
   Console::WriteLine("---Sorting with keys---");
   for each(String ^s in sa)
   {
       Console::WriteLine(s);
   }
   ```

The *keys* array is sorted, and the elements in *sa* are sorted into exactly the same order. When you run the code and print out the array, the elements will have been sorted from *Cat* to *Pig*.

> ### The *IComparable* interface
>
> Any type that wants to be used in the *Sort* method must implement the *IComparable* interface, which has one member, *CompareTo*. When *CompareTo* is invoked on an object, it is passed a reference to another object. The function returns 0 if the two instances are equal, a negative value if the object passed in is greater than the instance calling the function, and a positive value if the object passed in has a lesser value.

Using enumerators

You have already seen how you can use enumerators to iterate over any collection, and that they are what makes *for each* loops work with collections. The *GetEnumerator* method on a collection returns an enumerator that you can use to iterate over the elements of the collection.

In this next exercise, you'll use an enumerator to list the elements in the *String* array.

1. Continue by using the Strings project; add the following *using* declaration after the *using namespace System;* line:

```
using namespace System::Collections;
```

   The *IEnumerator* interface is defined in the *System::Collection* namespace, so it's easier to use enumerators if you add a *using* declaration for the namespace.

2. Add the following code to the end of the *main* function:

```
Console::WriteLine("---Using Enumerator---");
IEnumerator ^ie = sa->GetEnumerator();
while (ie->MoveNext())
    Console::WriteLine(ie->Current);
```

3. Build and run the application.

   You'll notice several things about this code. To begin with, the enumerator starts off positioned before the first element, so you need to call *MoveNext* once to get to the first element. When there are no more elements to retrieve, calls to *MoveNext* return false. The property *Current* retrieves the current object but doesn't move the pointer, so you'll get the same value back until you call *MoveNext* again. The *Current* property also returns a general *Object* handle, so you'll often need to cast this to the actual type of the object by using the C++ *dynamic_cast* or the .NET equivalent keyword, *safe_cast*. (See Chapter 11, "Exception handling," for details on how to use *safe_cast*.)

What isn't obvious from the preceding code is that the enumerator gets a snapshot of the underlying collection. Enumerators are designed for read-only access to collections, and you can have several independent enumerators active on the same collection at one time. If any changes are made to the underlying collection, the snapshot will fall out of synchronization, which causes the *IEnumerator* to throw an *InvalidOperationException*, alerting you that it no longer reflects the underlying data.

Note Any type that wants to provide enumerator access to its members must implement the *IEnumerable* interface. This interface has the one method, *GetEnumerator*, which returns a pointer to some object that implements the *IEnumerator* interface.

Other .NET collection classes

The *System::Collections::Generic* namespace contains several very useful collection classes that you can use in C++ programs. Some of the most commonly used are listed in the following table. A couple of them will be examined later in more detail to give you an idea of how they work.

Class	Description
Dictionary<K,V>	Stores a collection of key/value pairs as a hashtable
HashSet<T>	A collection of unique values
LinkedList<T>	A doubly-linked list
List<T>	An expandable array
Queue<T>	Stores a list of elements and accesses them in the same order in which they were stored
SortedList<K,V>	A collection of key/value pairs with which you can retrieve elements by index as well as by key
Stack<T>	Accesses a list of elements from the top only by using Push and Pop operations

The *List<T>* class

The *List<T>* class, defined in the *System::Collections::Generic* namespace, is a dynamically expandable (and shrinkable) array. By default, instances of this class are resizable and writable, but the class provides two static methods with which you can create read-only and fixed-size *List*s.

Note The non-generic version of the *List* is *System::Collections::ArrayList*. This class was introduced before generics were added to .NET, and although it provides the same functionality, use of generic collections is preferred whenever possible because they are type-safe.

The following exercise shows you how to create a *List* and manipulate it.

1. Create a new CLR Console Application project named **MyList**.

2. Open the MyList.cpp source file and add the following line immediately after the *using namespace System;* line:

```
using namespace System::Collections::Generic;
```

The *List* class is defined in the *System::Collections::Generic* namespace. By inserting a *using* directive, you can use the name without having to fully qualify it every time.

3. Add the following code to the *main* function:

```
int main(array<String ^> ^args)
{
    Console::WriteLine("List Demo");

    // Create an empty List
    List<int> ^lst = gcnew List<int>();

    // Look at the count and capacity
    Console::WriteLine("Capacity={0}", lst->Capacity);
    Console::WriteLine("Count={0}", lst->Count);

    // Adjust the capacity
    lst->Capacity = 10;
    Console::WriteLine("Capacity={0}", lst->Capacity);

    // Add some elements
    lst->Add(0);
    lst->Add(2);
    lst->Add(3);
    lst->Insert(1, 1);
    Console::WriteLine("Count is now {0}", lst->Count);

    return 0;
}
```

The default *List* constructor creates an empty *List*. Because this is a generic type, you need to specify the type that the *List* is to contain, in this case *int*.

The next two lines use the *Capacity* and *Count* properties to print the current capacity of the *List* and a count of how many objects it currently contains. If you run this code, you'll find that the count is 0—not surprising because you haven't added anything yet—and that the capacity is also 0. Using the following alternative constructor, you can specify a different initial capacity:

```
// Create a List with a capacity of ten elements
List<int> ^pal = gcnew List<int>(10);
```

If you exceed the capacity when adding elements, it will automatically be doubled. If your array is too large, you can reduce its capacity to match the actual number of elements stored by calling *TrimToSize*. You can also reset the capacity of the *List* at any time by using its *Capacity* property.

The *List* doesn't contain any elements until you add some by using the *Add* or *Insert* functions. *Add* appends a new item to the end of the list, whereas *Insert* takes a zero-based index and inserts a new item at that position.

4. Because *List* implements *IEnumerator*, you can print out the contents of the *List* by using a *for each* loop.

```
for each (int i in lst)
    Console::WriteLine(i);
```

5. The syntax for removing items from a *List* is similar to that used for retrieving them.

```
// Remove item at index 2
lst->RemoveAt(2);
Console::WriteLine("---Item removed---");
for each(int i in lst)
{
    Console::WriteLine(i);
}
```

If you want to remove more than one element, the *RemoveRange* function takes a starting index and a number of elements to remove. In addition, if you have stored a handle to an object in the collection, you can use the *Remove* function, which will search the *List* and remove the first occurrence.

6. Build and run the application.

Other list operations

The *List<T>* class implements the same interfaces as the *System::Array* class discussed earlier in the chapter, which means that it provides much of the same functionality.

- The *IList* interface provides the *Add*, *Clear*, *Contains*, *IndexOf*, *Insert*, *Remove*, and *RemoveAt* methods, plus the *Item*, *IsFixedSize*, and *IsReadOnly* properties.

- The *ICollection* interface provides the *CopyTo* method, plus the *Count*, *IsSynchronized*, and *SyncRoot* properties.

- The *IEnumerable* interface provides the *GetEnumerator* method.

- The *ICloneable* interface provides the *Clone* method.

You use these interfaces to specify common functionality for the collection classes. After you know how the interface methods work, it becomes easier to use other collection classes.

The *SortedList<K,V>* class

The *SortedList<K,V>* class, also defined in the *System::Collections::Generic* namespace, represents a collection of keys and values. A *SortedList* is very similar to a *Dictionary*, which also maintains key/value pairs, but the *SortedList* maintains its data in sorted-key order and allows you to access items by index as well as by key.

SortedList sorts its entries two ways:

■ The objects stored in the *SortedList* can implement the *IComparable* interface with its *CompareTo* method. All the value types, such as number and string classes, implement this interface, and you should implement it on any other user-defined types whose values can be ordered.

■ An external comparer object can be provided, which implements the *IComparer* interface with its *Compare* method.

The following exercise shows you how to create a *SortedList* and manipulate it. As an example, suppose you wanted to maintain a list of employees' names together with their phone extensions. A *SortedList* would work well in this case, using the name as the key and the extension as the value.

1. Create a new CLR Console Application project named **SortedList**.

2. Open the SortedList.cpp source file and add the following line immediately after the *using namespace System;* line:

```
using namespace System::Collections::Generic;
```

The *SortedList* class is defined in the *System::Collections::Generic* namespace, and by inserting a using directive, you can use the name without having to fully qualify it every time.

3. Add the following code to the *main* function to create a *SortedList* and add some data to it:

```
SortedList<String^, int> ^sl = gcnew SortedList<String^, int>();

sl->Add("Dilbert", 1044);
sl->Add("Wally", 2213);
sl->Add("Ted", 1110);
sl->Add("Alice", 3375);
```

When you create a *SortedList*, you must specify the types for the key and the value within the angle brackets. In this case, we are using a *String^* for the key, and an *int* for the value.

As with the *List* discussed in the previous section, a *SortedList* has a default capacity and will automatically increase its capacity as necessary. Using alternative constructors, you can create *SortedList* classes with particular initial capacities, and you can trim excess by using the *Trim ToSize* function.

The *Add* method takes key/value pairs and adds them to the *SortedList*. If the key already exists in the collection, the method throws an *ArgumentException*.

Note Keys cannot be nulls, but you can use nulls as values.

4. Add some code to print out the contents of the *SortedList* by using a *for each* loop.

```
for each (KeyValuePair<String^, int> kp in sl)
    Console::WriteLine("Key={0}, value={1}", kp.Key, kp.Value);
```

Each element of the *SortedList* is returned as a *KeyValuePair* object, and you can use its *Key* and *Value* properties to retrieve the key and value.

1. In addition to retrieving values by index, you can retrieve them by key, as demonstrated here:

```
Console::WriteLine("Value for key 'Alice' is {0}", sl["Alice"]);
```

The indexer uses the key to return its associated value if a match is found; if no match is found, the indexer throws an exception.

As an alternative to handling an exception, you can use *TryGetValue*, which returns a *bool* to let you know whether it found a value.

```
int value = 0;
if (sl->TryGetValue("Fred", value))
    Console::WriteLine("Value is {0}", value);
else
    Console::WriteLine("Key not found");
```

In this code, *value* is passed through to *TryGetValue* by reference so that the function can update it.

2. You can also modify entries in the list by using the indexer, like this:

```
// Change the value associated with key 'Alice'
sl["Alice"] = 5555;
Console::WriteLine("Value for 'Alice' is {0}", sl["Alice"]);
```

If the key already exists, its associated value is overwritten; if it doesn't exist, a new key/value pair is created.

3. Build and run the application.

Other *SortedList* operations

You can use the *IndexOfKey* and *IndexOfValue* methods to return the index of a given key or value, and both of them will return –1 if the key or value you specify doesn't exist in the collection. Likewise, the *ContainsKey* and *ContainsValue* functions will return true if the collection contains a given value or key.

If you want to delete items from the collection, you can use *Remove* to get rid of an item by key. *RemoveByIndex* does the same thing by index, and *Clear* can be used to remove all entries.

Generics and templates

If you are familiar with standard C++, you might be wondering how .NET generics relate to C++ templates, because they look so similar (on the surface, at least) and seem in many cases to be doing the same job.

> **Note** If you are new to C++ or have not encountered templates before, you might want to skip this section on first reading.

Although generics and templates do have some features in common, they are very different in the way in which they work, and neither of them can act completely as a substitute for the other. For this reason, they are both supported in C++/CLI. Because the use of templates in C++/CLI is an advanced topic, this section only gives a brief summary of the similarities and differences between the two mechanisms.

- Templates are compile-time, generics are run-time: this means that a generic type is still generic at run time, whereas a template has been instantiated at compile time.

- Templates support features such as specialization, non-type template parameters, and template template parameters. Generics don't support these and are rather simpler.

- Generic types cannot inherit from a type parameter, as is the case with templates.

- There is no metaprogramming support for generics.

- Generic types support constraints on type parameters, which templates do not.

The STL/CLR library

One reason why templates are supported in C++/CLI is to permit the use of the STL/CLR library. The Standard Template Library (STL) is part of standard C++. It is best known for providing a set of high-performance, extensible collection classes. This section can only give the briefest overview of what the STL is and how it works.

The STL containers are standard in unmanaged C++ code, and a version that works with managed types has been provided in the STL/CLR library. This has been done for two reasons. First, many C++ developers are familiar with (and like using) the STL containers, and this enables them to continue to be productive. Second, the STL is a lot more extensible and configurable than the .NET collection classes, and its features might appeal to developers looking for more performance and extensibility.

> **Note** If you want more details of the STL/CLR library, consult the reference documentation, which, as of this writing, you can find at *http://msdn.microsoft.com/en-us/library/bb385954. aspx*.

Here is a simple example to give you a feel for what STL/CLR code looks like:

```
#include "stdafx.h"

#include <cliext\vector>

using namespace System;
using namespace cliext;

int main(array<System::String ^> ^args)
{
    // Create a vector of int
    vector<double> v1;

    // Append values
    for(int i=0; i<10; i++)
        v1.push_back(i*2.0);

    // Use an iterator to print all the values in order
    vector<double>::iterator it = v1.begin();
    for(; it != v1.end(); it++)
        Console::WriteLine(*it);

    return 0;
}
```

A *vector* is the equivalent of an *ArrayList*: a dynamically resizable array. The *push_back* function adds an element to the end of a sequence, and if you were using a linked list, you could also use *push_front* to add values to the beginning. As you might expect, the *pop_back* function removes an element from the end. Iterators are classes, always called *iterator*, that are defined within a container, so an iterator to a *vector<int>* is a *vector<int>::iterator*. You obtain an iterator by calling the *begin* function, which returns an iterator that points to the start of the sequence. The *end* function returns an iterator pointing to the end of the sequence, and you use this to check when you get to the end.

You use iterators like pointers: you can use ++ and −− to move them along the sequence, and * to dereference them in order to get to the value at that position. The == and *!=* operators are overloaded to compare position: if == for two iterators returns true, they are pointing at the same position.

The three concepts behind STL

The STL is based on three concepts, which have far-reaching consequences for how containers are written and used.

The first concept is that of the *container*. In STL, the main job of a container is to hold its elements. Although this might seem obvious, many container types in other libraries do a lot more besides, which limits their adaptability. For example, although STL containers will allocate memory for their members, you can provide your own memory allocator if you want. And, if you want to sort the contents in some particular way, you can do this by providing your own custom external function rather than having to rely on the sort function that's built in to the container.

Be aware also that STL containers own their contents, which circumvents a lot of ownership problems. This is achieved by containers taking copies of what you add.

The following table shows the most commonly used STL/CLR container types:

Name	Description
vector	A dynamically resizable array.
list	A doubly-linked list.
map	A map of key/value pairs, with unique non-null keys.
multimap	A map of key/value pairs. Keys must be non-null but do not have to be unique.
set	An unordered set of unique elements.
multiset	An unordered set of elements that permits duplicates.
queue	A FIFO (first in, first out) queue, where elements are added at one and taken off the other.
deque	A queue in which elements can be added and removed at either end.
stack	A LIFO (last in, first out) stack.

The second concept is the *iterator*. An iterator is an object that knows how to iterate over the elements in a container, visiting each element in turn. Using an iterator means that you do not have to know how to traverse the data inside the container: simply ask the iterator for the next item. The implementation of STL iterators is very clever and makes it possible for them to interoperate with C++ pointers.

The final concept is the *algorithm*. Most non-STL container types are properly object oriented, in that the container completely encapsulates its data and all the functionality needed to operate on it. Want to sort the data in a list? Ask the list. Want to reverse the order? Again, ask the list. Although this fits well with object-oriented practice, it can be awkward: what if we want to provide another sorting algorithm? Object-oriented best practice states that the collection should hide its implementation, so it would be difficult to write another sort function that is at all efficient because we cannot get at the data.

STL encourages the use of external functions, called *algorithms*, to implement operations on containers. Algorithms work with containers by using iterators, so you will see code like this:

```
vector<int> vec;
...
sort(vec.begin(), vec.end());
```

Here, *vec.begin* is an iterator that points to the beginning of the sequence, and *vec.end* marks the end. The code inside the sort function can simply call ++ on the first iterator to advance it to the next item. When the *begin* and *end* iterators are pointing at the same location, the traversal is complete. In this way, sort doesn't need to know any details of the container that it is traversing.

In case you think that this does not sound very efficient, the way that the STL has been written, making heavy use of inline code and templates, means that very efficient code is generated at run time.

Quick reference

To	Do this
Create a fixed-size array of C++ built-in types.	Use a native C++ array.

Create a managed array	Use the generic *array<>* type. For example:
	
	`array<Person ^> ^people =`
	`    gcnew array<Person ^>();`

Iterate over the members of a managed array.	Use a *for each* loop. For example:
	
	`List<Person> ^lst = new List<Person>();`
	`...`
	`for each (Person p in lst)`
	`    Console::WriteLine(p);`

Create a dynamic array.	Use the *List<>* class.
Maintain a list of key/value pairs.	Use the *SortedList<>* or *Dictionary<>* classes.

Properties

After completing this chapter, you will be able to:

- Describe what properties are.

- Explain how properties are supported by C++/CLI.

- Implement properties.

Properties have been available in some programming languages—such as Microsoft Visual Basic—for some time, but the Microsoft .NET Framework has added support for them into Microsoft Intermediate Language (MSIL) so that they can be easily implemented in any .NET programming language. You'll see in this chapter that properties can often lead to a more natural style of programming without sacrificing robustness or violating the principles of object-oriented programming.

What are properties?

It is a long-accepted principle of object-oriented programming that it's a bad idea to give users direct access to the data members that make up your classes. There are two main reasons for this:

- If users directly access data members, they're required to know about the implementation of the class, and that might limit your ability to modify the implementation later.

- Users of your classes might accidentally—or deliberately—corrupt the data in objects by using inappropriate values, possibly leading to application failures or other undesirable results.

As a result, it's recommended that you hide data members, making them private and giving indirect access to them by using member functions. In traditional C++, indirect access has often been implemented by using *get* and *set* members. Thus, a data member named *date* might be accessed using a pair of member functions named *set_date* and *get_date*. This method works fine, but client code always has to call the *get* and *set* functions directly.

Properties in the .NET Framework give you a way to implement a virtual data member for a class. You implement the *get* and *set* parts of the property, and the compiler converts them into calls to the *get* or *set* method as appropriate.

```
MyClass ^pmc = gcnew MyClass();
pmc->Name = "fred";        // calls the setter
s = pmc->Name;             // calls the getter
```

It appears to the user that *MyClass* has a real data member called *Name*, and the property can be used in exactly the same way as a real data member.

Anyone who programmed in Visual Basic would find the idea of implementing properties using the *get*, *set*, and *let* methods familiar. In the .NET Framework, properties can be created and used in any .NET language, so you can create a class in Visual Basic and still use its properties in a C++ application, and vice versa.

The two kinds of properties

C++/CLI supports two kinds of properties: scalar and indexed.

A *scalar property* gives access to a single value by using getter and setter code. For example, a *Name* property would implement getter and setter code to give access to the underlying name data. It's important to note that a property doesn't have to represent a simple data member of the managed class; a property can represent derived values. For example, if a class has a date-of-birth member, it would be possible to implement a property that calculates the age. Properties can also represent far more complex values, which might involve using data from other sources, such as searching databases or accessing URLs.

An *indexed property* makes it possible for a property to be accessed as if it were an array, using the traditional C++ square bracket notation.

> **Note** If you've ever come across the overloaded [ ] operator in traditional C++, you'll find that indexed properties provide similar functionality, but you don't have to code the operator overload yourself.

Indexed properties are also implemented by using getter and setter code, and the compiler automatically generates the required code so that clients can use the square bracket notation.

The next sections in this chapter demonstrate how to implement both scalar and indexed properties.

Implementing scalar properties

As mentioned in the previous section, a scalar property is one that gives you access to a single data member by using getter and setter code. The following exercise shows you how to implement scalar properties. In this example, we'll use a simple *Person* class containing name and age members.

1. Start Microsoft Visual Studio 2012 and create a new CLR Console Application project named **Properties**.

2. Add the following class definition after the *using namespace System;* line and before the *main* function:

```
ref class Person
{
    String ^name;
    int age;
public:
    // Person class constructor
    Person()
    {
        Name = "";
        Age = 0;
    }

    // The Name property
    property String ^Name
    {
        String ^get() { return name; }
        void set(String ^n) { name = n; }
    }

    // The Age property
    property int Age
    {
        int get() { return age; }
        void set(int val) { age = val; }
    }
};
```

The class has two private data members that hold the name and age of the person. Properties are introduced by the *property* keyword, which is followed by a type and then the property name. It is convention to begin property names with a capital letter.

The getter and setter are declared inside the property and look a lot like nested functions. The getter is always called *get* and has a return type that matches the property type. The setter is called *set*, takes an argument of property type, and has a return type of *void*.

You can use the property from C++ code as if it were a real data member of the class. Note how the properties are used in the constructor in preference to using the data members directly; you will see why this is a good idea shortly.

Note The property names in this example are the same as the names of the underlying data members, but capitalized. It is a widespread convention in C# code that function and property names are capitalized. Therefore, to fit into the .NET world, it is a good idea if your property names are capitalized, as well.

3. Add the following code to *main* to test the property:

```
int main(array<String ^> ^args)
{
    // Create a Person object
    Person ^p = gcnew Person();

    // Set the name and age using properties
    p->Name = "fred";
    p->Age = 77;

    // Access the properties
    Console::WriteLine("Age of {0} is {1}", p->Name, p->Age);
    return 0;
}
```

After a *Person* object has been created and initialized, the name and age members can be accessed through the *Name* and *Age* virtual data members that have been generated by the compiler.

4. Build and run the application.

Errors in properties

What happens if a property *get* or *set* method encounters an error? Consider the following code:

```
// Set the name and age using properties
p->Name = "spiro";
p->Age = -31;
```

How can the *Age* property communicate that it isn't happy with a negative value? This situation is a good one in which to use exceptions, which are discussed in Chapter 11, "Exception handling." You could modify the setter function to check its argument like this:

```
void set(int val)
{
    if (val < 0)
        throw gcnew ArgumentException("Negative ages aren't allowed");
    age = val;
}
```

If anyone tries to set the age to a negative value, an *ArgumentException* will be thrown to alert the caller that there is a problem.

Auto-implemented properties

Many properties simply assign to and return a data member, as shown in the following:

```
String ^name;

property String ^Name
{
    String ^get { return name; }
    void set(String ^n) { name = n; }
}
```

When that is the case, you can get the compiler to implement the getter and setter, and it will generate a *backing variable* to store the data. You don't see this variable, but you access it indirectly through the property getter and setter.

This means that you can implement the *Name* property very simply, as demonstrated here:

```
property String ^Name;
```

In the next short exercise, you can declare and use an auto-implemented property in your *Person* class.

1. Modify your *Person* class, providing an automatic implementation for the *Name* property and removing the data member.

2. Build and run the application, which should work exactly the same as before.

   Because you used the property in the constructor rather than assigning to the data member, changing to an auto-implemented property still works.

Whenever you use auto-implemented properties, you must use the property within your class when assigning to or reading the value because you don't know the name of the backing variable that the compiler creates.

Read-only and write-only properties

You don't always have to provide *get* and *set* methods for a property. If you don't provide a *set* method, you end up with a read-only property. If you omit the *get* method, you'll have a write-only property (which is possible, but a lot less common than the read-only variety).

The following exercise shows how to implement a read-only property, and it also illustrates how to create a derived property. You'll change the *Person* class from the previous exercise so that it includes a date of birth rather than an age. The derived *Age* property will then calculate the person's age from the date of birth; it's obviously a derived property because you can't change someone's age without changing his or her date of birth, as well. It's also obviously a read-only property because it's always calculated and cannot be set by users of the class.

1. Either start a new CLR Console Application project or modify the one from the previous exercise.

2. Type or edit the definition of the *Person* class so that it looks like the following code. Place it after the *using namespace System;* line and before the *main* method.

```
ref class Person
{
    int dd, mm, yyyy;

public:
    // Person class constructor
    Person(String ^n, int d, int m, int y)
    {
        Name = n;
        dd = d; mm = m; yyyy = y;
    }

    // Auto implementation of the Name property
    property String ^Name;

    // The read-only Age property
    property int Age
    {
        int get() {
            DateTime now = DateTime::Now;
            return now.Year - yyyy;
        }
    }
};
```

The class now has three integer data members to hold the date of birth, initialized in the constructor.

The *Age* property now has only a *get* method, which retrieves a *DateTime* object representing the current date and time and then calculates the age from the difference between the current year and the stored year.

3. Use the *Name* and *Age* properties as you did in the previous example.

```
int main(array<String ^> ^args)
{
    // Create a Person object
    Person ^p = gcnew Person("fred", 4,9,1955);

    // Access the Name and Age properties
    Console::WriteLine("Age of {0} is {1}", p->Name, p->Age);
    return 0;
}
```

You can't set the *Age* property because you haven't provided a setter. This will result in a compiler error if you try to assign to the *Age* property.

4. Build and run the application.

Properties, inheritance, and interfaces

Properties are first-class members of types, on the same level as member functions and data members. This means that you can use them in inheritance and in interfaces. Properties can be virtual and even pure virtual, and it isn't necessary for both the *get* and *set* methods to have the same virtual specifier.

This exercise shows you how to use a virtual property when inheriting from a base class.

1. Create a new CLR Console Application project named **PropertyInheritance**.

2. Immediately after the *using namespace System;* line, define an abstract class called *Shape*.

```
public ref class Shape abstract
{
public:
    virtual property double Area;
};
```

This class defines a property called *Area* that is virtual and which can be overridden by subclasses.

3. Add the definition for a *Circle* class, which inherits from *Shape* and which also implements the *Area* property.

```
public ref class Circle : Shape
{
    double radius;
public:
    Circle(double r)
    {
        radius = r;
    }

    virtual property double Area
    {
        double get() override {
            return Math::PI * radius * radius;
        }
    }
};
```

The constructor for *Circle* takes a value for the radius, which is used in the *Area* property to calculate the area of the circle. Note the placement of the modifiers on the *Area* property declaration: It is declared as *virtual*, and the *get* is declared as an *override*.

4. Add a simple function to take a *Shape* and print out its area.

```
void printArea(Shape ^s)
{
    Console::WriteLine("Area is {0}", s->Area);
}
```

5. Create a *Circle* in *main* and pass it to the *printArea* function.

```
Circle ^c = gcnew Circle(4.0);
printArea(c);
```

6. Build and run the application.

You will see that even though the *printArea* function has a *Shape* as its argument type, it will use the *Circle* implementation of *Area* at run time.

Implementing indexed properties

Now that you know how to implement a scalar property, let's move on to consider indexed properties, which are also known as *indexers*. These are useful for classes that have data members that are collections of items, and where you might want to access one of the items in the collection.

The Bank example

Consider as an example a *Bank* class that maintains a collection of *Accounts*. If you're not using properties, you'd tend to see code such as the following being used to access members of the *Bank* class:

```
// Get a reference to one of the Accounts held by the Bank
Account ^acc = theBank->getAccount(1234567);
```

An indexed property makes it possible for you access the *Account* members by using array notation, such as is demonstrated here:

```
// Get a reference to one of the accounts held by the Bank
Account ^acc = theBank->Account[1234567];
```

You can implement *get* and *set* methods for indexed properties so that you can use them on both sides of the equal sign (=). The following code fragment uses two properties, with the first indexed property giving access to an account, and the second giving access to an overdraft limit:

```
// Set the overdraft limit for one of the accounts
theBank->Account[1234567]->OverDraft = 250.0;
```

Implementing the *Bank* class

The longer exercise that follows walks you through implementing the *Bank* and *Account* classes, and it also shows you how to create and use both scalar and indexed properties.

1. Start Visual Studio 2012 and create a new CLR Console Application project named **Banker**.

2. Add a new C++ header file named **Bank.h** to the project. When the file opens in the editor, edit the class declaration so that looks like this:

```
#pragma once

ref class Bank
{
public:
    Bank();
};
```

3. Add an implementation file called **Bank.cpp** to the project. When it opens in the editor, edit the code so that it looks like this:

```
#include "stdafx.h"
using namespace System;

#include "Bank.h"

Bank::Bank()
{
    Console::WriteLine("Bank: constructor");
}
```

4. To ensure that everything is correct, open the Banker.cpp file and add code to the *main* function to create a *Bank* object.

```
int main(array<String ^> ^args)
{
    Console::WriteLine("Bank Example");

    // Create a Bank object
    Bank ^theBank = gcnew Bank();

    return 0;
}
```

5. You must also include Bank.h from the Banker.cpp file so that the compiler will know where to locate the declaration of the *Bank* class. Therefore, add the following code to Banker.cpp after the *#include "stdafx.h"* line:

```
#include "Bank.h"
```

6. Compile and run the application. You should see the constructor message being printed on the console.

Adding the *Account* class

The next stage involves creating the *Account* class in very much the same way.

1. Add a header file named **Account.h** to the project. Edit the header file so that it looks like this:

```
#pragma once
using namespace System;

ref class Account
{
public:
    Account();
};
```

2. Add an implementation file named **Account.cpp** that looks like this:

```
#include "stdafx.h"
using namespace System;

#include "Account.h"

Account::Account()
{
    Console::WriteLine("Account: constructor");
}
```

3. Add some structure to the *Account* class. Accounts will have an account number, a balance, and an overdraft limit, so add three private members to the *Account* class definition in Account.h, as shown in the following:

```
private:
    long accNumber;     // the account number
    double balance;     // the current balance
    double limit;       // the overdraft limit
```

4. Open Account.cpp. Edit the constructor definition and implementation as follows so that three values are passed in and used to initialize these three variables:

```
Account::Account(long num, double bal, double lim)
{
    Console::WriteLine("Account: constructor");
    // Basic sanity check
    if (num < 0 || lim < 0)
        throw gcnew ArgumentException("Bad arguments to constructor");

    // Initialize values
    accNumber = num;
    balance = bal;
    limit = lim;
}
```

Remember that you will need to modify the declaration of the constructor in the Account.h header file, as well.

The basic sanity check simply checks that the account number and overdraft limit aren't negative. If they are, it throws an *ArgumentException*.

Creating *Account* class properties

After the *Account* class has been constructed, you can add properties to give access to the three data members. All three members are scalar, so the properties are easy to implement.

1. Add a public property to Account.h to allow read-only access to the account number, as shown here:

    ```
    property long AccountNumber
    {
        long get() { return accNumber; }
    }
    ```

    You can add the function definition inline in the class definition. Remember to put it in the public section.

2. You also need to add a read-only property for the balance member, because in real life, you don't want people simply modifying the balances in their accounts from code.

    ```
    property double Balance
    {
        double get() { return balance; }
    }
    ```

3. Add a read/write property for the overdraft limit because it's quite possible that the limit might be changed from time to time.

    ```
    property double OverdraftLimit
    {
        double get() { return limit; }
        void set(double value) {
            if (value < 0)
                throw gcnew ArgumentException("Limit can't be negative");

            limit = value;
        }
    }
    ```

    If you choose to implement these properties inline in the class definition, you'll need to add a *using namespace System;* line or fully qualify the name of *ArgumentException* before the code will compile.

4. Test out your implementation by adding some code to the *main* function in Banker.cpp to create a new *Account* object and access its properties. Include the Account.h file, and then add code to create an *Account* object, as demonstrated here:

```
// Create an Account object
Account ^theAccount = gcnew Account(123456, 0.0, 0.0);
```

5. Build and run the application and check the output.

Adding accounts to the *Bank* class

The purpose of the *Bank* class is to hold *Accounts*, so the next step is to modify the *Bank* class to hold a collection of *Account* objects. Rather than design something from scratch, you'll use the *System::Collections::Generic::List* class (which is introduced in Chapter 12, "Arrays and collections") to hold the *Accounts*.

Implementing the *Add* and *Remove* methods

The *Add* and *Remove* methods provide a way to manipulate the collection of *Accounts* held by the *Bank* class.

1. Open the Bank.h header file. Add the following two lines of code immediately after the *#pragma once* line at the top of the file:

```
using namespace System::Collections::Generic;
#include "Account.h"
```

The *using* declaration will make it easier to use a *List* in the *Bank* class, and you'll need to reference the *Account* class later.

2. Add a *List* variable to the *Bank* class, ensuring that it's private.

```
List<Account^> ^accounts;
```

Because *List* is a generic collection, you need to specify what it is going to hold. In this case, the *List* is going to hold *Account* handles.

3. Add the code for the public *AddAccount* method inline in the header file as follows:

```
bool AddAccount(Account ^acc)
{
    // check if the account is already in the list
    if (accounts->Contains(acc))
        return false;
    else
        accounts->Add(acc);
    return true;
}
```

AddAccount takes a handle to an *Account* object and then uses the *List::Contains* method to check whether the account already exists in the collection. If it doesn't, the *Account* is added to the collection.

4. Add code for the *RemoveAccount* function, which works in a very similar way.

```
bool RemoveAccount(Account ^acc)
{
    // check if the account is already in the list
    if (accounts->Contains(acc))
    {
        accounts->Remove(acc);
        return true;
    }
    else
        return false;
}
```

RemoveAccount checks whether an *Account* is in the list and, if present, removes it. It isn't necessary to call *Contains* because *RemoveAccount* will silently do nothing if you try to remove an item that isn't in the list. However, users might be interested in knowing that the account they're trying to remove isn't in the collection already.

5. Add the following line of code to the *Bank* constructor to create the *List* member:

```
accounts = gcnew List<Account^>();
```

6. Build the application to ensure that there are no errors.

Implementing an indexed property to retrieve accounts

You can now manipulate the collection of *Accounts*, adding and removing items. If you want to look up a particular account, you'll probably want to do so by the account number, and an indexed property provides a good way to access accounts by account number.

Indexed properties work in a very similar way to scalar properties, but you show the compiler that you are defining an indexed property by including the index type in square brackets after the property name.

```
property double Balance[long]
```

This informs the compiler that we are defining an indexed property called *Balance* that will use a *long* as its index type. When you define the indexed property, you include the index as the first parameter to the getter and setter.

```
property double Balance[long]
{
    double get(long idx) { ... }
    void set(long idx, double value) { ... }
}
```

Within the getter and setter, you can use the index to find the appropriate value. You can use the indexer like this:

```
// Get the balance for account 12345
double bal = myBank->Balance[12345];
```

In this exercise you will implement an indexed property to retrieve *Account* objects. Because you only need to retrieve *Account* handles and not set them, you'll implement a read-only indexed property.

1. Open the Bank.h header file.

2. Add the following code to implement the property:

```
// Indexed property to return an account
property Account ^default[long]
{
    Account ^get(long num)
    {
        for each(Account ^acc in accounts)
        {
            if (acc->AccountNumber == num)
                return acc;
        }
        throw gcnew ArgumentOutOfRangeException("No such account");
    }
}
```

Default properties

You might wonder why the property is called "default." It is possible for a class to have multiple indexers, but you have to use them explicitly by name. An indexed property called default, on the other hand, can be used directly on an object, such as in the following:

```
// Get account 12345
Account ^acc = myBank[12345];
```

You normally use the default indexer for the property that is most often used.

When you find an account whose number matches the one passed in, its handle is returned. If no such account is found, an exception is thrown because trying to access a nonexistent account is equivalent to reading off the end of an array: It's a serious error that should be signaled to the caller.

3. Test out the *Bank* class by adding some code to the *main* function in Banker.cpp. You'll need to start by ensuring that the Bank.h and Account.h header files are included. Next add some code so that your *main* function is similar to the following:

```
int main(array<String ^> ^args)
{
    Console::WriteLine("Bank example");

    // Create a bank
    Bank ^theBank = gcnew Bank();

    // Create some accounts
    Account ^accountOne = gcnew Account(123456, 100.0, 0.0);
    Account ^accountTwo = gcnew Account(234567, 1000.0, 100.0);
    Account ^accountThree = gcnew Account(345678, 10000.0, 1000.0);

    // Add them to the Bank
    theBank->AddAccount(accountOne);
    theBank->AddAccount(accountTwo);
    theBank->AddAccount(accountThree);

    // Use the indexed property to access an account
    Account ^pa = theBank[234567];
    Console::WriteLine("Account Number is {0}", pa->AccountNumber);

    return 0;
}
```

After creating a *Bank* and a number of *Account* objects, you add the *Account* objects to the *Bank* collection by calling *Add*. You can then use the indexed property to access an account by number and use that pointer to display the balance. Test the property by passing in an account number that doesn't exist and check that an exception is thrown.

4. Build and run the application and then check the output.

Quick reference

To	Do This

Create a property for a C++ class.	Use the *property* keyword and implement *get* and/or *set* methods. For example:
	
	``cpp
	property int Weight
	{
	    int get() { ... }
	    void set(int w) { ... }
	}
	``

Implement a simple property that requires no logic in its *get* or *set* methods.	Use an auto-implemented property. For example:
	
	``cpp
	property String ^Name;
	``

Implement a read-only property.	Implement only the *get* method.
Implement a write-only property.	Implement only the *set* method.

Implement an indexed property.	Implement a property that specifies an index type in square brackets, and whose *get* and *set* methods take an index value that is used to determine which value to get or set. For example:
	
	``cpp
	property Amount ^Pay[Person]
	{
	    Amount ^get(Person^) { ... }
	}
	``

Delegates and events

After completing this chapter, you will be able to:

- Understand what delegates are.

- Create and use delegates.

- Explain what events are.

- Create and use events.

Delegates and events are extremely powerful and important constructs in the Microsoft .NET Framework. Events in particular are used widely in GUI applications as a means of communicating between components, but both delegates and events can be used to good effect in non-GUI code.

What are delegates?

The function pointer mechanism in C and C++ has been used by programmers for many years, and it's a very useful way of implementing mechanisms such as event handlers. Unfortunately, function pointers are a C++ language feature, so they're of no use in the .NET environment, where features need to be accessible from many languages. If you're interested in knowing more about function pointers and how they work, see the sidebar that follows.

Delegates are the .NET equivalent of function pointers, and they can be created and used from any .NET language. They can be used by themselves, and they also form the basis for the .NET event mechanism discussed in the second part of this chapter.

What is the purpose of delegates?

A delegate is a class whose purpose it is to invoke one or more methods that have a particular signature. It is basically an indirect way of executing a function by delegating to an intermediate object. Here's a simple example to show when you might want to use a delegate.

Imagine that I want to be able to perform operations on numbers by passing a number into a function and getting a transformed value back, as demonstrated in the following:

```
double d = 3.0;
double result = Square(d);
result = Cube(d);
result = SquareRoot(d);
result = TenToThePowerOf(d);
```

In each case, I'm calling a function that has the same signature: one that takes a *double* and returns a *double* as its result.

With delegates, I can define a mechanism by which I can call any of those methods because they all have the same signature. Not only can I call any of the four methods above, but I can also define other methods and call them through the delegate—provided that they are also functions that take a *double* and return one. This makes it possible for one class or component to define a delegate, and for other classes to attach functions to the delegate and use it. You'll see examples of this use of delegates later in the chapter when we cover events.

In this case, I want to use the delegate to call one method at a time, but it's possible to attach more than one function to a delegate. All the functions are called in order when the delegate is invoked. The .NET Framework defines the *System::Delegate* class as the base for delegates that call a single method, and *System::MulticastDelegate* as the base for delegates that can call more than one method. All delegates in C++/CLI are multicast delegates.

Defining delegates

This exercise uses the numerical operations example from the previous section to show you how to create and use a simple delegate in C++/CLI code.

1. Start Microsoft Visual Studio 2012 and create a new CLR Console Application project named **Delegate**.

2. Open the Delegate.cpp source file and add the definition of a delegate to the top of the file, immediately after the *using namespace System;* line.

    ```
    delegate double NumericOp(double);
    ```

    The *delegate* keyword is used to define a delegate. It might look as though this is a function prototype for a function named *NumericOp*, but it's actually defining a delegate type that inherits from *System::MulticastDelegate*. This delegate type, named *NumericOp*, can be bound to any function that takes one *double* as an argument and returns a *double*.

Implementing delegates

Now that you have defined a delegate, you can write code to use it to call functions. One of the rules for using delegates is that you can only use a delegate to call functions that are members of C++/CLI classes; you can't use a delegate to call a global function or a function that's a member of an unmanaged C++ class.

Calling static member functions by using delegates

Let's start by looking at the simplest case: calling static member functions by using a delegate.

1. Continue with the project from the previous exercise. All the functions we want to call need to be static members of a class, so add the following class to your source code file, just above the *main* function:

```
ref class Ops
{
public:
    static double Square(double d)
    {
        return d*d;
    }
};
```

This managed class contains one public static method, which simply takes a number and returns its square.

2. Create a delegate in the *main* function of the application, as shown here:

```
// Declare a delegate
NumericOp ^op = gcnew NumericOp(&Ops::Square);
```

When you declared the delegate, you created a new type named *NumericOp*, so you can now create a *NumericOp* object. The constructor takes one argument: this is the address of the function that is to be associated with the delegate, so you use the & operator to specify the address of *Ops::square*.

The object pointed to by *op* is now set up so that it will call the *square* function when it is invoked, and it will take exactly the same arguments (and return the same type) as *Ops::square*.

 Note You can't change the function that a delegate invokes after it has been created. This is one respect in which delegates differ from C++ function pointers.

3. Every delegate has an *Invoke* method that you can use to call the function that has been bound to the delegate. *Invoke* will take the same arguments and return the same type as the function being called. Add the following lines to use *op* to call the *square* function:

```
// Call the function through the delegate
double result = op->Invoke(3.0);

Console::WriteLine("Result is {0}", result);
```

4. Build and run the application.

5. You can now easily create another static member, create a delegate, and call the function. Test this out by adding to the *Ops* class a second public static member called *Cube*.

```
static double Cube(double d)
{
    return d*d*d;
}
```

6. Create another delegate in the same way as the first; however, this time, pass it the address of the *Cube* function in the constructor.

```
// Create a second delegate and use it to call cube
op = gcnew NumericOp(&Ops::Cube);
result = op(3.0);

Console::WriteLine("Result of Cube() is {0}", result);
```

There are two things that you might notice about this code. The first is that you have reused the *op* reference to refer to the new delegate object. This means that the original delegate that you used to call *Square* is no longer referenced; thus, is can be garbage-collected.

The second is that there is no explicit call to *Invoke*. To mirror how delegates work in C# (and how function pointers work in unmanaged C++), you can actually omit the *Invoke* keyword, treating the delegate as if it were a function call itself.

7. Build and run the application and check that it runs as you expect.

Calling non-static member functions by using delegates

You can also call non-static member functions of classes by using delegates. By definition, a non-static member function must be called on an object, so you need to specify to the delegate the function it's going to call and the object it's going to use. You do so in the delegate's constructor, as illustrated here:

```
// Declare a delegate bound to a non-static member
MyDelegate ^pDel = gcnew MyDelegate(myObject, &MyClass::MyFunction);
```

The constructor specifies the address of an object, *myObject*, and a member function belonging to the class to which *myObject* belongs. Invoking this delegate is equivalent to directly calling *myObject->MyFunction*.

Using multicast delegates

We've seen how it's possible to use a delegate to call a single function, but it's also possible for a delegate to call more than one function with a single call to *Invoke*. A delegate that does so is called a *multicast delegate* and is derived from the *System::MulticastDelegate* class.

Note All delegates that you create in C++/CLI by using the *delegate* keyword are multicast delegates.

All delegate objects have an *invocation list* that holds the functions to be called. The invocation list for a normal delegate has one member. You can manipulate the invocation lists for multicast delegates by using the *Combine* and *Remove* methods, although this is seldom done in practice.

If you look at the documentation for the *Combine* method, you'll see that it takes two or more *Delegate* objects as its arguments. You don't build up a multicast delegate by specifying more functions to add to its invocation list. Instead, a multicast delegate is built up by combining other delegates.

The following exercise shows you how to create and use a multicast delegate.

1. Create a new CLR Console Application project named **Multicast**.

2. Open the Multicast.cpp source file and add the definition of a delegate to the top of the file, immediately after the *using namespace System;* line.

    ```
    delegate void NotifyDelegate(int);
    ```

    You can bind this delegate, named *NotifyDelegate*, to any function that takes one *int* as an argument and doesn't return anything.

3. You're going to call two functions through the multicast delegate. Because all functions called by delegates have to be members of a managed class, define two classes at the start of your project, each of which contains a static member function.

    ```
    ref class Client1
    {
    public:
        static void NotifyFunction1(int n)
        {
            Console::WriteLine("Client1: got value {0}", n);
        }
    };

    ref class Client2
    {
    public:
        static void NotifyFunction2(int n)
        {
            Console::WriteLine("Client2: got value {0}", n);
        }
    };
    ```

    These two classes are almost identical, both defining a single static member function that has the signature required by the delegate.

4. You want to call the two static member functions through one delegate, but you can't create a delegate to bind to two functions directly. Instead, you need to create two normal delegates (as you did in the previous exercise) and combine them into a multicast delegate. So, define two delegates in the *main* function, each of which binds to one of the static methods.

```
Console::WriteLine("Multicast Delegates");

// Create two delegates
NotifyDelegate ^del1 = gcnew NotifyDelegate(&Client1::NotifyFunction1);
NotifyDelegate ^del2 = gcnew NotifyDelegate(&Client2::NotifyFunction2);
```

At this stage, you could invoke both of the delegates, just as you did in the previous exercise.

5. Build a multicast delegate from *del1* and *del2* by using the += operator, as shown in the following:

```
// Create a third delegate from the first two
NotifyDelegate ^del3;
del3 += del1;
del3 += del2;
```

6. You can now invoke the multicast delegate as normal.

```
// Invoke the multicast delegate
Console::WriteLine("Invoking del3");
del3(5);
```

Remember that you don't have to call *Invoke* explicitly. When you build and run the application, you should see two lines of output, as shown in the following screen shot:

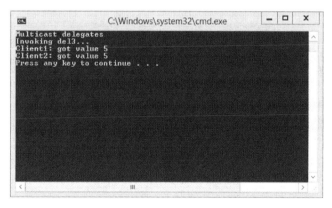

Note that the functions are called in the order in which the delegates are combined, so if you want to change the order, you'll need to change the way you create the multicast.

7. You can use this delegate as the basis for making up another one.

```
// Create a second multicast delegate and invoke it
NotifyDelegate ^del4 = del3 + del3;
Console::WriteLine("Invoking del4");
del4(5);
```

In this case, you're combining the invocation list of *del3* twice, which results in the output shown in the following screen shot when you invoke it. Notice how you can use the + operator to compose delegates at construction time.

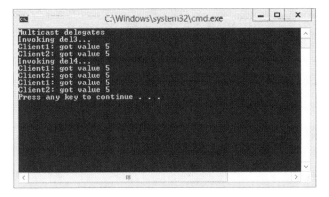

8. As the final part of this exercise, you can use the −= operator to remove an item from a delegate's invocation list.

```
// Remove an item
del3 -= del2;
Console::WriteLine("Invoking del3");
del3(5);
```

You specify the handle of the delegate that you want to remove on the right side of the −= operator. If the delegate to be removed exists in the invocation list of the first delegate, it will be removed. In this example, you have removed *del2* from *del3*; when you invoke *del3*, only *del1* is executed.

Delegates that return a result

You can, of course, use a delegate to call a function that returns a result. Here is an example:

```
ref class JMath
{
public:
    static double Square(double d) { return d*d; }
};

// Delegate to call a function that returns a double
delegate double MathOp(double d);

// Bind a delegate to Math::square
MathOp ^m = gcnew MathOp(&JMath::Square);

// Invoke the delegate
double result = m(3.3);
```

What happens if you create a multicast delegate that calls several such functions? Which result will be returned? It is most normal to use functions that don't return a value with multicast delegates, but there is nothing to stop you from calling functions that do return a value. Usually, the result of the last function executed will be returned, although this is implementation dependent. If you want to be sure of retrieving a particular value (or getting values from intermediate steps), you might want to walk over the list of delegates, which you can do by using the *GetInvocationList* function within a *for each* loop, as shown here:

```
for each (MathOp ^m in myMultiDelegate->GetInvocationList())
{
    double val = m(…);
}
```

What are events?

Most, if not all, GUI platforms support the idea of events, and events are very heavily used in GUI programming. As an example, consider a button. Buttons don't exist on their own; they are used as part of a user interface and are contained by some other item. This item is usually a form, but it could also be some other control, such as a toolbar.

The whole point of having a button on a form is so that the user can click it to signal his intent to the application and convey instructions. For example, "the user clicked the OK button, so dismiss the dialog box" or "the user clicked the Print button on the toolbar, so print the document."

Events provide a formalized, standard mechanism by which event sources (such as a button) hook up with event receivers (such as a form). Events in the .NET Framework implement a publish-and-subscribe mechanism, where event sources make public the events that they will raise—they publish them—and event receivers inform the source as to which events they're interested in—they subscribe to events. Event receivers can also unsubscribe when they no longer want to receive a particular event.

Events in the .NET Framework are based on delegates, and as is illustrated in the diagram that follows, it isn't too hard to see how this works. An event source declares a delegate for each event that it wants to generate, such as *Click*, *DoubleClick*, and so on. An event receiver then defines suitable methods and passes them to the event source, which adds them to its delegates. When the time comes to fire the event, the event source calls *Invoke* on the delegate, thus calling the requisite functions in the receivers.

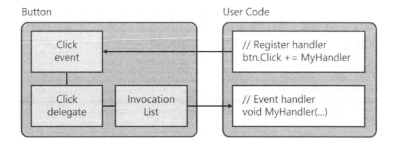

How do events differ from delegates?

People are sometimes confused about the difference between events and delegates because they seem to be doing very much the same task. You have seen how a delegate provides a way to execute a function indirectly, and this could be used to implement event handing: a button could expose a delegate object for the click event, and you could bind your handler function to it by using the += operator.

There are two problems with this, however. The first is that the button's delegate would have to be public in order to let clients bind to it, and this means that anyone could invoke the delegate. This isn't really desirable; only the button should be able to invoke its click delegate to say it has been clicked. The second problem is that even though clients could add and remove event handlers by using the += and −= operators, it is also possible to use the plain = operator. This would reset the invocation list to contain a single item, losing any bindings that might have been set up by other clients.

Events solve these two problems. An event uses a delegate to provide the underlying mechanism, but it refines the behavior of a delegate in two ways:

- An event can only be fired by the type that declares it.

- Clients can only add and remove event handler functions using += and −=. They cannot use = to reset the invocation list.

Implementing an event source class

The actual event mechanism simplifies the syntax so that you don't have to deal with delegates directly, and it's designed to fit in with the event mechanism that already exists in Microsoft Visual Basic. The following exercise takes you through creating an event source class and event receiver classes that register themselves with the source and use the events when they're fired.

1. Create a new CLR Console Application project named **Event**.

2. Event sources and receivers use delegates, so define a delegate for each of the events raised by the source. In this example, two events will be used, so open the Event.cpp source file and define the following two delegates immediately after the *using namespace System;* line:

```
// Delegates
delegate void FirstEventHandler(String^);
delegate void SecondEventHandler(String^);
```

The delegates define the signatures of the methods that event receivers must implement to handle the events, so they're often given names that end with *Handler*. Each of these events will simply pass a string as the event data, but you can make the data passed as complex as you want.

3. Add the implementation of the event source class to the source file.

```
// Event source class
ref class EvtSrc
{
public:
    // Declare the events
    event FirstEventHandler ^OnFirstEvent;
    event SecondEventHandler ^OnSecondEvent;

    // Event raising functions
    void RaiseOne(String ^msg)
    {
        OnFirstEvent(msg);
    }

    void RaiseTwo(String ^msg)
    {
        OnSecondEvent(msg);
    }
};
```

The first thing to note is the use of the *event* keyword to declare two events. You need one *event* declaration for each event that you want to raise, and its type is a handle to the delegate associated with the event. So, in the case of the first event object, the type is *FirstEventHandler* to match the *FirstEventHandler* delegate. Using the *event* keyword causes the compiler to generate a lot of delegate handling code for you; if you're interested in exactly what's going on, see the sidebar that follows.

You can then use the event objects in the *EvtSrc* class to raise the events by using them as if they were function calls and passing the appropriate argument.

Implementing an event receiver

You now have a class that can be used to fire events, so the next thing you need is a class that will listen for events and act upon them when they've been generated.

1. Continue with the project from the previous exercise and add a new class to the project named *EvtRcv*.

    ```
    // Event receiver class
    ref class EvtRcv
    {
        EvtSrc ^theSource;
    public:
    };
    ```

    The receiver has to know the event sources it's working with to be able to subscribe and unsubscribe, so we add an *EvtSrc* member to the class to represent the one source with which you'll be working.

2. Add a constructor to the class that takes a handle to an *EvtSrc* object and checks that it isn't null. If the pointer is valid, save it away in the *EvtSrc* member.

    ```
    EvtRcv(EvtSrc ^src)
    {
        if (src == nullptr)
            throw gcnew ArgumentNullException("Must have event source");
        // Save the source
        theSource = src;
    }
    ```

3. Define the member handler functions in *EvtRcv* that *EvtSrc* is going to call. As you know from our discussion of delegates, the signatures of these methods must match the signatures of the delegates used to define the events, as shown here:

```
// Handler functions
void FirstEvent(String ^msg)
{
    Console::WriteLine("EvtRcv: event one, message was {0}", msg);
}

void SecondEvent(String ^msg)
{
    Console::WriteLine("EvtRcv: event two, message was {0}", msg);
}
```

FirstEvent is the handler for the *FirstEventHandler* delegate, and *SecondEvent* is the handler for the *SecondEventHandler* delegate. Each of them simply prints out the string that's been passed to them.

4. After you have the handlers defined, you can subscribe to the event source. Edit the constructor for the *EvtRcv* class so that it looks like the following:

```
EvtRcv(EvtSrc ^src)
{
    if (src == nullptr)
        throw gcnew ArgumentNullException("Must have event source");
    // Save the source
    theSource = src;

    // Add our handlers
    theSource->OnFirstEvent +=
        gcnew FirstEventHandler(this, &EvtRcv::FirstEvent);
    theSource->OnSecondEvent +=
        gcnew SecondEventHandler(this, &EvtRcv::SecondEvent);
}
```

You subscribe to an event by using the += operator. In the code, you're creating two new delegate objects, which will call back to the *FirstEvent* and *SecondEvent* handlers on the current object. This is exactly the same syntax you'd use if you were manually creating a delegate. The difference is in the += operator, which combines the newly created delegate with the event source's delegate.

As you read in the preceding sidebar, += calls the compiler-generated *add_OnFirstEvent* method, which in turn calls *Delegate::Combine*.

Although you've subscribed to all the events automatically in the constructor, you could also use member functions to subscribe to individual events as required.

5. A matching −= operator lets you unsubscribe from events. Add the following member function to *EvtRcv*, which will unsubscribe from the first event:

```
// Remove a handler
void RemoveHandler()
{
    // Remove the handler for the first event
    theSource->OnFirstEvent -= gcnew FirstEventHandler(this,
        &EvtRcv::FirstEvent);
}
```

The syntax for using the −= operator to unsubscribe is exactly the same as that for the += operator to subscribe.

6. Build the application to ensure that there are no errors.

Hooking it all together

Now that you've written the event source and event receiver classes, you can write some code to test them out.

1. Edit the *main* function to create event source and receiver objects.

```
int main(array<String^> ^args)
{
    Console::WriteLine("Event Example");

    // Create a source
    EvtSrc ^src = gcnew EvtSrc();

    // Create a receiver, and bind it to the source
    EvtRcv ^rcv = gcnew EvtRcv(src);

    return 0;
}
```

The *EvtSrc* constructor takes no arguments, whereas the *EvtRcv* constructor must be passed a valid *EvtSrc* pointer. At this point, the receiver is set up, listening for events to be fired from the source.

```
int main(array<String^> ^args)
{
    Console::WriteLine("Event Example");

    // Create a source
    EvtSrc ^src = gcnew EvtSrc();

    // Create a receiver, and bind it to the source
    EvtRcv ^rcv = gcnew EvtRcv(src);

    // Fire events
    Console::WriteLine("Fire both events:");
    src->RaiseOne("Hello, mum!");
```

```
        src->RaiseTwo("One big step");

        return 0;
}
```

Calls to the source's *RaiseOne* and *RaiseTwo* functions tell it to fire both events. When you run
this code, you should see output similar to the following screen shot:

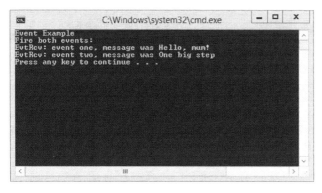

The receiver has had both handlers called, so it has printed both of the messages associated
with the events.

2. Insert some code to call the *RemoveHandler* function of the receiver and try firing both events
again.

```
// Remove the handler for event one
rcv->RemoveHandler();

// Fire events again
Console::WriteLine("Fire both events:");
src->RaiseOne("Hello, mum!");
src->RaiseTwo("One big step");
```

This time you should see only the second message printed because the receiver is no longer
handling the first event.

Standard events and System::EventHandler

You can base an event on a delegate with any signature, but the standard .NET event model requires
that delegates conform to a particular standard. All standard event handler functions have the following form:

```
void MyHandler(Object src, EventArgs ^args)
```

Handler functions do not have a return value and take two arguments. The first is a reference to
the object that raised the event, and the second is a reference to an object of type *EventArgs* or a
subclass. This second argument is used to pass extra information about the event. For example, in
the case of a mouse-click event, it will contain the position of the cursor and details of which mouse
button was clicked and whether any modifier keys were used. Because all system events follow this

pattern, it is good practice to make your events and their corresponding delegates use this model, as well.

All the delegates used in the standard event model will look the same, having the same two arguments and *void* return type. For this reason, you don't need to keep defining your own delegate types; instead, you can make use of the *System::EventHandler* delegate, which is designed to call functions that match the standard event handler signature.

The following exercise shows you how to use the *System::EventHandler* delegate. You will define a *Counter* class that contains a single integer value, which you can increment by calling the *increment* function. When you construct a *Counter*, you can specify a limit, and an event will be fired when the limit is reached.

1. Create a new CLR Console Application named **EventHandler**.

2. Add a new class called *Counter* to the source file. This class should have two data members representing the current count and the limit, and they should be initialized in the constructor.

```
ref class Counter
{
    int count;
    int limit;
public:

    Counter(int lim)
    {
        count = 0;
        limit = lim;
    }
};
```

3. Add the declaration of a standard *EventHandler* event to the class, placing it in the public section.

```
event EventHandler ^LimitReached;
```

4. Implement the *Increment* function, arranging for it to fire the *LimitReached* event at the appropriate point.

```
void Increment()
{
    Console::WriteLine("Count: {0}", ++count);
    if (count == limit)
        LimitReached(this, gcnew EventArgs());
}
```

Observe how the arguments to the event are a reference to the current object, and an *EventArgs* object. This default *EventArgs* object doesn't pass any extra information to the client but is necessary to conform to the delegate signature.

5. You now need some code that will be called when the event is fired, so add an *Observer* class to the source.

```
ref class Observer
{
public:
    static void CallMe(Object ^src, EventArgs ^args)
    {
        Console::WriteLine("Limit reached");
    }
};
```

The static *CallMe* method has the right signature for an event handler; thus, it can be bound to the *LimitReached* event.

6. Implement the *main* function. Start by creating a *Counter* object with an appropriate limit set and then bind the *CallMe* method to the *Counter's LimitReached* event. Finally, increment the *Counter* enough times that the limit is reached.

```
int main(array<System::String ^> ^args)
{
    // Define a counter with a limit of 3
    Counter count(3);

    count.LimitReached += gcnew EventHandler(&Observer::CallMe);

    for (int i=0; i<5; i++)
        count.Increment();

    return 0;
}
```

When you build and run the application, you should see the event handler being called when the limit is reached, as shown in the following screen shot:

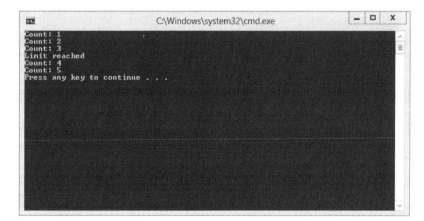

Quick reference

To	Do This
Define a delegate.	Use the *delegate* keyword with a function prototype. For example: `delegate void DelegateOne(double d);`

Create a delegate bound to a static class member.	Use *gcnew* to create a delegate object, passing *nullptr* for the first parameter, and the address of the static function as the second parameter. For example:
	
	`DelegateOne ^del = gcnew DelegateOne(`
	`    nullptr, &MyClass::MyFunc);`

Create a delegate bound to a non-static class member.	Use *gcnew* to create a delegate object, passing a handle to the instance for the first parameter, and the address of the member function as the second parameter. For example:
	
	`DelegateOne ^del = gcnew DelegateOne(`
	`    myObject, &MyClass::MyOtherFunc);`

Execute the function bound to a delegate.	Use the delegate's *Invoke* function, passing any parameters required. For example: `del->Invoke(22.7);`

Create an event.	First, define a delegate to define the handler routine for this event, as follows:
	
	`delegate void ClickHandler(int, int);`
	
	Then, in the event source class, use the *event* keyword to define an event object, like this:
	
	`event ClickHandler ^OnClick;`

Raise an event.	Use the event object as if it were a function, passing any parameters. For example: `OnClick(xVal, yVal);`

Subscribe to an event.	Use the += operator. For example:
	
	`src->OnClick += new ClickHandler(this,`
	`    &myHandler);`

Unsubscribe from an event.	Use the −= operator. For example:
	
	`src->OnClick -= new ClickHandler(this,`
	`    &myHandler);`

Create an event that follows the standard *EventHandler* pattern	Use a *System::EventHandler* delegate. For example: `event EventHandler LimitReached;`

The .NET Framework class library

After completing this chapter, you will be able to:

- Identify the components of the Microsoft .NET Framework.

- Work with the major components of the .NET Framework.

- Recognize the main namespaces that make up the .NET Framework class library.

In previous chapters, you learned how to use C++/CLI to build simple applications. Now, it's time to move on to learn how to build real Microsoft .NET applications that involve GUIs, databases, web servers, and all the other mechanisms needed by the modern Microsoft Windows application. And that's where the .NET Framework comes in.

The .NET Framework is the library of classes that you use to build Windows applications. It is large, complex, and far-reaching in its scope. This chapter gives you an overview of what the .NET Framework is and what it can do before we cover some of its features in more detail in later chapters.

What is the .NET Framework?

The .NET Framework is a computing platform that has been designed by Microsoft to simplify the development of modern applications, such as the following:

- Applications that use sophisticated GUI front ends

- Applications that use the Internet

- Applications that are distributed over more than one computer

- Applications that make use of databases and other data sources

There are two main components to the .NET Framework: the Common Language Runtime and the .NET Framework class library. You'll examine both components in this chapter.

The Common Language Runtime

You've already met the Common Language Runtime (CLR) because this is the part of .NET that manages your code as it runs, providing services such as garbage collection. The CLR is a run-time execution engine that is responsible for executing code within the .NET environment, providing services such as security, memory management, and *remoting* (communication between objects in different domains, processes, or computers). Code that is run by the CLR is known as *managed code*; code that executes outside the control of the CLR is *unmanaged code*. All Microsoft Visual Basic and C# code is managed, but it's possible to write both managed and unmanaged code in Microsoft Visual C++ and to have both types of code working together in the same application.

The Microsoft Intermediate Language

All .NET languages compile down into an intermediate form called Microsoft Intermediate Language (MSIL, or just IL.)

IL is similar to Java bytecode in that it's an intermediate form of code produced by the compiler that can't be directly executed on a target system. IL code is also portable and is always converted into native code before it's executed, which is done by a Just-In-Time (JIT) compiler. This conversion might happen on demand, function-by-function as an application executes, or all at once when an application is installed.

One of the great innovations of IL is that it isn't simply a low-level, machine-independent object code. In fact, support for object-oriented functionality—such as the ideas of classes, encapsulation and data-hiding, polymorphism, and inheritance—is built into IL, so you can view it as a type of object-oriented assembler language. This functionality makes it far more powerful than Java bytecode, and it makes it possible for you to perform cross-language object-oriented programming, easily calling members in C++/CLI classes from Visual Basic, and vice-versa, and even inheriting from a C++/CLI class in Visual Basic.

> **Note** If you're interested in seeing what IL looks like, you can use the IL Disassembler tool, ILDASM, to open a .NET executable and show you the code in IL. There's an example of how to do so in the section "Metadata" later in the chapter.

The Common Type System

The Common Type System (CTS) provides a specification for how types are defined, managed, and used, which is an important part of the .NET cross-language integration. The CTS provides a set of rules that languages must obey, which helps to ensure that types created in different languages can interoperate with one another.

The Common Language Specification

The Common Language Specification (CLS) is a set of rules and constraints that compiler and library writers need to follow to ensure that the languages and code they produce will interoperate with other .NET languages. The CLS forms a subset of the CTS, and if a language or a library is CLS-compliant, it will completely interoperate with other CLS-compliant languages.

You'll see in the online documentation that some .NET member functions are marked as not CLS-compliant, which means that they might not be accessible from some .NET languages. For example, functions that use unsigned integers are not CLS-compliant because unsigned integers aren't supported by Visual Basic. As a result, unsigned integers are not included in the types specified by the CLS.

The .NET Framework class library

The .NET Framework class library is an object-oriented library of classes that provides all the tools you need to write a wide variety of applications.

Since Windows was first released, programmers have written Windows applications using the Windows API (application programming interface). This API gives you a large number of C functions—several thousand, in fact—that you can call from your applications to interact with Windows. However, there are two main problems with the Windows API: first, it isn't object-oriented, and second, it's a C library, so it can't easily be used from every language.

One of the benefits of object-oriented programming is the help that it gives in structuring and managing large-scale projects. The Windows API has grown to several thousand functions, and it becomes harder and harder to manage such a large collection of unstructured routines. In addition to its other benefits (such as encapsulation and polymorphism), object-oriented programming lets you impose a structure on code. So, for example, a *Dialog* class can contain all the functions relating to dialog boxes. This ability makes it much easier to use a library the size of the Windows API.

The second problem with the Windows API is that it's basically written for C programmers, so it uses many features that are unique to C, such as pointers and null-terminated strings, which makes it hard—and sometimes impossible—to use some functionality from languages other than C or C++. You also tend to need a lot of ugly "plumbing" to interface between languages such as Visual Basic and the API.

The .NET Framework class library provides a set of classes that can be used from any .NET language because it works at the IL level. All .NET languages compile down to the same intermediate code, and because they all use references and agree on the basic set of value types, they can all use the classes defined in the class library. This is a huge advantage and provides language interoperability on a scale never seen before.

Assemblies

Assemblies are the basic building blocks with which .NET applications are constructed, and they're the fundamental unit of deployment and versioning. Assemblies contain IL code, metadata that describes the assembly and its contents, and any other files needed for run-time operation. An assembly is therefore much more self-contained than a standard Windows executable or Component Object Model (COM) object because there is no reliance on external sources of information such as the Windows Registry. Every .NET type is part of an assembly, and no .NET type can exist outside an assembly.

There are several aspects by which assemblies are fundamental to the .NET world:

- **Versioning** The assembly is the smallest unit to which versioning is applied, and the *assembly manifest* describes the assembly's version together with the versions of any assemblies on which it depends. This information means that it's possible to check that components with the wrong version information aren't being used at run time.

- **Deployment** Assemblies are loaded only as needed, which makes them highly suitable for distributed applications.

- **Type** A type's identity includes the assembly in which it resides. Two types with the same name living in two different assemblies are considered to be two completely different types.

- **Security** The boundary between assemblies is where security permissions are checked.

Metadata

.NET classes are self-describing, which means that they carry descriptive information with them in the .exe or .dll file. This information, called *metadata*, includes the following:

- The name, version, and culture-specific information (such as the language and calendar used) for the assembly

- The types that are exported by the assembly

- Other assemblies on which this one depends

- Security permissions needed to run

- Information for each type in the assembly: name, visibility, base class, interfaces implemented, and details of members

- Additional attribute information

Most of the metadata is standard and is created by the compiler when it produces the IL code, but you can use attributes to add extra metadata information.

The following exercise shows you how to modify the standard metadata produced by the compiler.

1. Start Microsoft Visual Studio 2012 and create a new CLR Console Application project named **Meta1**.

2. Open Solution Explorer and look at the Source Files folder.

   You can see that the project contains three C++ source files: Meta1.cpp is the code for the application, AssemblyInfo.cpp contains definitions of the standard metadata items that you can modify, and StdAfx.cpp is there to include the StdAfx.h header file.

3. Open AssemblyInfo.cpp.

   The file contains a number of lines that look like the following:

```
[assembly:AssemblyTitleAttribute("Meta1")];
[assembly:AssemblyDescriptionAttribute("")];
[assembly:AssemblyConfigurationAttribute("")];
[assembly:AssemblyCompanyAttribute("")];
[assembly:AssemblyProductAttribute("Meta1")];
[assembly:AssemblyCopyrightAttribute("Copyright (c)  2012")];
[assembly:AssemblyTrademarkAttribute("")];
[assembly:AssemblyCultureAttribute("")];
```

   Metadata is added to C++ code by enclosing declarations in square brackets ([]). Metadata is most often attached to code to describe classes and functions. Here, the keyword *assembly:* at the start of the attribute means that this attribute applies to an assembly, as opposed to being attached to code. There's a set of standard attributes that you can use to change the metadata compiled into an assembly, and most of them are listed in AssemblyInfo.cpp.

4. Edit the *AssemblyCompanyAttribute* line to contain some suitable name, such as the following:

```
[assembly:AssemblyCompanyAttribute("City Power & Light")];
```

5. Build the project, which automatically creates the assembly for you. How can you be sure that the metadata in the assembly reflects your change? One way to find out is to use ILDASM, which is part of the .NET SDK. On my system, this is located in the folder \Program Files (x86)\ Microsoft SDKs\Windows\v8.0A\bin\NETFX 4.0 Tools.

> **Note** I am using a prerelease version of Windows 8 and Visual Studio 2012, so the location of ildasm.exe might be different on your system.

6. When the ILDASM window opens, use the File menu to navigate to the Meta1.exe executable and open it. You should see something like the screen shot that follows.

7. Double-click MANIFEST, which opens a separate window displaying the assembly metadata.

    At the top of this listing are the details of the assemblies on which this executable depends. Scroll down until you find the *AssemblyCompanyAttribute* line, which should read something like the following:

```
.custom /*0C000005:0A000009*/ instance void
                                 ['mscorlib'/* 23000001 */]
'System.Reflection'.'AssemblyCompanyAttribute'
/* 0100000D *//::.ctor(string) /* 0A000009 */
= ( 01 00 16 41 63 6D 65 20 52 6F 63 6B 65 74 20 53
                                          // ...City Power &
    6C 65 64 2C 20 49 6E 63 2E 00 00 )    // Light...
```

    Although the contents are presented in hexadecimal, you can see that the metadata does reflect the change you made to the project.

The .NET Framework namespaces

The .NET Framework class library is made up of a set of classes, interfaces, structures, and enumerations that are contained in over 400 namespaces. This section begins by explaining how to use namespaces in C++/CLI code and then goes on to list some of the major .NET namespaces, together with brief details of their function and content.

You've already encountered .NET namespaces in use in C++/CLI code when you've used the C++ *using* keyword, as in the following example:

```
using namespace System::Collections;
```

As with traditional C++ namespaces, .NET namespaces provide an additional level of scoping that helps you to organize code and guard against name clashes. Two classes with the same name can be used in an application, provided that they belong to different namespaces. A type name that includes the namespace information is called the *fully qualified name*, as illustrated in the following examples:

```
System::Collections::Generic::List  // the List<T> class from
                                    // System::Collections::Generic
System::Threading::Thread           // the Thread class from System::Threading
```

Namespace names in .NET typically consist of more than one word. In C++/CLI, the components of the name are separated by the scope resolution operator (::). In many other .NET languages such as C# and Visual Basic, the components are separated by using a period (.), so in C#, the preceding examples would be as follows:

```
System.Collections.Generic.List
System.Threading.Thread
```

All classes, interfaces, structures, and enumerations that are part of the .NET Framework class library belong to a namespace. Most of the namespaces provided by Microsoft begin with one of two prefixes. Those that start with *System* have been developed as part of the .NET Framework class library, whereas those beginning with *Microsoft* have been developed by other product groups within Microsoft.

Namespace names can have any number of components, but there's no hierarchical relationship implied in names that contain the same root components. The hierarchical nature of namespace names simply gives you a way to organize your classes. So, for example, *System::Collections::Generic* and *System::Collections* both contain collections, yet they aren't necessarily related in any other way.

Note If you are a Java programmer, keep in mind that although .NET namespaces look very much like Java package names, there's no relationship between namespace names and directory paths as there is in Java.

There's no requirement that all the classes belonging to one namespace are defined in the same .dll file or that a single .dll file contains classes from only one namespace.

Using namespaces in C++ applications

C++/CLI applications employ the *#using* preprocessor directive to import metadata into applications. Remember that metadata is information that describes the types in an assembly, and it includes the fully qualified names of all the types. For example, if the compiler sees a line such as

```
#using <mscorlib.dll>
```

it loads the .dll file and reads the metadata for all the types that are defined there. Because mscorlib.dll contains most of the core .NET Framework classes, it imports the metadata for a very large number of types.

> **Note** You can only use *#using* to reference assemblies defined in .dll files.

The *#using* keyword means that you have to know which .dll file holds the class or classes that you want to use. Your typical source for this information is the online help.

Some of the fully qualified names can get rather long. Thus, it's common to use a traditional *using* directive to specify namespace names so that you can use unqualified names, as shown here:

```
// Read the metadata for MSCORLIB
#using <mscorlib.dll>

// Import all the names
using namespace System::Collections::Generic;

// Now you can use List without having to qualify it
List<int> ^pal = gcnew List<int>();
```

The *System* namespace

The *System* namespace, defined in mscorlib.dll, contains a lot of fundamental classes, including the following:

- Base classes for commonly used value and reference types, plus the base class for arrays
- Events and event handlers
- Delegates and interfaces
- Attributes
- Exceptions
- Math

- Application environment management

- Garbage collection

- Local and remote application invocation

- Data type conversion

You've already seen a lot of types from *System* in earlier chapters, and some of the other classes are rather obscure, so I won't go through them in detail. There are a few points that are worth mentioning about some of the classes in *System*; these are covered in the following sections.

Basic types

System implements all the basic types defined by the CTS, and you can find these listed in the following table (which also appears in Chapter 9, "Value types").

Value type	Description	C++/CLI equivalent type
Byte	An 8-bit unsigned integer	*unsigned char*
SByte	An 8-bit signed integer	*char*
Int16	A 16-bit signed integer	*short*
Int32	A 32-bit signed integer	*int* or *long*
Int64	A 64-bit signed integer	*__int64* or *long long*
UInt16	A 16-bit unsigned integer	*unsigned short*
UInt32	A 32-bit unsigned integer	*unsigned int* or *unsigned long*
UInt64	A 64-bit unsigned integer	*unsigned __int64* or *unsigned long long*
Single	A single-precision, 32-bit, floating-point number	*float*
Double	A double-precision, 64-bit, floating-point number	*double*
Boolean	A Boolean value	*bool*
Char	A 16-bit Unicode character	*wchar_t*
IntPtr	A signed integer whose size depends on the platform	No built-in type
UIntPtr	An unsigned integer whose size depends on the platform	No built-in type

Keep in mind that several of the types—namely the unsigned integer types and *SByte*—aren't CLS-compliant, so be wary of using them when you're writing code that's going to be used from other .NET languages.

All .NET languages map these types to native types, so C++/CLI maps *int* to *System::Int32*, but you can also use the underlying types directly, if you want.

Floating-point types

The *Single* and *Double* types implement IEEE-754 floating-point arithmetic. This means that every operation has a defined result, so you never get a divide-by-zero error when performing floating-point math; instead, you get an answer of infinity. The floating-point classes have values to represent positive and negative infinity and "not a number" (often represented as NaN), as well as methods to test for them, as shown in the following example:

```
double top = 1.0;
double bottom = 0.0;

double result = top/bottom;

if (result == Double::PositiveInfinity)
    Console::WriteLine("+infinity");
else if (result == Double::NegativeInfinity)
    Console::WriteLine("-infinity");
else if (result == Double::NaN)
    Console::WriteLine("Not a number");
```

Floating-point and decimal arithmetic

Chapter 8, "Inheritance," points out that floating-point calculations are subject to rounding errors. This is because of the way that IEEE-754 encodes values by using base 2, which means it is not possible to represent some decimal numbers exactly. In the same way that pi cannot be exactly represented as a decimal (3.14159...), a decimal value such as 0.1 cannot be exactly represented in base 2 arithmetic: it comes out as .00011001100110011... with the "0011" repeating forever. This means that you can only ever get an approximation to 0.1, in the same way that we can only ever get an approximation to the correct value of pi, and so we see rounding errors as these approximations accumulate.

There are two ways around this problem. The first is to use the *System::Decimal* type, which performs arithmetic in base 10 and so does not get these rounding errors, but which is slower. The second is to use integer arithmetic with scaling. For example, instead of using 123.45, use 12345 and divide the result by 100.

The *Collections* namespaces

Chapter 12, "Arrays and collections," looks at the *Collections* namespaces, in particular *System:: Collections::Generic*. *System::Collections::Generic* is implemented in mscorlib.dll, so to use it, you'll have to include a *#using* statement, as demonstrated here:

```
#using <mscorlib.dll>
```

The following table lists the main classes that you'll find in the *System::Collections::Generic* namespace.

Class	Description
Dictionary<K,V>	A collection of key/value pairs
HashSet<T>	A set of objects
LinkedList<T>	A doubly linked list of objects
List<T>	A strongly typed list of objects, retrievable by index
Queue<T>	A FIFO collection of objects
SortedList<K,V>	A collection of key/value pairs sorted on the key
SortedSet<T>	A collection of objects maintained in sorted order
Stack<T>	A LIFO stack

The *Collections* interfaces

The *System::Collections::Generic* namespace also defines a series of interfaces that are used to define the behavior of the collection classes. The collection classes themselves implement one or more of these interfaces, and you can use them as the basis for writing your own collection classes. The main interfaces are listed in the following table.

Interface	Description
ICollection<T>	Defines the size, enumerator, and synchronization methods for all collections
IComparer<T>	Defines a method for comparing two objects
IDictionary<K,V>	Implemented by collections that manage key/value pairs, such as *Hashtable* and *ListDictionary*
IEnumerable<T>	Defines the *GetEnumerator* method, which returns an *IEnumerator*; implemented by almost all collections
IEnumerator<T>	Defines the properties and methods of enumerators
IList<T>	Implemented by classes that define indexed collections of objects
IReadOnlyCollection<T>	Represents a strongly typed, read-only collection of elements
ISet<T>	Implemented by classes that manage sets of objects

The *Diagnostics* namespace

The *System::Diagnostics* namespace provides a number of classes with which you can do the following:

- Trace application execution

- Interact with the debugger

- Use the system event log

- Start system processes

- Monitor system performance

All the classes in *System::Diagnostics* are implemented in *system.dll*.

The *IO* namespace

The *System::IO* namespace, defined in mscorlib.dll, provides the classes that implement the .NET input/output (I/O) functionality. The main classes in this namespace are described in the following table.

Class	Description
BinaryReader	Reads .NET primitive types from a byte stream
BinaryWriter	Writes .NET primitive types to a byte stream
Directory	Contains static methods for operating on directories
DirectoryInfo	Represents a path to a directory and contains methods for operating on the directory path
File	Contains static methods for operating on files
FileInfo	Represents a path to a file and contains methods for operating on the file path
FileStream	Reads and writes to files by using streams
FileSystemInfo	The base class for *FileInfo* and *DirectoryInfo*
FileSystemWatcher	Watches for changes in the file system and fires events when changes occur
IOException	The exception thrown when I/O errors occur
MemoryStream	Reads and writes streams of bytes to and from memory
Path	Represents directory strings in a platform-independent way
Stream	The abstract base for the stream classes
StreamReader	Reads Unicode characters from a byte stream
StreamWriter	Writes Unicode characters to a byte stream
StringReader	Reads Unicode characters from a string
StringWriter	Writes Unicode characters to a string
TextReader	The base class for *StreamReader* and *StringReader*
TextWriter	The base class for *StreamWriter* and *StringWriter*

As with all the .NET Framework class library classes, these classes are language-independent. They can be used alongside or in place of the C++ stream classes. Chapter 19, "Writing a service by using Windows Communication Foundation," delves deeper into some of the *System::IO* classes. The *System::IO* classes are in mscorlib.dll.

The *Windows* namespaces

The *System::Windows* prefix identifies 50 namespaces that together provide the functionality of Windows Presentation Foundation (WPF), an advanced user interface (UI) framework for .NET introduced in version 3.0. WPF provides all the tools you need to create modern UIs, including support for forms-based applications, 2D and 3D graphics, typography and printing, run-time animation, and comprehensive support for playing media.

> **Note** In earlier versions of the .NET Framework, you built UIs by using a technology called *Windows Forms*, which was heavily influenced by Visual Basic.

One key feature of WPF is its use of XAML, an XML markup language, to define user interfaces. This makes it possible to separate the UI from the code, which allows teams to use design tools such as Microsoft Expression Blend in addition to coding tools such as Microsoft Visual Studio.

The *Net* namespaces

Networking support is provided by a number of namespaces in the *System::Net* family. *System::Net* itself provides an interface to many of the protocols commonly used today, such as manipulating IP addresses, making DNS lookups, talking to HTTP and FTP servers, managing cookies, and authentication.

System::Net::Sockets provides an implementation of the Berkeley Sockets protocol and provides a .NET wrapper around the Windows WinSock API, whereas *System::Net::WebSockets* provides a managed implementation of the WebSocket interface.

The *ServiceModel* namespaces

The *System::ServiceModel* namespaces (over 30 of them) together implement Windows Communication Foundation (WCF), a technology introduced in .NET 3.0 for creating distributed, service-oriented applications.

With WCF, you can build applications out of components hosted in other processes, and even on other computers. This has long been possible, but the technologies used were very different, depending on where your components were located (same process, different process on the same computer, or different process on another computer) and the communication mechanism you wanted to use (TCP/IP, HTTP, messaging).

WCF provides an integrated framework for creating, deploying, and managing distributed components and their clients. Chapter 19 shows you how to write a web service by using WCF.

The *Xml* namespaces

XML is heavily used throughout the .NET Framework, and several namespaces provide support for creating and manipulating XML, including the following:

- *System::Xml* Provides the basic classes needed for processing XML

- *System::Xml::Linq* Makes it possible to use Language-Integrated Query (LINQ) to work with XML data

- *System::Xml::Schema* Provides support for XML schemas

- *System::Xml::Serialization* Gives you the ability to serialize .NET objects to and from XML

- *System::Xml::XPath* Contains the XPath parser and evaluation engine

- *System::Xml::Xsl* Contains the Extensible Stylesheet Language (XSL) processor

Using these classes, it's possible to perform all the manipulation of XML that you'll ever need to do. These classes make the .NET Framework one of the most productive environments for XML programming. You can find the XML classes in *System.Xml.dll*, with the LINQ classes in *System.Xml.Linq.dll*.

The *Data* namespaces

The *System::Data* namespaces hold the classes that implement ADO.NET, a framework with which you can build components to manage data from a number of data sources. Data from different data sources is provided by data providers, five of which are shipped with the .NET Framework.

- **System.Data.OleDb** Object Linking and Embedding Database (OLE DB)–based technology that makes it possible to use many different kinds of data sources—such as relational database tables, Microsoft Excel spreadsheets, and even text files—as if they were databases.

- **System.Data.Odbc** The ODBC provider gives access to Open Database Connectivity (ODBC) data sources, including Microsoft Access databases.

- **System.Data.SqlClient** This provider is optimized for use with Microsoft SQL Server.

- **System.Data.OracleClient** The provider for Oracle makes it possible to work with Oracle databases from .NET code.

- **System.Data.EntityClient** Entity Framework (EF) is an object-relational mapping framework that can be used from ADO.NET, making it possible to map managed objects to a backing database automatically.

The most important class in the *System::Data* namespace itself is *DataSet*, which represents an in-memory cache of data retrieved from a data source. A *DataSet* consists of one or more *DataTable* objects, and these in turn consist of a collection of *DataColumn* and *DataRow* objects. You can use *DataSet*s to work in *disconnected mode*. This means retrieve data from a database into a *DataSet*, disconnect from the database server and work with the data locally, and then update the database from the *DataSet* later.

The *Web* namespaces

Because one of the main reasons for introducing the .NET Framework was to make it easier to build web applications, it's perhaps no surprise that the .NET Framework contains a number of namespaces related to web programming. These are all related to Microsoft ASP.NET, the latest version of Microsoft Active Server Pages technology that is optimized to work in the .NET environment.

The most significant of the *Web* namespaces are listed here:

- *System::Web* This provides the basic functionality for browser-to-server communication over HTTP, including the *HttpRequest* and *HttpResponse* classes that enable an ASP.NET page to exchange data with the client by using HTTP.

- *System::Web::Mail* This makes it possible for you to prepare and send email attachments by using the Simple Mail Transfer Protocol (SMTP) service that is built in to the Windows operating system.

- *System::Web::Security* This provides classes that implement security in ASP.NET.

- *System::Web::Services* This provides the classes with which you can build web services.

- *System::Web::UI* This contains all the classes with which you can build server-side controls.

The features provided by two of these namespaces merit particular mention. A *web service* is a programmable entity living on a web server that can be accessed by using standard Internet protocols. What this means in practice is that you can expose a function on a web server that others can call. Communication between client and server uses standard protocols such as HTTP, and data is usually passed to and from the web service in XML format by using Simple Object Access Protocol (SOAP). The use of XML over HTTP makes it possible to access web services easily from clients written in just about any programming language on any platform. It's also possible to find out what services a web server supports, and it's very easy in Visual Studio 2012 to write clients that make use of web services.

With the *System::Web::UI* namespaces, you can build server-side controls. You program these as if they were normal controls, but their code executes on the server. The *System::Web::UI::HtmlControls* namespace contains classes that represent HTML server controls that map directly to standard HTML elements such as buttons and forms. *System::Web::UI::WebControls* is more abstract, and you can use it to program server-side controls that might not map directly to HTML.

Quick reference

To	Do this
Use data structures such as dynamic arrays, lists, and hash tables.	Use the classes in the *System::Collections::Generic* namespace.
Create a form-based application.	Use the classes in *System::Windows::Forms*, and derive a class from *System::Windows::Forms::Form*.
Work with XML.	Look at the classes in the *System::Xml* namespace.
Trace application execution, interact with the event log, or monitor system performance.	Use the classes in the *System::Diagnostics* namespace.
Work with databases by using ADO.NET.	Look at the *System::Data* namespaces.

PART III

Using the .NET
Framework

CHAPTER 16   Working with files 281

CHAPTER 17   Reading and writing XML. 305

CHAPTER 18   Using ADO.NET 333

CHAPTER 19   Writing a service by using Windows
Communication Foundation 351

CHAPTER 20   Introducing Windows Store apps 369

CHAPTER 21   More about Windows Store apps 397

Working with files

After completing this chapter, you will be able to:

- Understand how the Microsoft Windows .NET Framework performs input/output (I/O).

- Identify the classes that make up the *System::IO* namespace.

- Perform text I/O.

- Read and write files.

- Work with files and directories.

- Perform binary I/O.

You've already used the *Console* class to perform I/O to and from the console. This chapter introduces you to the *System::IO* namespace, which contains the classes, structures, and enumerations that implement the Microsoft .NET I/O model.

 Note If you know anything about the Java I/O mechanism as implemented in the *java.io* package, you'll find it easy to start working with .NET I/O because the two have many similarities.

The *System::IO* namespace

The *System::IO* namespace contains all the classes that are used for binary and text I/O as well as classes that help you to work with files and directories. The following table lists the main classes in the namespace:

Class	Description
BinaryReader	Reads primitive data types as binary values
BinaryWriter	Writes primitive data types as binary values
BufferedStream	A stream class that buffers reads and writes to another stream
Directory	Has static methods for working with directories
DirectoryInfo	Has non-static methods for working with directories
File	Has static methods for working with files
FileInfo	Has non-static methods for working with files
FileStream	A class for reading and writing files by using a stream
FileSystemInfo	The abstract base class for *DirectoryInfo* and *FileInfo*
FileSystemWatcher	Watches for changes to the file system and raises events when changes occur
IOException	The exception thrown by classes in the *System::IO* namespace
MemoryStream	A stream class that reads and writes memory
Path	Helps you work with directory strings in a platform-independent way
Stream	The abstract base class for all the stream classes
StreamReader	A *TextReader* that reads characters from a byte stream
StreamWriter	A *TextWriter* that writes characters to a byte stream
StringReader	A *TextReader* that reads from a string
StringWriter	A *TextWriter* that writes to a string
TextReader	The abstract base class for *StreamReader* and *StringReader*
TextWriter	The abstract base class for *StreamWriter* and *StringWriter*

The I/O-oriented classes in *System::IO* can be divided into the following three groups:

- The *Stream* classes, which are designed for I/O of streams of bytes

- The *BinaryReader* and *BinaryWriter* classes, which are used to input and output .NET primitive types, such as *Int32* and *Double*, in binary form

- The *TextReader* and *TextWriter* classes, which are used for character-mode I/O

This chapter focuses on the latter two groups.

Implementing text I/O by using readers and writers

TextReader and *TextWriter* are the abstract base classes for a group of classes that are used to read and write characters. There are four classes in *System::IO* that derive from these two bases—*StreamReader*, *StreamWriter*, *StringReader*, and *StringWriter*, as well as with several other much more specialized writer classes in other namespaces.

Using *TextWriter*

The *TextWriter* class has a number of useful methods, as summarized in the following table:

Method	Description
Close	Closes the writer and releases any resources that it's using
Dispose	Releases all unmanaged resources used by the writer and optionally releases managed resources, as well
Flush	Causes all buffered data to be written to the underlying device
FlushAsync	Causes all buffered data to be written asynchronously to the underlying device
Synchronized	Creates a thread-safe wrapper for the writer
Write	Writes text without a newline
WriteAsync	Writes text without a newline asynchronously
WriteLine	Writes text with a newline
WriteLineAsync	Writes text with a newline asynchronously

As you might guess from the inclusion of the *Write* and *WriteLine* functions in the table, the *Console* class uses a *TextWriter* object to perform output.

Asynchronous I/O

You might have noticed that the *TextWriter* class contains several methods whose names end with *Async*. Normally, I/O operations prevent your code from executing further until they finish, a condition known as *blocking*. Asynchronous I/O helps overcome this by performing I/O in the background, letting your code continue executing while the input or output operation runs in parallel. This is very useful when you don't need to know that the operation has finished, although it is possible to find out when the operation finishes. Setting up and working with asynchronous I/O can be complex and is beyond what we can cover in this introductory chapter.

To show you how the I/O classes work together, let's look at how you use the *StreamWriter* class. Before we start, though, it's important that you understand how the .NET Framework implements I/O. Rather than create a number of classes that each perform an end-to-end I/O task—such as "write a string to a file" or "read a number from the keyboard"—.NET implements a number of smaller special-purpose classes that you can plug together to achieve the effect you want. This means that .NET doesn't have a "write characters to a file" class. Instead, it has a "write characters to a byte stream" class and a "read bytes from a stream and write them to a file" class. If you plug the output from the first class into the input of the second, you end up writing characters to a file.

This model is flexible because you can take binary or character data, convert it into bytes, and then pass the bytes to any of several classes to output them to files, memory, or a string. Data is transferred between the classes as streams of bytes, a method that provides a flexible base on which to build. The basic functionality for handling byte streams is provided by the *Stream* class, and you can build your own specialized I/O classes on top of *Stream*, if you need to.

With that information in mind, the exercise that follows shows you how to write character data to a text file by using a *TextWriter*. Using the plug-and-play model for I/O that the .NET Framework uses, you need to create the following two objects:

■ A *FileStream* object that takes bytes as input and writes them to a file

■ A *StreamWriter* object that takes text and converts it to a byte stream

So, let's get started.

1. Start Microsoft Visual Studio 2012 and create a new CLR Console Application project named **CppWriter**.

2. The *TextWriter* and file I/O classes are part of *System::IO*, so include a *using* declaration at the beginning of the application, as shown here:

```
using namespace System::IO;
```

3. In the *main* function, create a *FileStream* object to write to a file.

```
// Create a FileStream
try
{
    FileStream ^fs = gcnew FileStream("output.txt", System::IO::FileMode::Create);
}
catch(System::Exception ^pe)
{
    Console::WriteLine(pe->ToString());
}
```

The *FileStream* constructor takes a file name and a mode. In this case, the file is going to be created if it doesn't exist or overwritten if it does. I've used output.txt as the file name, but you can specify any path and file name you like for the new file.

 Note See the section "The *FileStream* class" later in this chapter for more details on how to construct *FileStream* objects.

The code is enclosed in a *try* block because a lot of things could go wrong when trying to open this file.

4. After you have initialized the *FileStream* object, create a *StreamWriter* that uses the *FileStream*, as demonstrated here:

```
try
{
    // Create a FileStream
    FileStream ^fs = gcnew FileStream("output.txt", FileMode::Create);

    // Create a StreamWriter
    StreamWriter ^sw = gcnew StreamWriter(fs);
}
catch(System::Exception ^pe)
{
    Console::WriteLine(pe->ToString());
}
```

The *StreamWriter* constructor takes a handle to a *Stream* object as its one argument.

5. You can now use the *Write* and *WriteLine* functions to output text to the file. Place the following lines inside the *try* block:

```
// Write some text
sw->WriteLine("First line");
sw->WriteLine("Second line");
sw->WriteLine("Third line");
```

6. Ensure that all output is flushed to the file and close the stream.

```
// Close the file
sw->Flush();
sw->Close();
```

> **Note** *WriteLine* performs buffered output, which means that it doesn't necessarily write lines to the file every time you call the function. Instead, it maintains an internal buffer and writes the buffer to hard disk as necessary. One hard disk access per buffer is more efficient than writing individual lines, but you need to call *Flush* at the end of the code to ensure that output currently in the buffer is transferred to the file.

7. Build and run the application.

A text file named output.txt should appear in the CppWriter project directory. The file contains the three lines of text written by the CppWriter application.

The *FileStream* class

FileStream is used to pass bytes from some other class—such as *StreamWriter*—to a file. There are several overloaded constructors to this class with which you can specify combinations of the following:

- The file name

- The file mode, which determines how the file is going to be opened

- The type of access required

- The sharing options

The file mode is represented by members of the *FileMode* enumeration, which are described in the following table:

Member	Description
Append	Opens an existing file or creates a new file and appends text to the end.
Create	Creates a new file or opens an existing one and over-writes it.
CreateNew	Creates a new file, throwing an exception if the file already exists.
Open	Opens an existing file.
OpenOrCreate	Opens an existing file or creates a new one.
Truncate	Opens an existing file and truncates its size to 0 bytes. An exception will be thrown if the file doesn't exist.

The access is represented by members of the *FileAccess* enumeration, as listed in the following table:

Member	Description
Read	Represents read access
ReadWrite	Represents read/write access
Write	Represents write access

Similarly, the sharing access is specified by the *FileShare* enumeration, as presented in the following table:

Member	Description
None	No sharing
Read	Represents shared read access
ReadWrite	Represents shared read/write access
Write	Represents shared write access
Delete	Allows subsequent deletion of a file

The following example shows how to construct a *FileStream* by using these permissions:

```
FileStream ^fs2 = gcnew FileStream(
    "foo.txt",             // the filename
    FileMode::Create,      // create or overwrite
    FileAccess::ReadWrite, // request read/write access
    FileShare::Read);      // allow shared reading
```

Note Although you'll usually use the *FileStream* class with other writer classes, you can use its *Read* and *Write* methods to input and output bytes directly.

Using *TextReader*

The structure and operation of the *TextReader* class parallels that of *TextWriter*. The following table lists the methods provided for you by *TextReader*:

Method	Description
Close	Closes the reader and releases any resources that it's using
Dispose	Releases all unmanaged resources used by the reader and, optionally, releases managed resources, as well
Peek	Returns the next character from the input stream without removing it
Read	Reads one or more characters from the input stream
ReadAsync	Reads one or more characters from the input stream asynchronously
ReadBlock	Reads a block of characters
ReadBlockAsync	Reads a block of characters asynchronously
ReadLine	Reads a line
ReadLine	Reads a line asynchronously
ReadToEnd	Reads to the end of the input stream
ReadToEndAsync	Reads asynchronously to the end of the stream
Synchronized	Provides a thread-safe wrapper for *TextReader* objects

As with *TextWriter*, you use *TextReader* by plugging a reader into an object that is going to act as a source of bytes. There are several of these, including the one you've already seen, *FileStream*.

The exercise that follows shows you how to write an application similar in functionality to the Linux *less* command, which reads a file and echoes its contents to the screen, a few lines at a time. After it has displayed some lines, the user is presented with the choice of pressing the Enter key to continue or pressing Q to quit.

1. Create a new CLR Console Application project named **CppReader**.

2. Include a *using* declaration for *System::IO* at the top of the project.

    ```
    using namespace System::IO;
    ```

3. Add code to *main* to ensure that the user has entered a file name.

    The argument to *main* is an array of the command-line arguments, not including the application name.

    ```
    // Check for required argument
    if (args->Length < 1)
    {
        Console::WriteLine("Usage: CppReader path");
        return 0;
    }

    String ^path = args[0];
    ```

    If the user hasn't given an argument, an error message is printed and the application exits. If the user has provided it, the argument is saved for later use.

4. It's wise to check that the path represents an existing file before continuing, so add the following code:

    ```
    if (!File::Exists(path))
    {
        Console::WriteLine("Invalid filename!");
        return -1;
    }
    ```

    The *File::Exists* method checks whether a file with the specified name exists, returning false if it doesn't. It will also return false if you give the name of a directory rather than a file. Notice the return value of –1. It's a common convention for C/C++ applications to return 0 to indicate success, with negative values being used to denote error conditions.

5. Start listing the file. The first step is to create a *FileStream* and connect it to a *StreamReader*.

    ```
    try
    {
        FileStream ^fs = gcnew FileStream(path, System::IO::FileMode::Open);
        StreamReader ^sr = gcnew StreamReader(fs);
    }
    catch(System::Exception ^pe)
    {
        Console::WriteLine(pe->Message);
    }
    ```

    In this case, you're opening the file by using *FileMode::Open*, which will throw an exception if the file doesn't already exist.

6. Listing the file is done in this loop, which you should place after creating the *StreamReader* object, like this:

```
int count = 0;
for(;;)
{
    String ^line  = sr->ReadLine();
    count++;
    // If there are no more lines, break out of the loop
    if (line == nullptr) break;

    Console::WriteLine(line);

    if (count % 20 == 0)
    {
        Console::Write("--more-- ");
        String ^response = Console::ReadLine();
        if (response->Equals("q")) break;
        count = 0;
    }
}

Console::WriteLine("-- end --");
```

The *count* variable is going to be used to count the lines as they're read so that the application knows where to break. The loop reads a line into a *String* by using the *ReadLine* function of *StreamReader*; if there are no more lines to read, a null will be returned. The line is then echoed to the console and the count checked. I've set the number of lines displayed at one time to an arbitrary value of 20; when the count is exactly divisible by 20, the application writes "--more--" to the console and waits for the user to input something. If the user presses a lowercase q, the application stops; otherwise, it outputs the next set of lines.

Remember that *for(;;)* sets up an infinite loop, which you need to terminate somehow. In this example, when there are no more lines to read, the call to *ReadLine* returns *nullptr*, and this causes the loop to terminate.

7. Build and run the application, giving the name of a suitable text file as the argument.

You can do this in one of two ways. The first is to open a command prompt, navigate to the directory containing the executable file, and then execute the application from the command line just as you would with any other application.

The second is to run the application from within Visual Studio, providing the command-line arguments that you need. In Solution Explorer, right-click the project name, and then, in the shortcut menu that appears, click Properties. When the Properties page appears, in the pane on the left, select Configuration Properties, click Debugging, and then enter the file name into the Command Arguments box in the center pane.

Working with files and directories

The *System::IO* namespace contains several classes to help you work with files and directories.

Getting information about files and directories

The *Directory* and *DirectoryInfo* classes provide you with functions to help you work with directories. The difference between them is that the *Directory* class only contains static methods, whereas *DirectoryInfo* contains non-static instance methods. Why the need for two different classes? It's necessary for .NET to perform a security check before allowing you access to a directory or a file. The *Directory* class performs this check every time you use one of its static methods, which can be time-consuming. Objects of the *DirectoryInfo* class, on the other hand, work with one directory, and the security check is done once when the object is constructed. It can, therefore, be a lot more efficient to use *DirectoryInfo* if you're going to perform multiple operations on one directory. The following table lists the main methods of the *Directory* class:

Method	Description
CreateDirectory	Creates a directory
Delete	Deletes a directory and, optionally, its subdirectories
EnumerateDirectories	Returns an enumerable collection of the directories in a specified path
EnumerateFiles	Returns an enumerable collection of the files in a specified path
EnumerateFileSystemEntries	Returns an enumerable collection of all the files and directories in a specified path
Exists	Checks whether a directory exists
GetCreationTime	Gets the creation time of a directory
GetCurrentDirectory	Returns a string representing the path to the application's current directory
GetDirectories	Gets an array of strings representing the names of subdirectories in a given directory
GetDirectoryRoot	Returns the root portion of a path
GetFiles	Gets an array of strings representing the names of the files in a given directory
GetFileSystemEntries	Gets an array of strings representing the names of the files and directories in a given directory
GetLastAccessTime	Gets the last access time for the directory
GetLastWriteTime	Gets the last write time for the directory
GetLogicalDrives	Gets a list of the logical drives on the computer
GetParent	Gets the parent directory of a specified directory
Move	Moves a directory and its contents
SetCreationTime	Sets the creation time for a directory

Method	Description
SetCurrentDirectory	Sets the application's current directory
SetLastAccessTime	Sets the last access time for the directory
SetLastWriteTime	Sets the last write time for the directory

The following two tables list the properties and methods of the *DirectoryInfo* class:

Property	Description
Attributes	Gets or sets the *FileAttributes* for the directory
CreationTime	Gets or sets the creation time for the directory
Exists	Value is true if the directory path exists
Extension	Gets the extension part of the directory name
FullName	Gets the full path of the directory
LastAccessTime	Gets or sets the time when the directory was last accessed
LastWriteTime	Gets or sets the time at which the directory was last written
Name	Represents the name of the directory
Parent	Gets a *DirectoryInfo* object representing the parent of this directory
Root	Gets a *DirectoryInfo* object representing the root portion of a directory path

Method	Description
Create	Creates a directory
CreateSubdirectory	Creates one or more subdirectories
Delete	Deletes a directory and its contents
EnumerateDirectories	Returns an enumerable collection of the directories in a specified path
EnumerateFiles	Returns an enumerable collection of the files in a specified path
EnumerateFileSystemEntries	Returns an enumerable collection of all the files and directories in a specified path
GetDirectories	Gets an array of *DirectoryInfo* objects representing the subdirectories of this directory
GetFiles	Gets an array of *FileInfo* objects representing the files in this directory
GetFileSystemInfos	Gets an array of *FileSystemInfo* objects representing the directories and files in this directory
MoveTo	Moves the directory and its contents
ToString	Returns the fully qualified path as a string

Two classes, *File* and *FileInfo*, are used to work with files. Like the *Directory* and *DirectoryInfo* classes discussed earlier, *File* contains static methods, and *FileInfo* contains non-static instance methods. The following table lists the methods provided by the *File* class:

Method	Description
AppendAllLines	Appends lines to a file, creating it if necessary, and then closes it
AppendAllText	Appends a string to a file, creating it if necessary, and then closes it
AppendText	Appends text to a file, creating the file if it doesn't already exist
Copy	Copies a file
Create	Creates a new file
CreateText	Creates a new text file
Delete	Deletes a file
Exists	Returns true if a file exists
GetAttributes	Returns the file attributes
GetCreationTime	Returns the file's creation time
GetLastAccessTime	Returns the file's last access time
GetLastWriteTime	Returns the file's last write time
Move	Moves a file to a new location, with the option of renaming it
Open	Opens a *FileStream* for read/write access to a file
OpenRead	Opens a *FileStream* for read-only access to a file
OpenText	Opens a *FileStream* to read from a text file
OpenWrite	Opens a *FileStream* for read/write access to a file
Replace	Replaces the content of one file with another, deleting the original and creating a backup of the replaced file
SetAttributes	Sets the file attributes
SetCreationTime	Sets the file's creation time
SetLastAccessTime	Sets the file's last access time
SetLastWriteTime	Sets the file's last write time
WriteAllLines	Creates a new file, writes lines to it, and then closes it
WriteAllText	Creates a new file, writes a string to it, and then closes it

The following two tables list the main properties and methods exposed by the *FileInfo* class:

Property	Description
CreationTime	Gets or sets the creation time of the directory
Directory	Returns a *DirectoryInfo* object representing the file's parent directory
DirectoryName	Returns a string representing the file's full path
Exists	Returns true if the file exists
FullName	Gets the full path of the directory or file
LastAccessTime	Gets or sets the time the file or directory was last accessed
LastWriteTime	Gets or sets the time the file or directory was last written
Length	Returns the length of the file in bytes
Name	Returns the name of the file

Method	Description
AppendText	Creates a *StreamWriter* to append text to a file
CopyTo	Copies a file to another location
Create	Creates a new file and a *FileStream* to write to it
CreateText	Creates a *StreamWriter* to write to a new text file
Delete	Deletes a file
MoveTo	Moves a file to a new location
Open	Returns a *FileStream* with a specified level of access to a file
OpenRead	Returns a *FileStream* with read access to a file
OpenText	Creates a *StreamReader* to read from an existing file
OpenWrite	Returns a *FileStream* with read/write access to a file
Refresh	Takes a snapshot of the file from the file system
Replace	Replaces the content of one file with another, deleting the original and creating a backup of the replaced file
ToString	Returns the file path as a string

The following example illustrates the use of the directory and file manipulation classes. You'll construct a simple directory-listing application, similar in functionality to the MS-DOS *dir* command. Here's how it will work:

- If the path represents a file, the details of the file will be printed.

- If the path represents a directory, the contents of the directory will be listed.

- In addition to the name, the user can choose to display size, last modification date, and attributes. For directories, only the last modification date applies.

1. Create a new CLR Console Application named **CppFiles**.

2. Because all the file and directory classes are part of *System::IO*, add a *using* declaration at the beginning of the application.

```
using namespace System::IO;
```

3. When the application is run, the user can supply options in addition to a file or directory path. Add the following code to *main* to check that you have the minimum number of options:

```
if (args->Length < 1)
{
    Console::WriteLine("Usage: CppFiles [options] [path]");
    return 0;
}
```

If the user has specified options, we need to check what they are. Each option is specified by a single letter, and multiple options are specified as a string, for example, "sa" to choose the "s" and "a" options. The options supported by this simple application are "s" (for the file size), "d" (for the last modified date), and "a" (for the file attributes). You can also use "v" (for verbose) as a shorthand to indicate that you want them all. It doesn't matter in what order the options letters are specified, or even if they are repeated.

4. Add the following code to *main*:

```
String ^options = nullptr;
String ^path = nullptr;
bool hasOptions = false;

bool size = false;
bool date = false;
bool atts = false;

// If we have two arguments, we have options
if (args->Length == 2)
{
    hasOptions = true;
    options = args[0];
    path = args[1];

    // Parse the option string to set the option flags
    ParseOptions(options, size, date, atts);
}
else
    path = args[0];
```

5. Add the function that is going to process the options, placing it before *main*:

```
void ParseOptions(String ^opts, bool &size, bool &date, bool &atts)
{
    opts = opts->ToLower();

    if (opts->Contains("v"))
    {
        size = date = atts = true;
    }
    else
    {
        if (opts->Contains("s")) size = true;
        if (opts->Contains("d")) date = true;
        if (opts->Contains("a")) atts = true;
    }
}
```

The three *bool* variables are passed in by reference rather than by value; thus setting them in this function will change their value back in the *main* function.

6. Check whether the path represents a file or a directory by adding the following code to the *main* function:

```
bool isAFile = false;
bool isADirectory = false;

FileInfo ^fi = gcnew FileInfo(path);
DirectoryInfo ^di = gcnew DirectoryInfo(path);

if (fi->Exists)
    isAFile = true;
else if (di->Exists)
    isADirectory = true;
else
{
    Console::WriteLine("No such file or directory");
    return -1;
}
```

This isn't quite as straightforward as you might think. You have to create both *FileInfo* and *DirectoryInfo* objects and then use their *Exists* properties to check whether either of them recognizes the path. If neither of them returns true, the most likely explanation is that the path doesn't exist, so you print an error message and exit.

7. Now that you know what kind of object you have and what options the user wants, you can print out the details. The first case is that for a single file, and the code for that is very simple, as illustrated here:

```
if (isAFile)
{
    ProcessFile(fi, size, date, atts);
}
```

8. Again, in the interests of modularity, place the code for processing a file in a separate function before *main*:

```
void ProcessFile(FileInfo ^fi, bool size, bool date, bool atts)
{
    // Echo the filename and length
    Console::Write("{0,30}", fi->Name);

    if (size) Console::Write(" {0,10}", fi->Length);
    if (date) Console::Write(" {0}",
        File::GetLastAccessTime(fi->ToString()));
    if (atts)
    {
        FileAttributes fa = File::GetAttributes(fi->ToString());
        Console::Write(" ");
        if ((fa & FileAttributes::Normal) == FileAttributes::Normal)
            Console::Write("<normal>");
        else
        {
            if ((fa & FileAttributes::Archive) == FileAttributes::Archive)
                Console::Write("a");
            if ((fa & FileAttributes::Hidden) == FileAttributes::Hidden)
                Console::Write("h");
            if ((fa & FileAttributes::System) == FileAttributes::System)
                Console::Write("s");
            if ((fa & FileAttributes::ReadOnly) == FileAttributes::ReadOnly)
                Console::Write("r");
        }
        Console::WriteLine();
    }
}
```

The function first prints the file name and then displays other details, depending on the options chosen by the user. The last access time can be obtained by calling one of the static methods on the *File* class, passing it the path. The easiest way to get the path is to call *ToString* on the *FileInfo* object.

Observe the use of a field width when printing the name; format specifiers can take an optional field width after the field number. If this value is positive, the value is right-justified in the field; if it is negative, the value is left-justified. A field width of 30 characters should be wide enough for most files.

If the user has requested attributes, use the static *GetAttributes* method on the *File* class to obtain the *FileAttributes*. You can then use the bitwise *AND* operator (&) to match against the various values defined in the *FileAttributes* class. This code only checks for four attributes. There are many more, and it would be simple to extend the application to check for them.

9. If the user has entered a directory, list its contents. We will list subdirectories first, followed by files; directory names will be printed in uppercase letters, and file names in lowercase, but you can obviously change this to display them however you want. Add the following code for listing the subdirectories:

```
    else if (isADirectory)
    {
        // Process the subdirectories
        array<String^> ^dirs = Directory::GetDirectories(di->ToString());

        for (int i=0; i<dirs->Length; i++)
        {
            DirectoryInfo ^inf = gcnew DirectoryInfo(dirs[i]);
            String ^name = inf->Name->ToUpper();
            Console::Write("{0,30}", name);
            Console::Write(" {0,10}", "--");  // no size for dirs

            if (date) Console::WriteLine(" {0}",
                Directory::GetLastAccessTime(inf->ToString()));
        }

        // Now do the files
    }
```

The *Directory::GetDirectories* function returns an array of strings representing the names of the subdirectories. Loop over this list, creating a *DirectoryInfo* object from each entry, and printing out its details. Because there is no size for a directory, simply print a couple of dashes.

10. Process the files by using the same function you defined earlier. Place the following code after the "Now do the files" comment:

```
array<String^> ^files = Directory::GetFiles(di->ToString());
for (int i=0; i<files->Length; i++)
{
    FileInfo ^fi = gcnew FileInfo(files[i]);
    ProcessFile(fi, size, date, atts);
}
```

As you can see, it is simply a case of retrieving a list of file names by using *GetFiles*, creating a *FileInfo* object for each file, and then passing it to the *processFile* function.

11. Build the application, open a console window, and then change to the project's Debug directory. You can then run the application with a suitable command line, such as the following:

```
CppFiles v ..
```

You should see output similar to the following screen shot, listing the files in the parent directory:

Tip If you want to run the application under the Visual Studio debugger, you will need to provide the command-line arguments for the application. To do so, bring up the property pages for the project. In the Configuration Properties section, click the Debugging option, and then, in the Command Arguments edit control, enter the arguments. You can now run the application in debug mode.

Binary I/O

Binary I/O in the .NET Framework uses the *BinaryReader* and *BinaryWriter* classes, which read and write .NET primitive types in binary format. As with the *TextReader* and *TextWriter* classes, the binary I/O classes use an underlying *Stream* object to provide a byte stream. Both *BinaryReader* and *BinaryWriter* have a *BaseStream* property that gives access to the underlying *Stream*.

The *BinaryWriter* class

The following table lists the methods provided by *BinaryWriter*:

Method	Description
Close	Closes the writer and the underlying stream
Dispose	Releases all unmanaged resources used by the writer and, optionally, releases managed resources, as well
Flush	Causes all buffered data to be written to the underlying device
Seek	Sets the seek position within the underlying stream
Write	Writes a value to the stream
Write7BitEncodedInt	Writes a 32-bit integer in a compressed format

If you look at the Visual Studio 2012 documentation, you'll see that the *Write* function has no fewer than 18 overloads for you to cope with when writing the various basic types provided by the .NET Framework. Because not all the types provided by .NET are compliant with the Common Language Specification (CLS), you need to be careful when using some of the *Write* methods if you intend for the data to be read from code written in other .NET languages.

Note The CLS defines types that all .NET languages must support. The signed byte and unsigned integer types are not included in the CLS, so they might not be usable from some .NET languages. The most important of these is Microsoft Visual Basic .NET, which doesn't support any of the non–CLS-compliant types.

The *BinaryReader* class

The following table describes the functions provided by *BinaryReader*:

Method	Description
Close	Closes the writer and the underlying stream
Dispose	Releases all unmanaged resources used by the writer and, optionally, releases managed resources, as well
FillBuffer	Fills the internal buffer with a number of bytes read from the underlying stream
PeekChar	Reads the next character but doesn't advance the seek pointer
Read	Reads one or more bytes or characters from the stream
Read7BitEncodedInt	Reads a 32-bit integer that was written in a compressed format
ReadBoolean	Reads a *Boolean* from the stream
ReadByte, ReadBytes	Reads one or more bytes from the stream
ReadChar, ReadChars	Reads one or more characters from the stream
ReadDecimal	Reads a decimal value from the stream
ReadDouble, ReadSingle	Reads a double or single-precision floating-point value from the stream
ReadInt16, ReadInt32, ReadInt64	Reads an integer type from the stream
ReadSByte	Reads a signed byte from the stream; not CLS-compliant
ReadString	Reads a string from the stream
ReadUInt16, ReadUInt32, ReadUInt64	Reads an unsigned integer type from the stream; not CLS-compliant

Unlike *BinaryWriter*, *BinaryReader* provides separate functions to read each of the basic types.

The exercise that follows shows you how to use the *BinaryReader* and *BinaryWriter* classes to write binary data to a file and read it back. It uses a class, *Customer*, which represents a bank customer who has a name, an account number, and a current balance. The application writes customer details to a file in binary and reads them back.

1. Create a new CLR Console Application project named **CppBinRead**.

2. Add the *using* declaration for *System::IO* to the beginning of the code, like this:

   ```
   using namespace System::IO;
   ```

3. Add a new class definition before the *main* function.

   ```
   // The Customer class
   ref class Customer
   {
       String ^name;
       long accNo;
       double balance;
   ```

```
public:
    // Default constructor
    Customer() : name(nullptr), accNo(0), balance(0.0) { }

    Customer(String ^n, long ac, double bal)
        : name(n), accNo(ac), balance(bal) { }

    // Properties to retrieve instance data
    property String ^Name
    {
        String ^get() { return name; }
    }

    property long AccountNumber
    {
        long get() { return accNo; }
    }

    property double Balance
    {
        double get() { return balance; }
    }


    // Write object
    void Write(BinaryWriter ^bw)
    {
        bw->Write(name);
        bw->Write(accNo);
        bw->Write(balance);
    }

    // Read object
    void Read(BinaryReader ^br)
    {
        name = br->ReadString();
        accNo = br->ReadInt32();
        balance = br->ReadDouble();
    }
};
```

The class has three data members: a *String* for the name, a *long* for the account number, and a *double* for the balance. There are constructors to create default and fully populated objects, and there's a set of read-only properties to allow access to the data members.

The *Read* and *Write* functions use *BinaryReader* and *BinaryWriter* objects to read and write the state of the object in binary format.

4. Add the following code to *main* to check that the user passes in a file name and save the path as a *String*:

```
if (args->Length == 0)
{
    Console::WriteLine("Usage: CppBinRead [path]");
    return 0;
}

String ^path = args[0];
```

This code is very similar to the argument-handling code that has been used in other exercises in this chapter. Note that for simplicity I'm not checking the path for validity, but it's easy— and advisable—to add such a check in a real application.

5. Create some *Customer* objects.

```
// Create some customers
Customer ^c1 = gcnew Customer("Fred Smith", 1234567, 100.0);
Customer ^c2 = gcnew Customer("Jane Doe", 2345678, 1000.0);
Customer ^c3 = gcnew Customer("Gill Evans", 3456789, 500.0);
```

6. To write the objects, you need a *BinaryWriter* and a *FileStream* to do the output to the file.

```
FileStream ^fs = nullptr;
try
{
    // Create a FileStream to write to the file
    fs = gcnew FileStream(path, FileMode::Create, FileAccess::ReadWrite);

    // Create a BinaryWriter
    BinaryWriter ^bw = gcnew BinaryWriter(fs);
}
catch(IOException ^iex)
{
    Console::WriteLine(iex->Message);
    return -1;
}
finally
{
    if (fs != nullptr) fs->Close();
}
```

The *FileStream* writes to a file, creating it if necessary, and the file will be opened with read/ write access because you'll be reading from it later in the application. Again, it's good practice to put the I/O class creation code in a *try* block to catch any problems that might occur. The *finally* block ensures that the file is closed, no matter what happens, but you obviously do not want to do this if creating the *FileStream* failed.

Note You might find that Visual Studio complains that the *FileMode* and *FileAccess* enumerations are ambiguous. You can ignore this because the code will compile perfectly well.

7. Writing the object data to the file is simply a case of calling the *Write* function, passing in a pointer to the *BinaryWriter*. Add the following code at the end of the *try* block:

```
// Write the objects to the file
c1->Write(bw);
c2->Write(bw);
c3->Write(bw);
```

8. Because the file was opened with read/write access, you can now read from the file. To do so, create a *BinaryReader* object and attach it to the same *FileStream*, as shown here:

```
// Create a BinaryReader that reads from the same FileStream
BinaryReader ^br = gcnew BinaryReader(fs);
```

9. Before you can read from a file to which you've written, you have to move the position of the seek pointer.

```
// Move back to the beginning
br->BaseStream->Seek(0, SeekOrigin::Begin);
```

Notice that this code uses the *BaseStream* property and its associated seek pointer to get at the underlying *Stream* object. If you haven't encountered seek pointers before, read the explanation in the following sidebar.

Streams and seek pointers

Every stream in .NET has a *seek pointer* associated with it, which represents the position in the stream at which the next read or write operation will take place. This pointer is automatically repositioned when you use *Stream* class methods to read or write the stream, but it's also possible to move this pointer yourself if you need to (and if you know what you're doing).

The most likely time you'll need to move the pointer is when you open a stream for read/write access. After you've written to the stream, the seek pointer is positioned at the end, ready for the next write. If you want to read from the stream, you'll have to reposition the pointer.

You reposition the pointer by using the *Seek* method of the *Stream* object, giving it an offset in bytes and a position where the offset should be applied. Offsets can be positive or negative, the sign reflecting whether the offset should move toward the start (negative) or end (positive) of the stream. The possible positions are members of the *SeekOrigin* enumeration, and they can be *SeekOrigin::Current* (the current position), *SeekOrigin::Begin* (the start of the *Stream*), or *SeekOrigin::End* (the end of the *Stream*).

---

10. Continue with the project from the previous exercise.

11. Create a new empty *Customer* object and read its details from the file, as follows:

```
Customer ^c4 = gcnew Customer();
c4->Read(br);
Console::WriteLine("Balance for {0} (a/c {1}) is {2}",
        c4->Name, c4->AccountNumber, c4->Balance);
```

The new *Customer* object has all its fields set to default values. The call to *Read* directs it to read its data from the current position in the file.

The obvious potential problem is that the *Read* function will read from wherever the *BinaryReader* is currently positioned. If it isn't at the beginning of a *Customer* object's data, you can expect to get an exception thrown.

Tip If you want to save the state of objects in a real-world application, you wouldn't do it manually like this. The *System::Runtime::Serialization* namespace contains classes that help you save and restore the state of objects in an efficient way.

12. Build and run the application, providing a suitable file name.

Quick reference

To	Do this

Write text to a file.	Create a *StreamWriter* that outputs to a *FileStream* and then use the *Write* and *WriteLine* members of *StreamWriter*. For example:
	
	`FileStream ^fs = gcnew FileStream("foo.txt",`
	`FileMode::Append);`
	`StreamWriter ^sw = gcnew StreamWriter(fs);`
	`sw->WriteLine("Some text");`
	
	Flush and close the *StreamWriter* when you're finished with it. For example:
	
	`sw->Flush();`
	`sw->Close();`

Read text from a file.	Create a *StreamReader* that reads from a *FileStream* and then use the *ReadLine* member of *StreamReader*. For example:
	
	`FileStream ^fs = gcnew FileStream("foo.txt",`
	`FileMode::Open);`
	`StreamReader ^sr = gcnew StreamReader(fs);`
	`String ^line = sr->ReadLine();`

To	Do this

Write binary values to a file.	Create a *BinaryWriter* that outputs to a *FileStream* and then use the overloaded *Write* members of *BinaryWriter*. For example:
	
	``
	FileStream ^fs = gcnew FileStream("bar.dat",
	FileMode::Create);
	BinaryWriter ^bw = gcnew BinaryWriter(fs);
	bw->Write("Some text");
	bw->Write(100.00);
	``

Read binary values from a file.	Create a *BinaryReader* that reads from a *FileStream* and then use the *ReadXxx* members of *BinaryReader*. For example:
	
	``
	FileStream ^fs = gcnew FileStream("foo.txt",
	FileMode::Open);
	BinaryReader ^br = gcnew BinaryReader(fs);
	String ^line = br->ReadString();
	double d = br->ReadDouble();
	``

Find out information about a file.	Use the static functions provided by the *File* class. If you're going to perform several operations on the same file, consider creating a *FileInfo* object and using that, instead.
Find out information about a directory.	Use the static functions provided by the *Directory* class. If you're going to perform several operations on the same file, consider creating a *DirectoryInfo* object and using that, instead.

CHAPTER 17

Reading and writing XML

After completing this chapter, you will be able to:

- Understand why XML is so important to Microsoft .NET.

- Describe the classes that make up the .NET XML namespaces.

- Parse XML files by using *XmlTextReader*.

- Validate XML by using *XmlValidatingReader*.

- Write XML by using *XmlTextWriter*.

- Use the *XmlDocument* class to manipulate XML in memory.

This chapter introduces you to the XML capabilities of the Microsoft .NET Framework. XML plays a major role in .NET as an enabling technology, and the .NET Framework provides full support for just about everything you'll need to do with XML.

Note This chapter assumes that you already know something about XML. You should be comfortable with elements, attributes, validation, namespaces, and all the other paraphernalia that make up XML.

There isn't ample space to give you a complete foundation in XML and the XML technologies, so if you haven't worked with it before, you might want to consult a book such as *XML Step by Step, Second Edition* by Michael Young (Microsoft Press, 2002) before reading further.

XML and .NET

One of the major features of the .NET Framework is that it makes it possible for you to easily produce distributed applications that are language-independent and that will be platform-independent when .NET is ported to other platforms. XML plays a major part in this plan by acting as a simple, portable glue layer that's used to pass data around in distributed applications.

Microsoft has XML-enabled many parts of the .NET Framework, and I'll list a few of the main ones to give you a flavor of where and how they are used:

- It's possible for the results of database queries to be returned as XML, which makes them portable across platforms and languages. It's also possible to interact with databases more fully by using XML.

- Calls can be made to web services by using Simple Object Access Protocol (SOAP), an XML-based protocol for making remote procedure calls.

- Finding out what a web service provider can do for you involves using the Web Service Description Language (WSDL). When you query a service, the description of what services are available and how to call them comes back as XML.

The .NET XML namespaces

The .NET Framework contains a number of namespaces that support XML functionality. The major members are summarized in the following table:

Namespace	Description
System::Xml	The overall namespace for XML support
System::Xml::Linq	Support for querying and modifying XML documents using Language-Integrated Query (LINQ)
System::Xml::Schema	Support for the World Wide Web Consortium (W3C) and the Microsoft XML-Data Reduced (XDR) schemas
System::Xml::Serialization	Supports serializing objects to and from XML
System::Xml::XPath	Supports XPath parsing and evaluation
System::Xml::Xsl	Supports Extensible Stylesheet Language Transformations (XSLT)

This chapter is mainly concerned with the *System::Xml* namespace and touches on some of the capabilities of *System::Xml::Schema*.

The XML processing classes

There are three main classes in the *System::Xml* namespace for processing XML. I'll briefly list their capabilities and functionality here; we'll get into more detailed examination in the rest of the chapter.

- You use an *XmlReader* for fast, non-cached, forward-only parsing. *XmlReader* is an abstract class, and you typically use its static *Create* method to create a reader with the characteristics you want, such as validation. Forward-only parsing means that you parse the document from start to finish, and you can't back up to reparse an earlier part of the document.

Note There are other, concrete reader classes in *System::Xml*, such as *XmlTextReader* and *XmlValidatingReader*, and you might see these being used in older code. It is now recommended that you use the *XmlReader* class, instead.

- *XmlTextWriter* provides a fast, forward-only way to write XML to streams or files. The XML produced conforms to the W3C XML 1.0 specification, complete with namespace support.

- *XmlDocument* implements the W3C Document Object Model (DOM), providing an in-memory representation of an XML document.

Parsing XML by using *XmlReader*

Let's start by looking at how you can parse XML by using the *XmlReader* class. An *XmlReader* provides you with a way to parse XML data that minimizes resource usage by reading forward through the document, recognizing elements as it reads. Very little data is cached in memory, but the forward-only style has two main consequences. The first is that it isn't possible to go back to an earlier point in the file without reading from the beginning again. The second consequence is slightly more subtle: Elements are read and presented to you one by one, with no context. So, if you need to keep track of where an element occurs within the document structure, you'll need to do it yourself. If either of these consequences sounds like limitations to you, you might need to use the *XmlDocument* class, which is discussed in the section "Using *XmlDocument*" later in this chapter.

XmlReader uses a *pull model*, which means that you call a function to get the next node when you're ready. This model is in contrast to the widely used Simple API for XML (SAX) API, which uses a *push model*, meaning that it fires events at callback functions that you provide. The following tables list the main properties and methods of the *XmlReader* class:

Property	Description
AttributeCount	Returns the number of attributes on the current node
Depth	Returns the depth of the current node in the tree
Encoding	Returns the character encoding of the document
EOF	Returns true if the reader is at the end of the stream
HasAttributes	Returns true if the current node has any attributes
HasValue	Returns true if the current node can have a value
IsEmptyElement	Returns true if the current element has no value
Item	Gets the value of an attribute
LocalName	Returns the name of the current element without a namespace prefix
Name	Returns the full name of the current element
NamespaceURI	Gets the namespace URI for the current node

Property	Description
NodeType	Gets the type of the current node
Prefix	Returns the current namespace prefix
ReadState	Returns the state of the reader (for example, closed, at the end of the file, or still reading)
SchemaInfo	Gets the schema information that has been assigned to the current node as a result of schema validation
Settings	Gets the *XmlReaderSettings* object used to create this *XmlReader*
Value	Gets the value for the current node
ValueType	Gets the Common Language Runtime (CLR) type of the current node
XmlLang	Gets the current *xml:lang* scope

Method	Description
Close	Changes the state of the reader to *Closed*, and closes the underlying stream.
Create	Creates a new *XmlReader* instance.
Dispose	Releases the resources used by the reader.
GetAttribute	Gets the value of an attribute.
IsStartElement	Returns true if the current node is a start tag.
LookupNamespace	Resolves a namespace prefix.
MoveToAttribute	Moves to the attribute with a specified index or name.
MoveToContent	Moves to the next content node. This method will skip over non-content nodes, such as those of type *ProcessingInstruction*, *DocumentType*, *Comment*, *Whitespace*, or *SignificantWhitespace*.
MoveToContentAsync	Moves to the next content node asynchronously.
MoveToElement	Moves to the element that contains the current attribute.
MoveToFirstAttribute, *MoveToNextAttribute*	Iterates over the attributes for an element.
Read	Reads the next node from the stream.
ReadAsync	Reads the next node asynchronously.
ReadAttributeValue	Processes attribute values that contain entities.
ReadContentAs, *ReadContentAsInt*, *ReadContentAsString*...	A set of functions that read text content encoded in various forms.
ReadElementContentAs, *ReadElementContentAsInt*...	A set of functions that read element content encoded in various forms.
ReadContentAsAsync	Reads the content of an object asynchronously.
ReadElementString	Reads the content of an element or a text node as a string.
ReadInnerXml, *ReadOuterXml*	Read content, including markup. *ReadInnerXml* only includes children, whereas *ReadOuterXml* includes the current node. Note that there are async versions of these methods (*ReadInnerXmlAsync*, *ReadOuterXmlAsync*).

Method	Description
ReadStartElement, ReadEndElement	Read start and end elements.
ReadString	Reads the content of an element as a string.
ReadToDescendant	Reads to a named descendant element.
ReadToFollowing	Reads until it finds a named element.
ReadToNextSibling	Advanced the reader to the next named sibling element.
Skip	Skips children of the current element.
SkipAsync	Skips children asynchronously.

The most important functions in the second of these tables are *Create*, which you use to create a reader object, and those beginning with *Read*, which instruct the reader to fetch data from the document. If you use *Read* to get the next node, you can use the *NodeType* property to find out what you have. You'll get one of the members of the *XmlNodeType* enumeration, whose members are listed in the following table:

Node type	Description
Attribute	An attribute, for example, *type=hardback*
CDATA	A CDATA section
Comment	An XML comment
Document	The document object, representing the root of the XML tree
DocumentFragment	A fragment of XML that isn't a document in itself
DocumentType	A document type declaration
Element, EndElement	The start and end of an XML element
Entity, EndEntity	The start and end of an entity declaration
EntityReference	An entity reference (for example, <)
None	Used if the node type is queried when no node has been read
Notation	A notation entry in a Document Type Definition (DTD)
ProcessingInstruction	An XML processing instruction
SignificantWhitespace	White space in a mixed content model document, or when *xml:space=preserve* has been set
Text	The text content of an element
Whitespace	White space between markup
XmlDeclaration	The XML declaration at the top of a document

Creating *XmlReaders*

Prior to version 2.0, *System::Xml* contained several concrete reader classes such as *XmlTextReader* and *XmlValidatingReader*. These all did the same task—reading XML—but were configured differently. It is now recommended that you use the *XmlReader* class, instead, which can create configured readers of various types.

You do this by using an *XmlReaderSettings* object, which holds a collection of settings that defines a reader configuration. Here's an example of how to create a basic reader:

```
XmlReaderSettings ^settings = gcnew XmlReaderSettings();
settings->ConformanceLevel = ConformanceLevel::Fragment;
settings->IgnoreWhitespace = true;
settings->IgnoreComments = true;
XmlReader ^rdr = XmlReader::Create("data.xml", settings);
```

The *XmlReaderSettings* class

The following table lists some of the most commonly used configuration properties along with their default values:

Property	Description	Default
CheckCharacters	Throw an exception if invalid characters are read	True
ConformanceLevel	Is conformance checked at document or fragment level?	Document
DtdProcessing	Determines whether DTDs will be processed	Prohibit (presence of a DTD will cause an exception)
IgnoreComments	Determines whether comments will be ignored	False
IgnoreProcessingInstructions	Determines whether processing instructions will be ignored	False
IgnoreWhitespace	Determines whether ignorable white space will be ignored	False
LineNumberOffset	Sets the point at which the *LineNumber* counter begins counting	0
LinePositionOffset	Sets the point at which the *LinePosition* counter begins counting	0
MaxCharactersInDocument	Sets the maximum size of the document, with 0 denoting no limit	0
Schemas	The set of schemas associated with this reader	An empty *XmlSchemaSet* object
ValidationFlags	Flags indicating the schema validation settings	*ProcessIdentityConstraints* and *AllowXmlAttributes* are enabled
ValidationType	The type of validation to be used	None
XmlResolver	Sets the XML resolver to be used for entities, DTDs, and schemas	A new *XmlResolver* object

Here's how you can combine these for some common scenarios:

- If the input must be a well-formed XML document, set *ConformanceLevel* to *Document*.

- If the input is a well-formed part of an XML document, set *ConformanceLevel* to *Fragment*.

- If the input contains entities or other features defined in a DTD, set *DtdProcessing* to *Parse*.

- If you want to validate the input against a DTD, set *ValidationType* to *DTD* and set *DtdProcessing* to *Parse*.

- If you want to validate the input against one or more schemas, set *ValidationType* to *Schema* and set *Schemas* to an *XmlSchemaSet* object that references the schema set.

The following exercise shows you how to read an XML document by using an *XmlReader*. Following is the sample XML document used by this exercise and the other exercises in this chapter. This document lists details of three volcanoes and contains many common XML constructs:

```xml
<?xml version="1.0" ?>
<!-- Volcano data -->
<geology>
  <volcano name="Erebus">
    <location>Ross Island, Antarctica</location>
    <height value="3794" unit="m"/>
    <type>stratovolcano</type>
    <eruption>constant activity</eruption>
    <magma>basanite to trachyte</magma>
  </volcano>
  <volcano name="Hekla">
    <location>Iceland</location>
    <type>stratovolcano</type>
    <height value="1491" unit="m"/>
    <eruption>1970</eruption>
    <eruption>1980</eruption>
    <eruption>1991</eruption>
    <magma>calcalkaline</magma>
    <comment>The type is actually intermediate between crater row
    and stratovolcano types</comment>
  </volcano>
  <volcano name="Mauna Loa">
    <location>Hawaii</location>
    <type>shield</type>
    <height value="13677" unit="ft"/>
    <eruption>1984</eruption>
    <magma>basaltic</magma>
  </volcano>
</geology>
```

1. Start Microsoft Visual Studio 2012 and create a new CLR Console Application project named **CppXmlReader**.

2. Add the following line to the top of CppXmlReader.cpp:

   ```
   using namespace System::Xml;
   ```

   It's easier to use the classes if you include a *using* directive for the *System::Xml* namespace.

3. Add this code to the beginning of the *main* function to check the number of arguments and save the path:

```
// Check for required arguments
if (args->Length == 0)
{
    Console::WriteLine("Usage: CppXmlReader [path]");
    return -1;
}

String ^path = gcnew String(args[0]);
```

4. Now that you have the path, create an *XmlReader* to parse the file. We start with a simple parser, which requires a full XML document rather than a fragment but doesn't do any validation.

```
try
{
    // Create the settings object
    XmlReaderSettings ^settings = gcnew XmlReaderSettings();
    settings->ConformanceLevel = ConformanceLevel::Document;

    // Create the reader...
    XmlReader ^rdr = XmlReader::Create(path, settings);
}
catch (Exception ^ex)
{
    Console::WriteLine(ex->Message);
}
```

The *settings* object is set to require a full document and to ignore any comment lines. Because the *XmlReader* constructor takes the name of the document you want to parse, it's a good idea to catch exceptions here because several things can go wrong at this stage, including passing the constructor a bad path name. You can build and run the application from the command line at this stage if you want to check that the file opens correctly, or you can use the Debugging page of the project's properties to enter the file name and run it from within Visual Studio.

Keep in mind that *XmlReader* isn't limited to reading from files. You can overload *Create* to take XML input from URLs, streams, strings, and other *XmlReader* objects.

5. Parsing the file simply means making repeated calls to the *Read* function until the parser runs out of XML to read. The simplest way to do this is to put a call to *Read* inside a *while* loop. Add this code to the end of the code inside the *try* block:

```
// Read nodes
while (rdr->Read())
{
    // do something with the data
}
```

The *Read* function returns true or false depending on whether there are any more nodes to read.

6. Each call to *Read* positions the *XmlReader* on a new node, and you can then query the *NodeType* property to determine the type of node with which you are dealing. Add the following code, which identifies several of the most common node types:

```
// Read nodes
while (rdr->Read())
{
    switch (rdr->NodeType)
    {
    case XmlNodeType::XmlDeclaration:
        Console::WriteLine("-> XML declaration");
        break;
    case XmlNodeType::Document:
        Console::WriteLine("-> Document node");
        break;
    case XmlNodeType::Element:
        Console::WriteLine("-> Element node, name={0}", rdr->Name);
        break;
    case XmlNodeType::EndElement:
        Console::WriteLine("-> End element node, name={0}",
                            rdr->Name);
        break;
    case XmlNodeType::Text:
        Console::WriteLine("-> Text node, value={0}", rdr->Value);
        break;
    case XmlNodeType::Comment:
        Console::WriteLine("-> Comment node, name={0}, value={1}",
                            rdr->Name, rdr->Value);
        break;
    case XmlNodeType::Whitespace:
        break;
    default:
        Console::WriteLine("** Unknown node type");
        break;
    }
}
```

Every time a new node is read, the *switch* statement checks its type against members of the *XmlNodeType* enumeration. I haven't included the cases for every possible node type, just those that occur in the sample document.

Observe that the *Name* and *Value* properties are used for some node types. Whether a node has a *Name* and a *Value* depends on the node type. For example, elements have names and can have values, and comments have a value (the comment text) but not names. Processing instructions normally have both names and values.

Also notice that nodes of type *XmlNodeType::Whitespace* are simply discarded. The volcanoes. xml file contains plenty of white space to make it readable to humans, but the CppXmlReader application isn't really interested in white space, so the application prints nothing when it encounters a white space node.

7. Build the application and run it from the command line, giving the name of an XML file:

```
CppXmlTextReader volcanoes.xml
```

The first few lines of the output should look like this:

```
-> XML declaration
-> Comment node, name=, value= Volcano data
-> Element node, name=geology
-> Element node, name=volcano
-> Element node, name=location
-> Text node, value=Ross Island, Antarctica
-> End element node, name=location
-> Element node, name=height
-> Element node, name=type
-> Text node, value=stratovolcano
-> End element node, name=type
-> Element node, name=eruption
-> Text node, value=constant activity
```

The first node is the XML declaration at the beginning of the document, which is followed by a comment whose value is the comment text. Each XML element in the document produces a matching pair of *Element* and *EndElement* nodes, with the content of a node represented by a nested *Text* node.

You can see that the nodes are presented to you in linear sequence, so if you want to keep track of the hierarchical structure of the document, you're going to have to put code in place to do that.

Verifying well-formed XML

XML that is correctly constructed is called *well-formed XML*, which means that elements are correctly nested and that every element tag has a matching end-element tag. If the *XmlReader* encounters badly formed XML, it will throw an *XmlException* to alert you as to what it thinks is wrong. As with all parsing errors, the place where it's reported might be some distance from the actual location of the error.

Handling attributes

XML elements can include attributes, which consist of name/value pairs and are always string data. In the sample XML file, the *volcano* element has a *name* attribute, and the *height* element has *value* and *unit* attributes. To process the attributes on an element, add code to the *Element* case in the *switch* statement so that it looks like this:

```
case XmlNodeType::Element:
    Console::WriteLine("-> Element node, name={0}", rdr->Name);
    if (rdr->AttributeCount > 0)
    {
        Console::Write("   ");
        while (rdr->MoveToNextAttribute())
            Console::Write(" {0}={1}", rdr->Name, rdr->Value);
        Console::WriteLine();
    }
    break;
```

The *AttributeCount* property indicates how many attributes an element has, and the *MoveToNext Attribute* method makes it possible for you to iterate over the collection of elements, each of which has a name and a value. Alternatively, you can use the *MoveToAttribute* function to position the reader on a particular attribute by specifying either a name or a zero-based index.

Attributes are read along with the element node of which they're a part. When reading attributes, you can use the *MoveToElement* method to position the reader back to the parent element. When you run the code, you should see output similar to this for nodes that have attributes:

```
-> Element node, name=height
   value=13677 unit=ft
```

Parsing XML with validation

There are a number of ways to validate the correctness of XML documents, and *XmlReader* supports the two most common standards: DTDs and W3C schemas.

The following exercise modifies the application to validate the XML as it's parsed. To perform validation, you need to have a DTD or a schema against which to validate. Here's a DTD for the volcano XML data (this is in a file named geology.dtd):

```
<!ELEMENT geology (volcano)+>
<!ELEMENT volcano (location,height,type,eruption+,magma,comment?)>
<!ATTLIST volcano name CDATA #IMPLIED>
<!ELEMENT location (#PCDATA)>
<!ELEMENT height EMPTY>
<!ATTLIST height value CDATA #IMPLIED
                 unit CDATA #IMPLIED>
<!ELEMENT type (#PCDATA)>
<!ELEMENT eruption (#PCDATA)>
<!ELEMENT magma (#PCDATA)>
<!ELEMENT comment (#PCDATA)>
```

Note I've used a DTD for simplicity, but a schema can be used in exactly the same way.

Edit the volcanoes.xml file to add a *DOCTYPE* reference at the top of the file.

```
<?xml version="1.0" ?>
<!DOCTYPE geology SYSTEM "geology.dtd">
<!-- Volcano data -->
```

If you check the sample XML document against the DTD, you'll notice that there's a problem. The element ordering for the second volcano, Hekla, is location-type-height rather than the location-height-type order demanded by the DTD. So, when you parse this XML with validation, you'd expect a validation error from the parser.

1. Continue with the project from the previous exercise.

2. Add a *using* declaration to the top of the CppXmlReader.cpp, as shown here:

    ```
    using namespace System::Xml::Schema;
    ```

    Some of the classes and enumerations are part of the *System::Xml::Schema* namespace, and the inclusion of the *using* declaration makes it easier to refer to them in code.

3. Add another property to the *XmlReaderSettings* to cause the reader to parse the DTD. If you do not set this, parsing will fail because the default setting prohibits DTD parsing.

    ```
    settings->DtdProcessing = DtdProcessing::Parse;
    ```

4. If you already have a reader, you can add validation by chaining two readers together, as demonstrated in the following:

    ```
    // Create settings for DTD validation
    XmlReaderSettings ^validationSettings = gcnew XmlReaderSettings();
    validationSettings->ValidationType = ValidationType::DTD;
    validationSettings->DtdProcessing = DtdProcessing::Parse;

    // Create a validating reader and wrap the existing one
    XmlReader ^validatingReader = XmlReader::Create(rdr, validationSettings);
    ```

    The constructor for the second reader takes a reference to the initial reader, which it uses to perform the basic parsing tasks. Notice how you must enable DTD parsing in the second settings object as well as the first.

5. Edit all the code that parses the XML to use the new reader, *validatingReader*, rather than the original reader, *rdr*.

6. If you now build and run the application, it should throw an exception when it finds the invalid element ordering in the document.

    ```
    The element 'volcano' has invalid child element 'type'. List of possible elements
    expected: 'height'.
    ```

You can improve on this error handling by installing an event handler. The parser fires a *ValidationEvent* whenever it finds something to report to you, and if you install a handler for this event, you'll be able to handle the validation errors yourself and take appropriate action.

7. Event handler functions must be members of a managed class, so create a new class to host a static handler function. Add this code before the *main* function:

```
// Validation handler class
ref class ValHandler
{
public:
    static void ValidationHandler(Object ^sender, ValidationEventArgs ^args)
    {
        Console::WriteLine("Validation Event: {0}", args->Message);
    }
};
```

The *ValHandler* class contains one static member, which is the handler for a *ValidationEvent*. As usual, the handler has two arguments: a pointer to the object that fired the event, and an argument object. In this case, the handler is passed a *ValidationEventArgs* object that contains details about the parser validation error. This sample code isn't doing anything except printing the error message, but in practice, you'd decide what action to take based on the *Severity* property of the *ValidationEventArgs* object.

8. Link up the handler to the settings object in the usual way.

```
// Set the handler
validationSettings->ValidationEventHandler +=
        gcnew ValidationEventHandler(&ValHandler::ValidationHandler);
```

Ensure that you set up the handler before the call to *XmlReader::Create*; otherwise, the reader will not know about the validation.

9. Build and run the application. This time, you won't get the exception message, but you will see the messages printed out from the event handler as it finds validation problems.

10. Correct the ordering of the elements in the XML file and then run the application again. You shouldn't see any validation messages this time through.

Writing XML by using *XmlTextWriter*

If you've read about XML, you're probably aware that the W3C XML 1 specification describes the serialized form of XML—the way that XML appears when rendered as text—complete with angle brackets, start tags and end tags, and namespace and XML declarations. If you have some data that you want to write as XML, it isn't hard to do it manually, but the .NET Framework provides you with the *XmlTextWriter* class to help with a lot of the formatting chores such as keeping track of indentation and inserting namespace information everywhere it's needed. The tables that follow list the properties and methods of the *XmlTextWriter class, respectively*:

Property	Description
BaseStream	Gets the underlying stream object
Formatting	Determines whether the XML is output with indentation. The default is *Formatting::None*.
Indentation	Determines the indentation level. The default is 2.
IndentChar	Represents the indentation character. The default is a space.
Namespaces	Determines whether to support namespaces. The default is true.
QuoteChar	Represents the character used to quote attribute values. The value must be a single or double quotation mark. The default is double.
Settings	Gets the *XmlWriterSettings* object used when creaing this *XmlWriter* instance
WriteState	Gets the state of the writer (discussed in the following text).
XmlLang	Gets a string that represents the value of the *xml:lang* attribute. The value will be null if there's no *xml:lang* attribute in the current scope.
XmlSpace	Represents the value of the *xml:space* attribute.

The state of the writer indicates what the writer is doing at the point where you query the property. It will report one of the values from the *WriteState* enumeration, such as *Start* (no write methods have been called yet), *Closed*, *Attribute* (it is writing an attribute), or *Content* (it is writing element content).

Method	Description
Close	Closes the writer and the underlying stream
Flush	Flushes whatever is in the buffer
LookupPrefix	Returns the current namespace prefix, if any
WriteAttributes	Writes out a set of attributes
WriteAttributeString	Writes an attribute with a specified value
WriteBase64, WriteBinHex	Encodes binary bytes as Base64 or BinHex, and writes the text

Method	Description
WriteCData	Writes text as a CDATA section
WriteCharEntity	Writes a Unicode character as a hexadecimal character entity
WriteChars	Writes text one buffer at a time
WriteComment	Writes text as an XML comment
WriteDocType	Writes a DOCTYPE declaration
WriteElementString	Writes an element
WriteEntityRef	Writes an entity reference
WriteFullEndElement	Writes a full end-element tag
WriteName	Writes a name, making sure it's a valid XML name
WriteNode	Writes an entire node, with all its content
WriteProcessingInstruction	Writes an XML processing instruction
WriteQualifiedName	Writes an XML qualified name
WriteRaw	Writes raw markup manually
WriteStartAttribute, WriteEndAttribute	Writes the start and end of an attribute
WriteStartDocument, WriteEndDocument	Writes the start and end of a document
WriteStartElement, WriteEndElement	Writes the start and end of an element
WriteString	Writes text
WriteValue	Writes a value
WriteWhitespace	Writes white space

Note There are asynchronous versions of many of these methods, such as *FlushAsync*, *WriteAttributesAsync*, and *WriteCommentAsync*.

As you can see from the preceding table, to write elements, attributes, and documents, you need to call a start and an end function. When using *XmlTextWriter*, you don't simply write an element; you write the start tag, write its content, and then write the end tag. Therefore, you have to keep track of where you are in the document to ensure that you call the correct end functions at the correct time.

This exercise shows you how to write a simple XML document by using *XmlTextWriter. It* uses most of the major member functions of the class.

1. Start a new CLR Console Application project named **CppXmlWriter**.

2. Add the following line to the top of CppXmlWriter.cpp, which will help you access the namespace members:

```
using namespace System::Xml;
```

3. Add this code to the start of the *main* function to check the number of arguments and save the path:

```
// Check for required arguments
if (args->Length == 0)
{
    Console::WriteLine("Usage: CppXmlWriter [path]");
    return -1;
}

String ^path = gcnew String(args[0]);
```

4. Create an *XmlTextWriter* by adding the following code (which is very similar to the code used to create the *XmlReader* in the previous exercise):

```
try
{
    // Create the writer...
    // Use the default encoding
    XmlTextWriter ^writer = gcnew XmlTextWriter(path, nullptr);
}
catch (Exception ^ex)
{
    Console::WriteLine(ex->Message);
}
```

The writer is created by specifying the path for the new file and the character encoding that should be used. Passing a null pointer means that the writer will use the default UTF-8 encoding; this is a good default choice.

> **Note** If you want to use another encoding, such as UTF-7 or ASCII, you can specify a *System::Text::Encoding* object of the appropriate type.

5. Let's write the XML declaration to the file. Add the following lines to the end of the code inside the *try* block:

```
// Set the formatting
writer->Formatting = Formatting::Indented;

// Write the standard document start
writer->WriteStartDocument();

// Flush and close
writer->Flush();
writer->Close();
```

XmlTextWriter can produce output that employs indents or that has no formatting. The default is no formatting, so you need to set the *Formatting* property if you want indentation. The defaults for the indentation character (a space) and the indentation level (two characters) are usually quite acceptable.

WriteStartDocument produces a standard XML declaration. To ensure that all the text is output to the file, you should call *Flush* and *Close* before exiting.

6. Write the root element to the document, as shown here:

```
// Write the standard document start
writer->WriteStartDocument();

// Start the root element
writer->WriteStartElement("geology");

// Close the root element
writer->WriteEndElement();
```

7. The content of the root element will go between the calls to *WriteStartElement* and *WriteEndElement*. There isn't any content in this case, but you still need both calls. Build and run the application at this stage, giving the name of the XML file.

```
CppXmlWriter test1.xml
```

You'll see that the application writes an empty root element.

```
<?xml version="1.0"?>
<geology />
```

8. To see how some of the other methods of *XmlTextWriter* are used, add one of the volcano entries to the root element, as illustrated in the following:

```
// Start the root element
writer->WriteStartElement("geology");

// Start the volcano element
writer->WriteStartElement("volcano");

// Do the name attribute
writer->WriteAttributeString("name", "Mount St.Helens");

// Write the location element
writer->WriteStartElement("location");
writer->WriteString("Washington State, USA");
writer->WriteEndElement();

// Write the height element
writer->WriteStartElement("height");
writer->WriteAttributeString("value", "9677");
writer->WriteAttributeString("unit", "ft");
writer->WriteEndElement();

// Write the type element
writer->WriteStartElement("type");
writer->WriteString("stratovolcano");
writer->WriteEndElement();
```

```
// Write the eruption elements
writer->WriteStartElement("eruption");
writer->WriteString("1857");
writer->WriteEndElement();

writer->WriteStartElement("eruption");
writer->WriteString("1980");
writer->WriteEndElement();

// Write the magma element
writer->WriteStartElement("magma");
writer->WriteString("basalt, andesite and dacite");
writer->WriteEndElement();

// Close the volcano element
writer->WriteEndElement();
// Close the root element
writer->WriteEndElement();
```

I've left in the root element code so that you can see how everything nests. Adding extra elements isn't hard, but it's rather long-winded, and you have to be careful to nest all the calls correctly.

9. Build and run the application, providing it with a suitable file name. The file should contain XML that looks very much like this:

```
<?xml version="1.0"?>
<geology>
  <volcano name="Mount St.Helens">
    <location>Washington State, USA</location>
    <height value="9677" unit="ft" />
    <type>stratovolcano</type>
    <eruption>1857</eruption>
    <eruption>1980</eruption>
    <magma>basalt, andesite and dacite</magma>
  </volcano>
</geology>
```

You can see how all the elements contain their attributes, how they are nested correctly, and how everything is properly indented.

Using *XmlDocument*

Our handling of XML so far has been forward-only, which is very light on resource usage but isn't so useful if you need to move around within the XML document. The *XmlDocument* class is based on the W3C DOM, and it's the class that you want to use if you need to browse, modify, or create an XML document.

What is the W3C DOM?

The DOM is a specification for an API by which programmers can manipulate XML held in memory. The DOM specification is language-independent, and bindings are available for many programming languages, including C++. *XmlDocument* is based on the DOM, with Microsoft extensions.

Because *XmlDocument* works with XML in memory, it has several advantages and disadvantages when compared with the *XmlReader* forward-only approach.

By reading the entire document and building a tree in memory, you gain the advantage of having access to all the elements and can wander through the document at will. You can also edit the document by changing, adding, or deleting nodes, and you can write the changed document back to hard disk again. It's even possible to create an entire XML document from scratch in memory and write it out—serialize it—which is a useful alternative to using *XmlTextWriter*.

The main disadvantage is that all of an XML document is held in memory at one time, so the amount of memory needed by your application is going to be proportional to the size of the XML document with which you're working. Therefore, if you're working with a very large XML document—or have limited memory—you might not be able to use *XmlDocument*.

The *XmlDocument* class

The *XmlDocument* class has a number of properties, methods, and events, the most important of which are summarized in the following three tables:

Property	Description
Attributes	Gets an *XmlAttributeCollection* representing the attributes of a node.
ChildNodes	Gets all the child nodes of a node.
DocumentElement	Returns the root element for the document.
DocumentType	Returns the DOCTYPE node, if one is present.
FirstChild, LastChild	Gets the first or last child nodes of a node.
HasChildNodes	Value is true if a node has child nodes.
InnerText	Returns the concatenated values of a node and all its child nodes.
InnerXml	Gets or sets the markup representing the children of the current node.
IsReadOnly	Gets a value indicating whether the current node is read-only.
Item	Gets the first child with the specified name.
LocalName	Gets the name of the current node without a namespace prefix.
Name	Gets the fully qualified name of the current node.
NamespaceURI	Gets the namespace URI associated with the current node.
NextSibling, PreviousSibling	Gets the node immediately following or preceding this node.

Property	Description
NodeType	Gets the type of the current node. The node type will be one of the *XmlNodeType* values listed in the table on page XXX.
OuterXml	Gets the markup representing the current node and its children
OwnerDocument	Gets the *XmlDocument* to which the current node belongs.
ParentNode	Gets the parent of a node.
Prefix	Gets or sets the namespace prefix associated with this node.
PreserveWhitespace	Determines whether white space should be regarded as significant. The default is false.
Schemas	Gets the collection of schemas associated with this document.
Value	Gets or sets the value of a node.

Method	Description
AppendChild	Appends a child node to a node
Clone, CloneNode	Creates a duplicate of the current node
CreateAttribute	Creates an *XmlAttribute* object
CreateCDataSection	Creates an *XmlCDataSection* object
CreateComment	Creates an *XmlComment* object
CreateDefaultAttribute	Creates a default *XmlAttribute* object
CreateDocumentType	Creates an *XmlDocumentType* object
CreateElement	Creates an *XmlElement* object
CreateEntityReference	Creates an *XmlEntityReference* object
CreateNavigator	Creates an *XPathNavigator* for navigating the object and its contents
CreateNode	Creates a plain *XmlNode*
CreateProcessingInstruction	Creates an *XmlProcessingInstruction* object
CreateTextNode	Creates an *XmlText* object
CreateWhitespace	Create an *XmlWhitespace* object
CreateXmlDeclaration	Creates an *XmlDeclaration* object
GetElementById	Returns an XML element with the specified *ID* attribute
GetElementsByTagName	Gets a list of descendant nodes matching a name
GetEnumerator	Get an enumerator for the children of the current node
ImportNode	Imports a node from another document
InsertBefore, InsertAfter	Inserts a node before or after a reference node

Method	Description
Load	Loads XML from a file, a URL, a stream, or an *XmlReader* object
LoadXml	Loads XML from a string
ReadNode	Creates an *XmlNode* based on the current position of an *XmlReader*
RemoveAll	Removes all child nodes and attributes from a node
RemoveChild, ReplaceChild	Removes or replaces a child node
Save	Saves the XML document to a file, a stream, or an *XmlWriter*
SelectNodes, SelectSingleNode	Select one or more nodes matching an XPath expression
Validate	Validates the document against a collection of schemas
WriteContentTo	Saves all the children of the *XmlDocument* node to an *XmlWriter*
WriteTo	Saves the *XmlDocument* to an *XmlWriter*

Event	Description
NodeChanged	Fired when the value of a node has been changed
NodeChanging	Fired when the value of a node is about to be changed
NodeInserted	Fired when a node has been inserted
NodeInserting	Fired when a node is about to be inserted
NodeRemoved	Fired when a node has been removed
NodeRemoving	Fired when a node is about to be removed

The *XmlNode* class

You'll notice a lot of references to nodes in the preceding tables. The DOM tree that an *XmlDocument* object builds in memory is composed of nodes, each of which is an object of a class that inherits from the abstract *XmlNode* base class. Just about everything in an XML document is represented by a node. For example:

- Elements are represented by the *XmlElement* class.

- Attributes are represented by the *XmlAttribute* class.

- The text content of elements is represented by the *XmlText* class.

- Comments are represented by the *XmlComment* class.

The *XmlNode* class provides common functionality for all these node types. Because this functionality is so important when working with *XmlDocument*, I've listed the properties and methods of *XmlNode* in the following two tables:

Property	Description
Attributes	Gets the collection of attributes for the node.
ChildNodes	Gets all the children of the node as an *XmlNodeList*.
FirstChild, LastChild	Gets a pointer to the first and last children of the node.
HasChildNodes	Value is true if a node has child nodes.
InnerText	Represents the concatenated values of the node and all its children.
InnerXml, OuterXml	*InnerXml* gets or sets the markup representing the children of the node. *OuterXml* includes the node and its children.
IsReadOnly	Returns the read-only status of the node.
Item	Gets a child element by name.
Name, LocalName	The name of the node, with or without namespace information.
NextSibling, PreviousSibling	Gets a pointer to the node immediately following or preceding a node.
NodeType	Returns an *XmlNodeType* value representing the type of the node.
OwnerDocument	Gets a pointer to the *XmlDocument* that owns this node.
ParentNode	Gets the node's parent node.
Prefix	Gets or sets the namespace prefix for the node.
Value	Gets or sets the value of the node. What the value represents depends on the node type.

Method	Description
AppendChild, PrependChild	Adds a child to the end or beginning of a node's list of child nodes
Clone, CloneNode	Clones a node
CreateNavigator	Creates an *XPathNavigator* for navigating the object and its contents
GetEnumerator	Returns an enumerator for the collection of child nodes
GetNamespaceOfPrefix	Returns the namespace URI for the namespace prefix of this node
GetPrefixOfNamespace	Gets the prefix associated with the namespace of this node
InsertAfter, InsertBefore	Inserts a node after or before a specified node
Normalize	Normalizes the tree so that there are no adjacent *XmlText* nodes
RemoveAll	Removes all children and attributes of a node
RemoveChild	Removes a specified child node

Method	Description
ReplaceChild	Replaces a specified child node
SelectNodes	Selects a list of nodes matching an XPath expression
SelectSingleNode	Selects the first node that matches an XPath expression
Supports	Tests whether the underlying DOM implementation supports a particular feature
WriteContentTo	Saves all children of the current node
WriteTo	Saves the current node

Perhaps the most important descendant of *XmlNode* is *XmlElement*, which represents an element within a document. This class adds a number of methods to *XmlNode*, most of which are concerned with getting, setting, and removing attributes.

The following exercise shows you how to use *XmlDocument*. You'll write an application that reads the volcano XML file into memory and then inserts a new element into the structure.

1. Start a new CLR Console Application project named **CppDom**.

2. Add the following line to the top of CppDom.cpp:

```
using namespace System::Xml;
```

3. Add this code to the start of the *main* function to check the number of arguments and save the path:

```
// Check for required arguments
if (args->Length == 0)
{
    Console::WriteLine("Usage: CppXmlWriter path");
    return -1;
}

String ^path = gcnew String(args[0]);
```

4. Create a new managed class named *XmlBuilder* and give it an *XmlDocument^* as a data member:

```
ref class XmlBuilder
{
    XmlDocument ^doc;
};
```

You need a managed class because it will be necessary to pass the *XmlDocument* handle around between functions. You could pass the pointer explicitly in the argument list of each function, but it's better to make it a member of a class so that it can be accessed by all the member functions.

5. Add a constructor that creates an *XmlDocument* object, and instruct it to load the file that was specified on the command line.

```
public:
    XmlBuilder(String ^path)
    {
        // Create the XmlDocument
        doc = gcnew XmlDocument();

        // Load the data
        doc->Load(path);
        Console::WriteLine("Document loaded");
    }
```

Unlike *XmlReader*, the *XmlDocument* class reads and parses the file when it's constructed. Note that you're not catching exceptions here. Something might go wrong when opening or parsing the file, but exceptions are left for the caller to handle.

6. Add some code to the *main* function to create an *XmlBuilder* object. Ensure that you are prepared to handle any exceptions that occur.

```
// Create a Builder and get it to read the file
try
{
    XmlBuilder ^builder = gcnew XmlBuilder(path);
}
catch(Exception ^ex)
{
    Console::WriteLine(ex->Message);
}
```

7. Try building and running the application at this point. First copy the volcanoes.xml and geology.dtd files you created earlier from the debug folder into the project folder. If you see the "Document loaded" message displayed when you run the application, you know that the document has been loaded and parsed.

The next step is to access the nodes in the tree. The current XML document contains three volcano elements; what you'll do is find the second element and insert a new element after it. There are a number of ways in which you could do this, but for now, I'll just illustrate one method. It isn't the most efficient way to do the job, but it does show how to use several *XmlDocument* and *XmlNode* methods and properties.

8. Continue working on the CppDom project. Start working with the tree by getting a handle to its root. Because you'll use this root several times, add an *XmlNode^* member to the *XmlBuilder* class, like this:

```
private:
    XmlNode ^root;
```

9. Add the following code to the constructor to get the root node:

```
// Get the root of the tree
root = doc->DocumentElement;
```

DocumentElement returns you the top of the DOM tree. Note that this is not the root element of the XML document, which is one level down.

10. You also need to get the list of child nodes for the root. Because you'll be using this list again, add an *XmlNodeList^* member to the class to hold the list.

```
private:
    XmlNodeList ^nodelist;
```

11. The code that follows shows how you can get a list of child nodes and iterate over it. Add this to the constructor:

```
// get the child node list
nodelist = doc->ChildNodes;
IEnumerator ^ie = nodelist->GetEnumerator();

while (ie->MoveNext() == true)
    Console::WriteLine("Child: {0}",
        (dynamic_cast<XmlNode^>(ie->Current))->Name);
```

The *ChildNodes* property returns a list of child nodes as an *XmlNodeList*. The *XmlNodeList* is a typical .NET collection class, which means that you can get an enumerator to iterate over the nodes. The code iterates over the child nodes, printing the name of each. Note that because *Current* returns an *Object* handle, it has to be cast to an *XmlNode^* before you can use the *Name* property.

12. The *IEnumerator* interface is part of the *System::Collections* namespace, so you need to add the following code near the top of the CppDom.cpp file, after the other *using* directives:

```
using namespace System::Collections;
```

13. If you run this code on the volcanoes.xml file, you should see output similar to the following:

```
Document loaded
Child: xml
Child: geology
Child: #comment
Child: geology
```

The root of the tree has four child nodes: the XML declaration, the DOCTYPE declaration, a comment, and the root node.

Note After you've verified the existence of the child nodes, you can remove the lines that declare and use the enumerator because you won't need them again. Be certain that you don't remove the line that assigns the value to *nodelist*!

14. Now that you have the root of the tree, you need to find the root element of the XML by using a public class member function named *ProcessChildNodes*, as shown here:

```
void ProcessChildNodes()
{
    // Declare an enumerator
    IEnumerator ^ie = nodelist->GetEnumerator();

    while (ie->MoveNext() == true)
    {
        // Get a handle to the node
        XmlNode ^node = dynamic_cast<XmlNode^>(ie->Current);

        // See if it is the root
        if (node->NodeType == XmlNodeType::Element &&
            node->Name->Equals("geology"))
        {
            Console::WriteLine("  Found the root");
            ProcessRoot(node);
        }
    }
}
```

The function creates an enumerator and iterates over the children of the root node. The root XML element will be of type *XmlNodeType::Element* and will have the name *geology*.

15. After you've identified that element, the public function *ProcessRoot* is then used to process the children of the root XML element.

```
void ProcessRoot(XmlNode ^rootNode)
{
    XmlNode ^node =
        dynamic_cast<XmlNode^>(rootNode->ChildNodes->Item(1));

    // Create a new volcano element
    XmlElement ^newVolcano = CreateNewVolcano();

    // Link it in
    root->InsertBefore(newVolcano, node);
}
```

The function is passed in the root node. I know that the file I'm working with has more than two volcano elements, and I know that I want to insert a new one before the second element. So, I can get a direct reference to the second element by using the *Item* property on *ChildNodes* to access a child node by index. In real code, you'd obviously need to put in a lot more checking to ensure that you were retrieving the desired node.

After the node has been retrieved, you call *CreateNewVolcano* to create a new *volcano* element. Then, you use *InsertBefore* to insert the new one immediately before the node you just retrieved by index.

16. Add the public *CreateNewVolcano* function, which creates a new *volcano* element. To save space, I have omitted some the code for creating the entire element; however, I've included enough so that you can see how it works.

```
XmlElement^ CreateNewVolcano()
{
    // Create a new element
    XmlElement ^newElement = doc->CreateElement("volcano");

    // Set the name attribute
    XmlAttribute ^att = doc->CreateAttribute("name");
    att->Value = "Mount St.Helens";
    newElement->Attributes->Append(att);

    // Create the location element
    XmlElement ^locElement = doc->CreateElement("location");
    XmlText ^xtext = doc->CreateTextNode("Washington State, USA");
    locElement->AppendChild(xtext);

    newElement->AppendChild(locElement);

    return newElement;
}
```

The function creates a new *XmlElement* for the volcano. Notice that the node classes— *XmlElement*, *XmlComment*, and so on—don't have public constructors, so you need to create them by calling the appropriate factory method. The *name* attribute is appended to the element's collection of attributes, and then the *location* element is created with its content. Building DOM trees like this is a process of creating new nodes and appending them to one another.

17. It would be useful to be able to print out the modified tree, so add a public function named *PrintTree* to the class, as shown here:

```
void PrintTree()
{
    XmlTextWriter ^xtw = gcnew XmlTextWriter(Console::Out);
    xtw->Formatting = Formatting::Indented;

    doc->WriteTo(xtw);
    xtw->Flush();
    Console::WriteLine();
}
```

You've already seen the use of *XmlTextWriter* to create XML manually. You can also use it to output XML from a DOM tree by linking it up to an *XmlDocument*, as shown in the preceding code.

18. Add calls to *ProcessChildNodes* and *PrintTree* to the *main* function, and then build and test the application.

```
try
{
    XmlBuilder ^builder = new XmlBuilder(path);
    builder->ProcessChildNodes();

    builder->PrintTree();}
catch(Exception ^ex)
{
    Console::WriteLine(ex->Message);
}
```

When you run the application, you can see that the new node has been added to the tree. Remember that this operation has modified only the DOM tree in memory; the original XML file has not been changed.

Quick reference

To	Do this
Parse XML without validation.	Create an *XmlReader*, and pass it the name of a file. Then, use the *Read* method to read nodes from the file.
Parse XML with DTD validation.	Create an *XmlReaderSettings* object, and set its *ValidationType* property to *ValidationType::DTD*. You must also set the *DtdProcessing* property to *DtdProcessing::Parse*.
	Then, use the settings to initialize an *XmlReader*. Create a handler function for validation events and attach it to the *ValidationEventHandler* event of the *XmlReader*.
Work with XML in memory.	Create an *XmlDocument* and use its *Load* or *LoadXml* function to parse XML into a DOM tree in memory.

Using ADO.NET

After completing this chapter, you will be able to:

■ Connect to a database.

■ Execute SQL statements to query the database.

■ Execute SQL statements to update the database.

■ Create disconnected applications, which use a *DataSet* to cache tables in memory.

■ Create a report displaying data from the database.

A DO.NET is the data access API from Microsoft for the .NET Framework. ADO.NET has been opti-mized to work with .NET, making it possible for distributed applications and services to exchange data easily and reliably.

ADO.NET offers two distinct programming models, depending on the type of application you need to build:

■ If you require forward-only, read-only access to the data, you can use a *DataReader* to iterate over the results of a query. As you'll see, *DataReader*s are easy to use but require that you remain connected to the database as long as you are using the reader.

■ Alternatively, you can use a *DataSet* to represent an in-memory cache of data from the data source. You can create a *DataSet*, load data into it from the database, and then disconnect. If you edit the *DataSet*, you can also update the database by using the changed data. One major advantage of the *DataSet* is that you only need to be connected to the database while exchanging data; this can make it a more scalable solution.

In this chapter, you will learn how to use ADO.NET to connect to a data source, execute queries, and perform database update operations. You will also learn how to use a *DataSet* in a disconnected application. You will see how to fill a *DataSet* with data from a database and display that data in a grid.

Note ADO.NET provides access to any kind of relational database. To avoid the need to download and install database engines and deal with complex setups, the examples in this chapter use a Microsoft Access database. However, I want to emphasize that the principles are exactly the same whether you're using Access or Microsoft SQL Server, and if you write your code correctly, you should only have to change the configuration file to change to another database type.

What is ADO.NET?

ADO.NET is a strategic API from Microsoft for data access in the modern era of distributed, Internet-based applications. ADO.NET contains a set of interfaces and classes with which you can work with data from a wide range of databases, including Microsoft SQL Server, Oracle, Sybase, Access, and so on.

ADO.NET data providers

ADO.NET uses the concept of a data provider to facilitate efficient access to different types of databases. Each data provider includes classes to connect to a particular type of database. The .NET Framework includes six data providers, as shown in the following table:

Data provider	Description
System.Data.SqlClient	Contains classes that give optimized access to SQL Server 7 and later
System.Data.OleDb	Contains classes that give access to SQL Server 6.5 and earlier; also provides access to databases such as Oracle, Sybase, Access, and so on
System.Data.ODBC	Contains classes that give access to Open Database Connectivity (ODBC) data sources
System.Data.OracleClient	Contains classes that give access to Oracle databases
System.Data.EntityClient	Contains classes that support the Entity Framework (discussed in Chapter 24, "Living with COM")
System.Data.SqlServerCe	Contains classes that work with SQL Server Compact Edition

In addition, data providers are available for a number of other databases through third-party vendors. Supported databases include MySQL, IBM DB2, Informix, Sybase, SQLite, Firebird, and PostgreSQL.

Provider-independent code

In early versions of ADO.NET, developers had to use provider-dependent classes, such as *Sql Connection* and *SqlCommand*. The problem with this approach is that it made it hard to write code that was independent of the data source, burdening you with a large editing job if you needed to switch providers.

Version 2.0 introduced a provider-independent interface by using a series of interfaces and classes whose names begin with "Db," such as *DbConnection* and *DbCommand*. All providers implement these interfaces, making it possible for you to use all providers in the same way. One advantage of this approach is that you can specify provider details in an application configuration file, which makes your code truly independent of the data provider.

It is now strongly recommended that you use the provider-independent interface rather than using the provider-specific classes directly.

ADO.NET namespaces

The classes in ADO.NET are divided into a number of namespaces, as shown in the following table:

Namespace	Description
System::Data	This is the core namespace in ADO.NET. Classes in this namespace define the ADO.NET architecture, and it holds provider-independent classes that can used for any type of data source, such as *DataSet*.
System::Data::Common	Defines common classes and interfaces for data providers.
System::Data::EntityClient	Defines classes for the Entity Framework data provider.
System::Data::Linq	Defines classes that gives access to relational data through Language-Integrated Query (LINQ)
System::Data::SqlClient	Defines classes for the SQL Server data provider.
System::Data::OleDb	Defines classes for the Object Linking and Embedding, Database (OLE DB) data provider.
System::Data::OracleClient	Defines classes for the Oracle data provider.
System::Data::Odbc	Defines classes for working directly with ODBC.
System::Data::Services	Defines classes used to create Windows Communication Foundation (WCF) data services.
System::Data::Spatial	Defines classes that work with spatial data.
System::Data::SqlTypes	Defines classes that represent native SQL Server data types.

ADO.NET assemblies

Many of the ADO.NET classes are in the *System::Data* assembly, although some of the newer features (such as LINQ and Entity Framework) have their own assemblies. To use these assemblies, you need to include the appropriate *using* statements in your application, such as in the following example:

```
#using <System.Data.dll>          // This assembly contains ADO.NET classes
#using <System.Data.Entity.dll>   // This assembly contains the
                                  // Entity Framework provider classes
```

 Note If you are creating projects by using Microsoft Visual Studio 2012, the reference to *System.Data.dll* will be provided for you.

Referencing external assemblies

If you want to use a type defined in another assembly, both the compiler and the runtime need to know where that assembly is located. You might want to reference types from a Common Language Runtime (CLR) library assembly, from a third-party library assembly, or even from another assembly that you've created in the same solution. You can add references to all these types of assembly in the same way.

On the Project menu, click properties to open the Project Properties dialog box. Select Common Properties and then, in the pane on the left, click Framework And References. At the bottom of the window, click the Add New Reference button. In the Add Reference dialog box that opens, in the pane on the left pane, click one of the options. For example, selecting Assemblies and then Framework displays all the CLR library assemblies for you to browse. Select the entry you require and then press OK twice to dismiss both dialog boxes. If you now expand the External Dependencies item in Solution Explorer, you will see the new dependency in the list.

After you have imported the assemblies you require, you can add *using* directives for the namespaces, as shown in the following example:

```
using System::Data::SqlClient;
```

Creating a connected application

In the next few pages, you will create a C++/CLI application that connects to an Access database. You will see how to set up the database connection and provider details in the application configuration file and then use a *DbConnection* object to establish a connection.

After you are connected, you will create a *DbCommand* object to represent a SQL statement. You will then perform the following tasks:

- Use the *ExecuteScalar* method on *DbCommand* to execute a statement that returns a single value.

- Use the *ExecuteNonQuery* method on *DbCommand* to execute a statement that updates the database.

- Use the *ExecuteReader* method to execute a statement that queries the database. *Execute Reader* returns a *DbDataReader* object, which provides fast, forward-only access to the rows in the result set. You will use this *DbDataReader* object to process the result set.

 Note You can find the sample database for this exercise, blog.mdb, in the sample code files for this book. Before starting the exercise, copy this file to a directory on your hard disk.

Connecting to a database

In this exercise, you will create a new application to perform all the operations described in the preceding section. The first step is to connect to the database.

1. Start Microsoft Visual Studio 2012 and create a new CLR Console Application project named **ConnectedApplication**.

2. In the ConnectedApplication.cpp file, after the *using namespace System;* statement, add the following statements:

```
// Generic ADO.NET definitions
using namespace System::Data;
// Provider-independent classes
using namespace System::Data::Common;
```

3. Add an application configuration file to the project. In Solution Explorer, right-click the project name to open the Add New Item dialog box (via the shortcut menu). In the pane on the left, click Utility, and then select Configuration file (app.config) as the file type. Press Add, and a file named app.config will be added to the project and opened in the editor.

4. Edit the app.config file to add a connection string.

```xml
<?xml version="1.0" encoding="utf-8" ?>
<configuration>
  <connectionStrings>
    <clear/>
    <add name="Blog"
      connectionString=
      "Provider=Microsoft.Jet.OLEDB.4.0;Data Source=C:\path\to\blog.mdb"
      providerName="System.Data.OleDb" />
  </connectionStrings>
</configuration>
```

Remember to edit the path to the location where you stored the blog.mdb database file.

The *connectionStrings* section holds connection string information. The *clear* element clears out the collection in case any have been inherited from computer configuration settings. In this example, we are defining a connection string, identified by the name *Blog*, which connects to an Access database file by using the *System.Data.OleDb* provider.

5. To work with configuration files, you need to add a reference to *System.Configuration.dll*. Do this by following the instructions given in the sidebar "Referencing external assemblies" earlier in the chapter.

6. Add a *using namespace* directive for *System.Configuration*.

    ```
    using namespace System::Configuration;
    ```

7. At the top of the *main* function, retrieve the connection string settings from the .config file.

    ```
    ConnectionStringSettings ^settings = ConfigurationManager::ConnectionStrings["Blog"];
    if (settings == nullptr)
    {
        Console::WriteLine("Couldn't get settings");
        return -1;
    }
    Console::WriteLine("Have settings");
    ```

    The *ConfigurationManager* class is responsible for interacting with settings stored in configuration files, and as such, it maintains a collection of *ConnectionStringSettings* objects, which you can access by using an indexer. If the call returns null, there isn't an entry with that name in the .config file.

8. After you have the *ConnectionStringSettings* object, you can use its *ProviderName* property to get a *DbProviderFactory*:

    ```
    // Get the factory object for this provider type
    DbProviderFactory ^fac = DbProviderFactories::GetFactory(settings->ProviderName);
    ```

    The *DbProviderFactory* is a factory that creates the various other objects that we need—connections, commands, and so on. You use *DbProviderFactory* the same way, regardless of the actual provider being used underneath.

9. After you have the factory, use it to create a connection and open it.

    ```
    DbConnection ^conn = nullptr;
    try
    {
        // Create a connection and set its connection string
        conn = fac->CreateConnection();
        conn->ConnectionString = settings->ConnectionString;

        conn->Open();
        Console::WriteLine("Connection opened");}
    catch (Exception ^ex)
    {
        Console::WriteLine(ex->Message);
    }
    finally
    {
        if (conn != nullptr) conn->Close();
        Console::WriteLine("Connection closed");
    }
    ```

Just about everything you do with databases can generate an exception, so you should always enclose your database code in a *try* block. Connections need to be opened before they are used, and it is important to close them afterward so that you free up resources. The best way to do this is to use a *finally* block, which ensures that the connection is closed whether or not an exception occurs.

10. Build your application and fix any compiler errors.

11. Run the application.

If all is well, on the console, you see the message shown in the figure that follows.

Creating and executing a command

In this exercise, you will create a *DbCommand* object that represents the following SQL statement:

```
SELECT COUNT(*) FROM Entries
```

This statement returns an integer indicating how many rows are in the *Entries* table. You will execute this statement by using the *ExecuteScalar* method on the command object.

1. Continue with the project from the previous exercise.

2. In the *main* function, add the following code to the *try* block, after the statement that opens the database connection:

```
// Count the entries
DbCommand ^cmd = fac->CreateCommand();
cmd->CommandText = "SELECT COUNT(*) FROM Entries";
cmd->CommandType = CommandType::Text;
cmd->Connection = conn;
```

This code creates and configures a *DbCommand* object that encapsulates a SQL statement. The *CommandText* property defines the SQL to be executed, and *CommandType* says that this is a SQL command, as opposed to a stored procedure. The *Connection* property specifies which database connection to use when executing the command.

3. Add the following code to execute the SQL statement and display the results on the console:

```
// Print the result
int numberOfEntries = (int)cmd->ExecuteScalar();
Console::WriteLine("Number of entries: {0}", numberOfEntries);
```

4. Build your application and fix any compiler errors.

5. Run the application.

The message shown in the following figure should appear on the console:

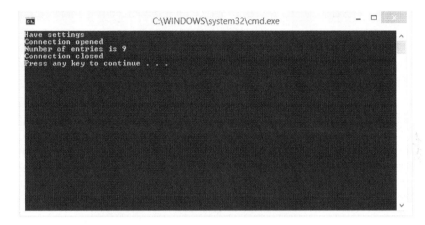

Executing a command that modifies data

In this exercise, you will add a new entry into the database by using the following SQL statement:

```
INSERT INTO [Entries] ([Date], [Text], [Author])
        VALUES ('Dec 02, 2012', 'Some text', 'Julian')
```

Note Some fields in the SQL are surrounded with square brackets in case they have the same name as predefined entities or types within Access.

You will use the *ExecuteNonQuery* method to execute this statement, which will return an integer to indicate how many rows the statement affected. Because you are inserting a single row, you'd expect this value to be 1.

1. Continue with the project from the previous exercise.

2. Find the code you wrote in the previous exercise and add the following statement:

```
// Update the prices of products
cmd->CommandText =
    "INSERT INTO [Entries] ([Date], [Text], [Author])"
    " VALUES ('Dec 02, 2012', 'A blog entry', 'Julian')";
```

This code reuses the *DbCommand* object from the previous exercise but specifies a different SQL statement.

 Tip It is a little-known feature of C++ that if the preprocessor sees two string literals on adjoining lines, it will combine them. This is a useful way to split up and format long strings.

3. Add the following code to execute the SQL statement and display the results on the console:

```
int rowsAffected = cmd->ExecuteNonQuery();
Console::WriteLine("Added {0} rows", rowsAffected);
```

4. Build your application and fix any compiler errors.

5. Run the application.

   The message shown in the following figure should appear on the console:

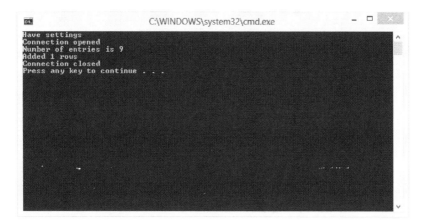

Executing queries and processing the results

In the final part of this connected application exercise, you will execute a command that retrieves information from the database by using the following SQL statement:

```
SELECT * FROM Entries
```

You will use the *ExecuteReader* method to execute this statement. This will return a *DbDataReader* object, which is a fast, forward-only reader that reads through each row in the result set in turn.

1. Continue with the project from the previous exercise.

2. Find the code you wrote in the previous exercise and add the following statement:

```
// Query the database
cmd->CommandText = "SELECT * FROM Entries";
```

This code reuses the *DbCommand* object from the previous exercise but specifies a different SQL statement.

3.   Add the following code to execute the SQL statement and return a *DbDataReader* object:

```
DbDataReader ^reader = cmd->ExecuteReader();
```

4.   Add the code that follows to loop through the results one row at a time. For each row, output the values of all four columns. The first, the record ID, is an integer, but the other three (*Date*, *Text* and *Author*) are all strings.

```
Console::WriteLine("\n------------------------------------");
while (reader->Read())
{
    Console::WriteLine("{0}: {1} by {2}", reader->GetInt32(0),
            reader->GetString(1), reader->GetString(3));
    Console::WriteLine("  {0}", reader->GetString(2));
}
Console::WriteLine("------------------------------------");
```

The *Read* method steps through the record set one row at a time. Notice the use of the strongly typed methods *GetString* and *GetInt32*.

5.   After the loop, close the reader.

```
reader->Close();
```

6.   Run the application.

The message shown in the following figure should appear on the console: (You might get different values than what's shown here.)

Creating a disconnected application

For the rest of the chapter, we'll turn our attention to disconnected applications. A disconnected application is one that does not have a permanently available connection to the data source. Applications are much more scalable when they only need a database connection to retrieve or send data back, and it is possible for an application such as a website to support many users with only a handful of database connections.

In ADO.NET, the *DataSet* class represents a disconnected, local data store. The following figure shows the *DataSet* object model:

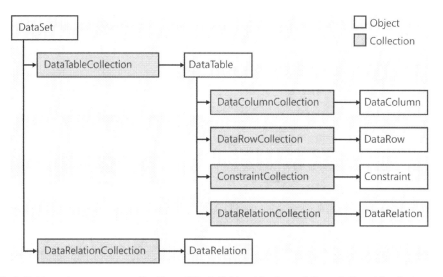

A *DataSet* is an in-memory collection of *DataTable* objects and the relationships between them. You can create many *DataTables* in a *DataSet* to hold the results of more than one SQL query.

Each *DataTable* has a collection of *DataRows* and *DataColumns*. Each *DataColumn* contains metadata about a column, such as its name, data type, default value, and so on. The *DataRow* objects actually contain the data for the *DataSet*.

You can create a *DataSet* from scratch, creating *DataTables*, setting up a schema using *Data Columns*, and then adding *DataRows*. It is, however, much more common to use a *DataSet* with a database.

The key to doing this is the *data adapter*, which sits between the database and the *DataSet*. The adapter knows how to retrieve data from the database and how to insert and update data. Each provider has its own data adapter class, but as you'd expect, you work with the provider-independent *DbDataAdapter* type.

The following figure shows how data adapters work with *DataSet*s:

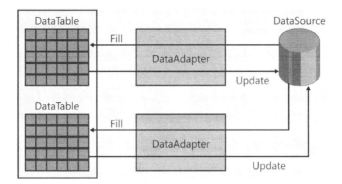

Each data adapter works with a single *DataTable* in a *DataSet*. You call the *Fill* method on a data adapter to fill the *DataSet* with data from the database. You call the *Update* method on a data adapter to save any changes in the *DataSet* back to the database.

Internally, the data adapter has four command objects, one each for the select, delete, insert, and update operations, each of which encapsulates a SQL command. The following table describes these command objects:

Command object in a data adapter	Description
SelectCommand	Contains a SQL SELECT statement to retrieve data from the database into the DataSet table
InsertCommand	Contains a SQL INSERT statement to insert new rows from the DataSet table into the database
UpdateCommand	Contains a SQL UPDATE statement to modify existing rows in the database
DeleteCommand	Contains a SQL DELETE statement to delete rows from the database

Disconnected operation using a *DataSet*

This exercise shows you how to create a *DataSet*, fill it by using a *DataAdapter*, and extract data from the tables in the *DataSet*. The details of setting up the configuration and getting a connection are exactly the same as for the previous exercise, so you will be able reuse a lot of the code.

1. Start a new CLR Console project project named **DataSetApp**.

2. Add an external reference to the *System::Configuration* assembly by using the Properties dialog box, as detailed in the sidebar "Referencing external assemblies" earlier in the chapter.

3. Add *using* statements to the top of the source file for the assemblies that you are going to be using.

```
// ADO.NET namespaces
using namespace System::Data;
using namespace System::Data::Common;
// For reading the configuration data
using namespace System::Configuration;
// For printing the content of the DataSet
using namespace System::IO;
```

4. Add an application configuration file to the project. In Solution Explorer, right-click the project name. On the shortcut menu that appears, point to Add, and then click New Item. In the New Item dialog box that opens, in the pane on the left, click Visual C++, and then click Utility. In the center pane, click Configuration file (app.config).

5. Remember to add the post-build step to the project settings so that app.config will be re-named to match the executable name. You can find details on how to do this in the previous exercise.

6. Copy the content of the app.config file from the previous exercise, "Creating a connected application." Here is the content that you need:

```
<?xml version="1.0" encoding="utf-8" ?>
<configuration>
  <connectionStrings>
    <clear/>
    <add name="Blog"
      connectionString=
      "Provider=Microsoft.Jet.OLEDB.4.0;Data Source=C:\path\to\blog.mdb"
      providerName="System.Data.OleDb" />
  </connectionStrings>
</configuration>
```

Remember to edit the path to reflect wherever you have stored the blog.mdb file.

7. Copy the code to read the connection string settings and create the *DbProviderFactory*. (The code is given here, but it is exactly the same as for the previous exercise.)

```
// Get the connection settings
ConnectionStringSettings ^settings =
    ConfigurationManager::ConnectionStrings["Blog"];
if (settings == nullptr)
{
    Console::WriteLine("Couldn't get settings");
    return -1;
}
Console::WriteLine("Connection settings OK");

// Get the factory object for this provider type
DbProviderFactory ^fac = DbProviderFactories::GetFactory(settings->ProviderName);
```

8. Add a *try* block in which you create a connection, a *catch* block to handle any errors, and a *finally* block to close the connection. (Again, I have reproduced the code here, but you should be able to copy it from the previous exercise.)

```
DbConnection ^conn = nullptr;
try
{
    // Create a connection and set its connection string
    conn = fac->CreateConnection();
    conn->ConnectionString = settings->ConnectionString;

    conn->Open();
    Console::WriteLine("Connection opened");
}
catch (Exception ^ex)
{
    Console::WriteLine(ex->Message);
}
finally
{
    if (conn != nullptr)
    {
        conn->Close();
        Console::WriteLine("Connection closed");
    }
}
```

9. With that setup complete, you can begin retrieving data. Start by asking the factory to create a *DataAdapter*.

```
// Create a DataAdapter and set its select command
DbDataAdapter ^adapter = fac->CreateDataAdapter();
```

10. A *DataAdapter* can have four commands associated with it, but because you are only going to be retrieving data, you only need to set the *Select* command. Do this by creating a *DbCommand* object, as in the previous exercise, and then assigning it to the *SelectCommand* property of the adapter.

```
DbCommand ^cmd = fac->CreateCommand();
cmd->CommandText = "SELECT * FROM Entries";
cmd->CommandType = CommandType::Text;
cmd->Connection = conn;

adapter->SelectCommand = cmd;
```

11. You can now create a *DataSet* and ask the adapter to fill it.

```
DataSet ^dataset = gcnew DataSet("Blog");
adapter->Fill(dataset, "Entries");
```

The first line creates an empty *DataSet* called "Blog". Calling *Fill* on the adapter causes it to execute its *SelectCommand*, which creates a *DataTable* called "Entries", fills it with the result of the query, and then adds it to the *DataSet*'s collection of *DataTables*.

Giving names to *DataSets* and *DataTables* is optional, but as you will see shortly, it is very useful when building XML documents from *DataSet* data.

> **Note** In a larger application, you could now close the connection to the database because you have the data locally in the *DataSet*.

12. Now that you have a *DataSet*, it would be useful to look at what it contains. The *WriteXml* function writes the content of a *DataSet* in XML format to any stream. The *XmlTextWriter* class provides a useful stream for our purposes because it writes the output to a file in properly formatted form.

```
XmlTextWriter ^xwriter = gcnew XmlTextWriter("c:\\SbS\\dataset.xml", nullptr);
xwriter->Formatting = Formatting::Indented;
```

The first two lines create an *XmlTextWriter* and ensure that it writes out the XML with indentation. Edit the path to put the XML file in a suitable location. Remember that you need to add a *using namespace* statement for *System::Xml*, or use the full name *System::Xml::XmlTextWriter*.

> **Note** The null second argument to the constructor means that the default UTF-8 encoding will be used. If you want to use another encoding, specify it like this:
>
> ```
> XmlTextWriter ^xwriter = gcnew XmlTextWriter("c:\\SbS\\dataset.xml",
> Encoding::Unicode);
> ```
>
> The *Encoding* class is in the *System::Text* namespace, so you will need to add a *using* declaration if you don't want to use the fully qualified name.

13. Use the table's *WriteXml* method to write the data out to the file.

```
DataTable ^table = dataset->Tables[0];

table->WriteXml(xwriter, XmlWriteMode::IgnoreSchema);
xwriter->Close();
```

The declaration of the *DataTable* handle makes the following code simpler and shows how the table created by the adapter is the first one in the *DataSet*'s *Tables* collection. Because you gave the table a name when the adapter created it, you could also specify the name here rather than the ordinal. The second argument to *WriteXml* shows that you only want the data and not the schema.

14. Build and run the application and then open the XML file in Notepad; you should see that the first few lines look like this:

```
<Blog>
  <Entries>
    <ID>2</ID>
    <Date>Jul 01, 2009</Date>
```

```
      <Text>A first entry</Text>
      <Author>Julian</Author>
   </Entries>
   <Entries>
      <ID>3</ID>
      <Date>Jun 27, 2009</Date>
      <Text>Second entry</Text>
      <Author>Julian</Author>
   </Entries>
   . . .
```

The root element has the same name as the *DataSet*, and each row is named after the table. If you hadn't assigned names to the *DataSet* and *DataTable*, the root element would have been called "NewDataSet" and each row would have been called "Table".

15. Change the *WriteXml* statement so that it includes the schema in the generated data.

```
table->WriteXml(xwriter, XmlWriteMode::WriteSchema);
```

Build and run the application again; you should see that the output file contains an XML schema that describes the data.

```
<Blog>
   <xs:schema id="Blog" xmlns="" xmlns:xs="http://www.w3.org/2001/XMLSchema"
              xmlns:msdata="urn:schemas-microsoft-com:xml-msdata">
      <xs:element name="Blog" msdata:IsDataSet="true"
                  msdata:MainDataTable="Entries" msdata:UseCurrentLocale="true">
         <xs:complexType>
            <xs:choice minOccurs="0" maxOccurs="unbounded">
               <xs:element name="Entries">
                  <xs:complexType>
                     <xs:sequence>
                        <xs:element name="ID" type="xs:int" minOccurs="0" />
                        <xs:element name="Date" type="xs:string" minOccurs="0" />
                        <xs:element name="Text" type="xs:string" minOccurs="0" />
                        <xs:element name="Author" type="xs:string" minOccurs="0" />
                     </xs:sequence>
                  </xs:complexType>
               </xs:element>
            </xs:choice>
         </xs:complexType>
      </xs:element>
   </xs:schema>
   <Entries>
      <ID>2</ID>
      <Date>Jul 01, 2009</Date>
      <Text>A first entry</Text>
      <Author>Julian</Author>
   </Entries>
   . . .
```

Quick reference

To	Do this

Use ADO.NET classes.	If you are using Visual Studio 2012, you will need to add only a using directive for the appropriate assemblies. For example:
	
	```using namespace System::Data;```
	```using namespace System::Data::Common;```

Store connection strings in the application configuration file.	Add an application configuration file to the project, and add a post-build event to rename it:
	
	```copy app.config $(TargetPath).config```
	
	Then, add one or more connection string sections to the .config file. For example:
	
	```<?xml version="1.0" encoding="utf-8" ?>```
	``` <configuration>```
	``` <connectionStrings>```
	``` <add name="NWind"```
	``` connectionString=```
	``` "Provider=Microsoft.Jet.OLEDB.4.0;"```
	``` "Data Source=C:\SbS\Blog.mdb"```
	``` providerName="System.Data.OleDb" />```
	``` </connectionStrings>```
	```</configuration>```

Connect to a database.	Obtain the provider factory by using the provider name. For example:
	
	```DbProvideFactory ^factory =```
	``` DbProviderFactories::GetFactory(name);```
	
	Then create a *DbConnection* object, and configure its *ConnectionString* property. For example:
	
	```DbConnection ^conn = factory->CreateConnection();```
	```conn->ConnectionString = connString;```

Create a SQL command.	Create a *DbCommand* object and configure its *CommandText*, *CommandType*, and *Connection* properties.

Execute a command.	If the command returns a scalar value, call *ExecuteScalar*. If the command modifies the database, call *Execute NonQuery*. If the command performs a query, call *ExecuteReader*. Assign the result to a *DbDataReader* object and use this reader to loop through the result set. For example:
	
	```DbDataReader ^reader = cmd->ExecuteReader();```
	```while (reader->Read())```
	```{```
	``` Console::Write(reader->GetString(0));```
	```}```

Use data in a disconnected application.	Create a *DbDataAdapter*, add *DbCommands* to access the database, and then set its connection. Create a *DataSet* and fill the *DataSet* by using the *data adapter*. For example:
	
	```DbDataAdapter ^daTitles =```
	``` factory->CreateDataAdapter();```
	```daTitles->SelectCommand = cmd;```
	```daTitles->Connection = conn;```
	```DataSet^ ds = gcnew DataSet("Titles");```
	```daTitles->Fill(ds);```

Writing a service by using Windows Communication Foundation

After completing this chapter, you will be able to:

■ Describe what Windows Communication Foundation is.

■ Write services by using Windows Communication Foundation.

■ Write clients to use Windows Communication Foundation services.

What is Windows Communication Foundation?

Windows Communication Foundation (WCF) is Microsoft's platform for writing distributed, service-based applications. Previously known as Indigo, it provides a framework for writing services and clients.

More Info WCF is a very complex topic, and this chapter can only provide an introduction. If you want to read more, I would suggest *Windows Communication Foundation 4 Step by Step* by John Sharp, published by Microsoft Press.

We live in an increasingly connected and distributed world. When you visit a website, your browser connects across the Internet to a server, and that server in turn might be using other servers to provide it with resources.

When you do this, you have in effect created a distributed application. Your browser provides the user interface, the web server provides the middle tier, and there can be other back-end servers providing the data tier. One very important feature of systems like this is that you can connect completely separate pieces together at run time to get the functionality that you want.

These pieces might be written by using different languages and frameworks, and run on different operating systems. All that is important is the functionality that they provide, not the details of their implementation.

With WCF, you can define contracts that specify, in a language and platform-independent manner, what services your components can provide, and these define the interface of your component to the outside world. The implementation details are immaterial to the user.

Distributed systems

Early frameworks for distribution tended to be proprietary. Microsoft's Distributed Component Object Model (DCOM) was intended to connect components written by using Microsoft technologies running on Windows. Java's Remote Method Invocation (RMI) was intended to do the same thing in the Java world.

Although these are still in use, the world has moved toward a need for more connectivity and independence, and so service-based systems have become increasingly popular.

Services

One of the hallmarks of modern service-based systems is the ability to compose parts together that have been developed independently.

This is done through the use of standards rather than proprietary technologies. So, for example, we can use XML and HTTP to connect two components rather than RMI, which was designed to work between Java components.

You will see shortly how WCF supports a wide range of the most popular and widely used standards, making it possible for you to create any type of service that you might need.

Characteristics of services

Services have the following distinguishing characteristics:

- **Platform and language independence** Services are written in such a way that they are not dependent on clients using a particular language or framework to access them.

- **Independent and autonomous** Services are independent in the same way that a website is independent.

- **Use well-known standards** Services make use of standard protocols, such as TCP/IP and HTTP, and data representations, such as XML. Doing this decouples clients of the service from the implementation.

- **Discoverability**   Many services publish metadata so that potential clients can discover what they offer and how to access them.

- **Reusability**   Because services are independent, when properly designed they can be combined into new distributed applications.

Connectivity

A component that you want to interact with could reside in another process on the same computer, on another computer on your local network, or out on the Internet. You have several options for connecting to such components.

For components that reside on the same computer, you would use an inter-process communication (IPC) mechanism such as *named pipes*, whereas for components deployed on other computers, you could use TCP/IP for binary communication or HTTP for text communication. In the enterprise world, it is also common to use messaging systems such as Microsoft MSMQ or IBM MQ to connect components located on different devices.

The problem here is that each of these communication mechanisms is implemented in a different way, using different libraries and techniques. A developer experienced in using TCP would have to learn how to use messaging.

WCF simplifies this by letting developers indicate how they want their components to be connected and leaving it up to the framework to implement the connection. For example, you can use an attribute to say that a class should be exposed as a web service using HTTP, and WCF will generate all the required code and configuration.

The ABCs of WCF

WCF contains a lot of detail—a lot of moving parts—and it is very easy to lose sight of what is important in a mass of detail. There is, however, a certain number of things that you need to know to work with WCF, and so in this section I present enough details on how WCF works and what it does that you will be able to write and consume a simple service, and appreciate other features of WCF that you might want to use in future projects.

Endpoints

A service in WCF is called an *endpoint*. Endpoints are characterized by three facets:

- **Address**   Where to find the service

- **Binding**   How to talk to the service

- **Contract**   What the service can do

The following figure shows how address, binding, and contract are related to a service:

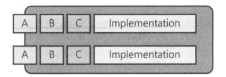

The client talks to the service through an address linked to a binding. The binding then invokes the service operation through the contract, but the implementation is well hidden from the client. A service can also expose more than one endpoint; these might be the same operations using different bindings (for example, HTTP and TCP) or different logical sets of operations (such as user and administrator interfaces).

Endpoint definitions are used by both services and clients to instruct the WCF framework what to do. You can set up endpoints in code, but setting them up declaratively in configuration makes it possible to reconfigure services without having to rebuild the code.

The next three sections look at each of the three endpoint aspects in turn.

Address

Every endpoint has an address composed from the following items:

- The transport protocol—*http:* is one example.

- The name of the server running the service, such as *//myserver.com* or *//localhost*. This might be followed by a port number, if necessary, such as *//localhost:8080*.

- The path to the service endpoint; for example, */MyService*.

Thus, to use HTTP to talk to a service called *MyService*, which is located at port 8080 on the local computer, you would use the following address:

```
http://localhost:8080/MyService
```

WCF supports four transports, as summarized in the following table:

Transport	Protocol	Comments
HTTP	*http:* or *https:*	Port 80 (443 for HTTPS)
TCP/IP	*net.tcp:*	Default port is 8080
IPC	*net.pipe:*	Must use *localhost* or local computer name
MSMQ	*net.msmq:*	Can use private queues

Base addresses

You might have several endpoints on the same server, which means that they will have the first part of their addresses in common. To make configuration simpler (and save typing!) you can specify a base address, and then assign relative addresses to the endpoints.

Metadata Exchange addresses

WCF services can publish metadata to clients, and this is done through a Metadata Exchange (MEX) address. This takes the form of an endpoint address with /mex appended to the end. Requests to this address will return the metadata for the service. This will be in the form of Web Service Definition Language (WSDL). You will see a MEX endpoint in use later in the chapter when Microsoft Visual Studio uses it to create a proxy in client code.

Binding

A binding describes the details of how to connect to a service, such as the transport to use, the message encoding, and whether security or transaction support is required.

A binding is simply a collection of settings, and you can create your own bindings. However, you seldom need to do this because WCF supports several bindings to cover for the most standard scenarios, as summarized in the following table:

Name	Transport	Encoding	Used
BasicHttpBinding	HTTP/HTTPS	Text, MTOM	Clients expecting legacy ASMX web service
WSHttpBinding	HTTP/HTTPS	Text, MTOM	Non-WCF client
WSDualHttpBinding	HTTP	Text, MTOM	Non-WCF client (bidirectional)
NetTcpBinding	TCP/IP	Binary	WCF client on another computer
NetMsmqBinding	MSMQ	Binary	WCF client using Microsoft Message Queuing (MSMQ)
NetNamedPipeBinding	Named pipes	Binary	WCF client on the same computer

This table demonstrates that if you want to use HTTP as the transport, you could pick *WSHttpBinding* or *WSHttpDualBinding*, depending on whether or not you need bidirectional communication.

Contract

Contracts define what a service can do, and contract details are expressed in metadata for clients to use.

WCF supports four kinds of contracts:

- **Service contracts**   A service contract exposes a .NET class or interface as a service.

- **Operation contracts**   An operation contract exposes a method on a type as a service. (You can only make methods into operations, not properties).

- **Data contracts**   A data contract is used to instruct WCF how to use custom types in service calls. WCF knows about a range of basic types, such as numbers and strings, but if you want to use a *Person* type as an operation parameter or return type, WCF will need to know what a Person object contains.

- **Fault contracts**   A fault contract is used to define error behavior.

You use contracts declaratively, by adding attributes to code. Here is a simple example of a service contract:

```
[ServiceContract]
interface class Foo
{
    [OperationContract]
    int SomeFunction(double d);
};
```

The interface is annotated with the *ServiceContract* attribute, which informs WCF that you are defining a set of operations. Individual functions within the interface are marked with *Operation Contract*, which makes them available to clients. Any function that isn't marked with *OperationContract* will not be exposed to clients.

The operation *SomeFunction* only uses built-in types, and WCF knows how to marshal those. Suppose, though, that you wanted to expose a function like the following as an operation:

```
Person^ GetPersonById(int id);
```

Note Marshaling is the process of converting data and sending it to another component. This can involve converting it to an intermediate form for transmission over a network, and it can result in the receiver getting a different representation than that of the sender.

In this case, you would have to instruct WCF how to marshal objects of type *Person*, and you could do this by using a *DataContract*:

```
[DataContract]
ref class Person
{
    [DataMember]
    String ^name;

    ...
};
```

The *DataContract* class defines this as being a serializable class, and you apply *DataMember* to all fields that you want to be serialized. If you don't want or need to send a field, don't annotate it; this will cut down the amount of data being sent over the wire.

> **Note** As of .NET 3.5, you often don't have to annotate your types with *DataContract* and *DataMember*, because public members will be made available by default. But it might be wise to still use it, making explicit those members that you want passed to clients.

Message exchange patterns

Communication between clients and services can be one-way or bi-directional. WCF supports three *message exchange patterns* (MEPs) that govern how clients communicate with services:

- Request-response

- One-way (also called *simplex*)

- Duplex (also called *bi-directional*)

Request-response is the default, and is typically used when the client expects a reply from the service. For example, consider this operation:

```
Person^ GetPersonById(int id);
```

The client calls the service with an ID and expects to get a *Person* back. Using request-response messaging, the client will block (and the connection will be maintained) until either the response has been received or a fault has been sent. This means that request-response message is synchronous, as demonstrated in the following illustration:

> **Note** The operation does not have to have a return type in order to use request-response messaging; it is quite possible to use it with an operation that has a *void* return type.

When using *one-way* (or *simplex*) messaging, the client sends a request but does not expect a response. This allows WCF to drop the connection to the service as soon as the call has been made because it does not have to wait for a reply. It also means that the operation must have a *void* return type because nothing will be returned, and it cannot declare a fault contract, because there is no way to get the error details back to the caller. One-way operations are useful for fire-and-forget operations such as logging or event notifications. They can also be useful for performing long-running operations asynchronously, where the client can use polling to ascertain when the server has the results ready. The following figure illustrates one-way messaging:

Duplex operation implies two-way communication between a client and service. Both ends can initiate a call, and neither has to wait for the other to finish before sending. To achieve this, service contracts specify a callback contract that the client must implement and which the service will call when it wants to call back to the client, as depicted in the following illustration:

Not all bindings support all MEPs. The following table summarizes what you can use:

Binding	MEPs	Comments
BasicHttpBinding	One-way and request-response only	HTTP does not support duplex operation
WSHttpBinding	One-way and request-response only	
WSDualHttpBinding	All MEPs	Simulates duplex by using two channels
NetTcpBinding	All MEPs	Supports full duplex messaging
NetMsmqBinding	Supports one-way and duplex	Does not support request-response
NetNamedPipeBinding	One-way, request-response, and half-duplex	Duplex messaging, but not in both directions at once

Behaviors

Services have default ways of working. If you want to modify these, you use *behaviors*, which modify or extend the operation of services.

Examples of behaviors include:

- How service objects are created. Is there just one or is there a new object created per call?

- How the service handles concurrent calls.

- Limiting the number of simultaneous connections.

- Handling transactions.

A detailed description of behaviors and how to use them is beyond the scope of this book.

Creating a service

In this exercise, you will see how to create and test a simple service that provides mathematical operations. To follow best practices, the service will be defined as an interface, with the implementation in a separate class.

1. Create a CLR Console Application project named **MathService**.

2. Add an external reference to *System::ServiceModel* and then add the following two *using* declarations:

```
using namespace System::ServiceModel;
using namespace System::ServiceModel::Channels;
```

3. Add a header file named **IMathService.h** to the project, and use it to define the following interface:

```
#ifndef IMATHSERVICE_H
#define IMATHSERVICE_H

[ServiceContract]
public interface class IMathService
{
    [OperationContract]
    virtual double Square(double d);

    [OperationContract]
    virtual double Cube(double d);
};

#endif
```

This declares a service as an interface. It is good practice to define services using an interface because this decouples the implementation from the definition. This is being declared in a separate header file because the client will need the interface definition, as well.

4. Open the MathService.cpp file and add the definition for a class that implements the service. You'll need to add an *include* statement to get the interface definition.

```
#include "IMathService.h"

ref class MathService : IMathService
{
public:
    virtual double Square(double d)
    {
        return d*d;
    }

    virtual double Cube(double d)
    {
    return d*d*d;
    }
};
```

5. You can now start to implement the *main* method to host the service.

```
int main(array<System::String ^> ^args)
{
    WSHttpBinding ^binding = gcnew WSHttpBinding();
    Uri ^baseAddress = gcnew Uri("http://localhost:8080/MathService");
}
```

These first two lines create a binding and a base address for the service. Because this is a basic HTTP service, you create a *WSHttpBinding* and an HTTP address.

6. Create a *ServiceHost* object and add an endpoint to it.

```
ServiceHost ^host = gcnew ServiceHost(MathService::typeid, baseAddress);
host->AddServiceEndpoint(IMathService::typeid, binding, baseAddress);
```

The *ServiceHost* is the object that implements the WCF behavior for you. It is initialized with details of the service implementation class (so that it knows what to call when requests come in) and the base address. You can then add an endpoint to the *ServiceHost* so that it knows to support the *WSHttpBinding* on the given base address and that it is supporting the *IMathService* contract.

7. Run the service.

```
host->Open();
Console::WriteLine("Service running... press Enter to terminate");
Console::ReadLine();
host->Close();
```

The call to *Open* starts the service listening for connections. But this is not a blocking call, so you need to keep the application running until you're ready to close the connection. An easy way to do this is simply to output a prompt and wait for the user to press Enter. When the user does press Enter, ensure that you close the host to free resources.

8. Build the application and run it to check that you have no errors.

When you try to run the application, you should find that it crashes with an exception of type *System::ServiceModel::AddressAccessDeniedException*. This is because Windows wants to prevent possibly malicious code running without authorization, so you need to run the application with sufficient privilege. There are two ways to do this: one is to register the service by using the *netsh* command so that Windows will allow it to run; the other is to run the application as an administrator, because administrators have rights to run services. To do that, you can either start a command prompt as administrator and run the application from the command line or run Visual Studio as administrator and run the application from there.

To run applications as administrator in Windows 8, right-click the application's tile on the Start screen and then, on the appbar menu that slides up from the bottom of the screen, click Run As Administrator.

Writing a service client

The next step is obviously to write a client to test out the service. There is a WCF Test Client included with Visual Studio, but you won't be able to use that until you've added metadata support to the service, and we will leave that until later in the chapter.

1. Create another CLR Console Application named **TestClient**.

2. In Windows Explorer, copy the IMathService.h file to the project directory and add it to the project. Right-click the project name. On the shortcut menu, point to Add, point to Existing Item, and then click the header file.

You need to add this file because your client code needs the definition of the interface.

3. Add an external reference to the *System::ServiceModel* assembly, just like you did when creating the service.

4. Add the two *using* directives for the *System::ServiceModel* and *System::ServiceModel::Channels* namespaces.

```
using namespace System::ServiceModel;
using namespace System::ServiceModel::Channels;
```

5. Add an *#include* statement for IMathService.h to the source file TestClient.cpp.

6. Start implementing the *main* function by creating a *WSHttpBinding* and *EndPointAddress*.

```
WSHttpBinding ^binding = gcnew WSHttpBinding();

String ^url = "http://localhost:8080/MathService";
EndpointAddress ^address = gcnew EndpointAddress(url);
```

7. Communication is handled by a *Channel*, and you get one of those from a *ChannelFactory*.

```
ChannelFactory<IMathService^> ^factory =
        gcnew ChannelFactory<IMathService^>(binding, address);
IMathService ^channel = factory->CreateChannel();
```

Note how the channel implements the interface of the service you want to call, and also has a binding and address. It therefore has all the details it needs to contact the service and use the operations it provides.

8. Call an operation on the service.

```
double value = channel->Square(3.0);
Console::WriteLine("Value is {0}", value);
```

9. When you're done, close the channel.

```
((IChannel^)channel)->Close();
```

You need to cast the channel to an *IChannel* handle because the *IMathService* doesn't implement the *Close* function.

10. Build the application to ensure that you have no errors.

11. Run the *MathService* executable that you created in the previous exercise, which you'll find located in the Debug directory of the project. When this has started, run the client as administrator and you should see the result message printed out.

Adding metadata to the service

One of the characteristics of services is that they are discoverable. This means that there is some way for potential clients to get details of the service, what it can do and how to call it. The standard way to provide this metadata is as a WSDL document, which describes the service in XML.

 More Info It isn't important for you to understand WSDL to create and use services, but if you are interested, you can learn more about it at the w3schools website at *http://www. w3schools.com/wsdl/wsdl_intro.asp*.

The next question is how you ask a service for its metadata. WCF services expose their metadata through an MEX endpoint. When you add such an endpoint, you can choose which transports (HTTP, TCP) that you want to support, and provide the URL.

You can use the WCF Test Client to examine and call service operations, but your service needs to publish metadata through an MEX endpoint before you can use this.

This next exercise adds an MEX endpoint to the service. It then shows how you can see the metadata and then use the WCF Test Client to exercise the service.

1. Continue with the project from the previous exercise.

2. Add a *using* directive for *System::ServiceModel::Description* to MathService.cpp.

   ```
   using namespace System::ServiceModel::Description;
   ```

3. Add the following lines after the call to *AddServiceEndpoint* and before the call to *Open*:

   ```
   // Add MEX endpoint
   ServiceMetadataBehavior ^mex = gcnew ServiceMetadataBehavior();
   mex->HttpGetEnabled = true;
   host->Description->Behaviors->Add(mex);

   host->AddServiceEndpoint(
       IMetadataExchange::typeid,
       MetadataExchangeBindings::CreateMexHttpBinding(),
       "http://localhost:8080/MathService/mex");
   ```

   Earlier in the chapter, you learned that behaviors are used to modify the behavior of a service. The *ServiceMetadata* behavior makes it possible for the service to expose its metadata via an MEX endpoint, and you can configure how it exposes this data. In this case, I've chosen to allow clients to access it via an HTTP GET request. The behavior object is added to the host's *Behaviors* collection, and then you add a service endpoint.

   The endpoint exposes the *IMetadataExchange* contract at the URL by using HTTP at the given address. Note how the standard MEX endpoint address is the service address with /mex appended.

4. Build the project and then start the service as administrator.

5. Start Internet Explorer and type the following URL in the address bar:

```
http://localhost:8080/MathService?wsdl
```

By setting the *HttpGetEnabled* property, you can request the metadata using HTTP by passing the *wsdl* parameter. When the request executes, you should see the following WSDL describing your service in the browser:

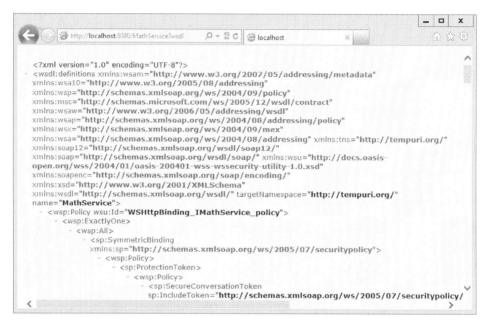

You can now run the WCF Test Client, WcfTestClient.exe, which you can find in C:\Program Files\Microsoft Visual Studio 11\Common7\IDE (or if you are running a 64-bit version of Windows, it will be in C:\Program Files (x86)\Microsoft Visual Studio 11.0\Common7\IDE).

6. When the application starts, in the pane on the left side of the window, right-click the MyService Projects entry, and then, on the shortcut menu that appears, click Add Service.

7. In the Add Service dialog box that opens, enter the service URL (**http://localhost:8080/ MathService**) into the text box and press OK.

After a short interval, you should see details of the service contract appear in the pane on the left in the WTF Test Client application window.

8. Double-click one of the operations—for example, *Square*. The pane on the right side shows you details of how to call the operation. Enter a number in the *Value* field and press *Invoke*. After a short pause, you should see the response appear in the lower part of the pane, as shown in the following figure:

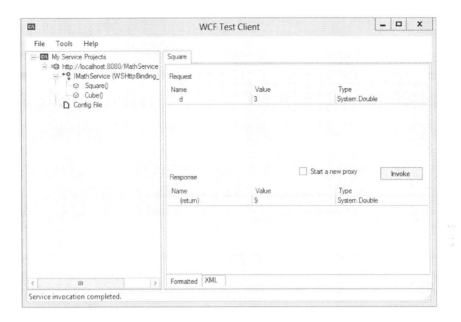

Accessing a service by using a proxy

You have seen how to connect to a service manually by using the WCF APIs. It is also possible to get Visual Studio to create a proxy class for you, one that encapsulates the details of where the service is and what the endpoints are; in this way, you don't have to be concerned with the low-level mechanics.

This is often the way that you would do it in C# and Microsoft Visual Basic .NET, asking Visual Studio to add a service reference to your project, and then using the generated proxy class. The problem is that this feature isn't supported by C++/CLI in Visual Studio, but it turns out to be quite simple to do if you use a C# wrapper.

Creating the wrapper DLL

In this next exercise, you will create a simple C# Dynamic-Link Library (DLL) project and add a reference to the MathService project. This will add a proxy class to the project, but because it is a public class, you will be able to use it from C++/CLI code. And even though you create a C# project, you don't have to write a single line of C# in order to make it work.

1. Continue with the project (MathService) from the previous exercise.

2. Create a C# Class Library project named **WcfClientLib**.

3. Add a reference to MathService. In Solution Explorer, under the project, right-click References, and then, on the shortcut menu, click Add Service Reference.

4. In the Add Service Reference dialog box that opens, type the URL of the service into the address box and press Go. After a few seconds, you should see the *MathService* added to the Services pane. You can expand this entry and click on *IMathService* to see the operations in the pane on the right.

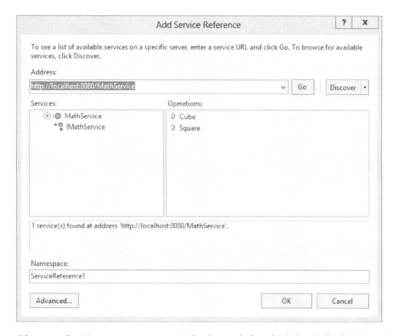

Observe the Namespace name at the lower left, which by default is *ServiceReference1*: the generated code will be placed in this namespace. You can change it if you want, but you'll need to remember it for subsequent steps.

5. When you're happy that you have a reference to the appropriate service, press OK and Visual Studio will generate a proxy class and application configuration file for you.

6. You don't need to add anything else to this project, so just build it to create the DLL.

Using the wrapper

You now have a DLL that contains all the code necessary to call MathService. In the second part of the exercise, you'll see how to use this DLL in a C++/CLI application.

1. Create a CLR Console Application project named **TestWcf**.

2. Add an external reference to *System::ServiceModel.*

3. Add a second external reference to the WcfClientLib DLL, which you'll find in the WcfClientLib/ bin.debug directory.

4. Add a *using* directive for the namespace *WcfClientLib.ServiceReference1.*

```
using namespace WcfClientLib::ServiceReference1;
```

If you changed the namespace for the generated proxy code, edit the *using* directive appropriately.

5. The proxy class is driven by configuration information, so add an application configuration file to the project. Right-click the project name, and then, on the shortcut menu, click to Add New Item.

6. In the dialog box that opens, in the Utility section, click Configuration file (app.config).

> **Note** You need to edit the project properties so that the app.config file is properly processed at build time. Open the project properties and then, under Configuration Properties, click Post-Build Event, and specify the following command line:
>
> ```
> copy app.config "$(TargetPath).config"
> ```

7. The configuration details you need are in the DLL's app.config file, so open that in the editor and copy the *<system.ServiceModel>* element shown here:

```
<system.serviceModel>
  <bindings>
    <wsHttpBinding>
      <binding name="WSHttpBinding_IMathService" />
    </wsHttpBinding>
  </bindings>
  <client>
    <endpoint address="http://localhost:8080/MathService" binding="wsHttpBinding"
        bindingConfiguration="WSHttpBinding_IMathService"
        contract="ServiceReference1.IMathService"
        name="WSHttpBinding_IMathService">
      <identity>
        <userPrincipalName value="WIN8PREVIEW\Julian" />
      </identity>
    </endpoint>
  </client>
</system.serviceModel>
```

The entries in the configuration file give all the details that the proxy needs to contact the service. Ensure that you replace the value of *userPrincipalName* with your details.

8. You are now ready to use the service. Add the following code to the *main* function:

```
try
{
    MathServiceClient ^msc = gcnew MathServiceClient();
    double result = msc->Cube(3.0);
    Console::WriteLine("Result: {0}", result);
}
catch(Exception ^ex)
{
    Console::WriteLine(ex->Message);
}
```

The proxy class is called *MathServiceClient*, based on the name of the service with "Client" appended. This class directly implements the operations exposed by the service, so you can just call the *Square* and *Cube* functions without even having to know that it is a service.

9. Ensure that the service is still running and then build and run the client. You should see the result displayed on the console.

Quick reference

To	Do This
Define a service interface.	Define an interface and annotate it with [*ServiceContract*]. Annotate the methods on the interface with [*OperationContract*].
Create a service.	Create a class that implements the service interface.
Host a service.	Create a *ServiceHost* object
Creating a service client	Create a *ChannelFactory* and use it to create a channel. Then, call methods on the channel.
Expose metadata from a service.	Add the Service Metadata behavior to your service.
Test A WCF service.	Use the the WCF Test Client.
Accessing a service using a proxy class.	Create a C# DLL project, and add a reference to the service using the Add Service Reference dialog.

Introducing Windows Store apps

After completing this chapter, you will be able to:

■ Explain essential features of the Windows Store user interface.

■ Create user interfaces by using XAML.

■ Create, deploy, and run a simple Windows Store app.

■ Describe the essential features of C++/CX.

The release of Windows 8 has presented developers with new opportunities and challenges, enabling them to write applications that make full use of the capabilities of mobile devices, including touch screens and cameras. This chapter introduces you to the world of writing Windows Store applications for the new Windows 8 environment.

A (brief) history of writing Windows user interface applications

The way in which Windows user interface (UI) applications have been written has evolved over the years, from the earliest applications written in C, through a move to C++, then Microsoft .NET, and now Windows 8. This section gives you a brief overview and history and also provides information to help you decide which technology you should consider using for a UI application.

The Win32 API

The earliest Windows UI applications were usually written in C by using the Win32 API. This was an exacting task, somewhat equivalent to writing code in assembly language. There was a tremendous amount of boilerplate code needed to do almost anything, and you had to know just what was going on because there was no higher-level library taking care of the housekeeping for you.

For example, the simple task of creating a window on the screen entailed calling a function that took no fewer than 12 parameters, as demonstrated here:

```
HWND WINAPI CreateWindowEx(
    DWORD dwExStyle, LPCTSTR lpClassName, LPCTSTR lpWindowName,
    DWORD dwStyle, int x, int y, int nWidth, int nHeight,
    HWND hWndParent, HMENU hMenu,
    HINSTANCE hInstance, LPVOID lpParam);
```

You can probably guess what some of the parameters mean (*x* and *y* are the initial position of the window, and *nWidth* and *nHeight* specify its size), but there are some obscure parameters and types here.

Creating applications by using the Win32 API often means copying an existing application to get all the boilerplate startup and housekeeping code, and then editing the business logic parts.

Microsoft Foundation Classes

Microsoft's first C++ user interface library was Microsoft Foundation Classes (MFC), initially released in 1992 and now at version 10. MFC provides a thin C++ wrapper around the Window APIs, but it does perform most of the tedious housekeeping for you.

MFC made it possible to create applications that looked like Microsoft Office and Windows Explorer, and which could interoperate with Office applications by using a complex technology called Object Linking and Embedding (OLE). MFC 9 introduced a number of new features including support for docking windows similar to those found in Microsoft Visual Studio, and a ribbon toolbar similar to that used in Microsoft Office.

MFC has been deprecated in favor of .NET, but there are many applications that still use it. Versions 7 through 9 were designed to help developers migrate to .NET, and so it is regarded as a legacy framework.

One drawback for MFC developers is that MFC has never had a UI designer in Visual Studio, although there are editors for icons, bitmaps, and other resources.

Windows Forms

The first versions of .NET introduced a new UI library called Windows Forms (or *WinForms*), which was modeled on the Microsoft Visual Basic way of creating UIs, and (as the name implies) it was targeted at producing form-based applications. Because it was a .NET library, you could write Windows Forms applications in any .NET language.

Windows Forms applications can have multiple windows, menus and toolbars, dialogs, and all the other features that you would expect in a desktop Windows application.

A Windows Forms application consists of one or more windows called *forms*, and you typically develop it by dragging controls from a toolbox onto a form and then using the Properties editor to set control properties and event handlers. Windows Forms was the first time that C++ developers had a visual designer for creating UIs.

 Note Although you'd usually use the designer in Visual Studio to create Windows Forms applications, Microsoft designed it so that you could create the entire UI in code if you wanted to, and compile from the command line.

A form and its child controls are represented by objects in code, and the Visual Studio designer creates the code that will generate the desired layout at run time. Note that Visual Studio 2012 does not support Windows Forms for C++/CLI. It is possible that support might be added back in a later version, but for the time being if you want to use WinForms, you will need to use Visual Studio 2010.

Windows Presentation Foundation

Version 3.0 of the .NET Framework saw the release of Windows Presentation Foundation (WPF, code-named "Avalon"), which was intended to build on the success of Windows Forms as well as add extra functionality. Microsoft Silverlight is a subset of WPF for writing components to embed in webpages, and which provide the same kind of functionality as Adobe Flash.

Although you can use it to design form-based applications, WPF is very different from Windows Forms. Here are some of the main differences:

■ WPF uses DirectX rather than the older GDI graphics subsystem, which makes for much faster rendering and offers the ability to use hardware graphics acceleration when available.

■ WPF uses XAML, an XML language, to describe UI layout. This makes it possible to almost completely separate the presentation and logic parts of an application.

■ WPF supports many advanced features that do not appear in Windows Forms, including rich support for media (vector and raster images, audio, and video), animation, bitmap effects such as drop shadows, and advanced text rendering.

■ WPF's support for data-binding is far more powerful and extensible compared to Windows Forms.

WPF can have a steep learning curve because it is intended as a professional graphics library with which developers can create any UI they want rather than a library that makes it easy to perform common tasks and build simple business applications.

Unfortunately, WPF isn't easy to use from C++/CLI, because the language lacks support for partial classes, and this feature is essential if you are to work with XAML. I'm not entirely certain why this wasn't added—it would certainly be possible—but it seems that Microsoft decided that it didn't want C++/CLI used for modern front-end development. Whatever the reason, there has never been a C++/CLI designer for WPF in Visual Studio, and so there is no "WPF Application" project type.

Windows 8 and Windows Store

Although Windows 8 fully supports the familiar Windows desktop environment, it also provides a new way of writing UI applications. Windows Store apps use a library called *Windows RT* (or WinRT) which provides a UI library that is aimed at touch devices and the style of interface made popular by the iPad and other tablets. It is called Windows Store because it is envisaged that developers will create applications and sell them online through Microsoft's Windows Store, in common with the way that many other mobile platforms make content available.

Windows Store applications are very different to traditional Windows applications; they require a different approach to development, as you will see in this and Chapter 21, "More about Windows Store apps."

So, Windows 8 supports two different styles of UI application: desktop and Windows Store. Note that they are completely separate. Among other things, this means that a Windows Store app won't appear on the desktop and needs to run in the WinRT environment.

Which UI library to choose?

So, which UI library should you choose for your applications? For most developers, the choice will come down to Windows Forms, WPF, or Windows Store.

At this point, Win32 and MFC are really legacy technologies, and there are few times when you would consider starting a new project using either of them (although MFC does have some support for interacting with Office that the newer libraries don't have)

If your application is going to have a traditional form-based UI, consisting mainly of text boxes and buttons, and doesn't need fancy graphics, animation, or media file support, Windows Forms will be suitable. You will find everything you need in Visual Studio, including a visual designer.

If you want a desktop application but with the advanced features that WPF provides, that is the way to go, although if you are using C++, you will have to jump through quite a few hoops to get there.

And, if you want an up-to-date, tablet-style interface that will suit touch devices as well as desktop computers, consider Windows Store. Oh, and don't let anyone tell you that Windows Store replaces WPF; they are designed for different types of application. I can't see anyone producing a Windows Store-style version of Visual Studio any time soon!

Introducing Windows Store apps

The Windows Store UI brings a completely new style of user interface to Windows applications. Many of the ways in which UIs have been constructed since the first versions of Windows are no longer supported. For example, in the Windows Store UI, there are no menus or dialog boxes, so how do you let users make choices? And then there are all the new modes of interaction supported by handheld devices, such as accelerometers and cameras that users will expect to use.

This means that you need to get used to new ways of writing applications. Of course, if you're new to writing Windows UI applications, you will in some ways have an easier task because you have less to unlearn.

If you read about development with WinRT, you will hear talk of the "green and blue stacks." This phrase arose from how Microsoft described how WinRT was going to fit with the existing Windows development technologies, and they produced a diagram similar to the following illustration:

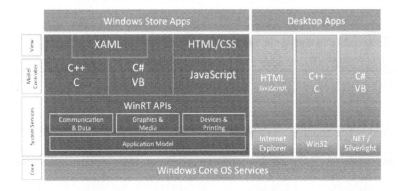

The area on the left, in green in the original diagram, is the new WinRT technology stack, whereas the area on the right (originally in blue) shows existing technologies. This does mean that developing for Windows 8 now has two distinct models, depending on the stack that you choose.

You will notice that .NET is placed in the older, blue section, but you will find that it is still relevant to writing Windows Store apps.

Main features of Windows Store apps

In this section, I'll list some of the major features of Windows Store apps. If you think of an app running on a typical tablet device or mobile phone, then you should be able to appreciate why these have been introduced.

App behavior

Apps are secure and sandboxed, and can't wreck other applications. If users are going to download apps from an online store, they need to be confident that a new one won't affect what they already have installed. Downloading and installing apps is made simpler by using single-folder installation.

One consequence of sandboxing is that some APIs are not available, such as sockets and file I/O.

Apps load quickly, with none of the waiting common to desktop applications. In fact, you don't start and stop apps like you do their cousins on the desktop. After you run an app it stays in memory but is suspended if you switch away from it, so you can switch back to it instantly. Suspended apps can be terminated if resources are needed; thus, apps need to handle moving to and from the background and termination gracefully.

Microsoft is setting up a Windows Store for Windows 8 applications, similar to the App Store used on Apple devices. In common with most of these stores, apps must be approved before being accepted, and developers need to obtain a license to be able to create apps. You will see how to do this when you create your first app, later in the chapter. And if you're going to distribute your apps through the Windows Store, they will also need to be signed with a digital signature because anonymous applications aren't allowed.

Hardware usage

The WinRT APIs make it possible for developers to take advantage of hardware features such as motion sensors and cameras, and apps can adapt to the hardware context, such as scaling to suit screen resolution or using the mouse and keyboard when touch input is not available.

The UI model

The WinRT UI model is intended for use with touch devices that have a limited display area, so there are some restrictions and unique aspects that you need to keep in mind:

- Apps do not support overlapping windows. An app can, however, have more than one window, and you can move from window to window as you would in a browser.

- Continuing the browser analogy, there are no menus or dialogs.

- Tiles are used to represent programs on the desktop. Unlike icons, tiles are active and can display content (such as weather or a stock report). By doing so, they can turn the desktop into a dashboard.

Two types of UI are supported. Code-based interfaces can be written in C#, C++, or Visual Basic; the UI is usually constructed declaratively by using XAML, although it is possible to create the UI manually in code. Web-based interfaces are written in JavaScript and constructed by using HTML5 and CSS3.

Contracts and charms

Windows 8 apps can work together using contracts, which express capabilities (such as search or copy and paste) in a language-independent way.

Charms are UI elements that invoke contracts, and every app has access to five standard charms.

The WinRT APIs

API calls can be direct or brokered. Brokered calls are those that might have security concerns, such as those that affect data or user settings or use device features. They must be declared by the app, and might need permission from the user in order to run.

WinRT places a premium on app response. Part of this is achieved by suspending apps and letting you resume them quickly. In addition, any API call that might take more than 50 milliseconds is implemented as an asynchronous call so that developers are forced to adopt a responsive coding style.

Writing a Windows Store app

Most people will write Windows Store apps in one of three ways:

1. Using C# or Visual Basic .NET and a subset of the .NET Framework libraries

2. Using JavaScript and HTML5

3. Using C++

We are obviously going to be concentrating on the third option.

Note When writing .NET applications, all languages are equivalent because they all compile down to Microsoft Intermediate Language (MSIL, or IL for short). In fact, you could say that to a very large extent, the language that you choose reflects the syntax you prefer. This is not the case when writing Windows Store apps, for which there are very real differences in the three aforementioned approaches. There is some functionality available in JavaScript that isn't available in C# or C++, and vice versa, but the main difference is that if you want to use any Win32 and COM libraries you can only do it from C++. This means that to use DirectX to write games, you will need to use C++.

Creating your first Windows Store app

This exercise shows you how to write the simplest of Windows Store apps, which in this case consists of a single screen and two controls. In Chapter 21, you see how to add more functionality, but this will show you the basics. Remember that to create and run Windows Store apps, you need to have Visual Studio 2012 installed on Windows 8. Be aware that you might also be prompted to get a developer license when you create your first project. For more information about developer licenses, read the sidebar at end of this exercise.

1. In Visual Studio 2012, open the New Project dialog box.

2. In the pane on the left, click Windows Store.

3. In the center pane, click Blank App (XAML), and then name the project **HelloXaml**.

4. In the Solution Explorer, open MainPage.xaml.

The designer loads (which can take a few seconds), and you then see a screen with a visual representation of the UI in the upper half, and the XAML in the lower half. The UI has a black background because of the default theme that is used for applications.

The XAML is simply an XML document consisting of a *Page* element that represents the entire page, and which contains a *Grid* element that will contain the content for the page.

Note You will learn about XAML in more detail later in the chapter. For now, let's just note that a *Page* can only contain one content item, and this will usually be some sort of layout control such as a *Grid*. As you'd expect, a *Grid* can contain multiple items laid out in rows and columns.

5. On the left side of the Visual Studio window, click the Toolbox tab to display the Toolbox. If the tab isn't visible, on the View menu, click Toolbox or press Ctrl+W, X to display it.

6. Drag a button from the Toolbox to the page.

    A button appears, while at the same time a *Button* element is added to the XAML. You can drag the button around to position it wherever you like, and you can also resize it; the *Button*'s properties in the XAML are updated to reflect any changes you make. In fact, the upper pane is simply a graphical interpretation of the XAML, so conversely, if you edit the XAML, the upper pane will update itself accordingly.

> **Note** The *Grid* control can lay components out using rows and columns, but this example is using absolute positioning. The *Margin* property determines how much space is left on all four sides of a component, in the order left-top-right-bottom. By specifying the first two, you are effectively defining the position of the button.

7. In the XAML pane, edit the *Button*'s *Content* attribute to something more suitable, such as "Click Me!"

> **Note** You can provide the content to a control such as a button in two ways, either by using the *Content* attribute or by providing it as the content of the element, such as in the following example:
>
> ```
> <Button Content="First One" ... />
> <Button>Second One</Button>
> ```
>
> In this example, which style you use is up to you, but if the content is going to be something other than text (such as another XAML element), you'll need to use the second form.

8. Drag a *TextBlock* from the Toolbox to the page, position it next to the button, and adjust its size because the default is rather small.

    You might also want to adjust the font size for the *TextBlock* as well, because the default might be too small when running on a desktop computer. You'll find the font settings under the Text section in the Properties window.

9. To work with the *TextBlock* in code, you need to give it a name. Ensure that the Properties window is visible by selecting Properties Window from the View menu or typing Ctrl+W, P.

    Now, select the *TextBlock*; you should see that the *Name* field at the top of the Properties window displays <No Name>. Enter a suitable name such as *TxtHello* and press Enter. The XAML updates with an *x:Name* attribute, as shown in the following figure:

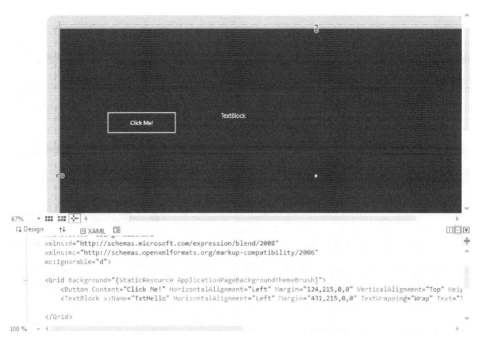

```
         xmlns:d="http://schemas.microsoft.com/expression/blend/2008"
         xmlns:mc="http://schemas.openxmlformats.org/markup-compatibility/2006"
         mc:Ignorable="d">

         <Grid Background="{StaticResource ApplicationPageBackgroundThemeBrush}">
             <Button Content="Click Me!" HorizontalAlignment="Left" Margin="124,215,0,0" VerticalAlignment="Top" Heig
             <TextBlock x:Name="TxtHello" HorizontalAlignment="Left" Margin="431,215,0,0" TextWrapping="Wrap" Text="1

         </Grid>
```

10. You now want the *TextBlock* to be updated when you press the button. To do this, you need to add a handler for the *Button*'s click event. In the designer pane, click the *Button*, and then, in the Properties window, click the small lightning-bolt button at the upper right.

This displays all the events that the *Button* can raise. In this case you just want to handle the click event, so double-click inside the text box, next to Click. This adds a handler with a default name to the *Page* class, which looks like this:

```
void HelloXaml::MainPage::Button_Click_1(Platform::Object^ sender,
    Windows::UI::Xaml::RoutedEventArgs^ e)
{

}
```

You'll learn more about event handling in Chapter 21, but you don't need much detail for now, because you aren't going to use either of the arguments.

11. To change the text in the *TextBlock*, add this line of code to the handler:

```
TxtHello->Text = "Hello, XAML!";
```

The name that you gave the *TextBlock* is used as the name for the object that represents it in code. Any UI element that you want to interact with in code has to have a name; you didn't give a name to the *Button* because you aren't interacting with it in code, only clicking it in the UI at run time.

12. On the Build menu, click Build Solution to build the app and ensure that you have no errors.

13. Run the app in the normal way, using Ctrl+F5.

Windows Store apps run full screen, so you'll see the entire screen taken up with your app's UI, as depicted in the screen shot that follows. Press the button and check that the *TextBlock* updates.

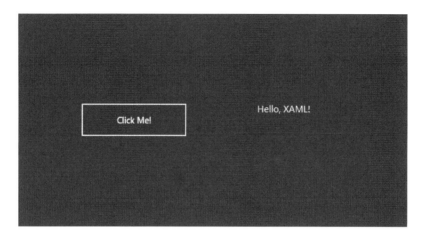

Note Windows Store apps work differently than traditional Windows applications. Running a Windows Store app doesn't just start it, it also adds it to the Start screen as an installed application.

If you're new to Windows 8 apps, you might be wondering how you get back to Visual Studio after you've performed testing. Moving the mouse to the lower-left corner of the screen displays the Start icon, which you can use to get back to the Start screen. When you get there, you'll notice that your app has been added to the list of available applications on the right of the page, although it doesn't look exciting because we haven't defined any content for the tile yet.

If you click the tile you'll be back at your app's UI, and you will probably find that the *TextBlock* still shows "Hello, XAML!" This is because apps stay active after they're started. I say "probably" because apps can be terminated if there is pressure on resources, in which case it would be restarted if you clicked it again.

If you decide that you don't want the app to appear on the Start screen, right-click its tile and then, on the shortcut menu that appears, click Unpin From Start. Even if an application isn't on the Start screen, you can always execute it by using the All Apps charm on the command bar.

Examining the project

When you create a Windows 8 app in Visual Studio, a lot of files are created. It is useful to know something about what they are, and in particular, which ones you can edit and which you should leave alone.

The following files are those that you can edit:

- **XAML files** App.xaml for the application; MainPage.xaml for the default page. Each page of the application has its own XAML file, whereas App.xaml holds code and XAML that represents the application itself.

- **Code-behind files** A .h and .cpp file for each XAML file; for example, App.xaml.h and App.xaml.cpp.

- **The manifest file: Package.appxmanifest** This contains metadata describing the application. You can double-click this to open it in the Manifest Designer.

- **The Assets folder** This contains Portable Network Graphics (PNG) files containing default images for the application. You can replace these with your own images to customize the appearance of your application.

- **Precompiled headers: pch.h and pch.cpp** You can add your own headers to pch.h, whereas pch.cpp is there simply to include pch.h.

Note *Precompiled headers* are a feature of many C++ compilers. A lot of code is included in header files, and in a typical application the same header files can be compiled for each source file. Many of these header files will never change, and so precompiled headers let the compiler process these once, and then reference the compiled version. Different compilers (and even different versions of Microsoft C++) use their own ways of handling precompiled headers, but for Windows Store apps any header files that are included in pch.h will be precompiled.

There are also a number of files that you shouldn't touch. XAML applications make heavy use of partial classes, and the .g.cpp and .g.h files represent the parts of classes that are generated by Visual Studio:

- **App.g.h and App.g.cpp**   The main function and XAML loading code.

- **StandardStyles.xaml**   Predefined styles and templates. You can derive from these, but don't change them.

- **MainPage.g.h and MainPage.g.cpp**   Generated partial class definitions for the default page. Another pair of .g.h and .g.cpp files are added for every page you add to the application.

- **XamlTypeInfo.g.h**   Type information generated by the XAML editor.

Introducing XAML

Although you can do a lot by just using the drag-and-drop functionality in Visual Studio and letting it generate the XAML for you, understanding how XAML works will make you a much more productive developer, and you'll also find that there are some things that you can only do by editing the XAML yourself. In this section, I introduce the concepts behind XAML and its grammar.

What is XAML?

XAML (Extensible Application Markup Language) is used in Windows RT and WPF to describe user interfaces. The idea behind XAML is that you create the user interface declaratively in XML, and the compiler then generates the code to create the UI at run time.

 Note Although XAML is mainly used for creating UIs, it provides a general way to describe the relationships and properties of objects; thus, it is also used to describe workflows within Windows Workflow Foundation.

There are three ways by which you can create UIs:

- Create the UI completely in XAML. The markup language includes features such as data-binding and triggers, which makes it possible for you to create sophisticated UIs without writing any code.

- Create the layout in XAML, with event handling code providing the logic behind the UI. This is the most commonly used approach, the default approach taken by Visual Studio, and the one that we use here.

- Create the UI completely in code, with no XAML. This is not the recommended approach, but it can be useful for complex and dynamic UIs.

XAML has a number of features that are especially useful for constructing UIs.

Using XAML for *declarative UI layout* separates the UI's look and feel. This way, you can specify the name of a button's click event handler without having to know in which language it is going to be implemented. This also makes it easy to separate the UI design and business logic implementation, making it possible for designers to work on the XAML without having to be concerned with the code.

XAML's event handling lets you link control events to handler functions in code, but you can also make event links in XAML itself. For example, you can have a label display the text of whichever item you select in a list box or for the font size of a label to be determined by the position of a slider. This means that for many simple interactions between controls, you don't need to write any code at all.

Using *Control templates*, you can define layout and visual behavior templates that can then be applied to controls across one or more applications. When combined with CSS-like *styles* and *triggers* that can change styles when events occur, you have a powerful way to create unique and responsive UIs. Template and style details can be defined as *resources* in XAML, which means that they can be reused easily. If placed in *resource dictionaries*, resources can be reused across projects.

Finally, data-binding is one of the most powerful features of XAML, making it possible for you to bind properties on objects to data that can come from a variety of sources. I have already mentioned one example, where the font size property of a control can be bound to the position of a slider. You can also bind to collections of objects, so that a list box can display an array of items, or you can bind to data retrieved from a data source.

XAML syntax

In XAML, an object is represented by an XML element, and the object's properties are defined by attributes. For example:

```
<Button Content="Click!" Click="Button_Click"/>
```

This element represents a *Button* object. It also sets its *Content* property and the name of the function used to handle the click event. It is easy to use custom classes from XAML, provided the runtime can locate the assembly containing the object code.

Relationships between objects are shown by nesting elements. For example, a *ListBox* can have a number of *ListBoxItem*s, as demonstrated in the following:

```
<ListBox>
  <ListBoxItem>Item 1</ListBoxItem>
  <ListBoxItem>Item 2</ListBoxItem>
</ListBox>
```

If you want to interact with a control from code, it must have a name, and you do this using the *x:Name* attribute, as shown in this example:

```
<TextBlock x:Name="txtHello" ... />
```

The *x:* prefix indicates that this is the XAML Name attribute, because a control could have its own *Name* attribute. The prefix will be defined in one of the parent elements of the *TextBlock*, as shown here:

```
<Page
    ...
    xmlns:x="http://schemas.microsoft.com/winfx/2006/xaml" />

    <Grid ... >
        <TextBlock x:Name="TxtHello" ... />
    </Grid>
</Page>
```

In a Windows RT application, each page of a UI is represented by an object of a class derived from *Page*. The definition of this class is in a *code-behind* file, and the link between the XAML and the class is provided by the *x:Class* attribute:

```
<Page
    x:Class="HelloXaml.MainPage" ... >
```

XAML also makes use of *markup extensions*, which are attribute values enclosed in curly brackets, like this:

```
<Grid Background="{StaticResource ApplicationPageBackgroundThemeBrush}">
```

This syntax informs XAML that the attribute value isn't simply text; it is normally used to create or manipulate objects.

XAML controls

A XAML UI is made up of controls. Everything is a control, from the top-level window to the image displayed on a button. Here's an important principle: XAML UIs are constructed by nesting controls within one another, and there is only one control at the top level, which will be a container such as a *Window* or *Page*.

We can divide controls into two broad types: *content controls* (which can only contain one item) and *items controls* (which can contain more than one).

> **Note** There are a number of commonly used controls that don't belong to these two groups (such as the *Calendar* and *DatePicker*) but for the purposes of explaining XAML, for the moment, I'll keep it simple.

A content control can only contain one other item as its content; for instance, a *Button* can display a piece of text or an image, but this can be an items control. As an example, a *Button* can contain a *StackPanel* which holds both an image and some text, as shown in the following illustration:

Here is the XAML to create that button:

```xaml
<Button HorizontalAlignment="Left" Margin="352,258,0,0"
        VerticalAlignment="Top" Height="120" Width="127">
    <StackPanel Orientation="Vertical">
        <TextBlock Text="Button" HorizontalAlignment="Center" />
        <Image Source="Assets/SmallLogo.png" Height="48" Width="75" />
    </StackPanel>
</Button>
```

You can see how the *Button* contains one item—a *StackPanel*—which contains a *TextBlock* and an *Image* stacked atop one another.

> **Tip** Keep in mind that textboxes aren't content controls, because they don't contain text or other controls as content; they implement their own UI that is used for input.

A selection of the most common content controls is shown in the following table:

Control	Description
AppBar	A container control that holds UI elements for commands and navigation
Border	Provides a border, background, or both around another control
Button	A standard Windows button. There are several other types of buttons, such as radio buttons, that look different but work in the same way.
CheckBox	A control that a user can select (check) or deselect (uncheck)
ScrollViewerl	A scrollable area that can contain other elements.
Tooltip	A tooltip associated with another control.

A selection of the most common items controls is shown in the following table:

Control	Description
ComboBox	A control that contains a drop-down list of items.
FlipView	A control that displays one item at a time, making it possible for users to "flip" between them.
GridView	A control that displays its items in a grid.
ListBox	A list box that contains a collection of *ListBoxItems*.
ListView	A control that shows a vertical list of items.

Layout controls

There is a special group of items controls that are used for UI layout. This group inherits from the *Panel* class. In both Windows Store and WPF applications, special controls are used to determine the layout of UI elements within a window or page. For instance, a *Page* might contain a *Grid* that will lay controls out in rows and columns, or a *StackPanel* that will create a vertical stack of elements. Separating out the container and layout functions affords greater freedom to UI designers because it is easy to create custom layouts if required. In this section, you'll look at a few of the most common layout controls.

The *StackPanel* is the simplest layout control. It arranges its child controls into a stack, either vertically or horizontally depending on the value of the *Orientation* property. The following image shows three buttons in a vertical *StackPanel*:

The XAML for this layout is very simple:

```
<StackPanel Background="{StaticResource ApplicationPageBackgroundThemeBrush}"
    Orientation="Vertical">
    <Button Content="First" FontSize="24" />
    <Button Content="Second" FontSize="24" />
    <Button Content="Third" FontSize="24" />
</StackPanel>
```

Because no other properties have been specified for the *StackPanel*, the panel fills all the available space, and its child controls are left-justified. Here are the same controls with the *Orientation* changed to *Horizontal*:

The *StackPanel* still fills all the available space, but this time, it lays out its children horizontally. By default, the child controls are centered vertically.

If you have so many items in a *StackPanel* that they aren't all visible at one time, you won't see the controls that fall outside the bounds of the *StackPanel*, but all of the objects will still be created. The *VirtualizingStackPanel* manages this efficiently by only creating child controls when they're visible.

The *Grid* is one of the most commonly used layouts. Items are arranged by row and column, and cells can have different sizes. You can specify the number of rows and columns as well as which cell a child control should occupy. The illustration that follows displays how three buttons look when displayed in a *Grid*.

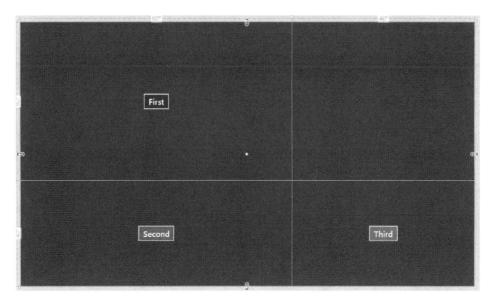

The XAML for this layout shows some interesting features.

```xml
<Grid Background="{StaticResource ApplicationPageBackgroundThemeBrush}" >
    <Grid.RowDefinitions>
        <RowDefinition Height="60*" />
        <RowDefinition Height="40*"/>
    </Grid.RowDefinitions>
    <Grid.ColumnDefinitions>
        <ColumnDefinition Width="60*" />
        <ColumnDefinition Width="40*" />
    </Grid.ColumnDefinitions>
    <Button Content="First" FontSize="24" Background="Blue" Grid.Row="0"
        HorizontalAlignment="Center"/>
    <Button Content="Second" FontSize="24" Background="Green" Grid.Row="1"
        HorizontalAlignment="Center"/>
    <Button Content="Third" FontSize="24" Background="Red" Grid.Column="1" Grid.Row="1"
        HorizontalAlignment="Center"/>
</Grid>
```

You can see how *RowDefinition* and *ColumnDefinition* elements are used to define the rows and columns in the grid. There are several ways to define the width and height, such as by using percentages or absolute values. In this case, the asterisk (*) denotes a proportion, so the widths of the two columns are distributed proportionally in the ratio 60:40. Like the *StackPanel*, there is no size specified for the *Grid* itself, so it fills all the available space. The other important concept shown by this example is the way in which the row and column values are specified for the buttons. This is done by using *attached properties*, which are explained in more detail in the sidebar that follows.

The *VariableSizedWrapGrid* is a variant on the *Grid*. It also lays items out in rows and columns but will automatically wrap items to the next row or column as necessary. This is obviously useful when the viewing area size changes, such as when switching your tablet from landscape to portrait mode. The following image shows five *Button* controls in a *VariableSizedWrapGrid*:

The XAML looks like this:

```
<VariableSizedWrapGrid Background="{StaticResource ApplicationPageBackgroundThemeBrush}"
                        MaximumRowsOrColumns="3" Orientation="Horizontal" ItemWidth="150">
    <Button Content="First" FontSize="24" Background="Blue" HorizontalAlignment="Center"/>
    <Button Content="Second" FontSize="24" Background="Green" HorizontalAlignment="Center"/>
    <Button Content="Third" FontSize="24" Background="Red" HorizontalAlignment="Center"/>
    <Button Content="Fourth" FontSize="24" Background="Cyan" HorizontalAlignment="Center"/>
    <Button Content="Fifth" FontSize="24" Background="Magenta" HorizontalAlignment="Center"/>
</VariableSizedWrapGrid>
```

The horizontal orientation shows that this control will lay its children out in rows, and the *MaximumRowsOrColums* says that it will wrap at three items. To achieve a nice layout, each grid cell is 150 wide, and the buttons are centered within their cells. If you decide that you want a layout that looks more like the Windows 8 Start screen, you could change the XAML to the following:

```
<VariableSizedWrapGrid Background="{StaticResource ApplicationPageBackgroundThemeBrush}"
    MaximumRowsOrColumns="3" Orientation="Horizontal" ItemWidth="150" ItemHeight="150" >
    <Button Content="First" FontSize="24" Background="Blue" HorizontalAlignment="Stretch"
        VerticalAlignment="Stretch"/>
    <Button Content="Second" FontSize="24" Background="Green" HorizontalAlignment="Stretch"
        VerticalAlignment="Stretch"/>
```

```
        <Button Content="Third" FontSize="24" Background="Red" HorizontalAlignment="Stretch"
            VerticalAlignment="Stretch"/>
        <Button Content="Fourth" FontSize="24" Background="Cyan" HorizontalAlignment="Stretch"
            VerticalAlignment="Stretch"/>
        <Button Content="Fifth" FontSize="24" Background="Magenta" HorizontalAlignment="Stretch"
            VerticalAlignment="Stretch"/>
</VariableSizedWrapGrid>
```

The difference is that both height and width have been set, and the horizontal and vertical alignments have been set to *Stretch*, so that the items will fill their respective cells. You can clearly see the difference in the following image:

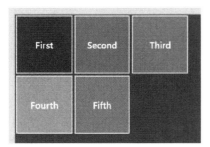

The last layout control we'll consider is the *Canvas*. With this control, you can specify absolute positions for its children, but it isn't used as often as the others because it doesn't adapt automatically to changing display conditions. Here is an example of some *Buttons* laid out on a *Canvas*:

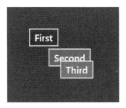

Here's the XAML for the layout:

```
<Canvas Background="{StaticResource ApplicationPageBackgroundThemeBrush}">
    <Button Content="First" FontSize="24" Canvas.Left="100" Canvas.Top="100" Background="Blue"/>
    <Button Content="Second" FontSize="24" Canvas.Left="150" Canvas.Top="150"
        Background="Green"/>
    <Button Content="Third" FontSize="24" Canvas.Left="180" Canvas.Top="180" Background="Red" />
</Canvas>
```

You can see that the positions of the *Buttons* are given by the *Canvas.Left* and *Canvas.Top* attached properties. The objects are displayed in the order in which they are declared, resulting in the third *Button* overlapping the second. If you want to specify the ordering explicitly, you can use the *ZIndex* property to determine the order in which elements will be rendered.

Event handling

When creating a UI in XAML, you use attributes on controls to link events to event handling functions, such as in the following example:

```
<Button Content="Click!" Click="Button_Click"/>
```

Here, the *Button*'s click event is being handled by a function called *Button_Click* in the associated code-behind file. Recall the example of an event handler function in the HelloXaml that you saw earlier:

```
void HelloXaml::MainPage::Button_Click_1(Platform::Object^ sender,
    Windows::UI::Xaml::RoutedEventArgs^ e)
```

Every event handler has the same signature: the return type is void, the first argument is a handle to the object that raised the event, and the second is a handle to an object, of type *RoutedEventArgs* or one of its subclasses, which might hold information about the event. For example, handlers for keyboard events will be sent a *KeyRoutedEventArgs* object whose *Key* property indicates which key was pressed. In the case of simple click-type notifications, there is no other information, so you can ignore this argument.

> **Note** Visual Studio will generate a handler for you, whose name is based on the control and event names, as in the previous example, but this is simply a convention, and you are free to use any name you like for event handlers.

The word "routed" in *RoutedEventArgs* refers to the fact that events can be routed to more than one control. Consider the example you saw earlier in the chapter, in which a *Button*'s content consisted of a *StackPanel* containing an *Image* and a *TextBlock*. If you click the *Image*, you're actually clicking an *Image* on top of a *StackPanel* on top of a *Button*, and you probably want to handle this event in the *Button*'s click handler. The event is first passed to the *Image*. Then, it's passed to its parent (the *StackPanel*), and so on, bubbling up the tree until it either reaches the top or someone says they've handled it.

C++/CX and Windows RT

Writing Windows Store apps exposes you to yet another variety of C++, known as *C++/CX* (Component Extensions).

You might well wonder (as I have myself on more than one occasion) why Microsoft needed to create yet another set of extensions to C++ when they had only recently introduced C++/CLI.

The main reason for this is that Windows Store apps do not use managed code; thus, they do not make use of the CLR. When you write a Windows Store app, it compiles down to native code rather than IL, so C++/CLI is not appropriate.

This means that you could write Windows Store apps in standard, unmanaged C++, but you'd have to provide a lot of housekeeping code to work with the underlying Component Object Model (COM)-based infrastructure. For this reason, Microsoft decided to add some extensions to C++ to handle these housekeeping tasks, in particular managing object lifetimes.

 Note If you don't want to use the C++/CX extensions, you can still write WinRT apps in C++ by using a library called Windows Runtime Library (WRL). This can be useful if you want to access low-level features not exposed by C++/CX, but it is more complex to use and beyond the scope of this book.

Unlike C++/CLI, C++/CX does not support garbage collection. This means that objects won't move around in memory, and so interop with unmanaged code is easier, and you can easily mix C++/CX and native C++ types.

You might also wonder where C++/CLI and .NET fit into the new world of Windows RT applications. It turns out that C++/CX applications can use a subset of the .NET APIs, and there is a client profile provided in Visual Studio so that you can code against this subset. This makes it possible for .NET developers to write Windows RT applications by using familiar APIs.

Windows RT

Windows RT is a new runtime on top of the Windows kernel. It doesn't use Win32: It is completely new. It covers the same functionality as Win32 (which was introduced in 1993!) but is object-oriented and written in C++.

The WinRT APIs contain a subset of the Win32 and COM APIs. You can use WinRT APIs from several languages, and language bindings are now called *projections*. There are currently three projections available: native (for C++), JavaScript, and .NET (for C# and VB.NET).

Metadata

All WinRT objects support reflection through metadata, so they can be used from dynamic languages such as JavaScript. WinRT uses the same metadata format as the CLR, which makes it easier and faster to use WinRT APIs from .NET without having to use P/Invoke.

WinRT code compiles down to native code, which has no facility for including metadata. For this reason, the metadata for WinRT code resides in separate files with a .winmd extension. These are CLI assemblies containing only metadata, so you can inspect them by using the IL disassembler tool (ISDASM).

C++/CX syntax

C++/CX is a lightweight set of extensions to C++, so there isn't too much to cover in this section. To create an object, use the *ref new* keyword, as demonstrated in the following:

```
MyClass ^mc = ref new MyClass();
```

The caret (^) is the same symbol used for managed handles in C++/CLI, but these are different because they are pointing to unmanaged code. We need a handle here rather than a pointer because C++/CX objects are *reference counted*.

Observe the use of *ref new* to create objects. This is an example of a compound keyword, formed of two separate tokens, and is not simply *new* with a *ref* modifier.

Reference counting

The COM mechanism that underlies WinRT uses a system of reference counting to manage object lifetimes. Each time client code obtains a handle to an object, the object increments its reference count. When the client has finished with the object, it needs to decrement the reference count. When the count reaches zero, the object knows that no one has a reference to it anymore, and so it can destroy itself. In the past, it was up to developers to ensure that reference counts were maintained correctly, and this was a common source of error. The Windows Runtime now manages this for you, so you no longer need to be concerned about object lifetimes.

Classes

You create run-time classes by using the *ref* keyword, as you do with C++/CLI.

```
public ref class MyClass
{
};
```

If a class is going to contain WinRT components, it must be declared as a *ref class*.

C++/CX also introduces the concept of *partial classes*, by which a class can be split into more than one part and combined by the compiler. This is necessary to support XAML, in which the GUI designer in Visual Studio generates code to represent a page. The developer then creates the second half of the class to add UI logic.

Note The lack of support for partial classes in C++/CLI is one of the reasons why it is not simple to create WPF applications in that language by using Visual Studio.

Here's how you might use a partial class. In the following example, one part is declared by using the *partial* keyword and placed in its own header file:

```
// MyClass.private.h
#pragma once
partial ref class MyClass   // use the 'partial' keyword
{
private:
```

```
    int _implementationDetail;
};
```

The second part of the class is placed in another header file that includes the first one.

```
// MyClass.h
#pragma once
#include "MyClass.private.h"

ref class MyClass  // don't use the 'partial' keyword here
{
public:
    int GetDetail();
};
```

Anyone wishing to use the class will include MyClass.h, but the interesting point is that anyone implementing the public part of the class doesn't have to see or know any details about the private part.

When Visual Studio creates the code for a XAML user interface, it generates .h and .cpp files. You will find that the .h file (for example, MyPage.h) includes another header (MyPage.g.h). The .g.h file is the partial class generated by the designer containing the private part of the page definition, whereas the .h file is the public part that you can edit. As you might expect, there is also a .g.cpp file, which contains the implementation of the functionality defined in the .g.h file.

Generics

C++/CX supports run-time generics, just like those you've met in C++/CLI.

```
generic <typename T>
public ref class List
{
    property T item;
    ...
};
```

The *generic* keyword introduces a generic type, and the *typename* in angle brackets shows that *T* is the type parameter which is used in the body of the class.

Strings

Whereas in C++/CLI code you use a *System::String* to represent strings, in C++/CX you use a *Platform::String*. Both types of string provide the same basic functionality, and both are immutable.

You create a string like this:

```
String ^s = "First string";
```

Or, you can create one like this:

```
wchar_t *txt = L"Second string";
String ^s2 = ref new Platform::String(txt);
```

In this example, *wchar_t* is the standard C++ wide character type, and a string literal is used to construct a *String* object. This example shows how C++/CX is an extension to standard C++ and can use the same data types.

To extract the underlying data from a *String*, use the *Data* function, as illustrated here:

```
const wchar_t *txt = s->Data();
```

Common namespaces

When building Windows Store apps you will find yourself working with a number of new namespaces. This final section summarizes the names and purposes of the main ones you need to know about.

The Windows namespaces

The *Windows* namespaces contain the APIs needed to build Windows Store apps. There are over 100 namespaces in all. The following table lists some those that are the most commonly used:

Namespace	Description
The *Windows::ApplicationModel* namespaces	Provide access to core run-time functionality and run-time information
The *Windows::Data* namespaces	Provide functionality for working with HTML, JSON and XML
The *Windows::Devices* namespaces	Enable applications to work with device capabilities such as cameras and geolocation
The *Windows::Foundation* namespaces	Contain fundamental Windows Runtime functionality
Windows::Foundation::Collections	Contains generic and specialized collection classes
The *Windows::Globalization* namespaces	Provide support for locale dependent features such as calendars and number formats
The *Windows::Graphics* namespaces	Provide support for image display and printing
The *Windows::Management* namespaces	Contain functionality for managing applications
The *Windows::Media* namespaces	Provide classes for creating and working with media such as photos, audio and video recordings
The *Windows::Networking* namespaces	Provide support for networking
The *Windows::Security* namespaces	Provide support for authentication and cryptography
The *Windows::Storage* namespaces	Provide functionality to work with files, folders and streams
The *Windows::System* namespaces	Provide system-level functions, including application launching, threading, and managing user profiles
The *Windows::UI* namespaces	Contain the core UI functionality, including input and notifications
The *Windows::UI::XAML* namespaces	Contain the classes, interfaces and enumerations necessary for working with XAML
The *Windows::Web* namespaces	Provide access to and help manage web resources, including RSS or Atom syndication feeds

The Platform namespaces

The *Platform* namespaces define a number of types that help you work with the Windows Store runtime. The following table lists the ones you might use in your code:

Namespace	Description
Platform	Contains built-in types that are compatible with the Windows Runtime
Platform::Collections	Provides implementations of the types defined in the *Windows::Foundation::Collections* namespace
Platform::Metadata	Contains attributes that modify type declarations

The *Platform* namespace defines a number of useful types:

- An *Object* base type

- Exception classes

- 1D array types

- A *String* class

The *Platform::Collections* namespace contains implementations of the following collection types that are defined in the *Windows::Foundation::Collections* namespace:

- *Map*, a modifiable collection of key/value pairs accessed by key, analogous to (and creatable from) *std::map*

- *MapView*, a read-only collection of key/value pairs accessed by key

- *Vector*, a modifiable sequence of elements, analogous to (and creatable from) *std::vector*

- *VectorView*, a read-only sequence of elements

The namespace also contains iterators to work with the collections, such as *VectorIterator* and *VectorViewIterator*.

> **Note** The concrete collections can't be passed between components written in different languages, such as from C++ to C#. When you need to accept or return a collection, use the corresponding interface type such as *Windows::Foundation::Collections::IVector*.

The *Platform::Metadata* namespace defines two attributes that can be used to annotate types:

- The *DefaultAttribute* is used to mark the preferred alternative among a collection of overloaded functions.

- The *FlagsAttribute* declares an enumeration that uses bit fields.

Quick reference

To	Do This
Create a single-page Windows Store app.	In the New Project dialog box, in the pane on the left, click Windows Store. Then, in the center pane, select the Blank App (XAML) project type.
Add controls to the page.	Drag controls from the Toolbox to the page, or edit the XAML directly.
Handle events from controls.	Double-click the control to add a handler for the default event. To add handlers for other events, use the event list in the Property editor.
Lay out elements in a row, horizontally or vertically.	Use a *StackPanel* container with the *Orientation* set appropriately.
Lay out elements in a grid	Use a *Grid* container.

More about Windows Store apps

After completing this chapter, you will be able to:

- Create a more complex app by using XAML and code-behind.

- Handle events from a more complex user interface.

- Use Windows Store app features, such as app bars.

- Share content with other applications.

I n this chapter you will create a more complex Windows Store app, one that uses a touch interface, and which can be deployed onto any Microsoft Surface tablet device. As well as showing you how to create a realistic Windows 8 app, you will also learn about some of the new features that the Windows Store interface has added to Windows programming.

Building the basic calculator

The app you'll be building during the course of this chapter is a programmer's calculator. This will offer the features of a normal calculator, such as arithmetic operations and being able to save values in memory, but it will also add some functions that are often useful to programmers. There is a lot that could be added, but we're going to limit the additions to the ability to work in different number bases (decimal, hexadecimal, and binary). In addition, programmer's calculators often work only with integers because they are used to manipulate addresses, so that's what we'll do here. The screen shot that follows shows how the finished app will appear.

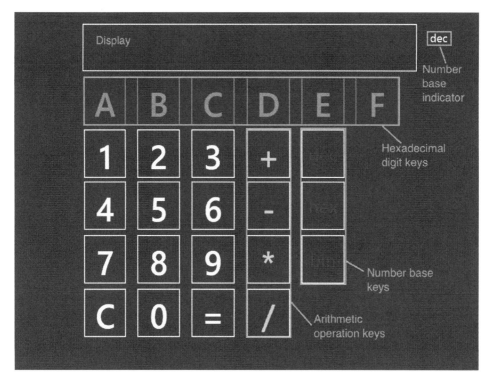

As you design and code this app, you will see how apps with a graphical UI like this are often not that complex in what they're doing, but you need to expend some effort to ensure that the UI works in the correct way. For example, if the user has selected binary mode, only the "0" and "1" number keys should be enabled. When he switches to hexadecimal, the keys "0" through "9" and "A" through "E" should be enabled.

Laying out the number buttons

Our UI is laid out in typical calculator style, with a *TextBlock* at the top to display the current value, and below that, number keys laid out in a grid.

> **Note** There are a lot of features that you need to consider—and lots of ways of implementing them—when designing a touch-based app for the Windows Store and the Microsoft Surface tablet, and we can't consider all of them without turning this chapter into a book. That means that this app is going to be limited in several respects. First, it is only going to be a single page app. Second, it is designed for use in landscape orientation only; the UI does not adapt itself to portrait mode.

Microsoft Blend for Microsoft Visual Studio

Visual Studio comes with a design tool called Blend for Visual Studio 2012, which provides a more design-oriented environment for creating UIs, as opposed to Visual Studio's code-oriented approach. Blend takes a more visual approach to UI design than Visual Studio, which makes it simpler to create styles and other graphical elements. The idea is that designers can use Blend to create sophisticated layouts by using XAML and then pass them on to developers who can add the logic in code.

In this first exercise, you will create a project with a single page, and lay out the number buttons and text display.

1. Start Visual Studio 2012 and create a new "blank XAML" project named **ProgCalc**.

2. In the editor, open MainPage.xaml.

3. To create an area where the numbers you enter and the results of calculations are displayed, drag a *Border* from the Toolbox to the main page, positioning it at the top with a left margin of about 430 and a top margin of about 50. Use the handles to resize the area to approximately 90 units high by 730 units wide, set its *BorderThickness* property to *2*, and then set *BorderBrush* to Gray (or any other color you like).

The numbers you enter into the calculator are going to be displayed in a *TextBlock*, and it would look good to give the *TextBlock* a border. The way you do this in XAML is not obvious: you add a *Border* control to represent the border, and then place the *TextBlock* inside it.

4. Drag a *TextBlock* to the form and drop it into the *Border*; you should find that it expands to fill the *Border* control. Add the *x:Name* attribute to give it a name so that you can interact with it in the code: I've called it **txtOutput**. You should also remove the *Text* attribute from the XAML and set its *FontSize* property to a suitable value such as 72.

> **Note** For this particular app, you actually don't need to give the *Border* a name, because you aren't going to interact with it from code. Only those UI elements with which you interact need to have a name.

The XAML should now look something like this:

```
<Grid Background="{StaticResource ApplicationPageBackgroundThemeBrush}">
    <Border BorderBrush="Gray" BorderThickness="2" HorizontalAlignment="Left"
            Height="89" Margin="432,48,0,0" VerticalAlignment="Top" Width="731">
        <TextBlock x:Name="txtOutput" TextWrapping="Wrap" FontSize="72"
            HorizontalAlignment="Left"/>
    </Border>
    ...
</Grid>
```

Don't worry about the exact sizes and positions: Where the buttons are and how they look isn't important to the functioning of the app.

5. Drag buttons to the page to start building up the grid. The buttons display with a preset style, but they are rather small for a calculator. I edited the properties to make them 100 wide by 108 high, and gave them a font size of 72. Ensure that you use the *x:Name* property to give each button a descriptive name, such as *btnOne*. You should end up with a grid positioned underneath the *Border*, and left aligned with it, similar to the following screen shot:

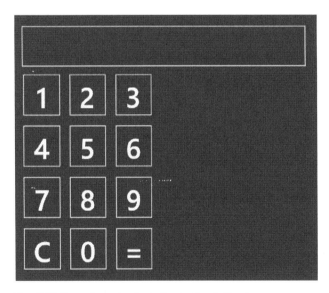

The XAML ought to look similar to the following:

```
<Grid Background="{StaticResource ApplicationPageBackgroundThemeBrush}">
    <Border BorderBrush="White" BorderThickness="2" HorizontalAlignment="Left"
            Height="100" Margin="431,50,0,0" VerticalAlignment="Top" Width="731">
        <TextBlock x:Name="txtOutput" TextWrapping="Wrap" FontSize="72"/>
    </Border>
    <Button x:Name="btnOne" Content="1" HorizontalAlignment="Left" Margin="431,167,0,0"
            VerticalAlignment="Top" Height="108" Width="100" FontSize="72"/>
    <Button x:Name="btnTwo" Content="2" HorizontalAlignment="Left" Margin="550,167,0,0"
            VerticalAlignment="Top" Height="108" Width="100" FontSize="72"/>
    <Button x:Name="btnThree" Content="3" HorizontalAlignment="Left" Margin="669,167,0,0"
            VerticalAlignment="Top" Height="108" Width="100" FontSize="72"/>
```

```
        <Button x:Name="btnFour" Content="4" HorizontalAlignment="Left" Margin="431,294,0,0"
            VerticalAlignment="Top" Height="108" Width="100" FontSize="72"/>
        <Button x:Name="btnFive" Content="5" HorizontalAlignment="Left" Margin="550,294,0,0"
            VerticalAlignment="Top" Height="108" Width="100" FontSize="72"/>
        <Button x:Name="btnSix" Content="6" HorizontalAlignment="Left" Margin="669,294,0,0"
            VerticalAlignment="Top" Height="108" Width="100" FontSize="72"/>
        <Button x:Name="btnSeven" Content="7" HorizontalAlignment="Left" Margin="431,422,0,0"
            VerticalAlignment="Top" Height="108" Width="100" FontSize="72"/>
        <Button x:Name="btnEight" Content="8" HorizontalAlignment="Left" Margin="550,422,0,0"
            VerticalAlignment="Top" Height="108" Width="100" FontSize="72"/>
        <Button x:Name="btnNine" Content="9" HorizontalAlignment="Left" Margin="669,422,0,0"
            VerticalAlignment="Top" Height="108" Width="100" FontSize="72"/>
        <Button x:Name="btnClear" Content="C" HorizontalAlignment="Left" Margin="431,550,0,0"
            VerticalAlignment="Top" Height="108" Width="100" FontSize="72"/>
        <Button x:Name="btnZero" Content="0" HorizontalAlignment="Left" Margin="550,550,0,0"
            VerticalAlignment="Top" Height="108" Width="100" FontSize="72"/>
        <Button x:Name="btnEquals" Content="=" HorizontalAlignment="Left" Margin="669,550,0,0"
            VerticalAlignment="Top" Height="108" Width="100" FontSize="72"/>
    </Grid>
```

6. Build and run the app to check that everything is OK. Start it by pressing Ctrl+F5 or, on the Debug menu, click Start Without Debugging.

    The app starts by showing a gray splash screen, and then shows the UI. If you move the mouse around you will see that buttons highlight as you move over them, and you can also press them, although nothing will happen at this point.

    You can get back to the desktop in several ways: you can either go via the Start screen, use the Alt+Tab key combination, or press Windows key+X to bring up a menu from which you can select the desktop.

Handling number input

Now that you have a basic layout in place, you can add the logic behind the buttons. When the user presses the number keys, you want to remember what they have pressed and build up the number. The easiest way to handle this is to realize that you don't need the actual number until you come to perform an operation: until that point, it can exist as a string on the display. This means that handling digit entry is very simple, as outlined in the following:

*   Get the current string from the *TextBlock*

*   Get the digit character represented by the number key

*   Add the digit to the string

*   Put the new string into the *TextBlock*

The following steps implement this logic in a handler:

1. Select one of the digit buttons in the XAML. Open the Properties editor by clicking the Properties tab at the side of the Visual Studio window and then click the lightning-bolt button at the upper-right of the editor to display the events for the button.

> **Tip** If the Properties tab is not visible, you can open the Properties editor by selecting Properties Window from the View menu or pressing Ctrl+W and then P.

2. In the list of events, find the *Click* entry, which should be at the top. Type **NumberButtons_Click** in the text box and press Enter.

   This causes Visual Studio to create an empty event handler. Edit the handler so that it ends up like this:

   ```
   void ProgCalc::MainPage::NumberButtons_Click(Platform::Object^ sender,
               Windows::UI::Xaml::RoutedEventArgs^ e)
   {
       Button ^btn = (Button^)sender;
       String ^digit = (String^)btn->Content;
       txtOutput->Text += digit;
   }
   ```

   You first need to cast the *sender* handle to a *Button*, so that you can use its *Content* property, which holds the digit you want. You then need to cast the *Content* to a *String*. Buttons can have all sorts of things as content, but in this case you know that it is a string, so the cast is safe.

3. Add the same handler to all 10 number buttons.

   You can either do this by using the Property editor or by editing the XAML, adding a *Click* attribute to the elements for each button. The advantage to doing it this way is that you can cut and paste the text rather than having to type it in the editor.

4. Build and run the app.

   You can click the number buttons to build up a number as a string in the *TextBlock*. And while we're thinking about the display, let's add the logic for the *Clear* button. All this needs to do for now is to clear the string in the display.

5. Select the *Clear* button in the XAML, open the Properties editor, and then display the event list.

6. Add a handler called *ClearButton_Click* to the *Click* event and then press Enter.

   Visual Studio creates a new handler for you.

7. Implement the handler to clear the string in the display, like this:

   ```
   void ProgCalc::MainPage::ClearButton_Click(Platform::Object^ sender,
               Windows::UI::Xaml::RoutedEventArgs^ e)
   {
       txtOutput->Text = "";
   }
   ```

8. Build and test the app.

   You should now be able to enter numbers and clear the display.

Adding arithmetic operations

Now that the numbers are displaying correctly, the next step is to add the buttons and logic for the arithmetic operations. When the user presses one of the arithmetic operation buttons, it signals that she has finished entering the first number. This means that you need to perform the following steps:

- Get the string from the display, convert it to a number, and then store it as the left operand
- Remember which operation was selected
- Clear the display and prepare it to accept the right operand

Adding the arithmetic buttons

The following exercise implements the aforementioned steps:

1. Edit the XAML to add four buttons for the basic arithmetic operations. I placed them in a vertical column, along the right side of the numbers, as illustrated in the following screen shot:

 Tip An easy way to do this is to duplicate a line in the XAML, and then edit it accordingly. For example, I copied the "3" button, renamed it to *btnPlus* and changed the Content to "+". You can then select it and drag it to the right to position it correctly; the designer will show you when buttons are aligned correctly.

2. To differentiate the arithmetic buttons from the number keys, assign them a color.

   You can do this by setting the *Foreground* property, either through the Property editor or by editing the XAML directly. (I set my buttons to *LightGreen*.)

3. When you have added all four buttons, pick one and display its events in the Property editor. Type **ArithmeticButtons_Click** as the handler name and then press Enter

   Visual Studio adds an empty handler for you.

4. Edit the other three arithmetic operation buttons so that they use the same handler.

Getting the number

Now, you need to get the string from the *TextBlock*, convert it to an integer, and store it for later use.

1. Start by adding an integer member to the *MainPage* class in MainPage.xaml.h, remembering to place it in the private section.

   ```
   int leftOperand;
   ```

2. Add code to the handler to convert the text to an *int* and store it in the *leftOperand*.

   ```
   void ProgCalc::MainPage::ArithmeticButtons_Click(Platform::Object^ sender,
           Windows::UI::Xaml::RoutedEventArgs^ e)
   {
       String ^txt = txtOutput->Text;
       int val;
       swscanf_s(txt->Data(), L"%d", &val);
       leftOperand = val;
   }
   ```

   There are a number of ways to perform the *string*-to-*int* conversion, and the one I've used here will simplify using other number bases later in the program. The *swscanf_s* function takes a string and converts it according to a format. The first argument is the raw string, which you can get from the *String* object by using its *Data* function. The second argument is the format string. The leading *L* denotes a wide character (as opposed to an ASCII) string literal, and *%d* alerts the function to expect a string that represents a decimal integer. Finally, the *&val* passes the address of the variable where the result should be written.

> **Note** There are two versions of *sswscanf*: *swscanf* and *swscanf_s*. You should always use the second of these because it does extra checking on its arguments and is less open to misuse, either accidental or deliberate.

Windows and strings

When you write code for Windows, you are going to find yourself wondering just how many ways of representing characters and strings there can be. You are also going to find yourself having to convert between different string formats, perhaps because a function that you want to use employs a different representation than that of the one you're using in your code, or because a string object doesn't support the functionality you want. The following table summarizes some (but not all) of the ways of representing characters and strings that you might encounter when working with C++ in Windows. In the Origin column, "S" stands for standard C++, and "M" for Microsoft-specific.

Representation	Description	Origin
char, 'a'	Single-byte character type and literal	S
char*, "abc"	Pointer to a single-byte character string, and string literal	S
wchar_t, L'a'	Wide character type and literal (normally two bytes)	S
wchar_t*, L"abc"	Pointer to a wide character string, and string literal	S
string	Single-byte string type	S
wstring	Wide string type	S
Platform::String	C++/CX string type that stores wide characters	M
System::String	C++/CLI string type that stores wide characters	M
BSTR	Component Object Model (COM) string type	M
TCHAR	Typedef for char or wchar_t, depending on platform, used in Win32 programming	M
LPTSTR	Typedef for char* or wchar_t*, depending on platform	M
CString	Microsoft Foundation Classes (MFC) string type	M

In best object-oriented style, the character data inside string objects is private, but many types give you a way to access it. For example, a *Platform::String* has a *Data* member function which returns you a *wchar_t** pointer to its data, whereas a standard C++ string has its *c_str* member function.

You might also see mention of Unicode and MBCS when reading about strings in Windows APIs. Unicode is the most widely used international standard for character representation, and many implementations in programming languages use two bytes per character. MBCS, which stands for Multi-Byte Character Set, was introduced by Microsoft. It uses a variable width representation, with one byte being used for ASCII characters, two bytes for most non-ASCII, and more where needed. The Windows API contains functions for converting between wide characters and MBCS (for example, *wcstombs* and *mbstowcs*).

Remembering the operation

What's the best way to remember which operation has been selected? The obvious solution is to use a variable to store the operation, and the fact that we want to choose one of a small set of values should suggest using an *enum* for this.

1. Open the MainPage.xaml.h file and add the declaration for an *enum* at the top, above the *MainPage* class declaration but still within the namespace.

   ```
   namespace ProgCalc
   {
       enum class ArithOp
       {
           PLUS, MINUS, TIMES, DIVIDE, NONE
       };

       public ref class MainPage sealed
       {
           ...
       };
   }
   ```

   The *enum* has one member for each operation, plus one to indicate that there is no operation. The names follow convention by being in capitals.

2. Add a private member to the *MainPage* class to represent the current operation.

   ```
   ArithOp currentOp;
   ```

3. Open the MainPage.xaml.cpp file and set the operation to *NONE* in the constructor, placing it after the call to *InitializeComponent*.

   ```
   MainPage::MainPage()
   {
       InitializeComponent();

       currentOp = ArithOp::NONE;
   }
   ```

4. You can now see which button was pressed. Edit the *ArithmeticButtons_Click* function to set the operation accordingly, using a chain of *if-else* statements.

   ```
   Button ^btn = (Button^)sender;
   if (btn == btnPlus) currentOp = ArithOp::PLUS;
   else if ...
   ```

5. Clear the display by setting the *Text* property for the *TextBlock* to an empty string.

6. Build the app to verify that there are no errors.

   You can't see any result at this stage, but you can if you want run the app in the debugger, setting a breakpoint in the arithmetic button handler to check that the conversion is working.

> **Tip** Checking that your code works by using the debugger is recommended practice. Writing output by using *Console::WriteLine* isn't!

Performing calculations

You can now complete the basic functionality by implementing the logic behind the Equals button. The operations you need to perform are as follows:

- Check that there is something to do. If there is no content in the *TextBlock* or no current operation, return.

- Get the text from the display and convert it to a number.

- Perform the calculation, using the current operation.

- Echo the result to the display.

Adding the handler and getting the number

1. In MainPage.xaml, bring up the properties for the Equals button and add a handler called *EqualsButton_Click*.

2. Add checks at the start of the handler to determine if there is anything to do.

   ```
   if (currentOp == ArithOp::NONE) return;
   if (txtOutput->Text->Length() == 0) return;
   ```

3. Get the string from the display and convert it to a number.

   You'll realize that you need to use the same code that you implemented in the arithmetic button handler, but this would lead to duplication. As a rule, any time that you see duplicated code, you should consider pulling it out into a separate function, a process called *refactoring*.

   Open the MainPage.xaml.h file and add the prototype for a function called *ConvertTextToInt*, placing it inside the namespace:

   ```
   int ConvertTextToInt(Platform::String ^str);
   ```

   Because this is a utility function and doesn't need access to internal details of *MainPage*, this doesn't have to be a member of the *MainPage* class, although you can make it one if you like.

4. Add the implementation to the MainPage.xaml.cpp file, as shown in the following:

   ```
   int ProgCalc::ConvertTextToInt(Platform::String ^str)
   {
       int val;
       swscanf_s(str->Data(), L"%d", &val);
       return val;
   }
   ```

Note There is nothing in the way of error checking here because we're sure that the only content of the string is digits, so conversion should not fail. This is reasonable for a tutorial example such as this, but in a real app you'd want to check that the user hadn't entered a number too large to fit in an integer.

5. Replace the original code in the arithmetic button handler with a call to your new function, like this:

```
leftOperand = ConvertTextToInt(txtOutput->Text);
```

6. Build the app and confirm that it still works as expected.

Performing the arithmetic operation

At last you can add the code to *EqualsButton_Click* to perform the operation.

1. Start by declaring the following two variables, one to hold the number currently in the *TextBlock*, and another to hold the result:

```
int rightOperand = 0;
int result = 0;
```

2. Store the content of the *TextBlock* in the *rightOperand* variable.

```
rightOperand = ConvertTextToInt(txtOutput->Text);
```

3. Add a switch statement that branches based on the operation.

```
switch(currentOp) {
case ArithOp::PLUS:
    result = leftOperand + rightOperand;
    break;
...
}
```

4. Addition, subtraction, and multiplication are simple, but you need to guard against dividing by zero. If you find that you are about to this, display an error message and return.

```
case ArithOp::DIVIDE:
    if (rightOperand == 0) {
        txtOutput->Text = "Divide by zero";
        Reset();
        return;
    }
    result = leftOperand / rightOperand;
    break;
```

Observe the call to *Reset*. If you get a divide by zero, you can't continue; you want to abandon the calculation and reset everything. But, because this can involve several operations, it makes sense to put it in a separate function.

5. Add the following declaration of the private *Reset* function to the *MainPage* class in MainPage.xaml.h, along with a Boolean member called *clearOnNextKey*:

```
void Reset();
bool clearOnNextKey;
```

6. Add the definition to the source file, as demonstrated here:

```
void ProgCalc::MainPage::Reset()
{
    currentOp = ArithOp::NONE;
    leftOperand = 0;
    clearOnNextKey = true;
}
```

The function clears the operation and saved left operand. The *clearOnNextKey* variable helps with controlling the UI. At present, the *TextBlock* is cleared when you press an operator key, ready for you to enter a new number. What we want to do in this case is to leave the message on the display and not clear it until the user taps a number key.

7. Add the following code to the start of *NumberButtons_Click*:

```
if (clearOnNextKey == true) {
    txtOutput->Text = "";
    clearOnNextKey = false;
}
```

If the flag is set, the *TextBlock* will be cleared before proceeding.

8. After you've done that, you can complete the equals handler, turning the result into a string and putting it back in the display.

> **Note** Development is often like this: you start implementing one piece of code and find that there are things you need to do before proceeding. Sometimes it feels as if you're moving backward, finding that in order to do A, you need to do B, which requires C, and so on. But, eventually you do get back to A again!

```
wchar_t buff[80];
swprintf(buff, 80, L"%d", result);
txtOutput->Text = ref new String(buff);
```

This code uses *swprintf*—which does the opposite to the *swscanf_s* function that you learned about earlier—taking a value and converting it to a string in a given format. Unlike *swscanf_s*, *swprintf* needs an array of *wchar_t*, which you need to convert to a *Platform::String* in order to use it with the *TextBlock*.

Testing the calculator

Have you ever had a problem with a piece of software and found yourself thinking "didn't anyone test this before they released it?"

We have all experienced buggy software that doesn't work properly or crashes, and it is very annoying when the problem is something basic that ought to have been caught during development. To avoid inflicting the same frustration on your users, now that you have implemented the basic logic for the calculator, you need to test what you've done before proceeding. This will ensure that you are building on a solid foundation.

When testing, you should start by making a test plan. This doesn't have to be anything complex or grand, but designing a plan helps to avoid the problem of "testing by playing around," when you test what occurs to you at the time. If you do that, you run the risk of missing out some vital area because it didn't occur to you.

How do you decide what needs to be tested? Here are several areas that you need to consider:

- Does the basic functionality work as it should?

- Does the UI render the results correctly and legibly?

- Does the app handle mistakes and errors properly?

- Does the UI respond to error conditions correctly?

Many developers make the mistake of only testing the first category, not thinking about what mistakes the user could make, which means that surprises might be left in the code for users to find later.

A good place to start is by making a list of what you want to test. Don't worry about thinking of everything straight off; if another test occurs to you, add it to the list. A first obvious test is for addition: adding two numbers results in another number that represents their sum. If you test this with, say, 1 + 2 and 3 + 3, there is no reason to suspect that other numbers will behave differently. The same is true of the other arithmetic operators, so we can start with the following four tests:

- Addition of two numbers

- Subtraction of two numbers

- Multiplication of two numbers

- Division of two numbers

Two things immediately spring to mind when I look more closely at this list. A subtraction such as 5 – 8 will yield a negative number, so I need to test that this displays correctly. I also realize that I'll have to test for division by zero, so I'll add that one. My list now looks like this:

- Addition of two numbers

- Subtraction of two numbers

  - Display of negative result from subtraction

- Multiplication of two numbers

- Division of two non-zero numbers

  - Divide-by-zero results in correct error

Another thing occurs to me: getting zero involved in calculations is not just a special case for division. Multiplying by zero results in zero, and adding or subtracting zero also has to be considered. And so we now end up with the following:

- Addition of two numbers

  - Addition of zero gives right answer

- Subtraction of two numbers

  - Display of negative result from subtraction

  - Subtraction of zero gives right answer

- Multiplication of two numbers

  - Multiplication by zero gives zero

- Division of two non-zero numbers

  - Divide-by-zero results in correct error

That will do for the basic operation of the calculator. Now, you need to think about the operation of the user interface. Here are a few examples:

- Does the Clear button return the calculator to its starting point whenever it is pressed?

- What happens if the user keeps pressing the Equals button?

- Does Equals handle an empty display or no operation?

There are a number of other conditions that you could add, and you should ensure that you test as many as you can before continuing.

Improving the graphics

When you run the app, you'll see that it appears on the Start screen as a rather boring, gray square with a white cross in the middle. This is the default image supplied for you, and any serious developer is going to want to update that to something more eye-catching and useful. But first, let's talk about tiles. Anyone who has worked with a computer is completely familiar with icons—those little square graphics that are used to represent and start applications. Windows 8 has taken the usefulness of icons to a new level by introducing tiles.

By default, tiles are 150x150 pixels in size, but if the app needs to show more information, it can use a wide tile that is 310x150 pixels.

Creating and using a tile

Double-click the *Package.appxmanifest* file to open the manifest editor. The manifest contains details of the resources used by the app and is arranged on four tabs. The Application UI tab is the one in which we're interested. This is where you specify details of UI elements such as the tiles and splash screen.

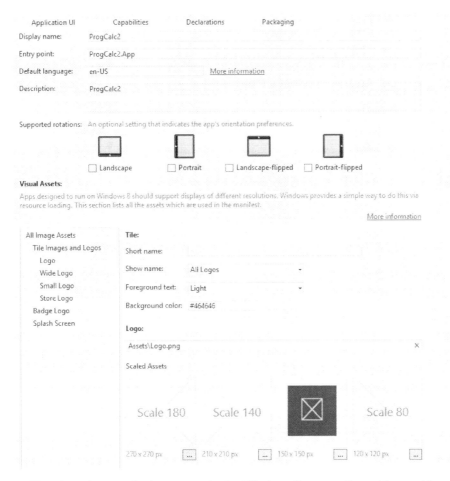

If you're going to submit your app to the Windows Store, you'll need to provide several logos and images. At a minimum you need to provide the following:

- The standard 150x150-pixel square logo

- The store logo (50x50 pixels), used to display your app in search listings in the Windows Store

- The small logo (30x30 pixels), used with your app's display name in various places, such as in search results and in lists of searchable apps.

- The splash screen (620x300 pixels) that displays while your app is starting up

Because you're not going to submit this particular app to the Windows Store, you don't need to create all of these. But we will address two of them to make the calculator look a bit more realistic.

Note The Manifest Editor has several entries for some of the logos under the heading Scaled Assets. To get the best UI experience, Microsoft encourages designers to provide properly scaled versions of the various image files because these will look much better than scaling them programmatically.

There are two ways in which you can provide a logo: the first is to edit the default graphic created for the project, and the second is to create another graphic and import it. To edit the logo, in Solution Explorer, double-click the Logo.png file. This opens the file in the built-in graphics editor. I created the logo shown in the following illustration by using a paint program; you can use any program you like, provided you can produce an image that is 150x150 pixels and saved as a Portable Network Graphics (PNG) file.

To use it to represent your app, copy it into the Assets folder for your app. Then, open the Manifest Editor, and type the name of the file into the Logo box, as demonstrated in the following screen shot:

Observe the Background Color entry in the editor. Although you can use any image you want for a tile, it is very common to use white graphics on a colored background, and to make the image background transparent. This makes it possible for users to change the background color of tiles, while still maintaining a consistent look. Here's how the app looks on the Start screen now:

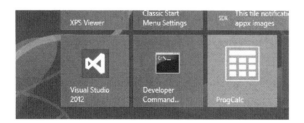

You can see that the custom logo appears alongside the tiles of other apps, and that the name of the app has been added to the tile. You can control whether this name is displayed, because you likely wouldn't want it to if your logo includes the app name.

The splash screen is displayed while the app is starting up. It consists of an image 620x300 pixels that is displayed on a colored background. Again, the image is often created with a transparent background so that users can change the Windows background color. After you have created an image of the correct size, in the manifest Editor, in the pane on the left, click Splash Screen and then type the name of the image file into the text box. Rebuild and run the app; you should see the splash screen appear before the calculator interface opens.

Updates and badges

Although we don't have the space here to delve into everything that you can do with tiles, there are two features that are worth mentioning in passing.

The first is updating. In a more traditional operating system, program icons are normally static. However, in Windows 8, Microsoft introduced the concept of *Live tiles*. With Live tiles, not only can you tap them to start the app, just like ordinary desktop icons, but they can also display "live" content when the app isn't running. For example, the tile for a weather app could display the current temperature and a weather symbol, or an email app could show how many new messages have arrived. Programs can update their own tiles, but they are most useful because they can be updated by background processes even when the app isn't running. This means that the Start screen is now a dynamic environment, with app tiles reflecting current content.

The second item is badges. Badges are small icons that display notifications in the lower-right corner of a tile, as shown in the following:

You pick a badge from a limited set of 11 symbols and the numbers from 0 to 99 (any number greater than 99 displays as "99+"). In the current version of Windows, you can't define your own badges. As with content, app badges can be updated by background processes.

Handling different number bases

One of the features that distinguish a programmer's calculator is the ability to work in other number bases. Addresses are often specified in hexadecimal (base 16, and less often nowadays in octal, base 8) and it might be useful to work in binary, as well.

So the next task is to add buttons with which the user can change the current number base, and then implement the logic to make the display and arithmetic work correctly in different bases.

Hexadecimal and binary

Hexadecimal (or hex, for short) arithmetic counts by 16's, which means that the hexadecimal value "10" represents "16" in decimal; "11" represents "17"; and "20" is "32." The letters A through F are used to represent the extra digits that we need for the values between decimal 9 and decimal 15. The following table shows the correspondence between hexadecimal and decimal values

Hexadecimal	Decimal
9	9
A	10
B	11
C	12
D	13
E	14
F	15
10	16
11	17
19	25
1A	26
1E	30
1F	31
20	32

In code, you specify hexadecimal values with a leading "0X" (or "0x") to differentiate them from decimal values. Binary uses only the digits 0 and 1, and represents numbers as powers of 2. The table that follows shows some powers of 2.

Power of 2	Value
2^0	1
2^1	2
2^2	4
2^3	8
2^4	16
2^5	32
2^6	64
2^7	128
2^8	256

You can represent any positive integer as a sum of powers of 2. For example, decimal "9" can be expressed as 8 + 1, whereas decimal "31" can be written as 16 + 8 + 4 + 2 + 1. To represent a number in binary, construct a string of 1's and 0's, with a 1 representing a power of 2 that you are using. So "9" would be represented as "1001" (2^4, no 2^3 or 2^2, and 2^0), whereas "31" would be "11111" (all the powers from 2^4 down to 2^0)

Adding the hexadecimal and base buttons

You need to add buttons to represent the three number bases that we're going to use. You also need to add another six buttons to represent the extra digits required by hexadecimal numbers. The following exercise shows you how to add and arrange the buttons to the UI.

1. Drag on the UI to select the 16 number and arithmetic operations. Move them down to leave space for another row of buttons below the *TextBlock*.

2. Add a row of six buttons in the gap, making them the same size as the number buttons. These represent the hexadecimal digits A through F, so give them the names *btnHexA* thru *btnHexF*. You should end up with an arrangement similar to following:

Ensure that they use the same handler as the other number buttons.

3.   Add three buttons next to the arithmetic operation keys and under the "E" key. Label them "dec", "hex", and "bin", from the top downward, and give them the names *btnDecimal*, *btnHex* and *btnBinary*. You'll need to decrease the font size for the text to fit on the buttons, and you can change the color to make them stand out. Refer back to the first figure in this chapter to see what the arrangement looks like.

4.   You'll need to a way to determine which base you're using, so add a *TextBlock* to the right of the main display. Give it a name (such as *txtBase*) and set its font size to about *24*.

5.   Open the Properties editor, and add a handler called *BaseButtons_Click* to all three buttons.

Changing the base

Adding the logic for changing the number base requires careful consideration. Here's what you need to do whenever the user clicks one of the base buttons:

*   Set the base to the appropriate value: binary, decimal, or hexadecimal.

*   Ensure that only the appropriate number buttons are enabled. In other words, when in binary mode, only the "0" and "1" keys are enabled, in decimal mode "0" through "9" are enabled, and in hexadecimal mode the "A" through "F" keys are available, as well.

*   Convert the string in the display to appear in the correct form.

*   Change the small *TextBlock* to display which base is being used.

The following exercise shows you how to implement this logic.

1.   You need a way to store the base that has been chosen. Like the arithmetic operation, you are choosing from a small set of values, so another *enum* is appropriate. Open MainPage.xaml.h and add an *enum* within the namespace.

```
namespace ProgCalc
{
    enum class Base
    {
        DEC, HEX, BIN
    };
    ...
};
```

2.   Add a data member to the *MainPage* class to hold the current base, and initialize it to decimal in the *Reset* function.

```
// In MainPage.xaml.h
Base base;
```

```
// In MainPage.xaml.cpp
void ProgCalc::MainPage::Reset()
{
    currentOp = ArithOp::NONE;
    base = Base::DEC;
    leftOperand = 0;
    clearOnNextKey = true;
}
```

3. Edit *BaseButtons_Click* and add the outline of the logic.

```
void ProgCalc::MainPage::BaseButtons_Click(Platform::Object^ sender,
    Windows::UI::Xaml::RoutedEventArgs^ e)
{
    // Get the button that was pressed
    Button ^btn = (Button^)sender;

    if (btn == btnDecimal)
    {
        // Enable the decimal buttons
        base = Base::DEC;
        txtBase->Text = "dec";
    }
    else if (btn == btnHex)
    {
        // Enable the hex buttons
        base = Base::HEX;
        txtBase->Text = "hex";
    }
    else if (btn == btnBinary)
    {
        // Enable the binary buttons
        base = Base::BIN;
        txtBase->Text = "bin";
    }
}
```

You can see how each of the cases sets the *base* variable and displays the current base in the *TextBlock*. The comments about enabling buttons are there as placeholders, because this is another example of code that is best provided as separate functions.

4. Add three new members to the *MainPage* class declaration in MainPage.xaml.h.

```
void EnableHexButtons(bool enable);
void EnableDecimalButtons(bool enable);
void EnableBinaryButtons();
```

Notice the slightly different form of the binary function. I've added the Boolean argument to the decimal and hexadecimal functions to help avoid code duplication.

5. Implement the following functions in MainPage.xaml.cpp:

```cpp
void ProgCalc::MainPage::EnableHexButtons(bool enable)
{
    btnHexA->IsEnabled = enable;
    btnHexB->IsEnabled = enable;
    btnHexC->IsEnabled = enable;
    btnHexD->IsEnabled = enable;
    btnHexE->IsEnabled = enable;
    btnHexF->IsEnabled = enable;
}

void ProgCalc::MainPage::EnableBinaryButtons()
{
    EnableHexButtons(false);
    EnableDecimalButtons(false);
    btnZero->IsEnabled = true;
    btnOne->IsEnabled = true;
}

void ProgCalc::MainPage::EnableDecimalButtons(bool enable)
{
    btnZero->IsEnabled = enable;
    btnOne->IsEnabled = enable;
    btnTwo->IsEnabled = enable;
    btnThree->IsEnabled = enable;
    btnFour->IsEnabled = enable;
    btnFive->IsEnabled = enable;
    btnSix->IsEnabled = enable;
    btnSeven->IsEnabled = enable;
    btnEight->IsEnabled = enable;
    btnNine->IsEnabled = enable;
}
```

The decimal and hexadecimal functions enable or disable the 0 through 9 and A through F keys, respectively. The binary function only wants the 0 and 1 keys, so the easiest solution is to disable everything and turn on the ones you want.

6. Call them from the base handler. For the binary case, just call *EnableBinaryButtons*. For the decimal case, call *EnableDecimalButtons(true)* and *EnableHexButtons(false)*, and for the hexadecimal case, call both the decimal and hex functions with *true* as the argument.

```cpp
if (btn == btnDecimal)
{
    // Enable the decimal buttons
    EnableDecimalButtons(true);
    EnableHexButtons(false);
    base = Base::DEC;
    txtBase->Text = "dec";
}
```

```
        else if (btn == btnHex)
        {
            // Enable the hex buttons
            EnableDecimalButtons(true);
            EnableHexButtons(true);
            base = Base::HEX;
            txtBase->Text = "hex";
        }
        else if (btn == btnBinary)
        {
            // Enable the binary buttons
            EnableBinaryButtons();
            base = Base::BIN;
            txtBase->Text = "bin";
        }
```

7. Add the default state to the *Reset* function so that it will be reset to decimal:

```
void ProgCalc::MainPage::Reset()
{
    currentOp = ArithOp::NONE;
    base = Base::DEC;
    txtBase->Text = "dec";
    leftOperand = 0;
    clearOnNextKey = true;
    EnableDecimalButtons(true);
    EnableHexButtons(false);
}
```

8. Call *Reset* from the *OnNavigatedTo* function, which means the page will initialize properly.

9. Build the app to ensure there are no coding errors.

Converting the string in the display

At this point, you can use the buttons to change the number base, but it isn't affecting the value shown on the display. You need to implement the base handler so that it works like this:

- Get the string from the display and convert it to a value, using the current number base

- Change the base, according to which button was pressed

- Convert the value to a string, using the new number base, and put it back in the display

The first step is to modify the *ConvertTextToInt* function that you wrote earlier so that it takes account of the number base. Converting from decimal and hexadecimal strings can be done by *swscanf_s*, but you need to do binary yourself.

1. Edit the *ConvertTextToInt* function so that it looks like the following example. Notice how it is now a member of the *MainPage* class so that it has access to members of the class:

```
int ProgCalc::MainPage::ConvertTextToInt(Platform::String^ s)
{
    int n;

    if (base == Base::HEX)
        swscanf_s(s->Data(), L"%x", &n);
    else if (base == Base::DEC)
        swscanf_s(s->Data(), L"%d", &n);
    else if (base == Base::BIN)
        n = FromBinary(s->Data());

    return n;
}
```

The *%x* descriptor converts a hexadecimal string, and *%d* handles the decimal case. You will provide your own function to deal with the binary conversion.

2. Add a prototype for the *FromBinary* function to MainPage.xaml.h. Because this is a utility function and doesn't need access to any members of the *MainPage* class, you don't have to make it a member.

```
unsigned long FromBinary(std::wstring s);
```

3. Add the implementation to the MainPage.xaml.cpp file

```
unsigned long ProgCalc::FromBinary(std::wstring s)
{
    wchar_t *stop;
    long l = wcstol(s.c_str(), &stop, 2);

    return l;
}
```

This function uses the *wcstol* (Wide Character String To Long) function for the conversion, which will cope with input strings in binary. Here is where you see a good example of the many string conversions that you might need to use in Windows programming: the *Data* function gets a *wstring* out of the *Platform::String*, and the *c_str* function then gets a *wchar_t** that represents the content of the *wstring*.

Notice the second argument to the function. This returns a pointer to where the number stopped in the string that you passed in. The idea is that the function will convert as much of the string as it can to a number and then stop when it reaches a character it can't handle; it will then pass you back a pointer to that character, so you can pinpoint where parsing stopped. Because we know that the entire string is valid, we don't need to use that argument, but we must still supply a variable.

4. You now need to do the opposite conversion, taking a value and converting it to a string in the correct format. Add a prototype for this function to the header file, such as shown in the following:

```
Platform::String^ ConvertOutputString(int val);
```

5. Add an implementation of the *ConvertOutputString* function to the source code file.

```
Platform::String^ ProgCalc::MainPage::ConvertOutputString(int val)
{
    wchar_t buff[80];
    if (base == Base::HEX)
        swprintf(buff, 80, L"%x", val);
    else if (base == Base::DEC)
        swprintf(buff, 80, L"%d", val);
    else if (base == Base::BIN)
    {
        String ^bf = ToBinary(val);
        return bf;
    }
    return ref new String(buff);
}
```

You can see that the structure of this function now mirrors that of *ConvertTextToInt*. It also uses another helper function called *ToBinary* to convert a value to a binary string.

6. Add the prototype for *ToBinary* to MainPage.xaml.h.

```
String^ ToBinary(int n);
```

7. Add the implementation to MainPage.xaml.cpp.

```
String^ ProgCalc::ToBinary(int n)
{
    String ^s = ref new String();

    do {
        s += (n & 1) ? L'1' : L'0';
    }
    while (n >>= 1);

    std::wstring result(s->Data());
    std::reverse( result.begin(), result.end() );

    s = ref new String(result.c_str());
    return s;
}
```

This function gives you a chance to use the bitwise operators, which is not something you have to do very often, so it is worth taking the opportunity to use them here. The *do* loop examines the code, bit by bit, adding a "1" or "0" character to a string, depending on whether the bit is set or not. The expression *(n & 1)* does a bitwise AND of the value and 1: Remember that the AND takes two integer values for each bit position, returning 1 if (and only if) both are set. Because "1" only has a single 1 in the lowest bit position, this is checking whether the lowest bit is set.

The loop condition *(n >>= 1)* does a right-shift on the value by one position. This shifts all the bits one place to the right, losing the rightmost bit, so that bit 2 becomes bit 1, and a zero is introduced on the far left to fill in. After the loop has examined all the bits, the number will be left as all zeros, so the loop will terminate.

At this point, however, the string is in the wrong order because the character representing the lowest bit is the first, and the others have been added on. So, you need to reverse the string; you could do this by using a loop, but the Standard Library has a useful reverse function, so you can use that, instead.

Note The way binary conversion is handled here is limited. In particular, because binary representations are much longer than their decimal or hexadecimal equivalent, it would be easy to generate a number that would overflow the space in the *TextBlock*.

8. The final stage is to complete the logic for changing base and updating the display. Add code to the start of the *BaseButtons_Click* handler to get the number from the display, as illustrated here:

```
// Get the value from the display
int val = 0;

if (txtOutput->Text->Length() > 0)
    val = ConvertTextToInt(txtOutput->Text);
```

9. After changing the base, put the value back in the new format.

```
// Update the display
txtOutput->Text = ConvertOutputString(val);
clearOnNextKey = true;
```

Here is the complete handler, for reference:

```
void ProgCalc::MainPage::BaseButtons_Click(Platform::Object^ sender,
    Windows::UI::Xaml::RoutedEventArgs^ e)
{
    // Get the value from the display
    int val = 0;

    if (txtOutput->Text->Length() > 0)
        val = ConvertTextToInt(txtOutput->Text);

    // Get the button that was pressed
    Button ^btn = (Button^)sender;
```

```
    if (btn == btnDecimal)
    {
        EnableDecimalButtons(true);
        EnableHexButtons(false);
        base = Base::DEC;
        txtBase->Text = "dec";
    }
    else if (btn == btnHex)
    {
        EnableDecimalButtons(true);
        EnableHexButtons(true);
        base = Base::HEX;
        txtBase->Text = "hex";
    }
    else if (btn == btnBinary)
    {
        EnableBinaryButtons();
        base = Base::BIN;
        txtBase->Text = "bin";
    }

    // Update the display
    txtOutput->Text = ConvertOutputString(val);
    clearOnNextKey = true;
}
```

10. Edit the *EqualsButton_Click* function so that the output will be converted to the right base. Locate the lines at the end of the function that use *swprintf* and place the result into a buffer, which should look like this:

```
wchar_t buff[80];
swprintf(buff, 80, L"%d", result);
txtOutput->Text = ref new String(buff);
```

Replace them with the following code:

```
txtOutput->Text = ConvertToOutputString(result);
clearOnNextKey = true;
```

11. Build and run the app, and test it thoroughly!

Using app bars

The Windows Store UI model doesn't support menus or dialog boxes. The idea is that the design should make it easy for the user to navigate his way through the app by using the controls on the page rather than having to pull down menus and use dialog boxes, which could be awkward on a touch device.

There are times, however, when users need to adjust settings or express preferences. For example, in the weather app you might want to switch from Fahrenheit to Celsius, or vice versa. Having these on the main UI would clutter things up, so there is a need for a way to expose these to the user, as needed. Windows Store apps use *app bars* to present navigation, commands, and tools to users.

These are areas that appear when the user swipes from top or bottom of the screen (or by right-clicking or typing Ctrl+Z). They are not intended to hold critical commands: the idea is that anything critical (like the "take a picture" command for a camera app) ought to be in the main UI.

Applications can have two app bars: one at the top of the screen, which is typically used for navigation, and one at the bottom, which is used for commands. In this section, you'll add a bottom app bar to the calculator, which will hold three buttons, giving you an alternative way to change the number base. Here is what the app will look like with the app bar displayed:

Defining the button styles

The buttons on an app bar are usually round, and this is provided by a set of styles. Before adding the app bar to your app, you need to edit the styles so that they will display correctly.

Styles

One of the secrets to designing great Windows Store apps is to use a coherent and consistent visual style throughout. This is done in XAML through the liberal use of styles, which work in a similar way to how CSS does in HTML. A developer or designer can define a style for buttons that establishes the basic appearance, including colors, fonts, borders, and other properties. This style can then be applied across the app, and a form of inheritance means that adjustments can be made. Doing this makes it possible for styles to be shared across pages and even across applications, and prevents duplication in the XAML. A Windows Store project comes with a file called StandardStyles.xaml, which defines a base set of styles for Windows Store apps. You should use these when you can so that your apps blend with the Windows Store look and feel.

1. Open StandardStyles.xaml, and search for **Standard AppBarButton Styles**.

   This is followed by a lot of commented out entries which define styles for various buttons.

2. Copy one of the style entries, remove the comments, and then edit it so that it looks like this:

```xml
<Style x:Key="HexAppBarButtonStyle" TargetType="ButtonBase"
        BasedOn="{StaticResource AppBarButtonStyle}">
    <Setter Property="AutomationProperties.AutomationId" Value="HexAppBarButton"/>
    <Setter Property="AutomationProperties.Name" Value="Hex"/>
    <Setter Property="Content" Value="h"/>
</Style>
```

   This creates a style for the Hex button, which is based on the default *AppBarButton* style and whose content is an "h". The *Name* is the text that will be displayed below the button when it appears on the app bar.

3. Repeat the previous step to create styles for the decimal and binary buttons.

```xml
<Style x:Key="DecAppBarButtonStyle" TargetType="ButtonBase"
        BasedOn="{StaticResource AppBarButtonStyle}">
    <Setter Property="AutomationProperties.AutomationId" Value="DecAppBarButton"/>
    <Setter Property="AutomationProperties.Name" Value="Dec"/>
    <Setter Property="Content" Value="d"/>
</Style>
<Style x:Key="BinAppBarButtonStyle" TargetType="ButtonBase"
        BasedOn="{StaticResource AppBarButtonStyle}">
    <Setter Property="AutomationProperties.AutomationId" Value="BinAppBarButton"/>
    <Setter Property="AutomationProperties.Name" Value="Bin"/>
    <Setter Property="Content" Value="b"/>
</Style>
```

4. Save the StandardStyles.xaml file.

Adding an app bar

Now that you have set up the styles for the three buttons, you can add the app bar.

1. Add this XAML to the bottom of the *Page* element, immediately after the end of the *Grid*:

```xml
<Page.BottomAppBar>
    <AppBar x:Name="bottomAppBar" Padding="10, 0 10, 0">
        <StackPanel Orientation="Horizontal" HorizontalAlignment="Left">
            <Button x:Name="btnAppBarDec" Style="{StaticResource DecAppBarButtonStyle}"
                Click="BaseButtons_Click"/>
            <Button x:Name="btnAppBarHex" Style="{StaticResource HexAppBarButtonStyle}"
                Click="BaseButtons_Click"/>
            <Button x:Name="btnAppBarBin" Style="{StaticResource BinAppBarButtonStyle}"
                Click="BaseButtons_Click"/>
        </StackPanel>
    </AppBar>
</Page.BottomAppBar>
```

The *BottomAppBar* element contains an *AppBar*, which in turn contains a *StackPanel*. A *StackPanel* is a container that contains a stack of items, in this case arranged horizontally and left-aligned. Like menus, it is a convention that commands on a bottom app bar should be left-aligned, and any buttons for help should be right-aligned on the other side of *AppBar*.

Each button has the appropriate style set and is linked to the base buttons click handler.

2. Build and run the app. When the UI appears, right-click with the mouse or swipe upward from the bottom of the screen. You should see the app bar appear. Click or touch anywhere else on the screen (or swipe downward), and it will slide away.

Hooking it up

You now have an app bar that you can display and hide, but it doesn't do anything. Fortunately, it's a simple matter to edit the base buttons handler so that it reacts properly to the app bar buttons.

1. Edit the code in the *BaseButtons_Click* function so that it accepts both the button on the screen and the app bar buttons.

```
if (btn == btnHexBase || btn == btnAppBarHex)
```

2. Build and run the app.

You can now change the base by using the app bar.

Adding sharing

For the final task in this chapter, you're going to add another feature to the calculator: the ability to share data with other applications. This isn't going to be very sophisticated, because you're only going to be able to share the value in the display, but it illustrates an important feature of Windows Store apps.

Contracts and charms

Applications can communicate and share data by using *contracts*. Windows Store apps use contracts to declare the interactions that they support with other applications.

These contracts are defined by Windows RT, and by using the Windows operating system as an intermediary, apps can communicate without knowing anything about one another.

For example, choosing the Share charm while in an app will display all applications that have registered themselves as targets for sharing. This means that you can send data from your app to any of the sharing targets without the two parties having prior knowledge of one another.

Windows 8 defines the following six contracts:

■ **Search**   The app is search enabled.

- **Share**   The app can share content with other applications or is ready to accept specific types of data from other applications.

- **Settings**   Implements a standard way of defining app settings.

- **Play To**   The app can stream audio, video, and images to enabled devices.

- **File Picker**   The app is used as a location for saving and loading files.

- **Cached File Updater**   The app can track file updates and deliver the latest version to the user.

Charms are a specific and consistent set of buttons that you can access in every app. The charms are Search, Share, Connect, Settings, and Start. They appear on the right side of the screen when you swipe inward from the right edge of the screen, move the mouse pointer to the upper-right or lower-left of the screen, or press Windows key+C.

These buttons provide the following set of core actions that users frequently need:

- Search for content located in your app or in another app, and search your app's content from another app.

- Share content from your app with people or services.

- Go directly to the Start screen.

- Connect to devices and send content, stream media, and print.

- Configure the app.

As you can appreciate, implementing contracts and using the charms makes your app a full member of the Windows Store community.

Implementing sharing

Sharing is one of the common contracts supported by apps, letting them share data with other apps in a variety of formats, including the following:

- Plain text

- Formatted text

- HTML

- URIs

- Bitmaps

- Files

- Developer-defined data

When a request to share data is received, either programmatically or by a user selecting the Share charm, your app receives an event. You implement an event handler in the normal way, which returns the requested data to the caller.

When implementing sharing, you'll need to use types from the *Windows::ApplicationModel.Data Transfer* namespace. Depending on the types of data you are sharing, you might also want others, such as *Windows::Storage* if you are using files.

The *DataPackage* class

The *Windows::ApplicationModel.DataTransfer::DataPackage* class is central to any data sharing operation, and a *DataPackage* object contains the data that the app wants to share, along with a description.

A sharing request comes with an empty *DataPackage* object. You retrieve it from the arguments passed to the event handler, fill it in with data, and then send it back. If you only want to provide data when the receiver requests it (as opposed to providing it at event handling time) you can add a delegate to the *DataPackage*, which will be called when the receiver wants the data.

DataPackage has several useful properties, which can be accessed via *DataPackage*'s *Properties* property, and which are summarized in the following table:

Name	Mandatory?	Description
ApplicationName	No	Gets or sets the name of the app that provided this DataPackage
Description	No	Gets or sets the description for this DataPackage
Thumbnail	No	Gets or sets the thumbnail image for this DataPackage
Title	Yes	Gets or sets the title for this DataPackage

When you choose to share data, the charms show details of the data that is going to be shared. At a minimum, you must supply a title, but you can also add a description to help clarify exactly what is being shared.

DataPackage also has several methods, which are used for populating the data. The following table lists them:

Name	Description
SetBitmap	Sets the bitmap contained in the DataPackage
SetData	Sets the custom data contained in the DataPackage
SetDataProvider	Sets a delegate to handle requests from the target app
SetHtmlFormat	Adds HTML content to the DataPackage
SetRtf	Sets the RTF content contained in the DataPackage

Name	Description
SetStorageItems	Sets the files and folders contained in the *DataPackage*
SetText	Sets the text contained in the *DataPackage*
SetUri	Sets the URI contained in the *DataPackage*

Handling share requests

This final exercise shows you how to implement sharing for the calculator:

1. At the top of the MainPage.xaml.cpp file, add the following *using* declaration for the *DataTransfer* namespace:

   ```
   using namespace Windows::ApplicationModel::DataTransfer;
   ```

2. Implement the handler that it going to be called when a sharing request arrives. Start by adding a member to the *MainPage* class declaration in MainPage.xaml.h.

   ```
   void ShareTextHandler(
       Windows::ApplicationModel::DataTransfer::DataTransferManager^ sender,
       Windows::ApplicationModel::DataTransfer::DataRequestedEventArgs^ e);
   ```

   As usual with event handlers, the two arguments represent the source of the event and event arguments. A *DataTransferManager* is an object that implements the sharing functionality within an app; you will shortly create one of these for your app.

3. Add the implementation of the handler to MainPage.xaml.cpp. Start by getting the *Data Request* object out of the event args—this is the object that is sent in reply to the request, and you can obtain a *DataPackage* by using its *Data* member.

   ```
   void ProgCalc::MainPage::ShareTextHandler(DataTransferManager^ sender,
          DataRequestedEventArgs^ e)
   {
       DataRequest ^request = e->Request;
       DataPackage ^data = request->Data;

       // Now add the data you want to share.
   }
   ```

4. You can now fill in the data that you want to share.

   Any content must have at least two properties (a title and the content itself). What other properties it has depends first on what you're sharing, and second on how helpful you want to be!

   ```
   // Set the title and description
   data->Properties->Title = "Calculator data";
   data->Properties->Description = "A demonstration of sharing";
   // Add the data
   data->SetText(txtOutput->Text);
   ```

5. Set up the *DataTransferManager* so that sharing is active for the app. Start by adding a new private member to the *MainPage* class, as shown here:

```
Windows::Foundation::EventRegistrationToken dataRequestedToken;
```

This object is returned to you when you register your event handler with the *DataTransfer Manager*. It isn't strictly necessary to include it here, because you only need it when implementing a multipage app. In that case, you will implement the *OnNavigatedFrom* function, which is called when you move to another page, and you'd use the token to tell the *Data TransferManager* that you no longer want this page to receive share events. There is, however, no harm in including it, and it will serve to remind you of what to do when you move on to multipage applications.

6. Add the following code to the *OnNavigatedTo* function to register for share events, placing it before the call to *Reset*:

```
DataTransferManager ^dataTransferManager = DataTransferManager::GetForCurrentView();

dataRequestedToken = dataTransferManager->DataRequested +=
    ref new TypedEventHandler<DataTransferManager^,
        DataRequestedEventArgs^>(this, &MainPage::ShareTextHandler);
```

Notice the rather compressed form of the second statement. You create a new *TypedEvent Handler*, which uses generics to create a delegate that will call a handler function. You use the angle brackets to specify the two argument types that the handler will use, and then provide the function that the delegate will call: in this case, it is the *ShareTextHandler* function on "this" object.

The delegate is hooked to the *DataRequested* event on the *DataTransferManager*, and this returns the token that you can use to unregister when navigating away from the page.

7. Build and run the app and put a number in the display. Then, select the Share charm, which is the second from the top.

After a few seconds initialization, you should see the title and description you provided, together with a list of the applications that can accept the data, as demonstrated in this screen shot:

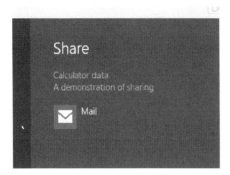

You can see that the title for the data, along with a description if you supplied one, is shown so that users can decide what they want to do with the data. On the system I'm using, only the Mail app is able to accept shared text data.

Where next?

I've run out of space in this chapter, but now that you have seen how to build a more complex Windows Store app, there are several ways in which you could enhance the calculator, building on what you've learned. Here are some suggestions:

- Add the typical calculator "memory" functionality. The calculator keeps a memory variable, and four buttons let you set it to zero (MC), add the currently displayed value to it (M+), subtract the currently displayed value from it (M−), and put the stored value into the display (MR).

- Add a change sign button (+/−) that changes the sign of the value in the display.

- Implement some more programmer functionality, such as bitwise operations (AND, OR, XOR, and NOT) and left and right shift.

- Add a history mechanism so that you can see what you've done up to now.

Quick reference

To	Do This
Add an app bar to hold command buttons	First create styles for the buttons in StandardStyles.xaml. Add a *BottomAppBar* to the XAML. Then, add a *StackPanel* containing the buttons, and link their *click* events to a suitable handler.
Implement the sharing contract.	Add a handler for a *DataRequestedEvent* and put the data into a *DataPackage*. Then, use the *DataTransferManager* to make sharing available for that page.

Advanced topics

CHAPTER 22   Working with unmanaged code 437

CHAPTER 23   Attributes and reflection. .453

CHAPTER 24   Living with COM. 475

Working with unmanaged code

After completing this chapter, you will be able to:

- Explain the issues that affect managed and unmanaged code.

- Use managed objects in unmanaged code.

- Use the Platform Invoke mechanism to call unmanaged functions in DLLs.

Although the primary focus of this book is using C++/CLI with the Microsoft .NET Framework, at times you'll have to call functions outside the .NET environment.

The *System::Runtime::InteropServices* namespace contains classes and structures to help with interoperation between .NET and the outside world. In this chapter, I'll introduce one feature of the namespace—the Platform Invoke mechanism for calling unmanaged functions within DLLs. We also investigate some of the other issues that surround interacting with unmanaged code. Chapter 24, "Living with COM," considers considers interoperating between the Component Object Model (COM) and .NET.

Managed vs. unmanaged code

Code and data that live in the .NET world are called managed because locations and lifetimes are managed by the Common Language Runtime (CLR). Code and data that exist outside of .NET are called unmanaged, because there is no central mechanism for managing their lifetimes. Sometimes you have to mix the two, calling existing unmanaged code from within .NET. This section introduces some of the issues and techniques that you'll need to consider in this situation.

Mixed classes

Although managed classes are normally composed of other managed types, it is possible to mix managed and unmanaged types as members of classes under some circumstances. It is also possible to have a pointer to an unmanaged object as a member of a managed class, as in this example:

```
ref class ManagedClass
{
    UnmanagedClass *puc;
    ...
};
```

Notice the use of the asterisk (*) rather than the caret (^): this is a pointer to an unmanaged type, not a handle.

Because the member is unmanaged, it's up to you to manage the lifetime of the object at the other end of the pointer. You should handle this carefully: unmanaged objects sometimes need explicit deletion at a particular point in the code, and this might not fit well with the .NET garbage collection model. However, you can declare destructors for managed classes and use *delete* on objects of managed types, so it's possible to arrange for correct object deallocation in most circumstances.

You can't have an unmanaged object as a member of a managed class, such as is illustrated in the following:

```
ref class ManagedClass
{
    UnmanagedClass obj;     // C4368: mixed types are not supported
    ...
};
```

An unmanaged object will only work as a class member if the host object is explicitly deleted at some point: at the end of the enclosing block for an automatic variable, at the end of the process for a global variable, or when *delete* is called on a pointer. Managed objects don't work in this way, and the garbage collector can't collect an unmanaged object.

It's impossible to have a handle to a managed type as part of an unmanaged class, as shown here:

```
class UnmanagedClass
{
    ManagedClass ^obj;      // C3265: cannot declare a managed 'obj'
                            // in an unmanaged 'UnmanagedClass'
    ...
};
```

Because the unmanaged object doesn't exist in the .NET world, the handle to the contained object is invisible to the garbage collector. Thus, the garbage collector doesn't know who has a reference to the object or when it can be collected.

The *GCHandle* type

There is a way to use a managed type as part of an unmanaged class by using the *GCHandle* type provided in the *System::Runtime::InteropServices* namespace. *GCHandle* asks the runtime to give you a "handle" to refer to a managed object from unmanaged code. You use the *GCHandle::Alloc* static method to create the handle, and the handle's *Free* method to release it again. Here's how you'd use *GCHandle* if you wanted to pass a pointer to a managed object to unmanaged code:

1. Create a *GCHandle* to refer to your object. *GCHandle*s can be converted to and from integers for ease of passing them between functions.

2. Pass the *GCHandle* to the unmanaged code. As long as the handle hasn't been freed, the runtime won't collect the object.

3. Call *Free* on the handle when the unmanaged code no longer needs it. At this point, the runtime is free to collect the object if no one else is using it.

To help you use *GCHandles* within unmanaged code without your having to get into the details of using *Alloc* and *Free*, Microsoft provides a helper template class called *gcroot*. The following exercise shows you how to use *gcroot* to include a pointer to a managed type as part of an unmanaged class:

1. Start Microsoft Visual Studio 2012 and create a new CLR Console Application project named **Manage**.

2. Add an *#include* directive for the gcroot.h system header file just below the stdafx.h *include* directive.

```
#include <gcroot.h>
```

This system header file defines the *gcroot* helper class.

3. Add a *using* directive to the top of the code to make it easier to use the *System::Runtime::Interop Services* namespace.

```
using namespace System::Runtime::InteropServices;
```

4. Add the definition of a simple managed class to the code.

```
ref class MClass
{
public:
    int val;
    MClass(int n) : val(n) { }
};
```

This class simply wraps an integer, whose value is set in the constructor.

5. Add the definition of an unmanaged class.

```
class UClass
{
public:
    gcroot<MClass^> mc;

    UClass(gcroot<MClass^> pmc) : mc(pmc) { }

    int getValue()
    {
        return mc->val;
    }
};
```

The definition of the *mc* variable is an example of using a template class. The definition effectively creates a *gcroot* variable that wraps a *GCHandle* to an *MClass* pointer. The *GCHandle* is created when the *gcroot* object is created, and it is freed when the *gcroot* object is destroyed.

A *UClass* object is passed a handle to a managed *MClass* object when it is created, and this handle is stored away in the *gcroot* object. The *getValue* function simply returns the public *val* member from the *MClass* object by value, so you can verify that the code really lets you access a managed object from an unmanaged context.

6. Modify the *main* function to use the classes.

```
int main(array<String^>^ args)
{
    Console::WriteLine("Testing...");

    // Create a managed object
    MClass ^pm = gcnew MClass(3);

    // Create an unmanaged object
    UClass uc(pm);

    Console::WriteLine("Value is {0}", uc.getValue());

    return 0;
}
```

The code first creates a managed object and initializes it with an integer. The pointer to this object is then used to initialize an unmanaged object, and the *getValue* function is used to extract the value from the managed object before printing it out. When the *UClass* object goes out of scope, the *gcroot* is destroyed, which frees the *GCHandle* and, in turn, frees up the managed object.

 Tip If the managed type that you want to use with *gcroot* has a destructor, using the *auto_gcroot* type (declared in *<auto_gcroot.h>*) will call the destructor on the object when the *gcroot* goes out of scope.

7. Build and run the application.

Pinning and boxing

This section discusses two C++/CLI concepts, *pinning* and *boxing*, and shows you how they're used in code.

Interior pointers

Before getting to pinning, let's briefly discuss *interior pointers*. We will do this by looking at a scenario in which you have a managed object, and you want to pass it to an unmanaged function that requires a pointer.

You probably know that the garbage collector can (and does) move objects around on the managed heap to maximize free space. This means that you can't use an unmanaged pointer to refer to a managed object, because the address held in the pointer could end up pointing to the wrong place if the garbage collector moves the object. In fact, the compiler will give you an error if you try to use an ordinary pointer with a managed object.

An *interior pointer* is a pointer whose address will be updated if the object to which it refers is moved. They are called "interior" pointers because you use them to point to a member within a managed object.

> **Note** You can't use an interior pointer to point to a "whole" managed object; you can only point to a field within an object.

Pinning pointers

The CLR assumes that it can move objects around in the managed heap whenever it wants. At times, however, you might need to tell the CLR to leave objects where they are. For example, if you want to pass a pointer to a managed object to an unmanaged function, you don't want the CLR to move the object around in memory while the object is being used by the unmanaged code.

A *pinning pointer* is a pointer to a managed object, but the value of the pointer cannot be changed, which means that the garbage collector cannot move it around in memory. Thus, creating a pinning pointer to an object gives you a pointer that can safely be passed out to unmanaged code because you can be sure that the address is going to remain valid.

You can use pinning on all or part of a managed object, and pinning a member of a managed object results in the entire object being pinned. For example, pinning the first element of an array will result in the entire array being pinned. The object will remain pinned until there are no references left to the pinning pointer.

The code fragment that follows shows the creation and use of a pinning pointer. First, assume that we have an unmanaged function that takes a pointer to an integer.

```
void someFunc(int *p)
{
    // Do something with the integer value...
    int n = *p;
}
```

Here is how we could use this with a managed array:

```
// Create a managed array of int
array<int> ^arr = gcnew array<int>(5);

// Create a pinning pointer to the first element
// Note there is no '^', and that '&' is used to take the address of the object
pin_ptr<MyClass> pin = &arr[0];

// Pass the integer member to an unmanaged function
someFunc(pin);

// Zero out the pinning pointer
// The array is not pinned any more
pin = nullptr;
```

After the array element has been pinned, you can pass its address to the unmanaged function, confident that the *int* won't be moved around in memory. Observe how there is an implicit conversion between *pin_ptr<int>* and *int**, so you don't need to convert it yourself. When you're finished, assigning *nullptr* to the pinning pointer frees the array object so that it can be moved.

Boxing and unboxing

Boxing and *unboxing*, which will be discussed in a moment, make it possible for value types to be treated as objects. Chapter 9, "Value types," covers value types in detail and teaches that they are fundamentally different from reference types. To recap, value types have three particular properties:

- Value types are stored on the stack, unlike references, which are stored on the run-time heap.

- Instances of value types are always accessed directly, unlike reference types, which are accessed through references. This means that you don't use the *new* operator when creating instances. It also means that value types are not garbage-collected.

- Copying value types copies the value rather than the reference.

Anything that wraps a simple value, such as a Boolean or an integer, and that is less than about 16 bytes in size is a good candidate for making a value type. Because value types aren't accessed via references, they can be far more efficient than the equivalent reference types but can't be regarded as objects in the same way that reference types can. This becomes a problem when you want to use a value type in a context where an object reference is needed. For example, consider the overload of the *Console::WriteLine* function that performs formatted output, whose prototype is shown here:

```
static void WriteLine(String^, Object^);
```

The first *String^* parameter is the format string, and the second is a handle to any .NET reference type. Because value types aren't accessed by references, you can't directly specify a value type. But, you will find that the following works, even though "12" is not an instance of a reference type:

```
int foo = 12;
Console::WriteLine("foo is {0}", foo);
```

Boxing

Boxing wraps a value type in an object "box" so that it can be used where an object reference is needed. In C++/CLI, this wrapping is done automatically.

The following three things happen when an object is boxed:

- A managed object is created on the CLR heap.

- The value of the value type is copied, bit by bit, into the managed object.

- The address of the managed object is returned.

Be aware that the managed object contains a copy of the value type. This means that any modifications you might make to the managed wrapper don't propagate back to the original value. You can see this happening if you look at the generated code the IL disassembler tool (ISDASM). The IL generated for the preceding two lines of C++/CLI code look something like this:

```
IL_0002:  ldc.i4.s    12
IL_0004:  stloc.1
IL_0005:  ldstr "Value is {0}"
IL_000a:  ldloc.1
IL_000b:  box         [mscorlib]System.Int32
IL_0010:  call        void [mscorlib]System.Console::WriteLine(string, object)
```

The first line pushes a literal 12 onto the stack, and the second line stores it (*stloc*) into a local variable. After the string literal is pushed onto the stack, the *ldloc* instruction takes the local variable and pushes it back onto the stack. You can see that the next line is a box instruction, which generates an object to hold the integer before calling *WriteLine*.

Unboxing

What if you want to retrieve the value from a boxed object? The following brief exercise shows you how to get the value back out of a boxed object by using a cast.

1. Create a new CLR Console Application project named **Boxing**.

2. Edit the *main* function to create an integer and box it.

    ```
    int main(array<String^>^ args)
    {
        Console::WriteLine("Boxing Example");

        // Create an int
        int foo = 12;

        // It will get boxed automatically
        Object ^obj = foo;

        // Use the boxed object
        Console::WriteLine("Value of foo is {0}", obj);

        return 0;
    }
    ```

3. Add the following code to get the value back out of the box:

```
// Unbox the value
int fooTwo = safe_cast<int>(obj);

Console::WriteLine("fooTwo is {0}", fooTwo);
```

The *safe_cast* checks to see whether a boxed *int* is on the other end of the *obj* pointer; if it is, it returns an *int*.

> **Note** The *safe_cast* is explored in Chapter 3, "Variables and operators," but let's take a moment to consider it here. Like *dynamic_cast*, a *safe_cast* is performed at run time. It checks whether the type on the other end of the handle is of the right type. If it is, the cast is performed and the value returned. Unlike *dynamic_cast*, which returns a null if the types don't match, *safe_cast* will throw an exception.

4. Build and run the application.

Using P/Invoke to call functions in the Win32 API

Although it's possible to do a great deal by using the functionality provided in the .NET Framework, at times you'll need to use code that wasn't written for .NET to accommodate situations such as the following:

- You need to call a Microsoft Windows API function that doesn't have a .NET equivalent.

- You have some code in a Dynamic-Link Library (DLL) that originated outside .NET and can't be rewritten.

- You have code that needs to be written in a language that's not yet supported by the .NET Framework.

Whatever the reason, the code you're calling exists outside the .NET-managed environment, so you need a way to pass function calls into and out of .NET. The mechanism to do this is called *P/Invoke* (for Platform Invoke, pronounced "p-invoke"). It is provided to let you call functions in DLLs.

Using P/Invoke involves adding a prototype to your code that uses attributes to inform .NET about the function you're proposing to call. In particular, you need to specify the name of the DLL containing the function, the name of the function, what arguments the function takes, and what the function returns.

A mechanism such as P/Invoke is necessary to facilitate communication between managed and unmanaged code. Take strings as an example: A string in C++/CLI is a handle to a *String* object, but in standard C++, a string isn't represented by an object. Instead, a string is a pointer to a series of memory locations that contain characters and is terminated by a null. If you're going to pass a string data between managed and unmanaged code, something has to convert between the corresponding managed and unmanaged data types. This conversion process is called marshaling, and it is one of the tasks that P/Invoke performs for you.

Identifying functions

There are two points that you need to be aware of when identifying functions to call using P/Invoke. Although you usually identify a function in a DLL by name, you can also assign a function in a DLL a number that can be used to execute the function at run time. If you need to, you can identify a DLL function to P/Invoke by using this ordinal number.

When you call Windows API functions, you can also have two or more versions of functions that take characters or strings as arguments because Windows can support more than one character encoding. For example, standard Microsoft Windows XP supports both the ASCII (one byte per character) and Unicode (two bytes per character) character encodings. This means that both ASCII and Unicode versions of each function must exist, identified by an "A" or a "W", respectively, added to the end of the function name (for example, *MessageBoxW*). Although you can call the different versions directly, the C++ compiler maps a call to *MessageBox* onto the correct function depending on whether you're using ASCII or Unicode in your application.

As you'll discover in the exercise later in this section, you can specify which version of a function you want to use with P/Invoke. If you don't explicitly pick one, the ASCII version will be used.

The following exercise shows you how to call an unmanaged function in one of the Windows system DLLs. The obvious candidate for this exercise is *MessageBox* for two reasons: first, it's a standalone function and doesn't require any setting up; second, it's obvious whether the call has worked.

The *MessageBox* function—that is, the *MessageBoxA* and *MessageBoxW* functions—reside in the User32.dll system DLL. Three system DLLs contain the unmanaged Windows API code:

- User32.dll, which contains functions for message handling, timers, menus, and communications

- Kernel32.dll, which contains low-level operating system functionality for memory management and resource handling

- GDI32.dll, which contains the GDI graphics subsystem code

How do you know which DLL holds a particular system function? If you look the function up in the Platform SDK, you'll usually find a clue in the "Requirements" section at the end of the topic. For example, the Help topic for *MessageBox* has the following lines:

Library: User32.lib

DLL: User32.dll

The first line indicates that if you want to use *MessageBox* in traditional C++ code, you'll have to link with a library named User32.lib, and the second denotes that the code actually resides in User32.dll.

Now that you know where you can find the *MessageBox* function, here's the exercise:

1. Start a new CLR Console Application project named **Message**.

2. Add a *using* directive to the top of the project.

    ```
    using namespace System::Runtime::InteropServices;
    ```

    Most of the interop features are part of the *System::Runtime::InteropServices* namespace, and it's much easier to use if you declare the namespace.

3. Add the P/Invoke prototype for the *MessageBox* function before the *main* routine:

    ```
    // Set up the import
    [DllImport("User32.dll", CharSet=CharSet::Auto)]
    int MessageBox(IntPtr hwnd, String ^text,
                          String ^caption, unsigned int type);
    ```

    There is quite a lot to explain about these few lines of code. The prototype for the *Message Box* function is declared by using the *DllImport* attribute. The two parameters passed to the attribute are the name of the DLL in which the function resides, and (because this is a function that uses characters or strings) an indication of which version to use. *CharSet::Auto* leaves it up to the target platform to decide which version to call and how to convert the string arguments.

    The first argument to *MessageBox* is a "handle to the owning window." This is a handle in the original Win32 sense, and it is basically a pointer. This is used to establish the *MessageBox* as a child of another window, and we're not concerned about it here. The rather strange choice of argument name (*hwnd*) comes from the original type, *HWND*.

> **Note** An *IntPtr* is an integer type large enough to hold a native pointer, so it will be 32 bits on 32-bit Windows and 64 bits on 64-bit systems. It is commonly used in interop to pass pointers to and from unmanaged code.

Notice how *String* handles are used to pass string information, where the original function would require a Windows *LPTSTR* type. The P/Invoke marshaling automatically converts the data when making the call. The final argument is the style of *MessageBox*, which governs which icon and buttons it will display. The default value is zero, which just displays an OK button.

4. Add code to the *main* function to call *MessageBox*:

```
int main(array<String^>^ args)
{
    Console::WriteLine("P/Invoke Example");

    String ^theText = "Hello World!";
    String ^theCaption = "A Message Box...";
    MessageBox(IntPtr::Zero, theText, theCaption, 0);

    return 0;
}
```

The first argument is passed as *IntPtr::Zero*, which is how you assign a null value to an *IntPtr*. We pass null because in this simple example we aren't concerned with setting the owner.

5. When you build and run the application, you'll see a *MessageBox* displayed on the screen, as shown in the following screen shot:

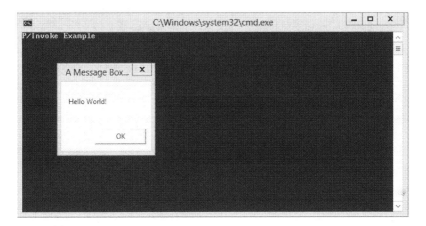

The *DllImportAttribute* class

You used the *DllImportAttribute* class in the previous exercise to provide a prototype for an unmanaged function. This class has a number of fields (data members) that can be used when constructing the prototype, and they're listed in the following table:

Field	Description
BestFitMapping	Selects a suitable replacement character where an exact conversion does not exist, for example, using "c" instead of a © symbol.
CallingConvention	Defines the calling convention used when passing arguments to the unmanaged function.
CharSet	Defines how characters and strings are to be handled during marshaling.
EntryPoint	Indicates the name or ordinal number of the DLL function to be called.

Field	Description
ExactSpelling	Indicates whether the name of the entry point should be modified to correspond to the character set in use.
PreserveSig	Used for COM methods, this field should be set to true if the return values from methods shouldn't be altered in any way.
SetLastError	If true, the caller can use the Win32 *GetLastError* function to determine whether an error occurred.
ThrowOnUnmappableCharacter	If true, will throw an exception when a best-fit match for a character is not available.

Let's look at the more common fields in detail. *CallingConvention* defines how arguments are passed between the managed and unmanaged code, and will take one of the values in the *Calling Convention* enumeration. Different languages use different ways of passing arguments, so Windows supports a number of different calling conventions. C and C++ normally use the C calling convention, often known as *Cdecl*, whereas many other Windows languages use the standard calling convention, often abbreviated to *StdCall*. You call Windows API functions by using *StdCall*, which is the default, unless you use the *CallingConvention* field to choose another.

With *CharSet*, you can specify how characters and strings are to be marshaled. It takes one of the values from the *CharSet* enumeration. You can specify *CharSet::Ansi*, in which case all characters and strings are converted to one-byte ANSI characters and an "A" is appended to the name of the DLL entry point. Choosing *CharSet::Unicode* converts characters and strings to use two-byte Unicode characters and appends a "W" to the entry point name. However, it's usually sufficient to specify *CharSet::Auto*, which chooses the best option for the host system.

Using the *EntryPoint* field, you can specify the name or ordinal number of the entry point in the DLL. If you don't specify this field, as in the preceding exercise, the entry point name is taken to be the function name given in the prototype. A name given using the *EntryPoint* field takes precedence over the prototype name, so this gives you the ability to provide synonyms for unmanaged functions if you want to refer to them by another name when calling them in your code. The following code fragment shows how you could define a synonym for the *MessageBox* function:

```
[DllImport("User32.dll", EntryPoint="MessageBox",
            CharSet=CharSet::Auto)]
int WindowsMessageBox(IntPtr hwnd, String ^text,
                String ^caption, unsigned int type);
```

You call the function as *WindowsMessageBox*, and the call is mapped onto the appropriate *MessageBox* entry point in User32.dll.

Passing structures

You'll often need to pass structured data to arguments to unmanaged functions, and you must do this carefully. In particular, you need to specify the way structures are laid out in memory to be sure that they are passed around correctly. You specify the layout of structures and classes by using the *StructLayoutAttribute* and *FieldOffsetAttribute* classes.

You add *StructLayoutAttribute* to managed types to define a formatted type with a particular layout. There are three possible layout types that you can specify for a formatted type:

- Automatic layout (*LayoutKind::Auto*), in which the runtime might reorder the members if it is more efficient. You never use automatic layout for types that are going to be used with P/Invoke because you need to be sure that everything stays in the same order.

- Explicit layout (*LayoutKind::Explicit*), in which members are ordered according to byte offsets specified by *FieldOffset* attributes on each field.

- Sequential layout (*LayoutKind::Sequential*), in which members appear in unmanaged memory in the same order they appear in the managed definition.

The following exercise shows how to call an unmanaged Windows API function that needs to be passed a structure. The function is *GetSystemPowerStatus*, which reports on the AC and battery status of the system. The Windows API defines a structure *SYSTEM_POWER_STATUS*, which contains the status information. The definition of this unmanaged structure is shown here:

```
typedef struct _SYSTEM_POWER_STATUS {
    BYTE  ACLineStatus;
    BYTE  BatteryFlag;
    BYTE  BatteryLifePercent;
    BYTE  Reserved1;
    DWORD BatteryLifeTime;
    DWORD BatteryFullLifeTime;
} SYSTEM_POWER_STATUS, *LPSYSTEM_POWER_STATUS;
```

The prototype for the *GetSystemPowerStatus* function in the API documentation is this:

```
BOOL GetSystemPowerStatus(
  LPSYSTEM_POWER_STATUS lpSystemPowerStatus  // status
);
```

The function takes a pointer to a *SYSTEM_POWER_STATUS* structure, fills it in, and hands back the filled structure, returning a Boolean value to let you know whether it worked. Your task is to call this function, passing over a structure, and then display the results.

1. Create a new CLR Console Application project named **PowerMonitor**.

2. Add the following *using* directive:

    ```
    using namespace System::Runtime::InteropServices;
    ```

    This makes it easier to refer to the attributes we'll be using later.

3. Define a managed equivalent for the structure.

```
[StructLayoutAttribute(LayoutKind::Sequential)]
ref class PStat {
public:
    System::Byte ACLineStatus;
    System::Byte BatteryFlag;
    System::Byte BatteryLifePercent;
    System::Byte Reserved1;
    System::UInt32 BatteryLifeTime;
    System::UInt32 BatteryFullLifeTime;
};
```

Our equivalent of *SYSTEM_POWER_STATUS* is a managed class named *PStat*. The original defi-nition contains two Windows data types: *BYTE*, which represents a one-byte integer, and so can be represented by the *System::Byte* type; and *DWORD*, which is a 32-bit unsigned integer, and so is represented by *System::UInt32*. The *StructLayoutAttribute* is attached to the class, and *LayoutKind::Sequential* is specified so that the layout of the members will remain the same as the data is passed through P/Invoke.

4. Define the prototype for the *GetSystemPowerStatus* function, as shown here:

```
// Define the BOOL type
typedef int BOOL;

// Prototype for the function
[DllImport("Kernel32.dll", CharSet=CharSet::Auto)]
BOOL GetSystemPowerStatus(PStat ^ps);
```

BOOL is a Windows type representing a Boolean value and is actually a *typedef* for an integer. It has been widely used in the Windows API because C lacks a true Boolean type. The proto-type uses the real name of the function as it occurs in Kernel32.dll, and the single argument is given as a handle to our managed type.

5. Write the code to call the function. Edit the *main* function to create a *PStat* object and use it to call the function, as illustrated in the following:

```
int main(array<String^>^ args)
{
    Console::WriteLine("Power Status Test...");
    PStat ^ps = gcnew PStat();

    BOOL b = GetSystemPowerStatus(ps);
    Console::WriteLine("Got status, return was {0}", b);

    return 0;
}
```

If the call worked, the return value should be nonzero, which represents a Boolean true value.

6. Build and run the application at this point, correcting any errors and checking the output.

7. Add code to report on the members of the class.

```
// Report on the AC line status
Console::Write("AC line power status is ");
switch(ps->ACLineStatus) {
case 0:
    Console::WriteLine("'off'");
    break;
case 1:
    Console::WriteLine("'on'");
    break;
case 255:
    Console::WriteLine("'unknown'");
    break;
}

// Report on the battery status
Console::Write("Battery charge status is ({0})",
            ps->BatteryFlag);
if (ps->BatteryFlag & 1)
    Console::Write(" 'high'");
if (ps->BatteryFlag & 2)
    Console::Write(" 'low'");
if (ps->BatteryFlag & 4)
    Console::Write(" 'critical'");
if (ps->BatteryFlag & 8)
    Console::Write(" 'charging'");
if (ps->BatteryFlag & 128)
    Console::Write(" 'no system battery'");
Console::WriteLine();

// What's the percentage charge left in the battery?
// A value of 255 means unknown
if (ps->BatteryLifePercent == 255)
    Console::WriteLine("Battery life unknown");
else
    Console::WriteLine("Battery life is {0}%",
        ps->BatteryLifePercent);

// How many seconds battery life is left?
if (ps->BatteryLifeTime == -1)
    Console::WriteLine("Battery life in seconds: Unknown");
else
    Console::WriteLine("Battery seconds remaining: {0} secs",
                    ps->BatteryLifeTime);
```

The first check is on the *ACLineStatus* field, which will have the value 0 (on), 1 (off), or 255 (unknown). The second check is on the status of the battery, and this value can be made up of one or more of the values 1 (high charge), 2 (low charge), 4 (critically low charge), 8 (charging), and 128 (no battery present). Each of these represents a particular bit position within the result, and the bitwise OR operator (&) is used to check which bits are set.

The final two checks print out the percentage of lifetime left in the battery and the number of seconds. If the function can't determine the number of seconds, it will return –1 in this field.

8. Build and run the application. You will obviously achieve the best results if you run it on a laptop.

Quick reference

To	Do this

Obtain a safe handle to a managed object so that it won't be garbage-collected while being used.	Use the *System::Runtime::InteropServices::GCHandle::Alloc* function to wrap a pointer to a managed object in a *GCHandle*. The easiest way to do this is to use the *gcroot* helper class. For example:
	
	`Foo ^ff = gcnew Foo();`
	
	`gcroot<Foo^> pf = ff;`
	
	This code wraps the pointer to the *Foo* object with a *GCHandle*, and handles cleanup when the *gcroot* is destroyed.

Fix all or part of a managed object in memory so that it can be used safely by unmanaged code.	Use *pin_ptr<>* to create a pinning pointer. For example: `pin_ptr<Foo> p = gcnew Foo();` The managed *Foo* object won't be moved in memory or garbage-collected until the pinning pointer goes out of context or has null assigned to it.
Convert a value type to an object so that it can be used where an object is required.	This will happen automatically. Note that the value in the box is a copy of the original.
Retrieve the value from a boxed object.	Use *safe_cast* to cast the boxing object to the correct type, and then dereference the pointer. For example: `int myVal = safe_cast<int>(po);`
Call an unmanaged function in a DLL.	Use the P/Invoke mechanism by declaring a prototype for the unmanaged function that uses the *DllImport* attribute to specify the DLL in which the function resides and other optional parameters.

Attributes and reflection

After completing this chapter, you will be able to:

- Describe what attributes are.

- Use attributes to add metadata to managed types.

- Create your own attribute types.

- Access attribute metadata from code.

This chapter introduces metadata and attributes and shows you how to start defining and manipulating metadata for your own .NET types.

Metadata and attributes

The concept of metadata is central to the way the Microsoft .NET Framework works, so to be an effective .NET programmer, you need to know what it is and how to work with it. Metadata is data attached to .NET data types that carries information about those types (in a broader sense, it is data that describes data). A lot of metadata contains information that can't be specified in the programming language, and it offers a useful—many people would say essential—way to provide all the extra information needed by the .NET runtime.

One of the major advantages of metadata is that it is stored along with the code, so extra data doesn't need to be stored separately. Traditionally, in Windows all extra data has to be stored in the Windows registry. One of the main problems with this is ensuring that the data in the registry doesn't become corrupt or out of step with the code.

Another major advantage of metadata is that it provides a way to add version information to the code so that you know which version of a component you're using. This solves a lot of problems that have plagued programmers since the early days of Windows; it is a huge step forward.

The compiler always attaches metadata to the output code to describe it, and the Common Language Runtime (CLR) uses the metadata to control the loading and execution of the code. You can also attach metadata to code by using attributes, which are special syntax elements that can be attached to classes and class members. You'll see how to use attributes later in this chapter.

You can see some of the metadata that the compiler attaches to your code if you use the IL disassembler tool (ILDASM), which is included with the .NET Framework SDK. (You can find this tool in the \Program Files\Microsoft SDKs\Windows\v8.0a\bin\NETFX4.0 Tools folder.)

Using ILDASM

The following example shows you how to use ILDASM to examine a simple application:

1. Start Microsoft Visual Studio 2012 and create a new CLR Console Application project named **Hello**.

2. Add a new managed class to the application.

```
ref class Hello
{
public:
    static void SayHello()
    {
        Console::WriteLine("Hello, world");
    }
};
```

    The class doesn't really have to do anything particular; it is simply here so that you can disassemble it to look at the metadata.

3. Build the application to generate the executable.

4. Run ILDASM. To do so, on the Tools menu, click Visual Studio Command Prompt, and then type **ildasm** on the command line.

5. On the ILDASM File menu, click Open, navigate to the Hello.exe executable, and then open it.

A window opens that should look similar to the following:

6. We're interested in the managed type *Hello*, which is indicated by the blue component symbol. Click the plus sign (+) to expand the tree for *Hello* and display the details of the class, as depicted in the following screen shot:

The type has three entries: the details of the class, and the entries for two methods, which are the *SayHello* method you added and the default constructor provided by the compiler.

7. Double-click the red triangle to bring up the class information.

A window similar to the following appears:

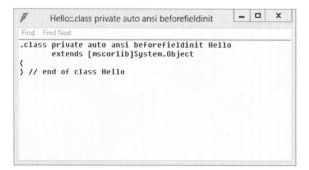

The definition of the managed class—which extends *System::Object*—is marked as *private auto ansi*. These keywords represent items of metadata that have been added by the compiler to describe the class. You can open the other methods in this class to see what metadata is attached to them.

You can inquire about attributes at run time by using reflection, which is a feature by which programmers can obtain information about the objects they are using, such as what class the objects belong to, what methods the objects support, and what metadata is attached to them. Using attributes in code is very powerful because it gives you a way to extend the programming language, introducing new properties for your classes that don't exist in the base language.

Later in the chapter, you'll see how to create custom attributes and how to use code to look at the attributes attached to classes.

Using predefined attributes

In this section, you'll learn how to use the attributes that are predefined by the .NET Framework. You can use these attributes in two ways: by editing the AssemblyInfo.cpp file that comes as part of a C++/CLI project, and by attaching attributes to managed elements in your code.

The AssemblyInfo.cpp file

Every C++/CLI project includes an AssemblyInfo.cpp file that contains code affecting the attributes applied to the assembly. You can edit this file to customize the assembly attributes, which will be used to set the metadata in the assembly at build time. The following exercise shows you how to modify assembly attributes:

1. Create a new CLR Console Application project named **AssemblyAttributes**.

2. Open the AssemblyInfo.cpp file and examine its contents.

   Observe that the file contains a number of entries of the following form:

   ```
   [assembly:AssemblyTitleAttribute("AssemblyAttributes")];
   ```

   Many of these have empty strings as arguments.

3. Find the version number attribute and edit it to produce a new version, such as in the following example:

   ```
   [assembly:AssemblyVersionAttribute("1.1.105.3")];
   ```

   This number would correspond to version 1.1, build 105, revision 3.

4. Compile and build the application. If you now look at the assembly by using ILDASM, you can see the version in two places. First, it will show in the pane at the bottom of the ILDASM main window, as demonstrated here:

You can also see it by double-clicking the MANIFEST entry in the main window and scrolling down to the bottom of the data window that opens. The line within the *.assembly Assembly Attributes* block that begins with *.ver* is the one that lists the version metadata:

```
.ver 1:1:105:3
```

You can check this version number in applications that use this assembly, but explaining how to do this is beyond the scope of this book.

Using the predefined attribute classes

Although much of the metadata produced by the compiler is predefined and you can't alter it, a number of optional standard attributes are provided by various .NET Framework namespaces. The following table lists just some of the more than 300 standard attributes that you might want to use in your own projects:

Class	Description
System::AttributeUsageAttribute	Specifies the usage of another attribute class
System::CLSCompliantAttribute	Indicates whether an application element is CLS-compliant
System::Diagnostics::ConditionalAttribute	Indicates that a method can be called if a preprocessor symbol is defined
System::Diagnostics::DebuggableAttribute	Modifies code generation for run-time JIT (Just-In-Time) debugging
System::Diagnostics::DebuggerHiddenAttribute	Applied to a method to indicate that breakpoints can't be set in the code and that debuggers will not stop in the method
System::Diagnostics::DebuggerStepThroughAttribute	Applied to a method to indicate that the debugger will not stop in this method, although breakpoints can be set
System::FlagsAttribute	Indicates that an enumeration is to be used as a set of flags and can be represented by a bit field
System::NonSerializedAttribute	Indicates that a field of a serializable class should not be serialized
System::ObsoleteAttribute	Indicates application elements that are no longer in use
System::ParamArrayAttribute	Indicates that a method accepts a variable number of arguments
System::Runtime::InteropServices::MarshalAsAttribute	Indicates how to marshal data between managed and unmanaged code
System::Runtime::InteropServices::StructLayoutAttribute	Determines how a type is laid out in memory
System::SerializableAttribute	Indicates that a class can be serialized

The following exercise shows you how to use one of the standard attributes in code. You'll use the *ObsoleteAttribute* class to mark a class method as obsolete and see how the compiler gives a warning when you use the obsolete method. This exercise will also show you how to build a C++/CLI Dynamic-Link Library (DLL) and use it in code. If you want to know more about DLLs, take a moment to read the following sidebar.

DLLs in Windows

Windows executable code can be packaged in two forms: as an executable, or as a DLL. DLLs contain executable code but can't run on their own. A DLL contains functions or classes used by other code in a process. It is loaded at run time.

There are both advantages and disadvantages to using DLLs. Here are some advantages:

- DLLs can be loaded and unloaded on demand, so applications can control their memory use.

- They can be shared by more than one process, so they are a good way to provide shared functionality such as printer drivers.

- Using DLLs means that it is possible to upgrade or fix part of an application without having to redistribute or reinstall everything.

There is also one major drawback to DLLs in the traditional Windows world: an application might use the wrong version of a DLL. When an application wants to load a DLL, it looks along the path for a file with the right name and then loads the first one it finds. So, if a user has changed the order of directories on their path—or if the path has been changed by installing or removing an application—the application might find another version of the DLL file before the correct one. This means that locating the right DLL is dependent on the individual computer setup, making it hard to diagnose and fix.

However, using the wrong version of a DLL isn't a problem for .NET programmers, because assemblies—the fundamental building blocks of .NET applications—have version information built in, and it is possible to specify in the code exactly what versions of an assembly are acceptable. If code does end up running on a computer with the wrong version of an assembly, the result will be a precise and repeatable error message rather than odd behavior.

In the .NET world, DLLs provide one way to package up assemblies. If an assembly contains a standard entry point such as *main* or *WinMain*, it is built as an executable with an .exe extension and can be executed from the command line. If the assembly doesn't contain an entry point, it is built as a library assembly with a .dll extension. A library assembly has no entry point to begin execution but contains types that can be referenced from other assemblies.

This exercise shows you how to use a standard attribute as well as how to create and use a DLL. Imagine that you have a class that didn't use properties but, instead, had an old-fashioned explicit getter function. You decide to add properties and want to inform developers that they should not be using the old getter function.

1. Create a new CLR Console application named **UseAttributes**.

   You'll add code to this project later on in the exercise.

2. You create DLLs by using a Class Library project. In Solution Explorer, right-click the solution name. On the shortcut menu that appears, point to Add, and then click New Project.

3. When the Add New Project dialog box appears, select Class Library, call the project **MyDll**, and then click OK

The MyDll.h file opens in the editor.

4. Edit the class definition so that it looks like this:

```
namespace MyDll {

    public ref class TestClass
    {
        int val;
    public:
        TestClass(int n) : val(n) { }

        int getVal() { return val; }

        property int Val {
            int get() { return val; }
        }
    };
}
```

You can see that in addition to the class having a getter function, it now also has a property that does the same job.

5. You don't want to remove the getter function because that might break existing client code, so you mark it as obsolete by using the *Obsolete* attribute:

```
[Obsolete("Use the Val property instead", false)]
int getVal() { return val; }
```

The *Obsolete* attribute alerts the compiler that this function shouldn't be used, and the message should be used to inform developers why and what to do instead. The second argument directs the compiler as to whether to treat use of this function as an error or to only issue a warning.

6. Build the application to ensure that you have no coding errors.

7. To use the DLL from the console application, you must add a reference to the console project. Open the project properties dialog box for the UseAttributes project by right-clicking the project name (not the solution name!) and then, on the shortcut menu, click Properties. In the dialog box, click Common Properties, and then, in the pane on the left, click Framework And References.

8. Click the Add New Reference button to open the Add Reference dialog box. In the pane on the left, click the Solution entry. Doing so shows all the projects in the current solution. You should see MyDll listed in the center pane: select the check box adjacent to it, and then click OK twice to dismiss the dialog boxes. If you expand the External Dependencies entry under the UseAttributes project, you should see that it now displays an entry for MyDll.

9. Open the UseAttributes.cpp source file and add a *using* directive for the *MyDll* namespace.

```
using namespace MyDll;
```

10. Edit the *main* function to create an object and call its obsolete *get* method, as shown here:

```
int main(array<System::String ^> ^args)
{
    TestClass ^tc = gcnew TestClass(4);

    int n = tc->getVal();

    return 0;
}
```

11. Build the application.

You should see the following warning from the compiler:

```
UseAttributes.cpp(12): warning C4947: 'MyDll::TestClass::getVal' : marked as obsolete
            Message: 'Use the Val property instead'
```

You could also try changing the second argument to the *Obsolete* attribute to *true*, rebuild the entire solution by selecting Rebuild Solution from the Build menu, and check that use of the obsolete function is now treated as an error.

 Note When you use the Build command, Visual Studio only recompiles those files that have changed since the last build. Using Rebuild causes Visual Studio to rebuild the entire project. This can be useful when you've made significant changes.

Defining your own attributes

As you'll see in this section, you can easily define custom attributes and use them in your projects. Custom attributes are quite simple to write because an attribute's parameters are simply represented by a class with properties and methods. For example, suppose you had the following attribute attached to a class designed to control the generation of logging information at run time:

```
[LogAttribute("myfile.log", type=LogAttribute::AllMethods)]
ref class MyClass...
```

The attribute has two parameters: one for the log file name, and a second that determines the level of logging. The attribute is represented by a class called *LogAttribute* whose members contain the file name and type information. Information about the attribute class is included with the metadata for *MyClass*, and a *LogAttribute* object can be queried at run time to retrieve its parameters. You'll see how to query attributes in code in the final section of this chapter.

You can use any class to represent an attribute, but you will often use a class that derives from *System::Attribute* because that will give you a number of useful methods.

Attribute targets

Attributes can be used at all levels in .NET, so you can apply them to whole assemblies, to .NET types, or to individual methods and properties within types. An attribute often isn't applicable at all levels, so there needs to be some way to restrict the items to which an attribute can be attached.

The *AttributeUsage* attribute, represented by the *System::AttributeUsageAttribute* class, is a *meta-attribute*: an attribute that is applied to attributes. You attach an *AttributeUsage* attribute to the class that implements an attribute to indicate where it can be used. Here's an example:

```
[AttributeUsage(AttributeTargets::Method)]
```

This attribute would indicate that the attribute class can be used only on methods. The following table lists the members of the *AttributeTargets* enumeration that control where attributes are valid:

Member	This attribute can be applied to...
All	Any element
Assembly	An assembly
Class	A class
Constructor	A type constructor
Delegate	A delegate
Enum	An enumeration
Event	An event
Field	A field (for instance, Data member)
Interface	An interface
Method	A method
Module	A Portable Executable (PE)
Parameter	A parameter
Property	A property
ReturnValue	A return value
Struct	A structure; for example, a value type

If you want to specify more than one target, you can combine two or more members together with the bitwise OR operator (|), as you'll see in the next exercise. As you might expect, an attribute without *AttributeUsage* can be applied to any code element.

Attribute class properties

Although some attributes have no parameters, most will specify at least one. Attribute parameters fall into two groups:

- *Positional parameters*, which are identified simply by their position in the parameter list

- *Named parameters*, which are specified as a name/value pair

Consider the custom attribute we used as an example:

```
[LogAttribute("myfile.log", type=LogAttribute::AllMethods)]
```

This attribute has one positional parameter and one named parameter called *type*. Positional parameters always appear before named parameters, are specified in a fixed order, and are passed to the class constructor. Named parameters are implemented as properties in the attribute class.

Design criteria for attribute classes

Before moving on to the exercise, here are a few design criteria that you should keep in mind when you write a custom attribute class:

- Always add "Attribute" to the class name for an attribute (for example, call a class *DocumentationAttribute* rather than *Documentation*).

- Use positional arguments for required parameters.

- Use named arguments for optional parameters.

- Provide a read-only property for each positional argument.

- Provide a read/write property for each named argument. Be sure the name of the property differs in case from that of the argument (for example, for an argument called *type*, provide a property called *Type*).

Writing a custom attribute

This exercise shows you how to create a custom attribute that can be used to document methods and properties. In the next section, you'll see how to write code that makes use of this attribute.

1. Create a new CLR Class Library project named **CustomAttributes**.

   The custom attribute needs to be created as a DLL so that it can be used in other projects.

2. Open the CustomAttributes.h header file and edit the skeleton class as follows:

```
namespace CustomAttributes
{
    [AttributeUsageAttribute(AttributeTargets::Method |
                AttributeTargets::Property)]
    public ref class DocumentationAttribute : Attribute
    {
    };
}
```

Our class is called *DocumentationAttribute* and inherits from *System::Attribute*. The name follows the convention of having the class name for an attribute end with "Attribute." The class is tagged with an *AttributeUsage* attribute that limits its use to class methods and properties. Note how you can use more than one member of the *AttributeTargets* enumeration by combining them with the bitwise OR operator.

3. The attribute will include three pieces of data: the documentation text (which will be a positional parameter), and author and date strings (which will be optional—and thus implemented as named parameters). Add the declarations for the three members to the class.

```
namespace CustomAttributes
{
    [AttributeUsageAttribute(AttributeTargets::Method |
                AttributeTargets::Property)]
    public ref class DocumentationAttribute : Attribute
    {
        String ^text;      // documentation text
        String ^author;    // optional author field
        String ^date;      // optional date field
    };
}
```

4. Add the constructor.

```
public:
    DocumentationAttribute(String ^txt) : text(txt) { }
```

The constructor takes a string as its only argument, saved away as the documentation text.

5. Add a read-only property so that users can retrieve the text at run time.

```
// Read-only property to return the text
property String^ Text {
    String^ get() { return text; }
}
```

6. Add read/write properties to allow access to the two named parameters.

```
// Properties for the positional parameters
property String^ Author
{
    String^ get() { return author; }
    void set(String ^au) { author = au; }
}

property String^ Date
{
    String^ get() { return date; }
    void set(String ^dt) { date = dt; }
}
```

Choose the names for the properties carefully because these are going to be used in client code when using the attribute.

7. Build the application to check that you haven't made any errors.

8. Add some code that will use the new attribute. In Solution Explorer, right-click the solution name. On the shortcut menu that appears, point to Add, and then select New Project. Ensure that the project type is set to CLR Console Application and call the project **TestAtts**.

9. Add an external reference to the CustomAttributes DLL, just as you did in steps 7 and 8 of the previous exercise.

10. Open the TestAtts.cpp file and add a *using namespace* line to the top of the file:

```
using namespace CustomAttributes;
```

11. Define a managed class that uses the new custom attribute, as demonstrated here:

```
// A class to test the attribute
ref class TestAtts
{
    int val;
public:
    [DocumentationAttribute(
      "The TestAtts class constructor takes an integer",
      Author="julian", Date="10/10/01")]
    TestAtts(int v)
    {
        val = v;
    }
    [DocumentationAttribute(
      "The read-only Value property returns the value of"
      " the int class member", Author="julian")]
    property int Value
    {
        int get() { return val; }
    }
};
```

The *Documentation* attribute has been attached to the two members of this class. The constructor uses all three possible parameters, whereas the property uses only the text and the *Author* named parameter.

> **Note** Remember that you can split a string literal over two lines, and as long as there is nothing between the closing and opening double quotation marks except white space characters, the preprocessor will concatenate them for you.

12. Build the application to ensure that it compiles cleanly.

You can now use ILDASM to see how the attribute data is held in the class.

13. Run ILDASM, as described earlier, and open the TestAtts.exe file.

14. Click the plus sign (+) next to the blue component symbol labeled *TestAtts* and then double-click the *.ctor* entry.

This opens the disassembly for the constructor, as shown here:

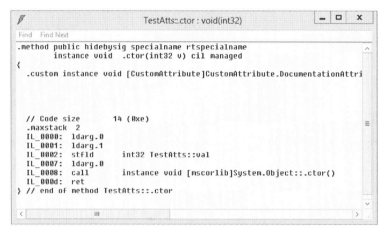

You can see how the code creates a *DocumentationAttribute* object, which then forms part of the *TestAtts* object. You can access this attribute object from code. (You'll see how to do this in the next section.)

15. Before leaving this exercise, try adding the *Documentation* attribute to the class, like this:

```
[DocumentationAttribute("The TestAtts class", Author="julian")]
ref class TestAtts
{
    ...
}
```

When you compile this code, the compiler will throw the following error message because the attribute cannot be applied to classes:

```
TestAtts.cpp(8): error C3115: 'CustomAttribute::DocumentationAttribute': this attribute
is not allowed on 'TestAtts'
        c:\users\julian\documents\sbs\customattribute\debug\customattribute.dll : see
declaration of 'CustomAttribute::DocumentationAttribute'
        attribute can only be applied to: 'member function', 'property'
```

Using reflection to obtain attribute data

The final section of this chapter shows you how to use attributes at run time by inquiring about what attribute data an object contains.

Reflection

Querying attribute data is only one aspect of *reflection*, a powerful feature supported by many languages that have a runtime, such as C++/CLI, C#, and Java. Reflection is mainly used for three things.

The first, also called *introspection*, is to find information about a type. For example, you can find out what members a type has, what its base class is, and what interfaces it implements. You will see this in action shortly, when you use it to find out the attributes attached to an object.

The second use of reflection is to create objects dynamically. This can be useful when you don't know the exact type you want until run time. For example, you could imagine a plug-in mechanism that loads a DLL at runtime, uses introspection to see what types the DLL defines, and then lets the user choose what to create.

The third use is dynamic invocation, which means executing functions and accessing properties on an object dynamically at run time. You'd typically do this on an object you've created dynamically.

The *Type* class

Before I talk about reflection and how it relates to attributes, you need to know something about the *Type* class. *System::Type* is a class that represents type declarations. This means that you can get a *Type* object to represent any object or type to which you have a reference, and you can then use that object to find out many details about the type. You can obtain *Type* objects to represent value types, arrays, classes, interfaces, and enumerations. It is the primary way to access metadata and the way in which you use reflection. Although the *Type* class is used mainly by developers writing language tools, you might find it useful at times, such as when you want to access class attributes.

System::Type has a lot of members (over 40 properties and almost 50 methods). The following two tables list a selection of properties and methods from this class to show you the sort of information you can access through a *Type* object:

Property	Description
Assembly	Gets a reference to the assembly where the type is defined
AssemblyQualifiedName	Gets the fully qualified name of the type, including the name of the assembly from which it was loaded
Attributes	Returns a *TypeAttributes* object representing the collection of attributes for this type
BaseType	Returns a *Type* for the type from which this object directly inherits
FullName	Returns the fully qualified name of the type, including namespace
IsAbstract	Returns true if the type is abstract
IsArray	Returns true if the type is an array
IsByRef	Returns true if the type is passed by reference
IsClass	Returns true if the type is a reference type (and not an interface or value type)
IsInterface	Returns true if the type is an interface
IsPublic, IsNotPublic	Indicates whether a type is marked as public or not
IsValueType	Returns true if the type is a value type
Module	Gets a reference to the module (the DLL) in which the type is defined
Namespace	Gets the namespace of the type as a string
UnderlyingSystemType	Gets a reference to the *Type* representing the CLR type underlying this language-specific type

Method	Description
GetConstructor, GetConstructors	Gets information about one or all of the constructors for the type
GetEvent, GetEvents	Gets information about one or all of the events defined for the type
GetField, GetFields	Gets information about one or all of the fields defined for the type
GetInterface, GetInterfaces	Gets information about one or all of the interfaces implemented by the type
GetInterfaceMap	Returns an *InterfaceMapping* showing how interface methods are mapped onto actual class methods
GetMember, GetMembers	Gets information about one or all of the members of the type
GetMethod, GetMethods	Gets information about one or all of the methods of the type

Method	Description
GetProperty, GetProperties	Gets information about one or all of the properties defined by the type
GetType	A static function that returns a *Type* object
InvokeMember	Invokes a member of the current type
ToString	Returns the name of the type as a *String*

You might think that you use the *Attributes* property to find out about custom attribute properties, but *Attributes* allows access only to standard system attribute data.

Accessing standard attributes

You can use the *Type* class's *Attributes* property to find out about the standard attribute settings for classes. This property returns a *TypeAttributes*, which is a value type; it's a set of flags describing which standard attributes are set for the type. This enumeration has over 30 members, and the table that follows shows you some of the common attributes that form part of *TypeAttributes*.

Member	Specifies that...
Abstract	The class is abstract
AnsiClass	Strings are interpreted using ANSI character encoding
AutoClass	The string encoding is automatically decided
Class	The type is a class
HasSecurity	The type has security information associated with it
Import	The type has been imported from another assembly
Interface	The type is an interface
NotPublic	The type is not public
Public	The type is public
Sealed	The type cannot be extended by inheritance
Serializable	The type can be serialized
UnicodeClass	Strings are interpreted by using Unicode character encoding

You can determine whether a type has an attribute set by using the bitwise AND operator (&), as shown in the following code fragment:

```
if ((tt->Attributes & TypeAttributes::Public) == TypeAttributes::Public)
    Console::WriteLine("Type is public");
```

If you want to check whether the type is a class, a value type, or an interface, you need to use the *ClassSemanticsMask* member, as illustrated here:

```
if ((tt->Attributes & TypeAttributes::ClassSemanticsMask) ==
        TypeAttributes::Class)
    Console::WriteLine("Type is a class");
```

Accessing custom attribute data

Custom attribute data is accessed by using the static *GetCustomAttribute* and *GetCustomAttributes* members of the *Attribute* class. As you'd expect, *GetCustomAttribute* retrieves information about one attribute, whereas *GetCustomAttributes* returns you an array containing details of all the custom attributes for a type. This exercise shows you how to use the *Type* class and the *GetCustomAttributes* method to retrieve the attribute settings from the class you created in the previous exercise.

1. Continue with the project from the previous exercise.

2. All classes dealing with reflection reside in the *System::Reflection* namespace, so add the following *using* declaration to the others at the top of the source:

    ```
    using namespace System::Reflection;
    ```

3. You need to create a *Type* object to use reflection to find out about custom attributes, so add this code to the start of the *main* function:

    ```
    int main(array<String^>^ args)
    {
        Console::WriteLine("Testing Attributes");

        // Create an object and get its type
        TestAtts ^ta = gcnew TestAtts(3);
        Type ^tt = ta->GetType();

        return 0;
    }
    ```

    You obtain a *Type* object by using the *GetType* method that every .NET type inherits from *System::Object.*

4. You can check whether there are any custom attributes on a class by using the *GetCustom Attributes* method on the *Type* object, like this:

    ```
    // See if there are any custom attributes on the class
    array<Object^> ^atts = tt->GetCustomAttributes(true);
    Console::WriteLine("Custom attributes on the class: {0}",
                          atts->Length);
    ```

    We know that the class doesn't have any custom attributes, so you'd expect a count of 0. Note the second Boolean argument, which specifies that we want to include any attributes inherited from base classes.

5. Build and run the application and check the output.

6. To run the console application, you will need to set it as the startup project. In Solution Explorer, right-click the project name, and then, on the shortcut menu, click Set As Startup Project.

    The project name should now be displayed in bold. This will be the project that is started when you instruct Visual Studio to run the projects in the solution.

7. The attributes are actually on the class members, not on the class itself, so get a list of the class members and query them, as shown in the following:

```
// Get info on the class members
array<MemberInfo^> ^mi = tt->GetMembers();
Console::WriteLine("Class members: {0}", mi->Length);
```

Calling *GetMembers* on the *Type* object returns an array of *MemberInfo* objects that describe the members. Running this code on the *TestAtts* class informs you that there are seven members.

 Note The seven members are the constructor, the private data value, the property get method, and four methods inherited from the *Object* base class (*Equals*, *GetHashCode*, *GetType*, and *ToString*).

8. Loop over the list of class members and get the custom attributes for each one.

```
for each (MemberInfo ^m in mi)
{
    array<Object^> ^atts = m->GetCustomAttributes(true);

    if (atts->Length > 0)
    {
        Console::WriteLine("Attributes for member {0}:", m->Name);
        for each(Object ^att in atts)
        {
            Console::WriteLine(" attribute is {0}", att->ToString());
        }
    }
}
```

The outer loop considers each member in turn and calls *GetCustomAttributes* on the *Member Info* object to get a list of attribute objects. If there are any attribute objects for this member, we print them out.

9. There are several ways to figure out whether a member has the *Documentation* custom attribute, and the following code shows one of them. Modify the code for the inner loop in the previous step so that it looks like this:

```
for each (Object ^att in atts)
{
    Console::WriteLine("  attribute is {0}", att->ToString());
    DocumentationAttribute ^da =
        dynamic_cast<DocumentationAttribute^>(att);
    if (da != nullptr)
    {
        Console::WriteLine("Doc attribute: {0}", da->Text);
    }
}
```

The loop first uses *dynamic_cast* to cast the current attribute as a *DocumentationAttribute* handle. If that returns a non-null value, you know that the cast worked, and so you can retrieve the *Text*.

10. Build and run the application.

You should see console output similar to that shown in the screen shot that follows, with a listing of the attributes present on class members and a showing of documentation text values.

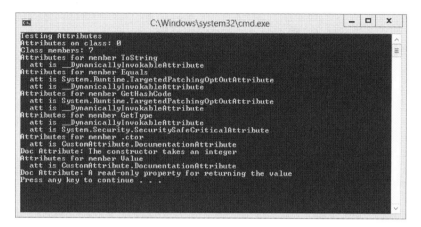

Quick reference

To	Do this
Modify the assembly-level attributes in a class.	Edit the entries in the AssemblyInfo.cpp file that is generated for all C++/CLI projects in Visual Studio 2012.

Find out about the standard attributes of a type.	Use the *Attributes* property on a *Type* object that represents the type, and use the bitwise AND operator (&) to compare the value with members of the *TypeAttributes* enumeration. For example:
	
	`if ((t->Attributes & TypeAttributes::Public) ==`
	`    TypeAttributes::Public)`

Create a custom attribute.	Create a class to represent an attribute, and use the *AttributeUsage* attribute to control where your attribute can be applied. For example:
	
	`[AttributeUsage(AttributeTargets::Method)] public`
	`ref class MyAttribute { ... };`

Represent mandatory parameters for a custom attribute.	Add arguments to the class constructor or constructors plus read-only properties to give access to the values.
Represent optional parameters for a custom attribute.	Add a property to represent each optional parameter.

To	Do this
Find out which custom attributes are attached to a class.	Create a *Type* object and use its *GetCustomAttributes* method to retrieve an array of objects representing the attributes attached to the class. For example: ```\nType ^tt = myObject->GetType();\narray<Object^> ^atts =\n tt->GetCustomAttributes(true);\n```
Find out which custom attributes are attached to a class member.	Create a *Type* object and use its *GetMembers* method to retrieve an array of *MemberInfo* objects representing the class members. Then call *GetCustomAttributes* on each *MemberInfo* object. For example: ```\nType ^tt = myObject->GetType();\narray<MemberInfo^> ^mi = tt->GetMembers();\nfor each(MemberInfo ^m in mi) {\n array<Object^> ^atts =\n m->GetCustomAttributes(true);\n if (atts->Length > 0) {\n // Do something\n }\n}\n```

Living with COM

After completing this chapter, you will be able to:

- Describe how you can use Component Object Model (COM) objects from .NET projects.

- Use COM objects through early and late binding.

- Use ActiveX controls in Windows Forms projects.

- Expose .NET objects as COM objects.

Although the types provided in the Microsoft .NET Framework are sufficient for the vast majority of applications, sometimes you'll need to interact with existing components, particularly COM components and ActiveX controls. This chapter shows you how the worlds of .NET and COM can interoperate, making it possible for you to take advantage of the best use of new and existing technologies.

Many people assumed that COM was dead when .NET arrived on the scene, and it is undeniable that .NET provides a better solution for creating a lot of component-based solutions. If you program in C++, though, it is still worth knowing about COM for two main reasons.

First, there is a lot of COM code out there, in the form of ActiveX controls and lower-level components, which is not going to go away. In fact, there are still some features of Windows that aren't wrapped by .NET for which you need to use COM to access.

The second, and perhaps more interesting reason, is that the Windows RT APIs are COM based. If you want to get the maximum performance out of Windows RT code (for example, if you're writing games in C++), you'll want to use COM.

 Note This chapter assumes that you know what COM objects are and something about how to use them outside the .NET world. If terms such as *GUID*, *HRESULT*, *IUnknown*, *IDispatch*, and *type library* don't mean anything to you, you should learn more about COM before proceeding with this chapter.

COM components and the COM Interop

The designers of the .NET Framework recognized that even though the framework is easier to use and more flexible than COM for many applications, it doesn't totally replace COM. For this reason, they developed the COM Interop facility so that .NET and COM objects can interact.

As you'll see shortly, it is easy to use a COM object from .NET code, and this gives .NET developers access to hundreds of existing COM objects. It is also possible to use a .NET object from COM code, although I'd expect this to be a less common occurrence.

Using COM components from .NET code

To use a COM object from .NET code, you first create a *Runtime Callable Wrapper* (RCW). You need the RCW because of several major differences between COM and .NET, which are summarized in the following table:

COM	.NET
Clients must manage the lifetimes of the COM objects they create.	The Common Language Runtime (CLR) manages the lifetime of .NET objects.
Clients use *QueryInterface* or browse the object's type information to find out whether a particular interface is supported.	Clients can use reflection to query an object.
COM objects are accessed through raw pointers and are therefore fixed in memory.	.NET objects are accessed through references and can be moved around by the CLR for performance reasons.

Wrapper classes are needed to bridge these differences so a COM object can appear as a .NET object, and vice versa.

How do RCWs work?

The wrapper takes the form of a proxy class that does all the work of creating and talking to the COM object, so you can use COM objects just as if they were .NET objects. You can see how this works in the diagram that follows. The RCW does all the housekeeping by interacting with the Windows Registry, creating the object, forwarding calls to the object, and managing its lifetime. The primary goal of the RCW is to hide the complexity of COM objects from .NET programmers; in some cases, .NET programmers might not even know they are using a COM object.

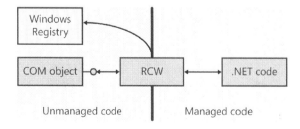

The wrapper class maintains a cache of interface pointers on the object it is using and releases these pointers when the object is no longer needed. The RCW itself is governed by the usual .NET garbage-collection rules because it is a managed object.

Because data types often differ in the .NET and COM worlds, the RCW performs standard marshaling so that both sides can use data types with which they are familiar. For example, when passing string data through an RCW, the .NET side works with *String* objects, but the COM side will probably use its own *BSTR* type; the RCW automatically converts between the two as necessary.

If you've used COM objects from C++, you're aware that COM objects implement several standard interfaces—such as *IUnknown* and *IDispatch*—that COM client programmers have to know about. The RCW simplifies the process of using COM objects by automatically handling many of the standard interfaces, as listed in the following table:

Interface	Description
IUnknown	The RCW uses *IUnknown* for object identity checking, type coercion via *QueryInterface*, and lifetime management.
IDispatch	Used for late binding to COM objects by using reflection.
IErrorInfo	Used for providing error information.
IProvideClassInfo	If the COM object being wrapped implements this interface, the RCW uses it to provide better type identity.
IConnectionPoint and *IConnectionPointContainer*	If the COM object uses connection points, the RCW exposes them to .NET clients as delegate-style events.
IDispatchEx	If the COM object implements *IDispatchEx*, the RCW exposes and implements the .NET *IExpando* interface.
IEnumVARIANT	The RCW enables COM types that expose this interface to be treated as .NET collections.

Creating and using RCWs

You can create RCW classes in two ways:

- If you're using Microsoft Visual Studio 2012, you can use a wizard to create the RCW for you.

- If you're compiling C++/CLI code from the command line, you can use the .NET Framework tool called tlbimp.exe (for Type Library Importer) to read a COM type library and create a wrapper class based on the information it finds.

The exercise that follows shows you how to use Visual Studio to create a wrapper for a COM object and then use the object.

Note I've created a simple COM object for use in this exercise called *TempConverter*. It implements simple temperature conversion functionality between Fahrenheit and Celsius. You'll find the source and executable for the *TempConverter* project, plus a ReadMe.txt file with directions for installing it, in this book's sample files. Be sure *TempConverter* is installed before starting this exercise.

1. Start Visual Studio 2012 and create a new CLR Console Application project named **ComWrapper**.

2. On the Project menu, click ComWrapper Properties to open the Project Properties dialog box. Select Common Properties, and then, in the pane on the left, click Frameworks And References, and then click the Add New Reference button.

3. In the Add Reference dialog box that opens, in the pane on the left, choose the COM entry.

   It might take a few seconds to populate the list box with details of the COM components registered on your system.

4. Browse the list to find the entry for the *TempConverterLib* component. Click to the left of this entry to add a check mark and then click OK.

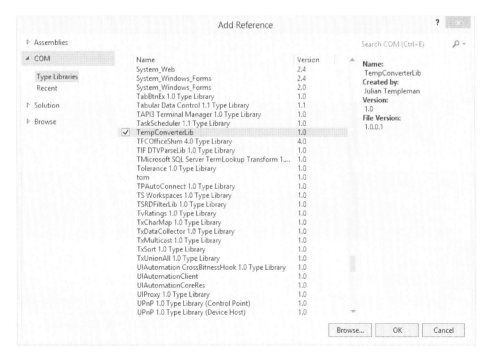

5. You will see that a new entry for *TempConverterLib* has been added to the project's list of references.

References:

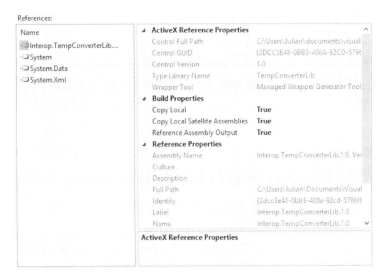

6. Open Windows Explorer and look in the project's Interop directory. You will see that it contains a file called Interop.TempConverterLib.1.0.dll, which contains the RCW assembly. These files are always named Interop.XXX.YYY.dll, where XXX and YYY are the name and version of the COM component to which the RCW refers.

7. Open the IL disassembler tool (ISDASM) and use it to examine Interop.TempConverter.1.0.dll.

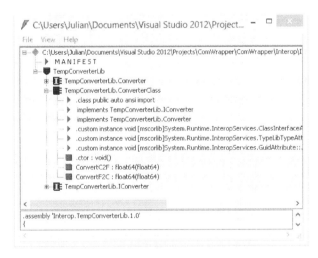

The shield-like symbol with the red top represents a namespace, so the namespace you need to import is *TempConverterLib*. You can see that the assembly contains three types. *Converter* and *IConverter* represent the original COM co-class and interface definitions, respectively; their symbol is marked with an I (a capital "i") to show that they are interfaces. *ConverterClass* is a real type, so its symbol doesn't contain the I. The RCW is produced by the tlbimp tool.

8. To deduce the name of the wrapper class without using ILDASM, you take the name of the COM co-class and append Class.

9. Add a *using* directive to your code to make it easier to reference the RCW.

```
using namespace TempConverterLib;
```

10. Add code to create a wrapper object, and use it to call methods on the COM object, as shown in the following:

```
int main(array<String^>^ args)
{
    Console::WriteLine("COM Interop Sample");

    // Create a COM object
    ConverterClass ^conv = gcnew ConverterClass();

    // Call a conversion method and print the result
    double d = conv->ConvertC2F(27.0);
    Console::WriteLine("27C is {0}F", d);

    return 0;
}
```

Observe how the wrapper is created just like any other managed object, and methods are called on it in exactly the same way as normal. There's no way to determine from this code that you're using a COM object, and the wrapper performs all the lifetime management for you.

11. Build and run the application, checking that the output is what you expect.

Handling COM errors

You know that COM methods return status and error information by using 32-bit *HRESULT*s. The RCW converts all error *HRESULT*s into exceptions that you can catch in your code. The test *Converter* project returns an error if the conversion methods are passed any values less than –273C or –459°F because temperatures less than absolute zero have no meaning. Here's the COM code:

```
STDMETHODIMP CConverter::ConvertC2F(double dCelsius, double* dFahr)
{
    if (dFahr == 0) return E_POINTER;

    // Temperatures below -273C are meaningless...
    if (dCelsius < -273.0) return E_INVALIDARG;

    *dFahr = (9/5.0 * dCelsius) + 32;
    return S_OK;
}
```

This code might return two error *HRESULT*s. The first, *E_POINTER*, occurs if the pointer to the result variable is null, which won't happen when called by the RCW. The second, *E_INVALIDARG*, occurs if an invalid temperature is passed. These are converted to exceptions by the RCW, and as usual, you need to catch them to prevent your application from terminating. Here's what you'll see on the console if you pass an invalid temperature:

You can handle this by adding a *try/catch* block to the code in the *main* function:

```
try
{
    double d = conv->ConvertC2F(-280.0);
    Console::WriteLine("-280C is {0}F", d);
}
catch(Exception ^ex)
{
    Console::WriteLine("Exception from COM object: {0}", ex->Message);
}
```

Again, build and run the application and check that the output is correct.

Late binding to COM objects

RCWs implement early binding connections to COM objects, because when you have a type library, you have all the details of what the COM object can do available to you at compile time. If you want to use a COM object that implements *IDispatch*, you can also call it at run time, but the process is a little more complex.

The exercise that follows shows how to use the *TempConverter* object with late binding. This COM object was created with a dual interface, so it can be accessed via both early binding and late binding.

1. Create a new CLR Console Application project named **LateBind**.

2. Add code to *main* to get a *Type* object that represents the COM component. (Consult Chapter 23, "Attributes and reflection," for more details on the *Type* class and its uses.)

```
// Get a type representing the COM object
Guid g = Guid("75F3EDC5-AA71-437A-ACB6-F885C29E50F7");
Type ^t = Type::GetTypeFromCLSID(g);
if (t == nullptr)
{
    Console::WriteLine("Error getting type for TConverter");
    return -1;
}
Console::WriteLine("Got type for TConverter");
```

The *GetTypeFromCLSID* static method takes a COM class ID (CLSID) as a *Guid* object and creates a *Type* object to represent the co-class. If there is a problem creating the *Type* object because the CLSID can't be found or because of some other registry-related problem, a null is returned. Overloads of this function let you specify that an exception be thrown instead of returning a null, if that suits your code better.

You can find the CLSID of a component by examining the .idl file that was used when creating it.

3. Use the *System::Activator* class to create the COM object for you, as demonstrated here:

```
// Use System::Activator to create an instance
Object ^obj = Activator::CreateInstance(t);
```

The *Activator* class creates instances of local or remote objects for you. The reference returned is a general object reference; you don't need to cast it to any specific type because this will be taken care of for you later.

4. Build the parameter list before you call a conversion method on the object. This takes the form of an array of *Object*s, as shown here:

```
// Make up the argument list

array<Object^> ^argarray = { 27.0 };
```

Here, the array contains only one value: the temperature to be converted.

5. Call the conversion method dynamically, using the *InvokeMember* method of the *Type* class.

```
// Invoke the method
try
{
    Object ^result = t->InvokeMember("ConvertC2F",
            Reflection::BindingFlags::InvokeMethod, nullptr, obj, argarray);

    double d = Convert::ToDouble(result);
    Console::WriteLine("27C is {0}F", d);
}
catch(Exception ^ex)
{
    Console::WriteLine("Exception from Invoke: ", ex->Message);
}
```

InvokeMember, as its name implies, dynamically invokes a member of an object. The arguments supplied to the function are the name of the member to be invoked, the type of operation (in this case, you're invoking a method rather than accessing a property or field), a handle to a *Binder* object (which you're not using), a handle to the object on which the operation is to be invoked, and a handle to the argument array.

If the call works, you'll be passed back an *Object* reference representing the result, which is then converted to the appropriate type by using one of the static methods of the *Convert* class.

6. Build and run the application, and check that you get the right answer (which is 80.6F).

Using .NET components as COM components

In addition to using COM objects from .NET clients, you can use .NET objects in the COM world. The process for exposing .NET classes as COM objects is complex because interacting with COM at the C++ level is difficult. For this reason, this section introduces the topic but leaves the practical implementation of .NET-to-COM code for more advanced texts.

Again, wrapper classes are used, only this time they are called COM Callable Wrappers (CCWs). In effect, a CCW puts a COM layer onto a .NET object so that the .NET object behaves in exactly the way a COM object is expected to behave. The process is shown here:

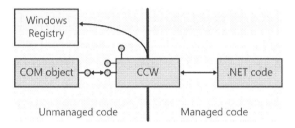

The CCW exposes all the interfaces expected by clients using COM, such as *IUnknown* and *IDispatch*, and it lets the client code manage its lifetime in the normal COM manner.

What must .NET types implement to be used as COM objects?

COM objects have a particular set of characteristics, and .NET types need to follow some rules if they're to be exposed as COM objects using COM Interop. Here's a summary of what the .NET type must to do:

- It must supply a default constructor—one that doesn't take arguments—because COM objects are always created uninitialized, and there's no standard way to pass over initialization data. For this reason, it must be possible to create .NET objects uninitialized if they're to be used as COM objects.

- The type's assembly must be signed with a strong name. See the upcoming sidebar "Names and signing" for details on strong names and how to use them.

- The type's assembly must be placed where the CLR can find it. See the upcoming sidebar "Installing assemblies" for more details.

- The correct COM-related registry entries must be made for the .NET object. This is done for you automatically if you're using Visual Studio.

Names and signing

Assemblies are normally identified by their name, version number, and possibly locale information. This is adequate for private assemblies that will be used only within a single application.
However, it isn't good enough for those that will be used more widely because two people
could use the same name for their assemblies, resulting in lots of potential for confusion.

To make assemblies unique, they should be given a strong name, which consists of the
text name, version, and locale information, plus a public key and a digital signature. Every key
generated by using Public Key Encryption is unique, so using keys and digital signatures serves
both to provide a unique identifier for an assembly, and a way to verify the assembly owner or
creator.

COM requires that components be uniquely identified, and it uses GUIDs to accomplish this.
.NET strong names fulfill the requirement for unique component identification, and they also
provide information about the component's originator, which GUIDs do not.

Installing assemblies

Assemblies are typically installed in one of two places. Private assemblies, which are intended
for use by a single application, can be placed in the directory where the executable resides
or any directory directly underneath. Shared assemblies are installed into the Global Assembly Cache (GAC), which is a per-computer repository for assemblies that need to be shared.
You don't manually copy assembly files into the GAC; you use the tools provided by the .NET
Framework for managing the cache (such as gacutil.exe).

Assemblies must reside in one of these two locations because they are where the CLR looks
for them when it needs to load them at run time.

Quick reference

To	Do this
Use a COM object from .NET code.	If you're using Visual Studio 2012, use the Properties dialog box to add a reference to the COM component. If you're compiling from the command line, use the tlbimp.exe tool to generate an RCW for the COM object, and then reference the wrapper in your code as you would any other .NET class.
Use a COM object via late binding.	Use the static *GetTypeFromProgID* or *GetTypeFromCLSID* methods of the *Type* class to generate a *Type* object representing the COM object. Then, use the *CreateInstance* static method on the *System::Activator* class to create an instance of the object. Finally, use *InvokeMember* on the *Type* object to invoke your chosen member.
Use a .NET component in a COM project.	Create a CCW.

Index

Symbols

+ (addition operator), 30
& (ampersand character), 175
& (AND operator), 296
&& (AND operator), 31
= (assignment operator), 26
* (asterisk) symbol, 438
^ (caret) symbol, 391
~ (complement operator), 32
%d descriptor, 422
/ (division operator), 30
. (dot operator), 20
:: (double-colon syntax), 79
= (equal sign), 236, 254
#include directive, 439
#include statements, 107
__int8 type, 24
__int16 type, 24
__int32 type, 24
__int64 type, 24
<< (left-shift operator), 32
<= (less-than-or-equal-to) condition, 199
% (modulus operator), 30
* (multiplication operator), 30
! (NOT operator), 31
-= operator, 252, 254
-> operator, 83
+ operator, 252
+= operator, 251, 254
-> (pointer operator), 28
#pragma once directive, 125
#pragma once line, 240
>> (right-shift operator), 32
:: (scope resolution operator), 269
[ ] (square brackets), 267
- (subtraction operator), 30

<> syntax, 207
%x descriptor, 422

A

Abs function, 169
Abstract attribute, 469
abstract classes
    and sealed classes, 137
    overview, 130–131
Account class, 14
    in bank example, 238–240
AddAccount method, 240
Add function, 221
addition operator (+), 30
Add method
    in bank example, 240–241
Add New Item dialog box, 107
Add New Reference button, 461
add_OnFirstEvent method, 256
addresses, WCF, 355
Add Service dialog box, 364
AddServiceEndpoint, 363
ADO.NET
    assemblies, 336
    connected application, creating
        connecting to database, 337–341
        creating and executing command, 340–341
        executing command that modifies data, 341–342
        executing queries and processing results, 342–343
        overview, 336–337
    data providers, 334–335
    disconnected application, creating, 344–345
    disconnected operation using DataSet, 345–350
    namespaces, 335

overview, 334–336
quick reference, 350, 368
Age property, 232
aggregate initializer, 202
algorithms, 226
All Apps charm, 378
ampersand character (&), 175
AND operator (&), 296
AND operator (&&), 31
Animal class, 16
AnsiClass attribute, 469
API (application programming interface),
        Windows, 265
AppBarButton style, 427
app bars
    AppBar control, 383
    in calculator example, 425–428
AppendAllLines method, 292
AppendAllText method, 292
AppendChild method, 324, 326
AppendText method, 292, 293
App.g.cpp, 380
App.g.h, 380
application programming interface (API),
        Windows, 265
Application UI tab, 412
ArgumentException, 222, 232, 239
ArithmeticButtons_Click method, 404, 406
ArithmeticException, 184
arithmetic operators, 30–31
    overloading, 161–162
arity, 161
array keyword, 207
Array::Reverse method, 217
arrays
    managed arrays
        and reference types, 208–210
        initializing, 208
        multidimensional, 211
        overview, 207–208
        using for each loop with, 210–211
    native
        dynamic allocation of, 203–205
        initializing, 202
        multidimensional, 202–203
        overview, 197–199
        passing to functions, 200–202
    overview, 28
    System::Array class
        basic operations using, 213–215

copying elements, 215
overview, 212
searching, 216–217
sorting, 217–218
using enumerators with, 218–219
Array::Sort method, 217
AsReadOnly method, 212
assemblies
    ADO.NET, 336
    .NET, 266
AssemblyCompanyAttribute, 267, 268
AssemblyInfo.cpp file
    predefined attributes, 457–458
assembly linker, 6
assembly manifest, 266
Assembly property, 468
AssemblyQualifiedName property, 468
Assets folder, 379
assigning variables, 26–27
assignment conversions, 26
assignment operator (=), 26, 30
asterisk (*) symbol, 438
attached properties, 386–387
AttributeCount property, 307, 315
Attribute node type, 309
attributes
    and metadata
        overview, 453–454
        using ILDASM, 454–457
    defining custom
        creating, 463–467
        design criteria for attribute classes, 463–464
        overview, 461–463
        properties for, 463–464
    predefined attributes
        AssemblyInfo.cpp file, 457–458
        classes for, 458–461
        overview, 457
    using reflection to obtain
        accessing custom attribute data, 470–472
        accessing standard attributes, 469
        overview, 467–468
        Type class, 467–469
Attributes property, 291, 323, 326, 468
AttributeTargets enumeration, 464
AttributeUsage attribute, 462, 464
AttributeUsageAttribute class, 458, 462
AutoClass attribute, 469
auto_gcroot type, 440
auto-implemented properties, 233

automatic layout, 449
Average function, 53

B

backing variable, 233
Balance property, 241
BankAccount class, 123, 124, 130, 132, 136
bank example
    adding Account class, 238–239
    Bank class
        adding accounts to, 240–243
        implementing, 236–238
    overview, 236
base addresses, 355
BaseButtons_Click method, 418
base classes, 126–129
BaseStream property, 298, 302, 318
BaseType property, 468
base variable, 419
BasicHttpBinding, 355, 358
behavior of Windows Store apps, 373
behaviors, WCF, 358–359
Berkeley Sockets protocol, 275
BestFitMapping field, 447
binary I/O
    BinaryReader class, 299–304
    BinaryWriter class, 298
    overview, 298
binary operator, 162
BinaryReader class, 274, 282, 299–303
BinarySearch method, 212
BinaryWriter class, 274, 282, 298
binding, WCF, 355
bitwise operators, 32–33
blocking, 283
Boolean type, 271
Boolean value type, 145
bool type, 24
Border control, 383
BorderThickness property, 399
BottomAppBar element, 428
boxing 443
    unboxing, 443–444
boxing process, 171
break keyword, 73
breakpoints, 47
BufferedStream class, 282
buffer overrun, 200

Button control, 383
Button element, 376
Byte type, 271
Byte value type, 144

C

Cached File Updater contract, Windows 8, 429
calculator example
    adding tile, 412–415
    app bars, 425–428
    arithmetic buttons, 403–404
    getting number from button, 404–405, 407–408
    handling different number bases
        adding buttons for, 417–418
        changing base, 418–421
        converting string in display, 421–425
    handling number input, 401–402
    laying out number buttons, 398–401
    overview, 397–398
    performing calculations, 408–409
    remembering operations, 406
    sharing in
        contracts and charms, 428–429
        DataPackage class, 430
        handling requests, 431–432
        implementing, 429–430
        overview, 428
    testing, 410–412
Calendar Assistant application, 61
CallingConvention field, 447, 448
calling functions, 45–47
CallMe method, 261
CanDebit method, 123, 133, 134
Canvas control, 388
Capacity property, 220
caret (^) symbol, 391
casting process, 26
cast operator, overview, 33–34
catch block, 347
    handling exceptions using, 180–182, 189
C++/CLI
    defined, 3
    Hello World example, 4
    identifiers in, overview, 5–6
    keywords in, overview, 5–6
    main function in, overview, 4–5
CCWs (COM Callable Wrappers), 483

CDATA node type, 309
charms
    in calculator example, 428–429
    in Windows Store apps, 374
CharSet field, 447, 448
Char type, 24, 271
Char value type, 145
CheckBox control, 384
CheckCharacters property, 310
CheckingAccount class, 15
ChildNodes property, 323, 326
Circle class, 236
Class attribute, 469
classes
    abstract classes, 130–131
    base classes, 126–129
    class-wide members
        data members, 88–89
        member functions, 90–91
        overview, 87–88
        static constructors, 92–93
    concrete classes, 130–131
    constants in
        class-wide constants, 93–94
        instance constants, 94–95
        overview, 93
    constructors
        defining, 84–86
        member initialization lists, 86–87
    creating objects, 83–84
    for custom attributes, 463–464
    derived classes, 129–130
    and finalizers, 106
    in header files, 79–80
    in source files, 81–82
    in object-oriented programming, 16
    object relationships
        creating LoyaltyScheme class, 95–96
        creating LoyaltyScheme objects, 97–100
        implementing LoyaltyScheme class, 96–97
        overview, 95–96
        testing example application, 100
    organizing, 78–79
    overriding member functions, 131–136
    for predefined attributes, 458–461
    protected access, 136–137
    sealed classes
        and abstract classes, 137
        overview, 137
    vs. structures, 149–150
    in Windows RT, 391–392
class keyword, 20
class library, .NET, 265
class members, 77
class-wide constants, 93–94
class-wide members
    data members, 88–89
    member functions, 90–91
    overview, 87–88
    static constructors, 92–93
ClearButton_Click method, 402
Clear method, 212
clearOnNextKey variable, 409
Clone method, 212, 324, 326
CloneNode method, 324, 326
Close method, 283, 287, 298, 299, 308, 318
CLR (Common Language Runtime), 20, 263–264,
    336, 437, 454
CLS (Common Language Specification), 160, 265,
    298
CLSCompliantAttribute class, 458
CLS-compliant operators, overloading, 166–167
code-behind files, 379, 382
code reuse, and inheritance, 122
collections
    List<T> class, overview, 219–221
    overview, 219
    SortedList<K,V> class, overview, 222–223
Collections interfaces, 273–274
Collections namespaces, 272–273
ColumnDefinition element, 386
Column property, 387
Combine method, 250
ComboBox control, 384
COM Callable Wrappers (CCWs), 483
COM (Component Object Model), 276
    overview, 475–476
    using from .NET code
        and RCWs, 476–477
        creating RCWs, 477–480
        handling errors, 480–481
        late binding to COM objects, 481–482
        overview, 476
    using .NET components as COM
        components, 483–485
CommandText property, 340
Comment node type, 309

Common Language Runtime (CLR), 20, 263–264, 336, 437, 454
Common Language Specification (CLS), 160, 298
Compare method, 222
CompareTo method, 218, 222
compiling source files, 9–10
complement operator (~), 32
Component Object Model (COM), 276. *See* COM
concrete classes, 130–131
ConditionalAttribute class, 458
ConfigurationManager class, 339
ConformanceLevel property, 310
connected application, ADO.NET
    connecting to database, 337–341
    creating and executing command, 340–341
    executing command that modifies data, 341–342
    executing queries and processing results, 342–343
    overview, 336–337
Connection property, 340
ConnectionStringSettings object, 339
connectionStrings section, 338
connectivity, WCF, 353
Console line, 4
Console::ReadLine function, 44
Console::Write function, 44
constants
    in classes
        class-wide constants, 93–94
        instance constants, 94–95
        overview, 93
    overview, 28–29
const_cast<> operator, 33
constructors
    defining, 84–86
    handling exceptions for, 184–185
    member initialization lists, 86–87
    for structures, 150
ContainsKey method, 223
Contains method, 241
ContainsValue method, 223
Content attribute, 376
content controls, 382
continue keyword, 73
contracts
    in calculator example, 428–429
    WCF, 356–358
    in Windows Store apps, 374
controls, in XAML, 382–383
Control templates, 381

conversion operator, 164
ConverterClass, 479
converting constructors, 164
ConvertOutputString function, 423
ConvertTextToInt function, 407, 421
Convert::ToInt32 function, 44
copy constructors, overview, 113–116
Copy method, 212, 215, 292
CopyTo method, 212, 293
Count property, 220
count variable, 289
CreateAttribute method, 324
CreateCDataSection method, 324
CreateComment method, 324
CreateDefaultAttribute method, 324
CreateDirectory method, 290
CreateDocumentType method, 324
CreateElement method, 324
CreateEntityReference method, 324
Create method, 291–293, 306, 308
CreateNavigator method, 324, 326
CreateNode method, 324
CreateProcessingInstruction method, 324
CreateSubdirectory method, 291
CreateText method, 292, 293
CreateTextNode method, 324
CreateWhitespace method, 324
CreateXmlDeclaration method, 324
CreationTime property, 291, 293
CreditCardAccount class, 78
CTS (Common Type System), 264
Cube function, 249
CurrentAccount class, 123, 126–127, 129–130
CurrentAccount.cpp project, 128
CurrentAccount header file, 129
Current property, 210, 218
custom attributes
    creating, 463–467
    design criteria for attribute classes, 463–464
    obtaining data using reflection, 470–472
    overview, 461–463
    properties for, 463–464

D

data adapter, 344
DataColumn class, 344
DataContract class, 357
data contracts, 356

data hiding, 14
data members, class-wide, 88–89
Data namespaces, 276–277
DataPackage class, in calculator example, 430
data providers, ADO.NET, 334–335
DataRow class, 344
DataSet class, disconnected operation using,
    344–350
DataTransferManager, 431
data types, for variables, 23–24
Date structure, 150, 152
DateTime class, 234
DbConnection class, 336
DbDataAdapter class, 344
DbProviderFactory class, 346
DCOM (Distributed Component Object Model), 352
DebuggableAttribute class, 458
DebuggerHiddenAttribute class, 458
DebuggerStepThroughAttribute class, 458
debugging, stepping through application, 47–51
Debug toolbar, 49
declarative UI layout, 381
declaring variables
    multiple, 26
    overview, 25
decrement operators, overloading, 171–172
DefaultAttribute, 395
default branch, 66
default values, for function prototypes, 40
delegate keyword, 247, 250
delegates
    defining, 247
    implementing
        calling non-static member functions by using
            delegates, 249
        calling static member functions by using
            delegates, 248–249
        delegates that return result, 252–253
        overview, 247
        using multicast delegates, 249–252
    overview, 245–246
    purpose of, 246–247
DeleteCommand, 345
delete method
    for arrays, 204
    overview, 109
Delete method, 290, 291, 292, 293
Depth property, 307
deque type, STL/CLR, 226
derived classes, 129–130

destructors
    overview, 105–106
    using, 109–110
Diagnostics namespace, 274
Dialog class, 265
Dictionary<K,V> class, 219
directories, getting information about, 290–297
Directory class, 274, 282
DirectoryInfo class, 274, 282, 290–291
DirectoryName property, 293
Directory property, 293
DisplayDate function, 59
Dispose method, 283, 287, 298–299, 308
Distributed Component Object Model (DCOM), 352
distributed systems, WCF, 352
DivideByZeroException, 183
division operator (/), 30
DLL (Dynamic-Link Library), 192, 365–368, 444
DllImport attribute, 446
DllImportAttribute class, 447–448
DOB member, 151–152
Documentation attribute, 466
DocumentationAttribute class, 464, 472
DocumentElement property, 323
DocumentFragment node type, 309
Document node type, 309
Document Object Model (DOM), 307
DocumentType node type, 309
DocumentType property, 323
do keyword, 72
DOM (Document Object Model), 307
dot operator (.), 20
double-colon syntax (::), 79
Double type, 24, 271
Double value type, 144
do-while loops, overview, 71–73
DtdProcessing property, 310
duplex operation, 358
dynamic allocation, of arrays, 203–205
dynamic_cast, 170, 444
dynamic_cast<> operator, 33
dynamic invocation, 467
Dynamic-Link Library (DLL, 192, 444

E

for each loop
    using with arrays, 210–211
EarnPointsOnAmount function, 97

EF (Entity Framework), 276
E_INVALIDARG error, 480
Element node type, 309
elements in arrays, copying, 215
EnableBinaryButtons method, 420
EnableDecimalButtons method, 420
EnableHexButtons method, 420
encapsulation, in object-oriented programming,
        14–15
Encoding property, 307
EndElement node type, 309
EndEntity node type, 309
EndPointAddress class, 362
endpoints, WCF, 353–354
EntityClient data provider, 334
Entity Framework (EF), 276
Entity node type, 309
EntityReference node type, 309
EntryPoint field, 447–448
EnumerateDirectories method, 290–291
EnumerateFiles method, 290–291
EnumerateFileSystemEntries method, 290–291
enumerations
        creating, 153–154
        memory usage, 156
        using in programs, 156
enumerators, using with arrays, 218–219
EOF property, 307
E_POINTER eror, 480
EqualsButton_Click method, 407, 425
Equals function, overloading, 169–171
equal sign (=), 236
Equals method, 74, 471
errNo field, 190
error handling, using COM components from
        .NET, 480–481
Error List window, 10
errors, in properties, 232
EventArgs object, 260
event handling, in XAML, 389
event keyword, 255
events
        event receiver, 256–258
        event source class, 254–256
        overview, 253–254
        quick reference, 262
        standard, 259–261
        System::EventHandler delegate and, 259–261
EvtRcv class, 257
EvtSrc class, 255

ExactSpelling field, 448
exceptions
        and safe_cast keyword, 191–192
        creating, 189–191
        Exception class properties, 182–183
        handling
                catch block, 189
                Exception class properties, 182–183
                exception hierarchy, 184
                finally block, 188
                try/catch blocks, 180–182
                with constructors, 184–185
        in mixed-language programming, 192–195
        nesting, 185–188
        overview, 175–178
        rethrowing, 185–188
        throwing, 178–180
        types of, 178
executable programs
        compiling source files, 6, 9–10
        creating project, 8–9
        running program, 7, 11
        source files for, 9
ExecuteNonQuery method, 337, 341
ExecuteReader method, 337, 342
ExecuteScalar method, 337, 340
Exists method, 212, 288, 290, 292
Exists property, 291, 293
explicit layout, 449
eXtensible Markup Language. See XML
Extensible Stylesheet Language Transformations
        (XSLT), 306
Extensible Stylesheet Language (XSL), 276
Extension property, 291

F

fall-through, using in switch statement, 67–68
fault contracts, 356
FieldOffsetAttribute class, 449
FIFO (first in, first out), 226
FileAccess enumeration, 286
FileAttributes class, 296
File class, 274, 282, 288
FileInfo class, 274, 282
FileMode enumeration, 286
File Picker contract, Windows 8, 429
files. See also binary I/O; See also text I/O
        getting information about, 290–297
        quick reference, 303–304

FileShare enumeration, 286
FileStream class, 274, 282, 286–287
file structure, for Windows Store apps, 379–380
FileSystemInfo class, 274, 282
FileSystemWatcher class, 274, 282
FillBuffer method, 299
finalAmount variable, 50
finalizers
    overview, 106
    using, 108–109
finally block, 347
    handling exceptions using, 188
FindAll method, 212
FindLast method, 212
Find method, 212
FirstChild property, 323, 326
FirstEventHandler delegate, 255
first in, first out (FIFO), 226
FlagsAttribute, 395
FlagsAttribute class, 458
FlipView control, 384
floating-point types, 272
floating-point values, 169
float type, 24
flow control statements
    if statement
        multiway tests, 62–64
        nested tests, 64–65
        one-way tests, 57–61
        overview, 57
        two-way tests, 61–62
    loop statements
        do-while loops, 71–73
        for loops, 70–71
        overview, 68
        unconditional jumps in, 73–74
        while loops, 68–70
    switch statement
        overview, 65–67
        using fall-through in, 67–68
FlushAsync method, 283
Flush method, 283, 298, 318
FontSize property, 399
for-each loop, 68
ForEach method, 212
Foreground property, 403
for loops, overview, 70–71
Format member, 154
Formatting property, 318, 320
forms, 370

FromBinary function, 422
FullName property, 291, 293, 468
fully qualified name, 269
func function, 180
function header, 41
Function keyword, 38
functions
    calling, 45–47
    function bodies
        defining, 41–42
        overview, 41
        parameters in, 42–43
        return type, 43–45
    function prototypes
        declaring, 38–39
        default values for, 40
        defined, 38
        parameters in, 39
        return type, 39–40
    global scope, 51–53
    local scope, 51–53
    non-static member functions, calling by using
        delegates, 249
    overloading, 53–55
    overriding, 131–136
    passing arrays to, 200–202
    static member functions, calling by using
        delegates, 248–249

G

GAC (Global Assembly Cache), 484
garbage collector, 103–104
GCHandle::Alloc method, 438
GCHandle type, and unmanaged code, 438–441
gcnew operator, 27, 28, 110, 143, 147, 208
gcroot variable, 440
GDI32.dll, 445
generations, 104
generic keyword, 206, 392
generics, in Windows RT, 392
generic types
    and templates
        overview, 224
        STL/CLR library, 224–227
    overview, 205–206
Geometry.cpp file, 117
GetAccountNumber function, 82
GetAttribute method, 308
GetAttributes method, 292, 296

GetConstructor method, 468
GetConstructors method, 468
GetCreationTime method, 290, 292
GetCurrentDirectory method, 290
GetCustomAttribute method, 470
GetCustomAttributes method, 470, 471
get_date function, 229
GetDay function, 59
GetDirectories function, 297
GetDirectories method, 290, 291
GetDirectoryRoot method, 290
GetElementById method, 324
GetElementsByTagName method, 324
GetEnumerator method, 212, 218, 324, 326
GetEvent method, 468
GetEvents method, 468
GetField method, 468
GetFields method, 468
GetFiles method, 290, 291
GetFileSystemEntries method, 290
GetFileSystemInfos method, 291
get function, 161
GetHashCode method, 171, 471
GetInterestRate function, 87
GetInterfaceMap method, 468
GetInterface method, 468
GetInterfaces method, 468
GetInvocationList function, 253
GetLastAccessTime method, 290, 292
GetLastWriteTime method, 290, 292
GetLength method, 212, 214
GetLogicalDrives method, 290
GetLowerBound method, 212, 214
GetMember method, 468
GetMembers method, 468
get method, 234
GetMethod method, 468
GetMethods method, 468
GetMonth function, 59
GetNamespaceOfPrefix method, 326
GetNumberOfAccounts function, 90
GetParent method, 290
GetPrefixOfNamespace method, 326
GetProperties method, 469
GetProperty method, 469
GetSystemPowerStatus function, 449, 450
getter, 231
GetTypeFromCLSID method, 481
GetType method, 469, 470, 471
GetUpperBound method, 213, 214

getVal function, 162, 164
getValue function, 440
GetValue method, 213
GetYear function, 58
Global Assembly Cache (GAC), 484
global scope, overview, 51–53
global variables, 52
green and blue stacks, 372–373
Grid control, 375–376
GridView control, 384

H

handles
    to objects, 118–119
    overview, 27–28
handling exceptions
    catch block, 189
    with constructors, 184–185
    Exception class properties, 182–183
    exception hierarchy, 184
    finally block, 188
    try/catch blocks, 180–182
hardware, and Windows Store apps, 374
HasAttributes property, 307
HasChildNodes property, 323, 326
hashcode, 171
HashSet<T> class, 219, 273
HasSecurity attribute, 469
HasValue property, 307
header files, classes in, 79–80
Hello World example, 4
hierarchy
    for exceptions, 184
    for inheritance, 123–124
HttpGetEnabled property, 364
HttpRequest class, 277
HttpResponse class, 277
HTTP transport, 354

I

IChannel handle, 362
ICollection<T> interface, 273
IComparable interface, 218
IComparer<T> interface, 273
IConnectionPointContainer interface, 477
IConnectionPoint interface, 477
IDE (integrated development environment), 11

identifiers, overview, 5–6

IDictionary<K,V> interface, 273

IDispatchEx interface, 477

IDispatch interface, 477

IEnumerable<T> interface, 273

IEnumerator interface, 210

IEnumerator<T> interface, 273

IEnumVARIANT interface, 477

IErrorInfo interface, 477

if statement
    multiway tests, 62–64
    nested tests, 64–65
    one-way tests, 57–61
    overview, 57
    two-way tests, 61–62

IgnoreComments property, 310

IgnoreProcessingInstructions property, 310

IgnoreWhitespace property, 310

ILDASM, 454–457

ILDASM tool, 264

IL Disassembler tool, 264

IL (Intermediate Language), 375

IList<T> interface, 273

IMathService contract, 361

IMetadataExchange contract, 363

Import attribute, 469

ImportNode method, 324

#include directive, 439

include guard, 360

#include statements, 79, 96

increment operators, overloading, 171–172

Indentation property, 318

IndentChar property, 318

indexed properties
    bank example
        creating Account class properties, 239–240
        implementing to retrieve accounts, 241–244
    defined, 230
    overview, 236

indexing, 207

IndexOfKey method, 223

IndexOf method, 213, 216

IndexOfValue method, 223

inheritance
    abstract classes, 130–131
    and code reuse, 122
    base classes, 126–129
    concrete classes, 130–131
    derived classes, 129–130

designing hierarchy for, 123–124
    interfaces, 138–139
    in object-oriented programming, 15
    overriding member functions, 131–136
    overview, 121–122
    properties and, 235
    protected access, 136–137
    sealed classes
        and abstract classes, 137
        overview, 137
    substitutability, 123–124
    terminology, 122

InitializeComponent method, 406

Initialize method, 213

inline functions, 19

InnerText property, 323, 326

InnerXml property, 323, 326

input/output. *See* I/O

input variable, 44

InsertAfter method, 324, 326

InsertBefore method, 324, 326

InsertCommand, 345

Insert function, 221

instance constants, 94–95

instance members, 77

Int16 type, 271

Int16 value type, 144

Int32 type, 271

Int64 type, 271

Int64 value type, 144

integrated development environment (IDE), 11

Interface attribute, 469

interfaces, properties in, 235

interior pointers, 441

Intermediate Language (IL), 375

inter-process communication (IPC), 353

IntPtr type, 271

IntPtr value type, 145

IntPtr::Zero argument, 447

introspection, 467

int type, 18, 24

IntVal class, 161, 163

InvalidCastException, 191

InvalidOperationException, 219

invocation list, 250

InvokeMember method, 469, 482

Invoke method, 248

IOException class, 274, 282

I/O (input/output)
    binary I/O, 298
        BinaryReader class, 299–303
        BinaryWriter class, 298
    text I/O
        FileStream class, 286–287
        overview, 283
        TextReader, 287–290
        TextWriter, 283–285
IO namespace, 274
IPC (inter-process communication), 353
IPC transport, 354
IProvideClassInfo interface, 477
IReadOnlyCollection<T> interface, 273
IsAbstract property, 468
IsArray property, 468
IsByRef property, 468
IsClass property, 468
IsEmptyElement property, 307
ISet<T> interface, 273
IsFixedSize property, 212
IsInterface property, 468
IsNotPublic property, 468
IsPublic property, 468
IsReadOnly property, 212, 323, 326
IsStartElement method, 308
IsSynchronized property, 212
IsValueType property, 468
Item property, 307, 323, 326
items controls, 382
iterator, 225, 226
IUnknown interface, 477

J

JIT (Just-In-Time) compiler, 264
Just-In-Time (JIT) compiler, 264

K

Kernel32.dll, 445
KeyRoutedEventArgs, 389
KeyValuePair class, 223
keywords, overview, 5–6

L

LastAccessTime property, 291, 293
LastChild property, 323, 326

LastIndexOf method, 213, 216
last in, first out (LIFO), 226
LastWriteTime property, 291, 293
late binding, to COM objects, 481–482
layout
    in calculator example, 398–401
    in XAML, 384–388
left-shift operator (<<), 32
Length property, 212, 213, 293
less-than-or-equal-to (<=) condition, 199
lifetimes, of objects, 103–105
LIFO (last in, first out), 226
LimitReached event, 260
LineNumberOffset property, 310
LinePositionOffset property, 310
LinkedList<T> class, 219, 273
Linq class, 276
ListBox control, 384
ListBoxItems control, 381
List class, 240, 241
List<T> class, 273
    overview, 219–221
list type, STL/CLR, 226
ListView control, 384
literal constant, 28
literal keyword, 93
Live tiles, 415
Load method, 325
LoadXml method, 325
LocalName property, 307, 323, 326
local scope, overview, 51–53
location element, 331
LogAttribute class, 462
logical operators
    overloading, 167–169
    overview, 31–32
LongLength property, 212
long long type, 24
long type, 24
LookupNamespace method, 308
LookupPrefix method, 318
loop statements
    do-while loops, 71–73
    for loops, 70–71
    overview, 68
    unconditional jumps in, 73–74
    while loops, 68–70
LoyaltyScheme class example
    creating, 95–96
    creating objects, 97–100

implementing class, 96–97
testing application, 100–101

M

main function, 41, 248
    overview, 4–5
main method, 108
MainPage class, 406
MainPage.g.cpp, 380
MainPage.g.h, 380
MakePurchase function, 80, 98
MakeRepayment function, 80
managed arrays
    and reference types, 208–209
    initializing, 208
    multidimensional, 211
    overview, 207
    using for each loop with, 210–211
managed code
    vs. unmanaged code
        GCHandle type, 438–441
        mixed classes, 437–438
        overview, 437
Map type, 394
map type, STL/CLR, 226
MapView type, 394
Margin property, 376
markup extensions, 382
MarshalAsAttribute class, 458
marshaling, 356
Math::Abs function, 169
MathServiceClient class, 368
MaxCharactersInDocument property, 310
MaximumRowsOrColums attribute, 387
MBCS (Multi-Byte Character Set), 405
MClass object, 440
mc variable, 440
member functions, class-wide, 90–91
member initialization lists, in constructors, 86–87
MemoryStream class, 274, 282
memory usage, for enumerations, 156
MEPs (message exchange patterns), 357–358
MessageBox function, 445, 446
Message property, Exception class, 182
metadata
    adding to WCF services, 363–365
    and attributes
        overview, 453–454
        using ILDASM, 454–457

.NET, 266–268
    in Windows RT, 390
MEX (Metadata Exchange) addresses, 355
MFC (Microsoft Foundation Classes), 370, 405
Microsoft Intermediate Language (MSIL), 229, 375
Microsoft Intermediate Language (MSIL) file, 81
Microsoft-specific data types, 24
mixed classes, and unmanaged code, 437–438
mixed-language programming, exceptions in, 192–195
mm class, 115
Module property, 468
modulus operator (%), 30
Move method, 290, 292
MoveNext method, 210
MoveToAttribute method, 308
MoveToContentAsync method, 308
MoveToContent method, 308
MoveToElement method, 308, 315
MoveToFirstAttribute method, 308
MoveTo method, 291, 293
MoveToNextAttribute method, 308, 315
MSIL (Microsoft Intermediate Language), 229, 264, 375
MSIL (Microsoft Intermediate Language) file, 81
MSMQ transport, 354
Multi-Byte Character Set (MBCS), 405
multicast delegates, 249–252
multidimensional arrays
    managed arrays, 211
    native arrays, 202–203
multimap type, STL/CLR, 226
multiplication operator (*), 30
multiset type, STL/CLR, 226

N

named parameters, 463
named pipes, 353
Name property, 291, 293, 307, 323, 326
Namespace property, 468
namespaces
    ADO.NET, 335
    .NET
        Collections interfaces, 273–274
        Collections namespaces, 272–273
        Data namespaces, 276–277
        Diagnostics namespace, 274
        IO namespace, 274
        Net namespaces, 275

overview, 268–269
ServiceModel namespaces, 275
System namespace, 270–273
using in C++ applications, 270–271
Web namespaces, 277–278
Windows namespaces, 275
Xml namespaces, 276
Namespaces property, 318
NamespaceURI property, 307, 323
naming, of variables, 25–26
NaN (not a number), 272
native arrays
dynamic allocation of, 203–205
initializing, 202
multidimensional, 202–203
overview, 197–199
passing to functions, 200–202
negative infinity, 272
nesting
exceptions, 185–188
if statements, 64–65
.NET
using COM components from
and RCWs, 476–477
creating RCWs, 477–480
handling errors, 480–481
late binding to COM objects, 481–482
overview, 476
using .NET components as COM
components, 483–485
.NET Framework
assemblies, 266
class library, 265
CLR (Common Language Runtime), 263–264
CLS (Common Language Specification), 265
CTS (Common Type System), 264
metadata, 266–268
MSIL (Microsoft Intermediate Language), 264
namespaces
Collections interfaces, 273–274
Collections namespaces, 272–273
Data namespaces, 276–277
Diagnostics namespace, 274
IO namespace, 274
Net namespaces, 275
overview, 268–269
ServiceModel namespaces, 275
System namespace, 270–273
using in C++ applications, 270–271
Web namespaces, 277–278

Windows namespaces, 275
Xml namespaces, 276
overview, 263
quick reference, 278
XML and
NET XML namespaces, 306
overview, 305–306
XML processing classes, 306–307
NetMsmqBinding, 355, 358
NetNamedPipeBinding, 355, 358
Net namespaces, 275
NetTcpBinding, 355, 358
new operator, 203
NextSibling property, 323, 326
NodeChanged event, 325
NodeChanging event, 325
NodeInserted event, 325
NodeInserting event, 325
nodelist, 329
NodeRemoved event, 325
NodeRemoving event, 325
NodeType property, 308–309, 324, 326
None node type, 309
NonSerializedAttribute class, 458
non-static member functions, calling by using
delegates, 249
Normalize method, 326
normal pointers, 246
not a number (NaN), 272
Notation node type, 309
NotifyDelegate, 250
NOT operator (!), 31
NotPublic attribute, 469
nullptr keyword, 184
nullptr value, 98
number bases
in calculator example
adding buttons for, 417–418
changing base, 418–421
converting string in display, 421–425
NumericOp function, 247

O

Object Linking and Embedding (OLE), 370
object-oriented programming
advantages of, 16–17
classes in, 16
defined, 13–14

encapsulation in, 14–15
example of, 17–22
inheritance in, 15
objects in, 16
polymorphism in, 15–16
objects
and stack semantics
creating objects with, 111–113
overview, 116–118
copy constructors, 113–116
creating, 83–84
destructors
overview, 105–106
using, 109–110
finalizers
overview, 106
using, 108–109
handles to, 118–119
lifetimes of, 103–105
in object-oriented programming, 16
relationships for
creating LoyaltyScheme class, 95–96
creating LoyaltyScheme objects, 97–100
implementing LoyaltyScheme class, 96–97
overview, 95–96
testing example application, 100–101
traditional C++ creation and destruction, 110–111
obj pointer, 444
Observer class, 261
Obsolete attribute, 460
ObsoleteAttribute class, 458
ODBC data provider, 334
OleDb data provider, 334
OLE (Object Linking and Embedding), 370
one-way messaging, 358
OnNavigatedFrom function, 432
OnNavigatedTo function, 421, 432
op_Addition operator, 166
op_AddressOf operator, 166
op_BitwiseAnd operator, 166
op_BitwiseOr operator, 166
op_Comma operator, 166
op_Decrement operator, 166
op_Division operator, 166
Open method, 292–293
OpenRead method, 292–293
OpenText method, 292–293
OpenWrite method, 292–293
op_Equality operator, 166

operation contracts, 356
operator overloading
and reference types, 172–173
arithmetic operators, 161–162
best practices, 173–174
CLS-compliant operators, 166–167
decrement operators, 171–172
increment operators, 171–172
logical operators
Equals function, 169–170
overview, 167–169
overview, 159
restrictions on, 160
rules for, 161
static operator overloads, 163–166
types needing, 160
operators
arithmetic operators, 30–31
assignment operators, 30
bitwise operators, 32–33
cast operator, 33–34
defined, 30
logical operators, 31–32
precedence of, 34
relational operators, 31–32
ternary operator, 32–33
op_ExclusiveOr operator, 166
op_GreaterThan operator, 167
op_GreaterThanOrEqual operator, 167
op_Increment operator, 167
op_Inequality operator, 167
op_LeftShift operator, 167
op_LessThan operator, 167
op_LessThanOrEqual operator, 167
op_LogicalAnd operator, 167
op_LogicalNot operator, 166
op_LogicalOr operator, 167
op_Modulus operator, 167
op_Multiply operator, 167
op_OnesComplement operator, 166
op_PointerDereference operator, 166
op_RightShift operator, 167
op_Subtraction operator, 167
op_UnaryNegation operator, 166
op_UnaryPlus operator, 166
OracleClient data provider, 334
Orientation property, 384
OR operator, 31–32
OuterXml property, 324, 326
overloaded [ ] operator, 230

overloading functions, 53–55
overriding member functions, 131–136
OwnerDocument property, 324, 326

P

Package.appxmanifest file, 379, 412
Page class, 377
Page element, 375
ParamArrayAttribute class, 458
parameters
    in function bodies, 42–43
    in function prototypes, 39
    names for, 39
ParentNode property, 324, 326
Parent property, 291
parsing XML using, XmlReaderSettings class,
    310–314
partial classes, 391
partial keyword, 392
passing structured data, 449–452
Path class, 274, 282
PeekChar method, 299
Peek method, 287
pf function pointer, 246
pinning pointers, 441–442
P/Invoke (Platform Invoke)
    calling functions in Win32 API
        DllImportAttribute class, 447–448
        overview, 444–447
        passing structured data, 449–452
Platform::Collections namespace, 394
Platform Invoke (P/Invoke). *See* P/Invoke
Platform::Metadata namespace, 394
Platform namespaces, in Windows RT, 394
Play To contract, Windows 8, 429
PNG (Portable Network Graphics) files, 379, 414
pointer operator (->), 28
pointers
    interior pointers, 441
    overview, 27–28
    pinning pointers, 441–442
polymorphism
    in object-oriented programming, 15–16
pop_back function, 225
Portable Network Graphics (PNG) files, 379, 414
positional parameters, 463
positive infinity, 272
post-decrement, 171

postfix increment operator expression, 31
post-increment, 171
#pragma once directive, 125
precedence, of operators, 34
precompiled headers, 379
pre-decrement, 171
predefined attributes
    AssemblyInfo.cpp file, 457–458
    classes for, 458–461
    obtaining attribute data using, 469
    overview, 457
prefix increment operator expression, 31
Prefix property, 308, 324, 326
pre-increment, 171
PrependChild method, 326
PreserveSig field, 448
PreserveWhitespace property, 324
PreviousSibling property, 323, 326
printArea function, 236
PrintStatement function, 78
private auto ansi, 456
private class, 136
private keyword, 19
ProcessChildNodes function, 330
processFile function, 297
ProcessingInstruction node type, 309
projections, 390
Project Properties dialog box, 338
projects, creating, 8–9
properties
    for custom attributes, 463–464
    for Exception class, 182–183
    indexed
        bank example, 236–244
        overview, 236
    overview, 229–230
    quick reference, 244
    scalar properties
        auto-implemented properties, 233
        errors in properties, 232
        inheritance and, 235
        in interfaces, 235–236
        overview, 231–232
        read-only and write-only properties, 233–235
    of value types, 145
Properties property, 430
Properties tab, 402
property keyword, 231
protected access, 136–137
ProviderName property, 339

proxy, accessing WCF services using, 365–368
Public attribute, 469
public class, 136
public keyword, 18
push_back function, 225

Q

Queue<T> class, 219, 273
queue type, STL/CLR, 226
QuoteChar property, 318

R

RaiseOne function, 259
raise_OnFirstEvent method, 256
RaiseTwo function, 259
Rank property, 212, 213
rateFraction variable, 50
RC (Release Candidate) version, 7
RCWs (Runtime Callable Wrappers)
    creating, 477–480
    overview, 476–477
Read7BitEncodedInt method, 299
ReadAsync method, 287, 308
ReadAttributeValue method, 308
ReadBlockAsync method, 287
ReadBlock method, 287
ReadBoolean method, 299
ReadByte method, 299
ReadBytes method, 299
ReadChar method, 299
ReadChars method, 299
ReadContentAsAsync method, 308
ReadContentAsInt method, 308
ReadContentAs method, 308
ReadContentAsString method, 308
ReadDecimal method, 299
ReadDouble method, 299
ReadElementContentAsInt method, 308
ReadElementContentAs method, 308
ReadElementString method, 308
ReadEndElement method, 309
Read function, 313
ReadInnerXml method, 308
ReadInt16 method, 299
ReadInt32 method, 299
ReadInt64 method, 299
ReadLine method, 287, 289

Read method, 287, 299, 308
ReadNode method, 325
read-only properties, 233–234, 239
ReadOuterXml method, 308
ReadSByte method, 299
ReadSingle method, 299
ReadStartElement method, 309
ReadState property, 308
ReadString method, 299, 309
ReadToDescendant method, 309
ReadToEndAsync method, 287
ReadToEnd method, 287
ReadToFollowing method, 309
ReadToNextSibling method, 309
ReadUInt16 method, 299
ReadUInt32 method, 299
ReadUInt64 method, 299
RedeemPoints function, 97
refactoring, 407
reference counted objects, 391
Reference Manager dialog box, 193
reference types, 20
    and managed arrays, 208–209
    and operator overloading, 172–173
ref keyword, 184
reflection
    obtaining attribute data using
        accessing custom attribute data, 470–472
        accessing standard attributes, 469
        overview, 467–468
        Type class, 467–469
ref new keyword, 391
Refresh method, 293
reinterpret_cast<> operator, 34
relational operators, overview, 31–32
relationships, object
    LoyaltyScheme class example
        creating, 95–96
        creating objects, 97–100
        implementing class, 96–97
        testing application, 100–101
    overview, 95–96
Release Candidate (RC) version, 7
remembering operations, in calculator example, 406
Remote Method Invocation (RMI), 352
remoting, 264
RemoveAccount function, 241
RemoveAll method, 325, 326
RemoveByIndex method, 223
RemoveChild method, 325–326

Remove function, 221
RemoveHandler function, 259
Remove method
    in bank example, 240–241
    manipulating invocation lists using, 250
remove_OnFirstEvent method, 256
RemoveRange function, 221
ReplaceChild method, 325, 327
Replace method, 292, 293
reserved words, 5
Reset function, 409
Reset method, 210
Resize method, 213
resource dictionaries, 381
restrictions, on operator overloading, 160
rethrowing exceptions, 185–188
return keyword, 4, 41
return type
    for function bodies, 43–45
    for function prototypes, 39–40
Reverse method, 213
rightOperand variable, 408
right-shift operator (>>), 32
RMI (Remote Method Invocation), 352
Root property, 291
RoutedEventArgs class, 389
RowDefinition element, 386
running programs, 7, 11
Runtime Callable Wrappers (RCWs). *See* RCWs
RuntimeWrappedException, 192

S

safe_cast, 444
safe_cast keyword, and exceptions, 191–192
safe_cast<> operator, 33
Save method, 325
SavingsAccount class, 15, 123, 126–127, 130
SavingsAccount.cpp project, 129
SavingsAccount header file, 129
SAX (Simple API for XML) API, 307
SayHello method, 456
SByte type, 271
SByte value type, 144
scalar properties
    auto-implemented, 233
    defined, 230
    errors in, 232
    inheritance and, 235

    in interfaces, 235
    read-only and write-only, 233–234
Schema class, 276
SchemaInfo property, 308
Schemas property, 310, 324
scope
    global scope, 51–53
    local scope, 51–53
scope resolution operator (::), 269
ScrollViewerl control, 384
Sealed attribute, 469
sealed classes
    and abstract classes, 137
    overview, 137
Search contract, Windows 8, 428
searching, arrays, 216–217
SecondEventHandler delegate, 257
security permissions, 266
Seek method, 298, 302
SeekOrigin enumeration, 302
seek pointer, 302
SEH (Structured Exception Handling), 178
SelectCommand, 345
SelectCommand property, 347
Selected Components pane, 193
SelectNodes method, 325, 327
SelectSingleNode method, 325, 327
sequential layout, 449
Serializable attribute, 469
SerializableAttribute class, 458
Serialization class, 276
ServiceContract attribute, 356
service contracts, 356
ServiceModel namespaces, 275
services
    WCF, 352
        accessing by using proxy, 365–368
        adding metadata to, 363–365
        overview, 359–362
        writing service client, 361–362
SetAttributes method, 292
SetBitmap method, 430
SetCreationTime method, 290, 292
SetCreditLimit function, 80
SetCurrentDirectory method, 291
SetCursorToArrow line, 112
SetData method, 430
SetDataProvider method, 430
set_date function, 229
SetHtmlFormat method, 430

SetInterestRate function, 87
SetLastAccessTime method, 291–292
SetLastError field, 448
SetLastWriteTime method, 291–292
SetName function, 20
SetRtf method, 430
SetStorageItems method, 431
setter, 231
SetText method, 431
Settings contract, Windows 8, 429
Settings property, 308, 318
set type, STL/CLR, 226
SetUri method, 431
SetValue method, 213, 214
Shape class, 235
Share contract, Windows 8, 429
sharing
    in calculator example
        contracts and charms, 428–429
        DataPackage class, 430
        handling requests, 431–432
        implementing, 429–430
        overview, 428
short-circuit evaluation, 32, 60
short type, 24
SignificantWhitespace node type, 309
Simple API for XML (SAX) API, 307
Simple Mail Transfer Protocol (SMTP), 277
Simple Object Access Protocol (SOAP), 277, 306
simplex messaging, 358
single-byte string type, 405
Single type, 271
Single value type, 144
sizeof operator, 201
SkipAsync method, 309
Skip method, 309
SMTP (Simple Mail Transfer Protocol), 277
SOAP (Simple Object Access Protocol), 277, 306
SortedList<K,V> class, 273
    overview, 219, 222–223
SortedSet<T> class, 273
sorting, arrays, 217–218
Sort method, 213
Source property, Exception class, 182
SqlClient data provider, 334
SqlServerCe data provider, 334
square brackets [ ], 267
square function, 248
StackPanel control, 384

stack semantics, and objects
        creating objects with, 111–113
        overview, 116–118
Stack<T> class, 219, 273
StackTrace property, Exception class, 182
stack type, STL/CLR, 226
StandardStyles.xaml file, 380, 426
Start Without Debugging option, 47, 401
static_cast<double> operator, 33
static_cast<> operator, 33
static constructors, class-wide, 92–93
static keyword, 90
static member functions, calling by using
        delegates, 248–249
static operator overloads, overloading, 163–166
stdafx.h file, 107
stepping through application, 47–51
STL/CLR library
    concepts behind, 225–227
    overview, 224–225
Stop Debugging option, Debug menu, 165
Stream class, 274, 282, 284, 302
StreamReader class, 274, 282
streams, 302
StreamWriter class, 274, 282, 283
String class, 18, 44
    overview, 29–30
String^ parameter, 442
StringReader class, 274, 282
strings, in Windows RT, 392–393
StringWriter class, 274, 282
struct keyword, 146
StructLayoutAttribute class, 449, 458
structured data, passing, 449–452
Structured Exception Handling (SEH), 178
structures
    constructors for, 150
    copying, 152–153
    creating, 146–148
    overview, 146
    using within another, 150–152
    vs. classes, 149–150
styles, 381
Sub keyword, 38
substitutability, 123–124
subtraction operator (-), 30
Supports method, 327
switch statement, 313
    overview, 65–67
    using fall-through in, 67–68

swscanf_s function, 404, 409

symbolic constant, 28

Synchronized method, 283, 287

SyncRoot property, 212

syntax, for XAML, 381–382

System::ApplicationException class, 179

System::ArgumentException class, 179

System::ArithmeticException class, 179

System::Array class
  basic operations using, 213–214
  copying elements, 215
  overview, 212
  searching, 216–217
  sorting, 217–218
  using enumerators with, 218–219

System::Collection namespace, 218

System::Collections::Generic namespace, 219

System::Configuration assembly, 345

System::Data::Common namespace, 335

System::Data::EntityClient namespace, 276, 335

System::Data::Linq namespace, 335

System::Data namespace, 335

System::Data::Odbc namespace, 276, 335

System::Data::OleDb namespace, 276, 335

System::Data::OracleClient namespace, 276, 335

System::Data::Services namespace, 335

System::Data::Spatial namespace, 335

System::Data::SqlClient namespace, 276, 335

System::Data::SqlTypes namespace, 335

System::Delegate class, 247

System::Diagnostics namespace, 458

System::DivideByZeroException error, 177

System::Enum class, 153

System::EventHandler delegate, events and, 259–261

System::Exception class, 177, 179

System::GC::Collect static method, 105

System::IndexOutOfRangeException class, 179

System::InvalidCastException class, 179

System::IO namespace, 281–282

System::MemberAccessException class, 179

System::MulticastDelegate class, 247, 249

System namespace
  basic types, 271
  floating-point types, 272
  overview, 270–271

System::NotSupportedException class, 179

System::NullReferenceException class, 179

System::Object class, 169

System::OutOfMemoryException class, 179

SYSTEM_POWER_STATUS structure, 449

System::Reflection namespace, 470

System::Runtime::InteropServices namespace, 437

System::Runtime::Serialization namespace, 303

System::ServiceModel::AddressAccessDenied
    Exception, 361

System::ServiceModel assembly, 362

<system.ServiceModel> element, 367

System::String class, 209

System::SystemException class, 179

System::TypeLoadException class, 179

System::ValueType class, 145, 171

System::Web::Mail namespace, 277

System::Web namespace, 277

System::Web::Security namespace, 277

System::Web::Services namespace, 277

System::Web::UI::HtmlControls namespace, 278

System::Web::UI namespace, 277

System::Xml::Linq namespace, 306

System::Xml namespace, 306

System::Xml::Schema namespace, 306, 316

System::Xml::Serialization namespace, 306

System::Xml::XPath namespace, 306

System::Xml::Xsl namespace, 306

T

TCP/IP transport, 354

TempConverterLib component, 478

TempConverter project, 478

templates, and generic types
  overview, 224
  STL/CLR library
    concepts behind, 225–227
    overview, 224–225

ternary operator, overview, 32–33

TestAtts class, 466, 471

testing, calculator example, 410–412

Test method, 193

text I/O
  FileStream class, 286–287
  overview, 283
  TextReader, 287–290
  TextWriter, 283–286

Text node type, 309

TextReader class, 274, 282, 287–290

TextWriter class, 274, 283–285

throwing exceptions, 178–180

throw keyword, 177

ThrowOnUnmappableCharacter field, 448

tiles, Start Page, calculator example, 412–415
ToBinary function, 423
Tooltip control, 384
ToString function, 134
ToString method, 291, 293, 469, 471
tracking handles, 27
tracking reference, 114
triggers, 381
TrimToSize function, 222
TrimToSize method, 221
TrueForAll method, 213
try block, 347
try/catch blocks, handling exceptions using, 180–182
TryGetValue method, 223
type casting, operator for, 33–34
Type class, obtaining attribute data using, 467–469
typedefs, overview, 29
TypedEventHandler, 432
type-safe, 121

U

UClass object, 440
UInt16 type, 271
UInt16 value type, 144
UInt32 type, 271
UInt32 value type, 144
UInt64 type, 271
UInt64 value type, 144
UIntPtr type, 271
UI (user interface)
    libraries for Windows applications, 372
    model for Windows Store apps, 374
UI (user interface) framework, 275
UInPtr value type, 145
UML (Unified Modeling Language), 123
unboxing, 443–444
unconditional jumps, in loop statements, 73–74
UnderlyingSystemType property, 468
UnicodeClass attribute, 469
Unified Modeling Language (UML), 123
unmanaged code, 264
    boxing, 443
    interior pointers, 441
    pinning pointers, 441–442
    unboxing, 443–444
    using P/Invoke to call functions in Win32 API
        DllImportAttribute class, 447–448
        overview, 444–447
    passing structured data, 449–452
    vs. managed code
        GCHandle type, 438–440
        mixed classes, 437–438
        overview, 437
UpdateCommand, 345
User32.dll, 445
user interface (UI) framework, 275
#using directive, 270

V

ValHandler class, 317
Validate method, 325
ValidationFlags property, 310
ValidationType property, 310
value keyword, 20, 146, 161
Value property, 308, 324, 326
ValueType property, 308
value types
    and reference types
        overview, 143–144
    enumerations
        creating, 153–154
        memory usage, 156
        using in programs, 156
    properties of, 145
    purpose of, 144–145
    structures
        constructors for, 150
        copying, 152–153
        creating, 146–148
        overview, 146
        using within another, 150–152
        vs. classes, 149–150
variables
    arrays, 28
    assigning values to, 26–27
    constants, 28–29
    data types for, 23–24
    declaring
        multiple, 26
        overview, 25
    defined, 23
    handles, 27–28
    naming of, 25–26
    pointers, 27–28
    String class, 29–30
    typedefs, 29

VariableSizedWrapGrid control, 387
VectorIterator class, 394
Vector type, 394
vector type, STL/CLR, 226
VectorViewIterator class, 394
VectorView type, 394
Vehicle class, 122
versioning, 266
VirtualizingStackPanel control, 385
void keyword, 38

W

W3C DOM, 322
WCF (Windows Communication Foundation)
    addresses, 355
    behaviors, 358–359
    binding, 355
    connectivity, 353
    contracts, 356–358
    defined, 275
    distributed systems, 352
    endpoints, 353–354
    MEPs (message exchange patterns), 357–358
    overview, 351
    services, 352
        accessing by using proxy, 365–368
        adding metadata to, 363–365
        overview, 359–362
        writing service client, 361–362
wchar_t* pointer, 405
wchar_t type, 24
wcstol (Wide Character String To Long) function, 422
Web namespaces, 277–278
web service, 277
Web Service Definition Language (WSDL), 355
Web Service Description Language (WSDL), 306
WeekDay class, 154
while loops, overview, 68–70
white space, 5
Whitespace node type, 309
Wide Character String To Long (wcstol)
            function, 422
wide string type, 405
Win32 API, 369–370
    calling functions using P/Invoke
        DllImportAttribute class, 447–448
        overview, 444–447
        passing structured data, 449–452

Windows::ApplicationModel.DataTransfer
            namespace, 430
Windows::ApplicationModel namespaces, 393
Windows applications
    Microsoft Foundation Classes, 370
    Win32 API, 369–370
    Windows Forms, 370–371
    Windows Presentation Foundation, 371
Windows Communication Foundation (WCF), 275
Windows::Data namespaces, 393
Windows::Devices namespaces, 393
Windows Forms, 370–371
Windows::Foundation::Collections namespaces, 393
Windows::Foundation namespaces, 393
Windows::Globalization namespaces, 393
Windows::Graphics namespaces, 393
Windows::Management namespaces, 393
Windows::Media namespaces, 393
WindowsMessageBox function, 448
Windows namespaces, 275
Windows::Networking namespaces, 393
Windows Presentation Foundation, 371
Windows Presentation Foundation (WPF), 275
Windows RT (WinRT). See WinRT
Windows Runtime Library (WRL), 390
Windows::Security namespaces, 393
Windows::Storage namespaces, 393
Windows Store apps
    and Windows applications
        Microsoft Foundation Classes, 370
        Win32 API, 369–370
        Windows Forms, 370–371
        Windows Presentation Foundation, 371
    calculator example
        adding tile, 412–415
        app bars, 425–428
        arithmetic buttons, 403–404
        getting number from button, 404–405,
            407–408
        handling different number bases, 416–425
        handling number input, 401–402
        laying out number buttons, 398–401
        overview, 397–398
        performing calculations, 408–409
        remembering operations, 406
        sharing in, 428–432
        testing, 410–412
    choosing UI library, 372
    creating, 375–379
    file structure for, 379–380

main features
    app behavior, 373
    contracts and charms, 374
    hardware usage, 374
    overview, 373
    UI model, 374
    WinRT APIs, 374
overview, 372–373
Windows RT
    classes, 391–392
    generics, 392
    metadata, 390
    overview, 389–390
    Platform namespaces, 394–395
    strings, 392–393
    Windows namespaces, 393
XAML
    controls, 382–383
    defined, 380–381
    event handling, 389
    layout controls, 384–388
    syntax, 381–382
Windows::System namespaces, 394
Windows::UI namespaces, 394
Windows::UI::XAML namespaces, 394
Windows::Web namespaces, 394
WinRT (Windows RT)
    APIs, 374
    classes, 391–392
    generics, 392
    metadata, 390
    overview, 389–390
    Platform namespaces, 394
    strings, 392–393
    Windows namespaces, 393
WPF (Windows Presentation Foundation), 275
Write7BitEncodedInt method, 298
WriteAllLines method, 292
WriteAllText method, 292
WriteAsync method, 283
WriteAttributes method, 318
WriteAttributeString method, 318
WriteBase64 method, 318
WriteBinHex method, 318
WriteCData method, 319
WriteCharEntity method, 319
WriteChars method, 319
WriteComment method, 319
WriteContentTo method, 325, 327
WriteDocType method, 319

WriteElementString method, 319
WriteEndAttribute method, 319
WriteEndDocument method, 319
WriteEndElement method, 319
WriteEntityRef method, 319
WriteFullEndElement method, 319
WriteLineAsync method, 283
WriteLine method, 283
WriteLine statement, 108, 111, 162
Write method, 283, 298
WriteName method, 319
WriteNode method, 319
write-only properties, 233–234
WriteProcessingInstruction method, 319
WriteQualifiedName method, 319
WriteRaw method, 319
WriteStartAttribute method, 319
WriteStartDocument method, 319
WriteStartElement method, 319
Write statement, 108
WriteState property, 318
WriteString method, 319
WriteTo method, 325, 327
WriteValue method, 319
WriteWhitespace method, 319
WriteXml method, 348
WRL (Windows Runtime Library), 390
WSDL (Web Service Definition Language), 355
WSDL (Web Service Description Language), 306
WSDualHttpBinding, 355, 358
WSHttpBinding, 355, 358, 360, 362

X

XAML (Extensible Application Markup Language)
    controls, 382–383
    defined, 380–381
    event handling, 389
    layout controls, 384–388
    project files, 379
    syntax, 381–382
XamlTypeInfo.g.h, 380
Xml class, 276
XmlDeclaration node type, 309
XmlDocument class, 322
XML (eXtensible Markup Language)
    NET and
        NET XML namespaces, 306
        overview, 305–306
        XML processing classes, 306–307

parsing using XmlReader
    creating XmlReaders, 309–310
    handling attributes, 314–315
    overview, 307–309
    verifying well-formed XML, 314
    with validation, 315–317
    XmlReaderSettings class, 310–314
quick reference, 332
writing using XmlTextWriter, 318–322
XmlDocument class
    overview, 322
    W3C DOM and, 322
XmlNode class, 325–332
XmlLang property, 308, 318
Xml namespaces, 276
XmlNode class, 325–332
XmlNodeType enumeration, 309
XmlReader class
parsing XML using
    creating XmlReaders, 309–310
    handling attributes, 314–315
    overview, 307–309
    verifying well-formed XML, 314
    with validation, 315–317
    XmlReaderSettings class, 310–314
XmlResolver property, 310
XmlSpace property, 318
XmlTextReader class, 307
XmlTextWriter class
    creating object, 348
    writing XML using, 318–322
XmlValidatingReader class, 307
XmlWriter class, 138
x:Name attribute, 381
XPath class, 276
Xsl class, 276
XSL (Extensible Stylesheet Language) processor, 276
XSLT (Extensible Stylesheet Language
        Transformations), 306

Z

ZIndex property, 388

About the author

 JULIAN TEMPLEMAN is a professional consultant, trainer, and writer. He has been writing code for nearly 40 years, has been using and teaching C++ for nearly 20 of those, and has been involved with .NET since its first alpha release in 1998. He is the author or coauthor of 10 programming books, including *COM Programming with Microsoft .NET*. He currently runs a training and consultancy company in London with his wife, specializing in C++, Java and .NET programming, and software development methods.

Microsoft

How To Download Your eBook

To download your eBook, go to

http://aka.ms/PressEbook

and follow the instructions.

Please note: You will be asked to create a free online account and enter the access code below.

Your access code:

> # WXPVBDG

[Microsoft Visual C++/CLI Step by Step]

Your PDF eBook allows you to:

- Search the full text
- Print
- Copy and paste

Best yet, you will be notified about free updates to your eBook.

If you ever lose your eBook file, you can download it again just by logging in to your account.

Need help? Please contact:
msinput@microsoft.com

Now that you've read the book...

Tell us what you think!

Was it useful?
Did it teach you what you wanted to learn?
Was there room for improvement?

Let us know at http://aka.ms/tellpress

Your feedback goes directly to the staff at Microsoft Press,
and we read every one of your responses. Thanks in advance!

 Microsoft